SOUTHERN EVANGELICALS AND THE SOCIAL ORDER

SOUTHERN EVANGELICALS AND THE SOCIAL ORDER
1800–1860

Anne C. Loveland

Louisiana State University Press
Baton Rouge and London

Designer: Patricia Douglas Crowder
Typeface: VIP Baskerville
Typesetter: LSU Press

Portions of Chapter Three were previously published as an article, "Presbyterians and Revivalism in the Old South," in *Journal of Presbyterian History*, LVII (Spring, 1979), 36–49.

LIBRARY OF CONGRESS CATALOGING IN PUBLICATION DATA

Loveland, Anne C.   1938–
    Southern evangelicals and the social order, 1800–1860.

    Bibliography: p.
    Includes index.
    1. Clergy—Southern States.   2. Evangelicalism—
Southern States.   3. Church and social problems—Southern
States.   4. Southern States—Church history.   I. Title.
BR535.L68   280'.4   80–11200
ISBN 0–8071–0690–9   0–8071–0783–2 (pbk)

For my husband
J. Kenneth Edmiston

Contents

Preface

This book is a study of Baptist, Methodist, and Presbyterian clergymen in the Old South. I have focused on ministers in the South Atlantic states, paying somewhat less attention to those in Mississippi, Alabama, and Louisiana. I have not been concerned with the larger body of professing Christians in the Old South, or with denominations or churches per se, but with the clergymen, both as individuals and as a group. Where significant, I have noted doctrinal or other differences between the three denominations, but my emphasis is on the beliefs, assumptions, and values which the ministers held in common. Not only did they all subscribe to the evangelical theology, they also shared similar views regarding the role of the church in the social order and on such social questions as temperance, benevolence, dueling, slavery, and the sectional controversy.

Southern evangelicals saw themselves as guardians of the religious and moral purity of the southern people and felt that it was their duty to concern themselves—even, in some cases, to the point of engaging in political action—with issues and problems relating to the social order. Some historians have viewed southern evangelicalism as a "culture religion" shaped by and completely subservient to the ideology of the Old South. I do not completely reject this interpretation, but my research has convinced me that in some cases southern evangelicals were more autonomous than such an interpretation suggests. To be sure, they did not challenge the fundamental structure or ethos of their society. Nevertheless, in some of their views—for example on temperance, Sabbath observance, and dueling —they set themselves against popular opinion and were sharply critical of the actions of "public men." On other issues, such as slavery, evangelicals were more in line with the dominant ideology, yet they never went so far as to defend slavery as a "positive good," and their demands for religious instruction of the Negroes often contained an implicit criticism of the Old South's "peculiar institution." I hope my book will illustrate to the reader that southern evangelicalism—and southern evangelicals—were more complicated than has generally been recognized.

Acknowledgments

I would like to thank the following persons for the assistance they provided while I was working on this book: the staff of the Louisiana State University Archives; Allen Stokes and Mrs. Loulie L. Owens of the South Caroliniana Library; Herbert Hucks, Jr., Curator of the Historical Society of the South Carolina Conference of the United Methodist Church; J. Glen Clayton, Special Collections Librarian, Furman University Library; Mrs. Martha Aycock, Reference Librarian, Union Theological Seminary Library; Mrs. Mary G. Lane and other members of the staff of the Historical Foundation of the Presbyterian and Reformed Churches; the staff of the Southern Historical Collection, University of North Carolina Library; Ms. Jane Kleiner and Mrs. Olar Bell of the Interlibrary Loan Department, Louisiana State University Library; and Ms. Connie DeGroff of the Mount Union College Library.

In addition, I would like to acknowledge the assistance provided by the National Endowment for the Humanities in the form of a Younger Humanist Fellowship, and by the Louisiana State University Council on Research in the form of two Summer Faculty Research Grants.

SOUTHERN EVANGELICALS AND THE SOCIAL ORDER

CHAPTER ONE

Conversion and Calling

In August, 1821, Daniel Witt and Jeremiah Jeter attended a section meeting at the Baptist meeting house near Liberty, Virginia. The two young farmers, both twenty years old, had met the night before at the home of a Baptist minister. They went to the meeting, Witt wrote later, without any thought of being converted, but almost as soon as the services had begun, Witt found himself "the subject of new and strange emotions." There was nothing unusual in the surroundings or the discourses being presented, yet he felt that "an uncontrollable power had fallen on me, and mastered my soul." He had never before wept at public worship, and "was really ashamed when the big, unbidden tears began to drop down my face." In vain he tried to stop "the flood of feelings." "I hid my head behind the shoulders of my friend, unwilling that he should witness my weakness; but still I shook convulsively, and soon found that he too was under the control of similar impressions." Before the close of that memorable day, the two young men had "determined to be Christians."

These "impressions" were the beginning of a period of anxiety for Witt and Jeter. For the first time in his life, Witt felt himself "under a sense of real wretchedness and want." His sense of helplessness and guilt increased as the weeks went by. Although he had always admitted the sinfulness of man, he was now appalled to discover the "deep-rooted *depravity of my heart*." The tender sensibility that had manifested itself at Hatcher's meeting house had given way to a stony and stubborn heart. He read the Bible, attended meetings, prayed—but to no avail. Even his friend Jeter, after undergoing similar anguish, had attained the hoped-for blessing. Indeed, the two had often met to compare their experiences and had found "a striking sameness" in their exercises. "We wept together," Witt remembered. "We bowed at the same altar of prayer. We endeavored to strengthen each other's resolution to persevere to the very end of life, if we did not attain sooner the blessing we pursued." Finally, in October, in a state of despair, Witt attended one of the weekly night meetings held in the neighborhood. When anxious persons were invited forward for prayer, he went with them, kneeling in an obscure corner of the room. After the prayer had been offered, he remained on his knees, and "gradually, and mysteriously, and without my knowing wherefore, or how, relief came to my burdened heart." Was this conversion? It had not come at the time or in the way he had expected. "I saw nothing; I heard nothing; but I *felt* something for which I could not account." The sense of guilt was gone; instead of the miseries of the past month, there was a feeling of peace. "I felt in my heart the very first full-formed hope of acceptance with God through Jesus Christ."[1]

Daniel Baker's first "serious impressions" occurred when he was twelve years old, on the occasion of his reading a dialogue between Christ, Youth, and the Devil in a Presbyterian *Shorter Catechism*. During the next two years his anxiety over salvation manifested itself in a recurring fear of dying a sinner and going to hell. Unlike Witt and Jeter, the orphaned Baker had no one to talk with "except a coloured man by the name of Joe." Finally, "after going on in darkness for many months, fearing the worst, and not knowing what to do," Baker "went out into the grove, and resolved that if I perished, I would perish at my Saviour's feet. If I did perish, I would perish praying. I went out in great distress, I returned with great joy. In prayer my mind experienced a sweet relief; I had new views of my Saviour, and saw that Christ could save even so great a sinner as I was. . . . I became one of the happiest creatures upon earth."

Baker's new-found happiness was short lived, though. He moved to Savannah to take a job as a clerk in a dry-goods and grocery store, and his employer, though kind, was "very profane" and "loose in his morals." Baker was sure he never went to church. The young men at the boarding house where Baker lived were also profane and "all desecrated the Sabbath." Shocked at first, Baker soon found himself following their bad example. He began to neglect prayer, absented himself from church on Sunday, and "sometimes would go into confectionary shops and beer-gardens."

1. J. B. Jeter, *The Life of Rev. Daniel Witt, D.D.* (Richmond, 1875), 32–34, 38, 41–44.

None of this came easily or "without many checks of conscience," but in three or four years, Baker recalled, "the tide of worldly feeling and worldly amusement had nearly swept me away." The death of one of his "wicked companions," announced from the pulpit, jarred him into a consideration of his tenuous position. "I felt awful. My young companion taken away in his sins!—suddenly and without warning! What—said I to myself, over and over again—what if I had been taken!" Baker resolved that he would no longer neglect the salvation of his soul.

An offer of financial aid enabled him to leave the temptations of Savannah to attend Hampden-Sydney College. Although he intended to study for the ministry, he had not yet made a public profession of religion. After arriving at college, he underwent a period of "great spiritual darkness, even on the borders of despair." He was tortured by the remembrance of broken vows, of "all my wanderings in Savannah." He began to fear that he "had sinned away my day of grace." One day, reading a volume of sermons, he came upon a sentence that offered "great comfort. . . . that if a man had any serious concern about the salvation of his soul, and has any tender thoughts in relation to the Redeemer, that was proof positive that he had not committed the unpardonable sin." Upon reading this, Baker wrote, his "burden" disappeared, and his "feelings became most delightful. . . . I had new views of my Saviour, felt that I could rest upon him, and was enabled to rejoice with joy unspeakable and full of glory."[2]

William Capers had no intention of becoming a minister. A vain, ambitious youth, he had his eyes set on a political career in the South Carolina legislature. Accordingly, when he went to a Methodist camp meeting in the summer of 1806, it was not for any religious reasons, but "as a friend among friends, and to make more friends." Capers was not converted at the meeting, but for the first time he became "clearly convinced that there was an actual, veritable power of God's grace in persons then before me, and who were known to me, by which they were brought to repentance and a new life." Seeing others converted convinced him of the reality of the work of salvation, and having acquired such knowledge, Capers wondered what use he should make of it. Then began a period of prayer, Scripture reading and meditation. On one of his fast days, while praying in the woods, he fell asleep. He awoke in terror. "Asleep at prayer! . . . I seemed to myself a monster of profanity, who had mocked God to his face, and must surely have committed the unpardonable sin." Capers was plunged

2. William M. Baker, *The Life and Labours of the Rev. Daniel Baker, D.D..* (Philadelphia, 1859), 22–26, 28–31, 34.

into "a darkness as of death." His agony was compounded when, upon returning home, he found an invitation to attend a ball. "The bare coinci-
dence of such an invitation at such a moment seemed to tell me that I was
doomed, and there was nothing better left for me." Giving up all hope of
becoming a "spiritual Christian," Capers decided to attend the ball. He
knew he could not find enjoyment in "the pleasures of the gay world," but
given his condemned state, he thought "it would be useless to give offence,
and break with my former associates." Returning to the South Carolina
College, he joined freely in the recreations of his classmates and friends.
"But behind all this there slumbered a feeling of remorse, which could
sometimes be aroused into a loathing of myself, and extreme sadness." He
ceased to pray and read Scripture. In the solitude of night he would contemplate the tragic scenario of the previous summer: "how I had had the
truth of spiritual religion demonstrated to me; had been graciously drawn
to seek it; and had (as still it appeared to me) profanely cast it all away."

Capers' anguish was ended in the summer of 1808 during family prayers.
While his father was reading Psalm 103 and in the presence of his sister
and brother-in-law (both recently converted at a camp meeting), Capers
experienced a "great visitation" which released his soul from the prison
despair had created. Though he did not consider his feelings on this occasion to imply conversion, he "knew them to be from God," and he felt,
once again, that "I, even I, had access to a throne of mercy for the Redeemer's sake." He subsequently joined the Methodist church and shortly
thereafter, while attending a quarterly meeting, found "that unspeakable
blessing which I had been so earnestly seeking. . . . the Spirit itself bearing
witness with my spirit that I was a child of God."[3]

Experience—the nineteenth century term for "that series of convictions,
emotions and conflict intervening between the time of the awakening and
the conversion of the sinner"—was the common denominator of professing Christians in the Old South, whether Baptist, Presbyterian or Methodist. It always involved a conviction of sinfulness leading to feelings of
despair and resignation which then gave way to a lifting of the burden of
guilt and a feeling of acceptance by God. In most cases such religious experience was the outgrowth of Christian nurture, of a cultural context in
which religious values and exercises were accepted and practiced. Witt's

3. William M. Wightman, *Life of William Capers, D.D., One of the Bishops of the Methodist
Episcopal Church, South; Including an Autobiography* (Nashville, 1858), 51–52, 54–58, 61–62,
72–75, 81.

parents were both members of the Baptist church. Baker's parents were members of the Congregational church, and it was his older brother's acquaintance with the Reverend C. Gildersleeve that enabled Baker to obtain the financial aid he needed to attend college. Capers described his father as a pillar of the Methodist church, who, after a period of backsliding, experienced a renewal of spirituality on the same occasion of family worship that offered his son a way out of *his* spiritual impasse. A number of future ministers had fathers or other relatives who were engaged in ministerial work: James Finley, Basil Manly, Jr., Benjamin Morgan Palmer, John Landrum, Moses Drury Hoge (named for his grandfathers, Moses Hoge and Drury Lacy, both ministers), Charles Deems, Francis Asbury Mood, Peter Doub, and John Holt Rice. Other youths grew up in "pious households" where one or both parents were professing Christians, where visits by ministers were not uncommon, and where church attendance and Sabbath school were regular activities. Francis Asbury Mood noted that his parents devoted a good deal of attention to the religious training of their children. "I cannot . . . recall the time when I did not think seriously about future and eternal things, when I did not pray or when I did not daily night and morning hear the Scriptures read, a verse or two of a hymn sung and a Father's prayer offered at the Family Altar," he wrote in later years. Abner Clopton's father, a leading member of the Shockoe Baptist church, often prayed with his young son for the latter's salvation; and Peter Doub remembered the "godly admonitions" of his father, as well as the instructions he received from ministers who lodged at the Doub home.[4]

Many of those who ultimately entered the ministry had been the subject of religious impressions in childhood. Though he claimed to have been brought up "without special religious instruction," since his parents were not church members, Jeremiah Jeter remembered being affected by the pious conversation of his mother, and even in his boyhood, he cherished the hope of being converted. In some cases, early thoughts of religion were stimulated by attendance at camp meetings with the rest of the family. At age six Peter Doub attended a camp meeting and was "considerably impressed with the necessity of serving God." The next day he and his ten year old brother resolved, after talking about religion, to try to live better

4. Jeremiah Bell Jeter, *The Recollections of a Long Life* (Richmond, 1891), 43; Jeter, *Life of Witt*, 29; William M. Baker, *Life of Baker*, 17, 31; Wightman, *Life of Capers*, 24–25, 73; Francis Asbury Mood Autobiography (typed copy in Francis Asbury Mood Papers, South Caroliniana Library, University of South Carolina), 23; Jeremiah B. Jeter, *A Memoir of Abner W. Clopton, A.M.* (Richmond, 1837), 7, 10–11; Peter Doub Journal, 1819–1834 (in William Clark Doub Papers, William R. Perkins Library, Duke University), 3.

lives. No doubt many youngsters played minister to a congregation of neighborhood children, as did John Holt Rice. Children of a more solitary nature, like Benjamin Mosby Smith, might "go into a grape summer house and read and sing and try to pray." At thirteen Smith had "no well-fixed religious views," but, like others his age, he was much affected by sermons he had read and was led by his "serious thoughts" to engage in religious exercises of various sorts.[5]

Conviction of sin—the feeling which initiated the religious experience —generally occured between the mid-teens and early twenties. It frequently came at a time of unsettlement for the youth—not merely the emotional unsettlement accompanying puberty or young adulthood, but unsettlement in the conditions of life which also produced emotional upheaval and sensitiveness. For example, when George Gilman Smith was eighteen years old, his father was removed from his office of postmaster in Atlanta. The "Catastrophe," as Smith termed it, plunged him into a deep depression. Concern for the future was translated into concern for "the welfare of my immortal soul." Smith felt that he was "a sinner helpless and miserable and growing worse daily."[6]

For a number of young men, the change in the conditions of life occurred as a result of attending college. Indeed, college students were of an age and in a situation which made them particularly susceptible to religious experience, as the numerous college revivals of the period testify. Robert Lewis Dabney came under conviction and was converted during a revival at Hampden-Sydney in 1837. John Bailey Adger had a similar experience while attending Union College. He had entered college as "a light-hearted boy . . . quite happy in my relation to all my college friends, and very well satisfied on the whole with myself," sure that he was too young to be concerned with matters of religion. When an older student named John R. McDowell began going about "talking to everybody on the subject of religion," Adger resolved to resist his influence. Soon, however, his "fancied security" was dispelled. "The conviction that I was a sinner took strong hold of me." He spent his leisure time in religious conversation with classmates, who were similarly affected, and he spent long hours in solitary prayer. Finally, he began attending prayer meetings in Mc-

5. Jeter, *Recollections*, 43–44; Doub Journal, 3–4; William Maxwell, *A Memoir of the Reverend John H. Rice, D.D.* (Philadelphia, 1835), 4; Francis R. Flournoy, *Benjamin Mosby Smith, 1811–1893* (Richmond, 1947), 9.

6. George Gilman Smith Autobiography, 35, and Diary, March 23 and April 3, [1855], p. 74 (both in George Gilman Smith Books, Southern Historical Collection, University of North Carolina Library).

Dowell's room. After enduring a period of "alternations of darkness and light, of doubts and hopes," he was able to make a profession of faith and be accepted as a member of the Presbyterian church. John L. Girardeau entered Charleston College at age fourteen and almost immediately "a gloom like that of eternal night fell upon his soul." He struggled through the period of conviction, unable to eat or study, "afraid to put out the light at night lest the darkness should never end. . . . afraid to go to sleep lest he should awake in the company of the damned." Release came, "after a month's conflict with sin and hell," upon reading a book of spiritual biographies.[7]

In the cases described above, the unsettlement which seems to have provided the occasion for conviction involved factors unrelated to religious matters. Sometimes, however, the connection between unsettlement and religious experience was more apparent. Incidents or crises directly involving the moral or spiritual condition of a youth were well calculated to provoke thinking on the matter of salvation. Sometimes it was a brush with death, either as a result of severe illness or as a consequence of the passing of a friend or relative. Edward Baptist, Richard Fuller and Abner Clopton experienced a season of conviction in connection with illness. We have seen that Daniel Baker was jolted into a concern for his own salvation upon hearing of the death of a friend. Similarly, John Landrum wrote that the sudden death of his father brought him "to feel deeply my lost condition as a sinner." Charles Deems recalled that the death of his mother "brought a crisis in my experience." Although "not a vicious boy," he nevertheless felt the "need of some act of consecration which should separate me from the world" and insure that he would meet her in heaven when he died. He was led by this concern to listen to religious conversation, to seek out "practical preaching," and to try to understand the Methodist view of salvation.[8]

Daniel Baker's experience clerking in a store suggests another condi-

7. Thomas Cary Johnson, *The Life and Letters of Robert Lewis Dabney* (Richmond, 1903), 42–43; John B. Adger, D.D., *My Life and Times, 1810–1899* (Richmond, 1899), 63–67; George A. Blackburn (comp. and ed.), *The Life Work of John Girardeau, D.D., LL.D.* (Columbia, 1916), 22–23.
8. Edward Baptist Diary, 1790–1861 (typed copy in Virginia Historical Society, Richmond), 2; J. H. Cuthbert, *Life of Richard Fuller, D.D.* (New York, 1879), 69; Jeter, *Memoir of Clopton*, 26–28, 33; H. P. Griffith, *The Life and Times of Rev. John G. Landrum* (Philadelphia, 1885), 30; Charles Force Deems, *Autobiography of Charles Force Deems, D.D., LL.D. Pastor of the Church of the Strangers, New York City and President of the American Institute of Christian Philosophy and Memoir by His Sons Rev. Edward M. Deems, A.M., Ph.D. and Francis M. Deems, M.D., Ph.D.* (New York, 1897), 38.

tion conducive to conviction. The picture that he drew of a young man succumbing to temptation and worldliness was a staple of nineteenth century ministerial biographies and autobiographies. Though such sketches were probably overdrawn in order to dramatize the change wrought by conversion, they point to what may have been a fairly common experience of youths raised in a sheltered, "godly" environment. Attendance at school or college or taking a job often brought about a confrontation with "the world"—with youths who gambled, or swore, or danced, or desecrated the Sabbath. Like Baker, Edward Baptist was placed in a store (his father's) at the age of twelve, and by "16 or 19 I had made such proficiency in vice, that I could frolic with the young and drink with the old, ridicule the Bible, and its most sacred characters and things." When Benjamin Morgan Palmer was seventeen and acting as a private tutor on a plantation outside of Charleston, he was thrust into the gay social life of the city. He became, according to his own recollection, "irreligious," even "hostile to religion." During this period he was brought to a sense of conviction, struggled for six months, and finally experienced conversion.[9]

How did a young man who had been raised in a Christian environment react to the confrontation with sin and worldliness? Baker was shocked at first, but succumbed to temptation. Others showed even less hesitation in embracing a life of frivolity and amusement. Conviction occurred when the religious standards ingrained in childhood prompted questions about the morality of such a life. Thus, Moses Waddel, who had acquired a fondness for dancing as a young schoolteacher, "began to doubt the innocence of dancing as an amusement, and often, after having attended . . . [a party], his thoughts were so unpleasant as to lead him to resolve that this should be the last one of the kind he should ever attend." Palmer apparently agonized in private over his involvement in Charleston social life. Peter Cartwright's period of conviction began when, returning from a wedding where there had been much drinking and dancing, he "began to reflect on the manner in which I had spent the day and evening." The guilt which he felt for the activities of that occasion soon widened to include other forms of "wickedness."[10] For youths like Baker, Palmer and Cartwright, the conversion experience provided a genuine release from feelings of guilt, since

9. Baptist Diary, 1–2; Thomas Cary Johnson, *The Life and Letters of Benjamin Morgan Palmer* (Richmond, 1906), 54–55.

10. John N. Waddel, *Memorials of Academic Life: Being an Historical Sketch of the Waddel Family* (Richmond, 1891), 33; Peter Cartwright, *Autobiography of Peter Cartwright, The Backwoods Preacher*, ed. W. P. Strickland (New York, 1856), 34–35.

it entailed a repudiation of worldliness and a return to the security of the kind of godly society the youth had experienced in his childhood.

Individuals under conviction felt condemned and isolated, cut off not only from God but from other human beings. The word they frequently employed to convey this feeling was "lost." In describing the state of conviction, they spoke of their "lost estate," their "lost and sinful state," their "lost condition as a sinner." Daniel Witt wrote that "I seemed to be a lone, lost sinner in the vast universe of God. . . . I was sunk into my own individuality, deploring the almost certain loss of my soul; and I had 'ceased from man,' assured that he could do me no good." He felt that "there must be something peculiar in my case, or that God had determined to withhold for ever his mercy from such a lost, guilty sinner, as I knew myself to be." Thus, the individual struggled alone with his sense of sin and guilt. If others noticed his depressed state, their concern and attempts to help provided little comfort. Indeed, some individuals kept their anxiety a secret, thereby intensifying the sense of isolation. Capers referred to his conviction as "a secret wound, hidden from the light of day," which he managed to hide while with his friends, but which haunted him in the solitude of night. Palmer, too, confessed that although he gave the appearance of being "thoughtless and flippant," in fact he was undergoing "as fierce a storm as ever swept over a human soul." For individuals who experienced conviction in terms of lostness or isolation, conversion was the experience of being found or accepted, of becoming "a child of God." [11]

Individuals under conviction also experienced a feeling of helplessness, which derived from the realization that they could do nothing to earn salvation. Prayer, reading the Bible and meditating, attempts at reformation —all were useless. Indeed, Jeter and Baptist found that the more they tried to achieve salvation by their own works, the farther away they were from it. Conversion came when the individual admitted his helplessness and gave himself up entirely to God. Thus John Girardeau, realizing "that he had already done everything that it was possible for him to do, and that all of these things had availed him nothing," determined to "surrender himself to Jesus and leave the case in his hands." Such resignation, according to his biographer, was evidence of the faith necessary for salvation.

11. Baptist Diary, 3; James Dunwody, *Reminiscences and Sermons* (Macon, 1872), 6; Griffith, *Life and Times of Landrum*, 30; James B. Finley, *Autobiography of Rev. James B. Finley; or, Pioneer Life in the West*, ed. W. P. Strickland (Cincinnati, 1854), 162, 177, 179; Jeter, *Life of Witt*, 36, 42, 44; Wightman, *Life of Capers*, 61, 81, 82; Thomas Cary Johnson, *Life and Letters of Palmer*, 56.

"Instantly the Holy Spirit assured him that he was accepted in Christ, that his sins were forgiven, and that God loved him with an everlasting love." [12]

What enabled the individual to pass from conviction to conversion? Nineteenth century evangelicals maintained that conversion occurred through the agency of the Holy Spirit, but the historian looks for a more mundane explanation. We have seen that individuals under conviction felt lost in the sense of being isolated or alone. Because of his feeling of helplessness the individual felt lost in another sense—in the sense of having lost the way or of being ignorant of the way of salvation. Here, too, the feeling of isolation was paramount. Significantly, for some individuals, the way out of the darkness and despair of conviction came upon reading accounts of the religious experience of others, or talking to converts about their experience, or seeing others converted at prayer or revival meetings. It would seem that such activity reestablished the connection between the individual and other human beings by allowing him to see that his experience was not unique, that his case was not peculiar (as Witt feared), that others had undergone a similar experience. The experience of others also functioned as a guide which enabled the individual to understand—perhaps for the first time—the significance of his own experience. Conversion came when he recognized his own experience in the accounts of others and realized that even he, sinner though he was, could be the subject of grace, as others, equally sinful, had been. Indeed, in some cases, the experience of others functioned as more than a guide, by serving to verify the fact that the individual was converted. Norvell Robertson's account provides a good illustration of this. In his autobiography he explains that his religious experience had carried him to the point where he had experienced certain "impressions" while engaged in prayer, but he was not sure that they were the work of the Holy Spirit. He endured this "state of suspense" for about two months until he decided "that no individual of the human family had ever been in a situation similar to mine." While visiting some friends, he discovered a religious work, *Grace Abounding to the Chief of Sinners.* Reading the book enabled him "to recognize my character as a subject of grace." He wrote that "the perplexing question of singularity was solved, for I discovered so many points of my experience that cor-

---

12. Norvell Robertson Autobiography, 1765–1846 (typed copy in Virginia Historical Society, Richmond), 26–28; Wightman, *Life of Capers,* 56; Jeter, *Life of Witt,* 36, 39–40; Smith Diary, April 3, [1855], pp. 74–75; Baptist Diary, 3; Jeter, *Recollections,* 50; Blackburn (comp. and ed.), *Life Work of Girardeau,* 23.

responded with Bunyan's exercises, that, having no doubt that he was a Christian, I could not doubt but that I also was a Christian. All the prom- ises of the gospel that I understood to be such, applied to my case, and seemed as if they had been specially intended for my benefit. And these views of my interest in the Saviour were accompanied with 'joy unspeak- able and full of glory', and I was inclined to think (erroneously) that surely the Lord never wrought with any sinner in so beautiful a way as he had with me." [13]

Like Robertson, Jeremiah Jeter was also unsure that he had experi- enced conversion. It was not until his religious instructor, Elder Harris, told him, "you are converted," that Jeter said he understood the meaning of the "new, strange, and inexplicable emotions" that perplexed him. Even then, he was not entirely convinced. "I had not experienced such a con- version as I had heard described, or as I had been seeking," he explained. But when Harris related his own experience, the youth noted that "it bore a striking resemblance to my own. Of the genuineness of his conversion I had no doubt. As my exercises bore a likeness to his, I could but cherish the hope that I might be a subject of renewing grace." [14]

For those who experienced conversion at a camp or prayer meeting, the moment of recognition might come, as it did for Thomas Cleland, during the course of a sermon or exhortation. Describing a sermon which seemed to portray his own case "exactly," Cleland observed that the preacher "'*struck the trail*' of my experience some distance back, and came on plainer and plainer, and at every step more sensibly, and with more effect. At length he came right up with me—my religious state and feeling were de- picted better than I could have possibly done it myself." [15]

By viewing conversion as a moment of recognition we come closer to understanding how nineteenth century individuals themselves experi- enced it. No doubt imitation or contagion (especially at camp meetings) also played a role and helps to explain why most religious experience fol- lowed a similar order or pattern. [16] But what the observer (historian) sees as

13. Robertson Autobiography, 30–31.

14. Jeter, *Recollections*, 55. Witt wrote that in comparing their conversion experiences, he and Jeter found "a striking similarity," and "after a solemn self-examination . . . we settled the case in our own favor, and accepted our conversion as real and sound." Jeter, *Life of Witt*, 47.

15. Edward P. Humphrey and Thomas H. Cleland, *Memoirs of the Rev. Thomas Cleland, D.D., Compiled From His Private Papers* (Cincinnati, 1859), 54.

16. See, for example, Brantley York, *The Autobiography of Brantley York* (Durham, 1910), 22, and Mood Autobiography, 26.

imitation or contagion was, for the subject of conversion, a revelation of shared experience. He experienced conversion not as imitation or contagion but as discovery, as illumination.

The moment of conversion was a time of overpowering emotions, evidenced by such actions as weeping and sobbing, falling to the ground, clapping hands, or shouting. Converts experienced great happiness, ranging from ecstasy to a feeling of peace and well-being. Even their surroundings seemed different. For Sidney Bumpas, "all nature wore a new aspect," and Charles Deems declared that after the moment of conversion "the fields seemed greener, the air sweeter, and the heaven itself brighter."[17]

While most individuals were able to pinpoint the moment of conversion as to date and time, others were unable or unwilling to do so. Some of these lacked the feeling of assurance that they associated with conversion. Moses Drury Hoge, for example, hoped that he had experienced "a change of heart," but he was beset by "doubts and hesitations." When he made a profession of faith and was accepted into the church, he became somewhat more sure of his conversion but still expressed it as a "hope." Other converts described their conversion as gradual. The sense of relief from guilt, of being changed into a new person, did not come all at once, nor in a transport of emotion, but gradually. Edward Baptist said that his relief from conviction "was not as expected, sudden, but gradual," and Samuel Dunwody wrote that the change wrought by God's grace "was gradual and almost imperceptible." James Henley Thornwell spoke of light gradually breaking in on him: "by degrees I came out, as I believe, a Christian."[18]

The overpowering emotions induced by conversion usually lasted a few hours, but never more than several days. As Richard Fuller observed, such "ecstastic feelings . . . would have rendered me unfit to live in [the] world." As the emotions subsided, the individual entered a state characterized by peace of mind and a sense of well-being, but assurance of salvation was usually imperfect. The sense of joy, peace, and well-being that derived from a feeling of acceptance by God often lasted but a short time, after which the individual was beset with doubts as to his spiritual condi-

17. Sidney D. Bumpas Autobiography and Journal (typed copy in Bumpas Family Papers, Southern Historical Collection, University of North Carolina Library), 3; Deems, *Autobiography*, 42.

18. Peyton Harrison Hoge, *Moses Drury Hoge: Life and Letters* (Richmond, 1899), 45, 50–51; Baptist Diary, 9; James Dunwody, *Reminiscences and Sermons*, 7; B. M. Palmer, *The Life and Letters of James Henley Thornwell, D.D., LL.D., Ex-President of the South Carolina College, Late Professor of Theology in the Theological Seminary at Columbia, South Carolina* (Richmond, 1875), 96.

tion. For several years after his conversion experience, Basil Manly, Jr., worried over the "coldness" of his heart, his "want of consistency . . . , of stedfastness [*sic*]." His religious state remained "a mystery" to him, alternating between "warm devotional frames when I might . . . almost as well doubt my existence as my being the subject of grace" and "cold, heartless, sinful periods which make my doubts rise like mountains." Sidney Bumpas experienced the same alternating between periods of gloom and comfort, which led him to doubt his conversion. Relief and assurance came when he decided to join the Methodist church. "Then," he wrote, "I received such a bright manifestation of my acceptance that I concluded if I had never been converted before I surely was then." Daniel Baker experienced a similar sense of relief and assurance upon joining the church at Hampden-Sydney College. But even then, feelings of doubt returned. In his journal Baker castigated himself for his "flinty heart," for his "languid and heartless" devotions. He continued to long for a "permanent" sense of assurance.[19]

Most converts joined a church either on the day of conversion or shortly thereafter. The renewed hope that Baker and Bumpas experienced upon making a profession of faith and becoming church members suggests the general significance of this action. It was both a way of making a public proclamation of one's newfound spiritual state and of immediately reinforcing one's own sense of acceptance, since admission came only after scrutiny of one's profession by the minister and other members of the church.

Being a church member, in turn, aided the new convert in seeking the life of holiness that was supposed to characterize the "professing Christian." Most southern evangelicals believed that sanctification was to be achieved gradually, and that although absolute perfection could never be reached in this life, it was the duty of the believer continually to strive for it. Thus Basil Manly, Jr., described the life of a Christian as "a constant struggle, an earnest unflinching continual strife till death." Similarly, John Bailey Adger termed the Christian life "a journey of many steps," and declared that "we have to go from step to step, rising from plane to plane, still never reaching the height of true and perfect holiness."[20] By joining a

19. Cuthbert, *Life of Fuller*, 69; Basil Manly, Jr., Diary, June 6, 1841, August 27, 1843, and "Jottings Down" (MS dated March 13, 1844) (both in Basil Manly, Jr., Papers, Special Collections, Furman University Library); Bumpas Autobiography and Journal, 3; William M. Baker, *Life of Baker*, 34, 37, 39, 43, 44, 48–51, 55, 61.

20. Manly, Jr., Diary, February 10, 1833; Adger, *My Life and Times*, 73. For a discussion

church and putting himself under its discipline, the new convert obtained help and guidance in living a Christian life.

Immersion in religious activities was another means of sustaining spirituality. Indeed, converts took a new pleasure in religious activities. Daniel Witt declared that he "enjoyed" worship services and private prayer "with new delight," and Francis Asbury Mood said that after his conversion he listened to preaching with "an eagerness and delight . . . I had never felt before." Perhaps one reason for this was that since much of the preaching was directed to the conversion of sinners, converts could find a certain satisfaction in feeling that they had attained the state which the less fortunate were being exhorted to seek. For perhaps much the same reason—because they were working to sustain assurance rather than to obtain it— new converts found prayer and meditation more gratifying. Of Scripture reading, Mood said that "before, I had only found condemnation in its pages, now I found them filled with blessed consolation and promises."[21]

Finally, joining a church and participating in religious activities was a way of avoiding the temptations of the world. William Capers said that after his conversion, "I longed with intense desire for the time to arrive when, by joining the Church, I should formally break with the world, and identify myself with . . . the most spiritual and least worldly . . . of all the sects of Christians." The utility of such an identification for the professing Christian is seen in the case of Francis Asbury Mood. While attending Charleston College, he joined the debating society and at the first meeting declared himself to be a Methodist "and trying to serve God." Mood recalled that his speech not only "made a brave beginning in the matter of debate," but, more importantly, his public avowal delivered him "from a thousand temptations." Because of it, Mood wrote, except on one occasion "I never was solicited during my whole college course to do anything that would have compromised a Christian profession." The importance to the new convert of what was termed "religious society" is also seen in the experience of James Finley. When he experienced conversion he was living in a neighborhood where there were "no religious persons . . . and no religious meetings to attend." Finley "felt, deeply, the need of Christian society." He held prayer meetings in the woods with his brother and another young man, but these were not enough to satisfy him. "I sighed for Church

of the doctrine of sanctification in southern evangelical theology see John B. Boles, *The Great Revival, 1787–1805: The Origins of the Southern Evangelical Mind* (Lexington, 1972), 125, 139–41.

21. Jeter, *Life of Witt*, 46; Mood Autobiography, 30.

privileges, and communion with the people of God," he wrote. The lack of religious society was partly responsible for his backsliding into "the way of sin."[22]

Even those favored with religious society and the means of grace were in danger of backsliding. Constant self-examination was necessary to prevent it. Few individuals have left such detailed evidence of the impulse to self-examination and the part it played in the search for holiness as Basil Manly, Jr. Shortly after his conversion he began "a catalogue of questions for self-examination." Writing in his diary for June 6, 1841, he noted that he had "resolved to examine the state of my heart, at least, weekly, and to write it down." Later in the evening he wrote the first of many examinations: "When I contrast the feeling of my heart with the exercises of that blessed man of God, Jon. Edwards, I am astonished at the coldness of my own heart. But when I read the feelings of Paul[,] of Peter & of the Apostles and above all when I consider Christ in an *agony for me*! O! I know not what to say or think. Lord take away the heart of stone & give me a heart of flesh. Why cannot I feel as others have felt. Give me some view of thee O Lord that I may feel thy power & wisdom & goodness." Manly also began a list of resolutions (modeled on those of Jonathan Edwards and ultimately numbering around one hundred) to help him live a Christian life. Indeed, for a while after his conversion he engaged in a veritable orgy of self-examination, citing his faults in his diary, resolving to overcome them, and drawing up schedules and lists to structure his life around the purpose of being a Christian. A list composed in July, 1841, entitled "What Shall I do, this next week, to advance the great ends of my being?" enumerated twenty-one items, a combination of trivial and serious objectives that might be expected of a college youth of fifteen who had recently obtained religion. First on the list was "must not bite my nails," for nail biting had been and would continue to be one of Basil's "besetting sins." Then came such items as rising early, making "Memoranda" daily and reading over his "'Resolutions' daily *this week* at least," making labels for his mother's medicine cabinet, and cleaning up his room at college, alternating with other duties such as reading devotional books, trying "in all my actions to 'Watch' & 'Pray'" and to "Mind & Keep humble." The last-named item, Manly confessed, was "a grand difficulty," for, he wrote, "if I succeed at all I am afraid I shall be proud; & pride will have a fall."[23]

22. Wightman, *Life of Capers*, 74–75; Mood Autobiography, 44–45; Finley, *Autobiography*, 170–73.
23. Manly, Jr., Diary, August 18, 1840, June 6, 1841, and "What Shall I do, this next

The striving for holiness placed heavy emotional demands on professing Christians. It is not surprising that they should have been excessively introspective, constantly examining and analyzing their spiritual condition. But, significantly, their preoccupation with self was not as strong as when they were under conviction. Conversion not only provided relief from feelings of guilt and despair, but also released the individual from debilitating egoism. Having obtained assurance of his own salvation, the convert felt an expansive love for others and a concern that they too should obtain the blessings of religion. Daniel Baker recalled that after conversion, he was "filled with zeal and love" and his "heart [was] gently drawn out towards my fellow students." The first time that Jeremiah Jeter engaged in private prayer following his conversion experience, he found himself petitioning God not only for himself but for others. He wrote, "That morning I prayed for my parents, my brothers and sisters, my remoter kindred, my friends, and I continued to extend the circle of my intercession until it comprehended the whole world. My prayer was a mystery to me. I had intended to pray, as I had ever before done, simply for myself, but my feelings had borne me quite beyond the limit prescribed by my judgment." Jeter's friend Witt said that after conversion "I loved everybody; I prayed for everybody; and had salvation been put into my hands, everybody would have been saved."[24]

Such feelings of love and concern for the religious state of others were frequently translated into efforts on their behalf. Following his conversion experience Daniel Lindley went out to share his newfound happiness with the unconverted youths of the neighborhood. Other new converts began holding prayer meetings with friends, relatives, and neighbors.[25]

The conversion experience was probably the most important factor influencing the decision to enter the ministry. One reason for this is that conversion tended to occur during adolescence or in the teens, at the very time when most young men were confronted with the problem of choosing an occupation. Also, the conversion experience tended to distract the individual from the world and its concerns and caused him to look almost exclusively to religion as the focus of his life. New converts were inclined

week, to advance the great ends of my being?" (MS dated University of Alabama, July 18, 1841, in Manly, Jr., Papers).

24. William M. Baker, *Life of Baker*, 48; Jeter, *Recollections*, 54–55; Jeter, *Life of Witt*, 46.
25. Edwin W. Smith, *The Life and Times of Daniel Lindley, 1801–80* (London, 1949), 14; see also, for example, William M. Baker, *Life of Baker*, 48; Finley, *Autobiography*, 180–81, and Thomas Cary Johnson, *Life and Letters of Dabney*, 63.

to throw themselves into an orgy of religious activity after joining a church. Finding greater satisfaction in that aspect of their lives than in any other, they were naturally led to look upon the ministry as the ideal career, the way in which religion could become, as Daniel Baker put it, "the very element in which I should live, and move, and have my being."[26]

Becoming a minister was also a way for the convert to signify that break with the world which a Christian profession entailed. Richard Fuller and John Emory gave up profitable legal careers for the ministry. Richard McIlwaine, who, prior to conversion and joining the Presbyterian church, had been preparing for a law career, felt impelled to abandon "worldly ambition" and preach the gospel. Having become a Christian, he felt that he "must not lead a life of self-satisfaction and indulgence, or work in a sphere devoted to self-gratification and aggrandizement, but must give my life to the service of God and my fellow-men." Similarly, it seemed to James Furman that, having dedicated himself to God, having "promised to give all my thoughts, all my actions, & all my words to the cause of His Glory," he could not enter any pursuit other than the ministry. "I think I would account it an honor (& esteem it my happiness) to not only to [*sic*] resign all temporal advantages, but to lay down my life for the glory of God," he wrote.[27]

Times of revival, when numerous young men were converted and when religious enthusiasm pervaded the community, produced many of the ministers in the Old South. Jeremiah Jeter and Daniel Witt were converted and entered the ministry during the revival of 1821 in Virginia, an awakening which, as Jeter observed, was "in a remarkable degree . . . promoted by agents created by itself." Jeter delivered his first religious address— "impulsive, unpremeditated, and without method"—on the bank of the stream in which he had just been baptized. He was invited to speak in prayer meetings and at the close of sermons. Then his pastor began asking him to preach at meetings. Jeter did so, "sometimes with freedom and pleasure, and not unfrequently with confusion and shame," and soon he

---

26. William M. Baker, *Life of Baker*, 30. George Gilman Smith's religious activities included going to preaching on Sunday, Sunday school in the morning and afternoon, prayer meeting Wednesday and Thursday night, love feast once a month. He also attended college prayer meetings and revival meetings. "I . . . was never more fully employed religiously than I was during these two years," he observed, adding, "I doubt if I had ever been as continuously happy before nor ever was afterward." George Gilman Smith Autobiography, 40–41.

27. Cuthbert, *Life of Fuller*, 74; Robert Emory, *The Life of the Rev. John Emory, D.D.* (New York, 1841), 36–37; Richard McIlwaine, *Memories of Three Score Years and Ten* (New York, 1908), 91; James C. Furman, MS dated June 1, 1828, in James Clement Furman Papers, Special Collections, Furman University Library.

was traveling throughout Virginia, promoting the revival. Witt's experience was similar. Like Jeter he was called upon to pray in public meetings or to address the congregation at their close. When some of the brethren suggested that he become a minister, he gave the matter serious consideration and, concerned about his limitations for the task, decided to "continue the exercise of my gifts, as opportunity might be presented to me." As he explained, "I went with the preachers to their appointments; continued to speak to the people; and before I was aware of it, I had become a preacher myself."[28]

Jeter said that he "glided into the ministry without design."[29] So did William Capers, though his entry into the ministry was more painful and problematic than either Witt's or Jeter's. Following his conversion experience, Capers was invited by the Reverend William Gassaway to accompany him and his junior colleague on their circuit. Capers accepted, viewing the journey as an opportunity to benefit from the spiritual guidance of his "reverend friend" and to attend religious meetings daily. He was amazed during family prayer at the home where the three men stopped the first night when "the books were handed to me . . . and I was asked to have prayers for them. Could it be right? And could I possibly perform it?" Deferring to the judgment of "those who were so much wiser and better than myself," Capers took the books, "though the extreme agitation I was under scarcely admitted of reading, and much less praying." The next day, accompanying the two preachers in visiting their flock, Capers was again called on several times to pray, which he did "with no little perturbation, doubting its propriety." He was even more agitated upon being called to the pulpit by Gassaway and ordered to "exhort." Yet exhort he did, "if I may call it so," Capers remembered. "The word served me for a text—'earnestly to beseech,' 'to prevail by entreaty;' and so I made an effort to beseech the people to believe and do as they had been taught by the preacher." Later, when Capers confided his doubts and anxiety to Gassaway regarding the propriety of his praying and exhorting, the preacher simply urged him to be guided by God's will. The junior preacher, responding to the same complaint, offered the reasonable argument that Capers' exhorting was nothing more than what every Christian ought to do, that it did not make him a preacher or even imply that he was to become one. So Capers continued riding with the two men, exhorting in the pulpit and "wherever and as often as occasion served."

28. Jeter, *Recollections*, 41, 57–60; Jeter, *Life of Witt*, 51–55.
29. Jeter, *Recollections*, 62.

Nevertheless, his uneasiness persisted, and it was not until he experienced what the Methodists termed the second blessing that he acquired "new views as to my calling in life." Former doubts were dissipated. "I could no longer say, nor think, that I was never to be a preacher," Capers wrote, "but, on the contrary, it appeared to me, and the conviction grew stronger and stronger, that I was called to preach." Returning home for a week, he informed his family that he had decided to give up studying law, and arrangements were made for him to continue riding with Gassaway, exhorting at religious meetings and studying for a career in the ministry. When, at a camp meeting a young Charlestonian acknowledged Capers as the instrument of his awakening and conversion, the would-be preacher felt even more confirmed in his determination. Shortly thereafter, at the quarterly meeting in November, 1808, about five months after his conversion experience, Capers was licensed to preach and recommended to the Annual Conference to be admitted on trial in the Methodist itinerancy.[30]

Although Jeter claimed that he entered the ministry "without carefully inquiring whether I had been divinely called to it," most evangelicals described their decision to enter the ministry as the response to a providential call. According to the evangelical theology, the ministry differed from other professions, which an individual might choose according to his talents or taste, in being "a vocation from Heaven, such as lays a necessity upon the man to preach the gospel." Evangelicals generally described the call in terms of internal and external manifestations or evidences. Internal evidence of a call to the ministry was a desire to preach the gospel and/or a conviction that it was one's duty to do so. Evangelicals stressed the self-sacrificing nature of the desire to preach; one who was truly called was not moved by "worldly inducement" or a selfish regard to his own interests, but by a desire "to consecrate all to the service of Christ's kingdom" and by an enlarged sympathy for the unconverted. The desire or conviction might be reinforced by the individual's realization, after "a candid, calm and prayerful examination" of his own character, that he possessed the qualifications or talents (God-given) to enable him to perform the duties of the ministerial office.[31]

In some individuals, the desire to preach developed out of the concern for sinners that characterized the new convert. For someone like Daniel

30. Wightman, *Life of Capers*, 76–83.
31. Jeter, *Recollections*, 60; *Southern Christian Advocate*, March 25, 1853, p. 174; "A Call to the Ministry of the Gospel," *Virginia Evangelical and Literary Magazine*, IX (March, 1826), pp. 115–16; *Religious Herald*, October 5, 1832, pp. 154–55, April 30, 1840, p. 71, May 7, 1840, p. 75.

Witt, who "thought that a love for souls constrained me to do something for *them*," the ministry appeared to be the best way both to "glorify God, and promote the welfare of men." Edward Baptist gave up the study of medicine because "it seemed the greatest privilege and happiness on earth to be able to preach Christ crucified to perishing sinners." Baptist's desire often expressed itself spontaneously. When walking in the fields or woods he would find himself "preaching with great feeling and comfort to a large congregation of weeping hearers."[32]

Other young men decided to enter the ministry because they became convinced that it was their duty to do so. The conviction of duty was frequently described as an "impression" or "impressions" that were presumed to have come from God. Francis Asbury Mood said that he was made to feel his duty to preach during one of the Young Men's Prayer Meetings he had been attending since his conversion. He recalled that

on one occasion, kneeling in the Southwest corner of the room engaged in earnest prayer an impression was suddenly and vividly made on my mind that I would find it my duty to preach the Gospel. The thought came suddenly, unexpectedly and greatly startled me. I tried to banish it, but it hung about my heart like a great weight. During the prayers that succeeded I struggled to shake off the impression, I tried to pray and could not and at last getting down upon my knees, upon a call to pray, I said in a whisper audible to myself "Yes Lord if it is thy will I will preach the Gospel."[33]

As Mood's account suggests, the "impression" was an idea proposed to the mind through the agency of the Holy Spirit. Evangelical theology stressed that the call to the ministry did not consist in "any extraordinary or miraculous influence on the mind." The individual should not look for a voice from Heaven, or dreams or visions. Nor should he suppose that the action of the Holy Spirit was so compulsive as to prevent him from exercising his own judgment in the matter. "We are not to expect any such irresistible force of divine influence as shall *cleave* its way through all the mysterious avenues and approaches to the will, and set aside the laws of moral agency, and compel the mind to surrender," declared the editor of the *Southern Christian Advocate*. "Room is left for such a concurrence on our part as obtains in all the ordinary procedures of experimental religion."[34]

The concurrence of the individual came by way of prayer and self-examination. He must decide not only whether he desired the holy office

32. Jeter, *Life of Witt*, 51; Baptist Diary, 5.
33. Mood Autobiography, 31–32.
34. *Southern Christian Advocate*, March 25, 1853, p. 174, April 1, 1853, p. 178.

but whether he had the necessary qualifications for it—piety, learning or, at least, "native strength of intellect," "uprightness of walk and conversation," speaking ability, good health, etc. Most ministers claimed to have resisted the call at first, much as the sinner resisted the claims of the gospel. Conscious of the awesome responsibilities involved, many young men felt incompetent to fill the ministerial office. A few, like William Winans and Brantley York, believed they lacked sufficient means to support themselves while engaged in the ministry or to enable them to acquire the necessary education for it. Mood's inward struggle over the decision to enter the ministry was very brief, as we have seen, but Peter Doub claimed to have undergone "powerful struggles in my mind about Preaching the Gospel." He could not assent to the idea of preaching because he felt he lacked the proper education, the fortitude, and the "experience as a professor" necessary to the task. As a result his mind was "in great perplexity, and distress." At night, he recalled, "my mind was disturbed by dreams." Often while engaged in business, "I found myself engaged in warning Sinners to turn from the error of their ways." He tried to get rid of the "distressing impressions" by immersing himself in temporal matters. After a period of alternating between resistance and concurrence, during which he nearly lost all comfort of religion, Doub assented to the call. "Finally, seeing that my Eternal Salvation much, (if not chiefly,) depended upon my complyance, [*sic*] I at length resolved fully, that I would offer myself to the Church, as a Candidate for the Ministry."[35]

While individuals like Doub resisted the call because they felt inadequate to fill the office, others did so out of an unwillingness to give up the comforts of the world to engage in the self-sacrificing task of saving souls. Abner Clopton's biographer said that his success as a doctor prevented him from entering the ministry. Clopton "found it no easy matter to relinquish affluence and worldly distinction, brought within his grasp by years of patient toil, for a profession which promised him little on earth

35. *Ibid.*, April 1, 1853, p. 178; *Religious Herald*, April 30, 1840, p. 71, May 7, 1840, p. 75; "A Call to the Ministry of the Gospel," *Virginia Evangelical and Literary Magazine*, IX (March, 1826), p. 115; William Winans Autobiography (typed copy in William Winans Collection, Mississippi Conference Historical Society, Millsaps-Wilson Library, Millsaps College), 26; York, *Autobiography*, 31–32; Doub Journal, 6–7. The notion of resistance was sufficiently common that individuals who did not experience it remarked on the fact. Jeter became "quite anxious" as to the validity of his call because it "seemed to differ widely from that of many of the old preachers. They represented, or seemed to represent, that they had been constrained to enter the ministry sorely against their wills. . . . Unfortunately for me, as I supposed, I had a wish to preach the gospel." His doubts were dispelled when, a few years later, he found the passage in Paul which declared that "if any man desire the office of a bishop, he desireth a good work." Jeter, *Recollections*, 60–61.

besides toil, poverty, and reproach." Moreover, Clopton's absorption in "worldly pursuits" caused him to lose the ardent piety he had felt immediately after his conversion experience. Destitute of the godliness which he believed necessary to the ministerial office, Clopton could not respond affirmatively and completely to the "exercises" he experienced with regard to the ministry. For several years he continued his medical practice while at the same time engaging in "public labours for Christ"—conducting prayer meetings and preaching. Only after an extended and painful struggle and following a severe illness similar to the one that had preceded his conversion, was he brought "to the solemn purpose of . . . devoting himself *exclusively* to the work of the gospel ministry."[36]

Whatever the cause of struggle, once the individual felt able to assent to the call to preach, he experienced a feeling of relief and happiness comparable to that of the newly converted. Mood said that his decision to become a minister "seemed to bring a settled peace of mind," and John Emory, whose decision provoked strong opposition from his father and entailed giving up a profitable legal practice, declared that "the moment I entered into this covenant upon my knees I felt my mind relieved, and the peace and love of God to flow through my soul, (though I had before lost almost all the comforts of religion)." Since his decision, Emory felt that he had "enjoyed closer and more constant communion with God than ever before."[37]

Besides "impressions" on the mind, one might also look for other evidence of a call to the ministry, such as "the indications of providence." Evangelicals taught that God sometimes encouraged individuals to enter the ministry by "interposing" in their favor and opening up the opportunity to do so. Thus S. G. Hillyer adduced as evidence of his call the fact that, against the advice of friends, he was led (providentially) to cultivate "the art of publick & extempore speaking" and that "about the time when I was preparing to enter upon the profession of the Law, The Lord was pleased to open my eyes—and show me my obligations to love him, and at the same time to shut up for the time at least every approach to the bar." Finally, evangelicals believed that if God called a man to preach, he gave him "seals to his ministry," that is, evidence of being instrumental in awakening and converting sinners. Success in winning souls to Christ as an ex-

---

36. Jeter, *Memoir of Clopton*, 37–45, 52–53, 70–73.
37. Mood Autobiography, 32; John Emory to the Reverend James Bateman, November 2, 1809, in Emory, *Life of Emory*, 40–41.

horter, or, later, as a minister, could be interpreted as proof of a call to the ministry.[38]

External evidence of a call was manifested in the views of others as to one's qualifications. If a congregation felt spiritually edified by a young man, or if a church or other ecclesiastical body judged him fitted to be a preacher, this was evidence of his calling. Evangelicals stressed that internal evidence—especially the desire to convert sinners—was more important than external evidence, and that no individual should consider himself called unless he were sure of an inward conviction.[39] But for the individual who was unsure of his suitability for the ministry, external evidence could become an extremely important factor influencing his decision. Many youths entered the ministry primarily as a result of the encouragement they received from those around them—pastors, friends, family, or brethren of the church.

The convert who revealed spiritual "gifts" was likely to be urged by his pastor or some other person to consider the claims of a ministerial vocation. New converts, because of their eagerness to participate in religious exercises, often found themselves called upon to pray or exhort at prayer meetings, Bible classes and the like. Not a few were willing volunteers, eager to testify to their recent conversion experience and to extend the blessings of religion to others. Peter Cartwright remembered that "in class and other meetings, when my soul was filled with the love of God, I would mount a bench and exhort with all the power I had." John B. McFerrin, who was converted at age fourteen, was soon leading prayers in public. "In class-meeting," he recalled, "I always spoke either voluntarily or in answer to questions propounded by the preacher or leader. In family prayer my father occasionally called on me to lead." McFerrin became a class leader himself at sixteen and was licensed to exhort the next year. Other pious young men would organize prayer meetings or teach Sunday school. Where ministers were unavailable or nonexistent, or their visits infrequent, it was not uncommon for relatives or neighbors to ask a young man with a talent for exhorting to lead prayer meetings or to engage in religious conversation with inquiring souls. Such efforts, if they proved successful, usually convinced the brethren that the individual "was going

38. "A Call to the Ministry of the Gospel," *Virginia Evangelical and Literary Magazine*, IX (March, 1826), pp. 116–17; the Reverend S. G. Hillyer to James C. Furman, February 1, 1839, in James Furman Papers; *Wesleyan Journal*, June 24, 1826, p. 3.

39. "A Call to the Ministry of the Gospel," *Virginia Evangelical and Literary Magazine*, IX (March, 1826), p. 113.

to make a preacher," even though he might as yet be undecided or even resistant to the idea.[40] No doubt the power of suggestion or the expectations of those around him played a part in influencing a youth to consider the ministry.

The family also played an important role in shaping an individual's decision. Some young men had before them the example of fathers or other male relatives who were ministers, and it was often expected that they would follow suit. Others claimed that the maternal influence was decisive. Indeed, it was not uncommon for a pious mother to "consecrate" a newborn son to the ministry and to encourage him in that direction even as a child.[41]

All of the evangelical denominations regarded piety as the chief qualification for a minister. To be considered as a candidate for the ministry, an individual must have experienced the grace of God in his own heart, otherwise he was unfit to preach the gospel. The prospective candidate was also expected to exhibit blameless deportment. He should be leading a life of "eminent holiness." Finally, evangelicals stressed "aptness to teach" as a qualification for the ministry. A candidate should have demonstrated the talents necessary to preaching and should be able to gain the confidence and command the attention of his hearers.[42]

Although agreeing as to qualifications, the denominations varied considerably in the kind of education and training they required of ministers. The early Baptists and Methodists were prejudiced against education, especially education for the ministry.[43] In the late eighteenth and early nineteenth centuries the formal education of many Baptist and Methodist min-

40. Cartwright, *Autobiography*, 58; O. P. Fitzgerald, *John B. McFerrin: A Biography* (Nashville, 1888), 34, 36, 37–38; Finley, *Autobiography*, 180–86; Robertson Autobiography, 32; W. B. and A. D. Gillette, *Memoir of Rev. Daniel Holbrook Gillette, of Mobile, Alabama* (Philadelphia, 1846), 24.

41. On paternal influence see, for example, Fitzgerald, *John B. McFerrin*, 49, Andrew Broaddus, *The Sermons and Other Writings of the Rev. Andrew Broaddus, With a Memoir of His Life, by J. B. Jeter,* ed. A. Broaddus (New York, 1852), 4, and Adger, *My Life and Times*, 85; on maternal influence, Maxwell, *Memoir of Rice*, 3, and Emory, *Life of Emory*, 11.

42. Boles, *Great Revival*, 120; Robert N. Watkin, Jr., "The Forming of the Southern Presbyterian Minister: From Calvin to the American Civil War" (Ph.D. dissertation, Vanderbilt University, 1969), 382–84; *Religious Herald*, October 5, 1832, pp. 154–55; *Wesleyan Journal*, June 24, 1826, p. 3, August 19, 1826, p. 2; *Southern Christian Advocate*, February 17, 1859, p. 149; "The Power of the Pulpit," *Southern Presbyterian Review*, II (September, 1848), p. 290.

43. On Baptist and Methodist views of education, see Albea Godbold, *The Church College of the Old South* (Durham, 1944), 17–19, 30–35, A. H. Newman, *A History of the Baptist Churches in the United States* (New York, 1894), 381–82, 406–408, 410–16, and Emory Stevens Bucke (ed.), *The History of American Methodism* (3 vols.; New York, 1964), I, 265–72, 546–71.

isters consisted of little more than attendance at a neighborhood school for anywhere from a few months to several years. Peter Doub, for example, was said by his biographer to have received no more than eighteen months of schooling over a period of eight years. At age ten Daniel Witt was sent to a neighborhood school which he attended a little over two years, after which he began working on the family farm.[44] Still, the limited education which Witt and Doub received ranked at or above the level of schooling which the majority of white Southerners received in the early nineteenth century.[45] Academies and classical schools, many of them conducted by clergymen, provided a step beyond the neighborhood schools and served in some cases to prepare individuals for college. By the 1830s Baptist and Methodist opposition to education had lessened and the two denominations began establishing church colleges. Then, although prejudice against ministerial (as opposed to general) education persisted, it became less unusual for Baptist and Methodist ministers to have attended college. Francis Asbury Mood, for example, attended the classical high school in Charleston and then went on to Charleston College. Basil Manly, Jr., received his early schooling at the Academy of the German Friendly Society in Charleston and at a private school in Tuscaloosa, after which he entered the University of Alabama. Abner Clopton's schooling included Banister Academy and a private classical school, followed by North Carolina University.[46]

In the Presbyterian church a college diploma or its equivalent was required of all ministerial candidates. Some southern Presbyterian ministers received their collegiate education outside the South, but as the movement to educate southern youths at home gained momentum, they were increasingly likely to attend a denominational college such as Hampden-Sydney or a state institution such as the South Carolina College or the University of Virginia. Three years of theological training at one of the Presbyterian seminaries—for example, Princeton, Union (in Virginia), or

44. Rev. M. T. Plyler, "Peter Doub, Itinerant of Heroic Days," *Historical Papers of Trinity College Historical Society and the North Carolina Conference Historical Society*, Series IX (1912), 36; Jeter, *Life of Witt*, 29–30.

45. For a comprehensive discussion of education in the Old South see Charles S. Sydnor, *The Development of Southern Sectionalism, 1819–1848* (Baton Rouge, 1948), 57–73. Sydnor writes, p. 59, that in the 1830s "various persons estimated that about a third of the adult white people of Alabama, Louisiana, Virginia, and North Carolina were illiterate, and there is no reason to think that conditions were better in other slave states."

46. Cody, *Life and Labours of Mood*, 99; Joseph Powhatan Cox, "A Study of the Life and Work of Basil Manly, Jr." (Th.D. dissertation, Southern Baptist Theological Seminary, 1954), 21, 27, 31; Jeter, *Memoir of Clopton*, 15, 18, 23.

Columbia (in South Carolina)—completed the formal education required of would-be ministers. While pursuing their theological studies, seminary students gained practical experience by organizing Sunday schools or leading prayer meetings and preaching trial sermons to congregations in the surrounding community.[47] If Robert Lewis Dabney's observations are accurate, such preaching could serve as a rigorous test of the candidate's abilities. Not only did the Union Seminary professors attend and offer criticism of the sermon, but the congregations were also highly critical. Dabney described the congregation of the small country church at which he preached his first sermons as "pretty select and pretty critical, the very worst place to preach in." The congregations in the vicinity of the seminary, he declared, "only regard the preaching of the seminarians as a sort of imitation of the reality, and look on with no other feeling than curiosity to see how complete the mimicry will be. . . . And then . . . they all criticize, from suckling babies up, through the children, the negroes, and all."[48]

Before the establishment of theological seminaries, Presbyterian youths acquired their theological education by studying with some approved minister. When Thomas Cleland was admitted by Presbytery as a candidate for the ministry in 1802, "the custom was, if any young man wished to study theology, and prepare for the ministry, he must get in privately with some settled minister, board in his family gratuitously, perhaps, and in this solitary way arrive at length to the pulpit." After graduating from Princeton, Daniel Baker studied theology under the pastor of the Presbyterian church in Winchester, Virginia, who set the young candidate to exhorting at the Wednesday evening prayer meetings and even left Baker in charge of his two congregations when he took an extended trip. This method of ministerial education proved unsatisfactory, however. As Ernest Trice Thompson points out, "only successful ministers were desired as teachers, and successful ministers were too busy to teach effectively." Presbyteries and synods began designating certain ministers to teach candidates. The next step, taken early in the nineteenth century, was the establishment of theological seminaries, the first being Princeton Theological Seminary, founded in 1812. But even after other seminaries had been established in the South, according to Thompson, "a surprisingly large num-

47. For a thorough discussion of ministerial education in the Presbyterian church see Ernest Trice Thompson, *Presbyterians in the South* (3 vols.; Richmond, 1963), I, 274–85, 501–509.
48. Robert Lewis Dabney to his mother, July 8, 1845, and April 14, 1846, in Thomas Cary Johnson, *Life and Letters of Dabney*, 87–88.

ber of ministers continued to receive their theological education outside the seminaries, according to the older method."[49]

Baptists employed the "solitary" method of ministerial education throughout the first half of the nineteenth century. During the period that he served as pastor to the Baptist churches in Charlotte county, Virginia (1823–1833), Abner Clopton usually had one or two ministerial candidates boarding with him. They utilized his extensive library of theological works and received instruction from him, in addition to assisting him in his pastoral duties. One such student was Daniel Witt. Richard Fuller also had a number of young men studying with him for the ministry. Besides reading theology under his direction, they also led prayer meetings and preached alternately on Sunday afternoons. Like the Presbyterians, though, the Baptists ultimately found such methods of ministerial education unsatisfactory. Despite considerable opposition and apathy within the denomination, they began establishing theological institutes in the mid-1820s and early 1830s. In 1859 the Southern Baptist Theological Seminary was established in Greenville, South Carolina.[50]

Prior to the Civil War, southern Methodists founded no theological seminaries. Scorning formal ministerial education, they stressed practical experience instead. The itinerancy was the chief school in which ministerial candidates received their training. After having decided to enter the ministry, William Capers believed it would be necessary for him to pursue a "regular course of divinity studies," but the Reverend Gassaway persuaded him that his own "brief methodistic course"—"to study and preach, and preach and study, from day to day"—was the better one. And so, Capers, like many other Methodist preachers, acquired his ministerial education while riding circuit. Among the Methodists, presiding elders assumed the role of teachers and exemplars, carrying in their saddlebags books and tracts which they distributed to the young circuit preachers on trial.[51]

Whether they stressed formal or practical methods of ministerial education, all of the denominations emphasized the need for self-education on the part of candidates and ministers. Many southern preachers engaged

49. Humphrey and Cleland, *Memoirs of Cleland*, 77; William M. Baker, *Life of Baker*, 78–79; Thompson, *Presbyterians in the South*, I, 275–76, 286.

50. Jeter, *Memoir of Clopton*, 108; Jeter, *Life of Witt*, 71–82, 85–86, 135–38; Cuthbert, *Life of Fuller*, 115; Godbold, *Church College of the Old South*, 24–30; Newman, *History of the Baptist Churches*, 406–16.

51. Bucke (ed.), *History of American Methodism*, I, 465–68; Wightman, *Life of Capers*, 83–86.

in a more or less intensive program of study, reading not only theological and doctrinal works, biblical commentaries, sermons, religious biographies and personal narratives, but a wide range of historical, biographical and literary works outside the field of religion. The Methodist General Conference in 1816 institutionalized the precept of self-education in the Course of Study (initially two years, in 1844 extended to four) to be formulated by each annual conference for ministerial candidates within its jurisdiction. No man could be received into full connection in an annual conference unless he had passed the prescribed Course of Study. Though it was not uniform throughout the church and was often not rigorously enforced, the Course of Study was believed by its supporters to be an effective means of ministerial education. Of course it also helped, in conjunction with other factors, to delay the establishment of theological seminaries.[52]

All of the denominations prescribed a period of probation for ministerial candidates prior to ordination. Among the Presbyterians the probationary period followed graduation from the seminary. The candidate was examined by a presbytery and, if found to be satisfactory, was licensed to preach. Licentiates preached to congregations that had no pastor, but they could not administer the sacraments or officiate at weddings. When they received a call to a regular pastorate, they were ordained by the presbytery under which they were to labor and authorized to perform all ministerial duties. Whereas among the Presbyterians the period of probation was fairly short—usually less than a year—among the Methodists it lasted much longer. The candidate was received on trial by conference and itinerated for two years. If his performance was acceptable, he became a deacon. After another two years he was elected elder and given the authority to administer the sacraments. Among the Baptists it was the congregation that granted a license to a candidate who felt called to preach and who had demonstrated his gifts in a trial sermon. Licensed ministers usually preached at large and were ordained when they were called to take charge of a particular congregation. Unlike licensed ministers, who were limited to preaching, ordained ministers could also administer the sacraments.[53]

52. Bucke (ed.), *History of American Methodism*, I, 566–69. For the texts which made up the Course of Study see Robert E. Chiles, *Theological Transition in American Methodism: 1790–1935* (Nashville, 1965), 32–34.
53. Thompson, *Presbyterians in the South*, I, 212–13; Watkin, "Forming of the Southern Presbyterian Minister," 198–99, 300, 304–306; Bucke (ed.), *History of American Methodism*, I, 465–68; Walter Brownlow Posey, *The Baptist Church in the Lower Mississippi Valley, 1776–1845* (Lexington, 1957), 22–23; William Warren Sweet, *Religion on the American Frontier: The Baptists, 1783–1830, A Collection of Source Materials* (New York, 1964), 39–40, 40n.

Ordination marked the end of one phase of the religious career of the would-be minister and the beginning of another. The experiences of conversion and calling played an important role in shaping evangelicals' view of themselves and their office. As the recipients of God's grace and feeling called by him to the ministry, they were bound to consider their office an awesome responsibility.

CHAPTER TWO

The Ministry

Describing his ordination by Bethel Presbytery, James Henley Thornwell declared, "I felt that a new era had commenced in my life—that I was no longer a citizen of the world, but an ambassador of God, standing in the stead of Jesus Christ and beseeching men to turn from the unsatisfying vanities of a fleeting life and to fix their hopes on the enduring sources of beatitude which surrounds the throne of God." Other evangelicals shared Thornwell's exalted view of the clerical office. Jeremiah Jeter wrote to his friend Daniel Witt shortly after the two had begun preaching that their office was "one of infinite importance." It stood "far above those which relate only to the regulation of empires, or, the temporal destinies of men." Jeter declared that he would "rather be instrumental in the salvation of a single Soul, than like Washington, to be the father of a nation." [1]

The exalted character of the ministry derived, first of all, from the fact that its practitioners had been called to their office by God himself. Thus the preacher was an ambassador of God, a representative of no mere earthly potentate but of "the King of kings, and the Lord of lords." As such he was "invested with a portion of the lofty elevation and dignity of the superior he serve[d]." Secondly, whereas other professions were concerned with the temporal interests of men, the minister's concern was

1. James Henley Thornwell to General James Gillespie, June 13, 1835, in James Henley Thornwell Papers, South Caroliniana Library, University of South Carolina; Jeremiah Jeter to Daniel Witt, February 16, 1827, in Virginia Baptist Historical Society Collection, University of Richmond.

"Eternal Life," and "the prize for which he contend[ed], the immortal soul." His work, unlike that of other men—the physician who cared "for the bodies of men," the lawyer who concerned himself with "the civil rights of men"—had "immediate respect to a future and endless existence." The exalted character of the ministry also rested on the fact that the minister's sphere was "co-extensive with all the relations which man sustains." As John Holt Rice explained,

It embraces every duty, in every situation of life. It reaches to the magistrate in his chair of state, to the judge on his bench, to the legislator in his hall, to the neighbour in his transactions with his fellow men, to the master in the arrangement of his family, to the husband and wife, the parent and child in their domestic circle; yea, and to a man in the inner chamber of his bosom, his secret thoughts and purposes. For, to all these do the precepts of the divine word extend; and the minister of religion is bound faithfully to interpret, and fully to declare the whole will of the Almighty as revealed in his holy word, concerning all human interests and relations.

Nor was the salutary influence of the ministry limited to individuals. "The moral and political salvation of the world depends more upon the ministry under God, than upon any other means," declared a writer in the *Christian Index*. The editor of the *Southern Christian Advocate* termed the ministry "the agent of a high and pure civilization."[2]

Saving sinners—saving the world—was a task of considerable magnitude and difficulty. The principle of voluntaryism, which operated throughout the United States by virtue of religious pluralism and the separation of church and state, made it even more arduous. People were not automatically members of a church and subject to its discipline. Denominations had to maintain and perpetuate themselves by purely voluntary means. Revivals, Sunday schools, and missionary activities were just some of the ways in which they spread their beliefs and added to the list of members. None of the three denominations was opposed to the principle of voluntaryism. Indeed, the Baptists and Presbyterians of Virginia had played an important role in bringing about the separation of church and state. Nevertheless, the principle did necessitate constant evangelism over a broad area,

2. *Religious Herald*, August 29, 1850, p. 138; *Christian Index*, January 14, 1842, p. 25, January 18, 1838, p. 24; *Central Presbyterian*, March 21, 1857, p. 46; John H. Rice, *The Importance of the Gospel Ministry. A Sermon, Preached at the Opening of the Synod of Virginia, on the Sixteenth of October, 1817* (Richmond, 1817), 8; *Southern Christian Advocate*, August 27, 1841, p. 42.

since no denomination was willing to concede any portion of the population to its competitors.[3]

Other cultural factors more or less peculiar to the South enhanced the difficulty of the southern ministers' task. At the beginning of the nineteenth century the South was one of the most unchurched—or, to use the contemporary term, "destitute"—sections of the country. Anglicanism had never had a great deal of popular support during the colonial period and in the 1790s it was in disrepute because its clergy had taken the Tory side for the most part during the American Revolution. Deism was popular in the late eighteenth century, and although Methodists, Baptists, and Presbyterians had made numerous converts during the First Great Awakening, a period of religious apathy and declension had followed in the 1790s. At the end of that decade less than one person in ten was a church member.[4] Moreover, the number of ministers in the South was small. It would require a considerable increase in their number to accomplish the task of converting the South to religion. In addition to the lack of ministers, the wide dispersal of population in the South, where there were few cities and towns, and the lack of good transportation posed further problems.

Southern evangelicals generally came from and had the greatest appeal among the middling ranks of southern society. Their fathers were professional people (ministers, lawyers, merchants), tradesmen or mechanics, small planters or farmers. Presbyterian ministers often came from somewhat higher levels of society than did Baptists and Methodists, but, as Robert Lewis Dabney observed, "Not many of the rich of this world cast in their lot among us." Except for a few Presbyterians and Baptists in the larger cities, or ministers who were independently wealthy (like Richard Fuller and Charles Colcock Jones), the salaries of most evangelicals, including those who supplemented their earnings by farming or school-teaching, placed them squarely in the middle or even lower ranks of society. In the early nineteenth century Baptists and Methodists found their following mainly among blacks and the poorer classes of whites, and as a result they were often scorned by upper class southerners. William Capers wrote of his appointment in 1813 to Wilmington, North Carolina, "It

3. On the principle of voluntaryism see Sidney E. Mead, *The Lively Experiment: The Shaping of Christianity in America* (New York, 1963), 113–15.
4. This would seem to be a rather conservative estimate, based on statistics which Charles Sydnor gives for the early 1820s when church membership lists in the South probably still contained at least a portion of those converted during the Great Revival of 1800–1805. See Sydnor, *Development of Southern Sectionalism*, 54. Leo Pfeffer, *Church, State and Freedom* (Boston, 1967), 95, estimates church affiliation at the time of the founding of the republic at four percent of the total population of the United States.

seemed to be admitted on all hands that the Methodists were, on the whole, a good sort of enthusiasts, and their religion very well suited to the lower classes, who needed to be kept constantly in terror of hell-fire. For the negroes, in particular, it was deemed most excellent." Most of Capers' flock in Wilmington were Negroes, and "the whites were very poor, or barely able to support themselves with decency." But by the 1830s Baptists and Methodists had gained respectability by virtue of their increasing wealth and higher educational level. Writing in 1850, the editor of the *Christian Index* pointed proudly to "the respect shown to our branch of Zion by our fellow citizens." To become a Baptist no longer obliged one to "lose . . . standing or influence in society." Nevertheless, while Baptists and Methodists improved their economic and social status and thereby attracted a sprinkling of wealthy and influential members, they continued to appeal mainly to the masses of southerners, both white and black. The Presbyterians stood slightly higher on the social scale, attracting a membership of small planters, merchants, professionals, yeomen farmers, skilled mechanics, and tradesmen.[5]

Southern ministers had four main duties to perform: teaching, pastoral work, discipline, and preaching. The minister, as teacher, was expected to catechize not only the children but also the adults under his care. In the early years of the nineteenth century this was usually done in private homes, or sometimes the minister would assemble members of the congregation in groups to receive spiritual instruction. Parents were expected to aid the minister's efforts by having family worship and by catechizing their children regularly. But following the War of 1812, a new and, in the view of many evangelicals, better means of providing religious instruction began to replace the older method. This was the Sunday school, which had been brought to the United States by the Methodists and which was adopted by other denominations, including the Presbyterians and Baptists. Daniel Baker and William Walton, who were licentiates at the time, established one of the first Sunday schools south of the Mason and Dixon

5. Robert Lewis Dabney to his mother, November 22, 1844, in Thomas Cary Johnson, *Life and Letters of Dabney*, 84; Louis C. LaMotte, *Colored Light: The Story of the Influence of Columbia Theological Seminary, 1828–1936* (Richmond, 1937), 49; Cuthbert, *Life of Fuller*, 163; Wightman, *Life of Capers*, 164, 167–68; *Christian Index*, January 17, 1850, p. 10; Rev. G. Lewis, *Impressions of America and the American Churches: From Journal of the Rev. G. Lewis, One of the Deputation of the Free Church of Scotland to the United States* (Edinburgh, 1848; rpr., New York, 1968), 109–10, 402; Watkin, "Forming of the Southern Presbyterian Minister," 344–45, 359; "The Inefficiency of the Pulpit," *Southern Literary Messenger*, XXIV (February, 1857), 83–91, 106–107, 109–110, 112.

line in 1815, in the Winchester (Virginia) Presbyterian Church. Baker had
become familiar with Sunday schools while a student at Princeton Theological Seminary. By 1818 many of the larger towns in Virginia had Sunday schools, some operating under interdenominational auspices. The
Sunday school movement spread throughout the South, encouraged by
the various denominations and aided by auxiliaries of the American Sunday School Union, which set as one of its goals the establishment of a Sunday school in every neighborhood of the southern states. Most of the religious newspapers supported the movement, publishing accounts of the
work of the Sunday School Union as well as of local interdenominational
and denominational societies. In 1831 the Synod of South Carolina and
Georgia pointed approvingly to the change wrought by the introduction
of the Sunday school system. Eighteen years before, when the Synod had
been founded, "the rising generation were the object of parental and pastoral solicitude and great pains were taken, but on a very contracted scale,
in training them up in the nurture and admonition of the Lord. Now Sabbath schools, though lamentable to say, not universally established in our
churches, are extending ten times the influence, and producing on the
community directly and indirectly a hundred times the effect that had resulted from the former mode of family instruction." The number of Sunday schools supported by the various denominations continued to increase,
but, even as late as 1860, they were to be found mainly in the cities and
larger towns. The sparseness and dispersal of population in the rural areas
made establishing and maintaining them difficult, if not impossible.[6]

Bible classes were another means of providing religious instruction,
particularly for adults, although they were not utilized as extensively as
Sunday schools. Ministers of the Old South also supported the work of the
American Tract Society and the Bible Society, as well as the various denominational publishing houses, whose agents and colporteurs traveled
throughout the South, distributing religious literature of all kinds. Among
the Methodists, the itinerants themselves distributed the publications of
the Methodist Book Concern, founded in 1789. In the 1820s and 1830s
Baptists and Presbyterians began to make increasing use of the printed
word as a means of evangelism, and during the two decades preceding the

6. Thompson, *Presbyterians in the South*, I, 76, 223–25, 237, 239–40, 293–94; Bucke (ed.),
History of American Methodism, I, 26–27, 273–76, 582–86; B. F. Riley, *A History of the Baptists
in the Southern States East of the Mississippi* (Philadelphia, 1898), 267–73; Posey, *Baptist Church
in the Lower Mississippi Valley*, 110; Robert G. Torbet, *A History of the Baptists* (Philadelphia,
1950), 342, 344.

Civil War those two denominations employed colporteurs to work in destitute areas. They not only sold or gave away Bibles, tracts and other religious books, but also established Sabbath schools and temperance societies, and conducted prayer meetings. The colportage enterprise, as the *Watchman and Observer* noted, was "particularly adapted to the sparse population of our Southern country, and to all other places where the stated administration of the word is not enjoyed." It was a means of providing the people with the foundation of religious knowledge, without which the preaching of the minister would have been in vain.[7]

Of the minister's pastoral duties, the most important was visitation. The minister was the spiritual overseer of the church, and it was his duty to maintain "constant, close, personal supervision and intercourse" with members of his congregation. One way of doing this was by visiting the homes of church members and engaging them in spiritual conversation and prayers. Visits might also provide an occasion for offering instruction in religious doctrine or even administering a needed reproof for misconduct. However, there were other, more important reasons adduced in support of visitation. Evangelicals believed it was a way of binding together the minister and his people. By visiting members of the congregation regularly, the minister could become acquainted with their particular needs and interests, and he would soon find himself genuinely concerned for their welfare. "He will feel a kind of property in the families which he visits. . . . [and] will find himself far more deeply interested in their welfare, than if no such visits had been paid." He would be able to prepare his sermons so as to have "special reference to the state of his people" and thereby "win souls to Christ." By visiting he would also win the affections of the people and consequently would "be armed with a much higher moral power which he might exert to their spiritual and everlasting benefit." Southern evangelicals were well aware that many church members desired pastoral visitations, and that it was an important way of keeping such people in the church. A writer in the *Central Presbyterian* warned that if the minister did not look after his flock by visiting and other means, "some one else will." In a society governed by the principle of voluntaryism, ministers soon learned that "nothing so effectually defeats the gen-

7. Thompson, *Presbyterians in the South*, I, 294, 418–20; Bucke (ed.), *History of American Methodism*, I, 279–81, 330, 536–37, 572, 574; William Wright Barnes, *The Southern Baptist Convention, 1845–1953* (Nashville, 1954), 82; Newman, *History of the Baptist Churches*, 426–28; Torbet, *History of the Baptists*, 342, 343; *Watchman and Observer*, April 20, 1848, p. 142.

erous endeavour to decoy the tender sucklings of the flock into foreign pastures as personal oversight —pastoral attention."[8]

Another argument offered in support of pastoral visitation was that it was a way of maintaining the interest of the congregation in religion. A revival might bring members into the church, but once there they needed to be sustained, and visitation was one way to do it. Also, impressions made on the congregation during preaching needed to be cultivated. Finally, a visit provided an opportunity for the minister to encourage interest in benevolent enterprises such as the tract, Bible, and missionary societies, and in church activities such as monthly concerts for prayer, Bible classes, and Sunday schools.[9]

Although most southern evangelicals agreed on the importance of pastoral visiting, there were difficulties in the way of carrying it out. Visitation was a time-consuming task. During the year he was assigned to Fayetteville, in order to visit each family under his care once a week, William Capers set aside the hours 9 A.M. to 1 P.M., five days a week, for the purpose, allowing a half hour for each visit. Basil Manly estimated that in one year of his ministry in Charleston, he made an average of between two and three visits per day among his congregation—a total of 337 visits in five months. Thomas Smyth took his wife along to expedite visitation: "he would read as they drove to the house, at the door would be roused by Mrs. Smyth who would remind him of whose house it was, the number and names of the children and household, the nature of any family joy or sorrow through which they were passing, and any other details that might be advisable." Not surprisingly, ministers with busy schedules or those who were particularly diligent in studying or preparing sermons found visitation to be something of a burden, and many neglected it in favor of what they considered more important duties. Smyth had no doubt of the importance of visiting, especially if done well, and he tried to be faithful in performing it, but he admitted he found it "a very irksome, painful, self-denying, and often very exhausting duty."[10] Ministers who had to engage in secular employment during the week found it almost impossible to visit frequently or with regularity.

8. *Religious Herald*, March 8, 1854, p. 34; Charleston *Observer*, February 20, 1830, p. 30; *Central Presbyterian*, April 26, 1856, p. 65.

9. William Winans to the Reverend Reuben B. Ricketts, July 9, 1839, in Winans Collection; Charleston *Observer*, February 20, 1830, p. 30; *Christian Index*, August 19, 1847, p. 269; Cuthbert, *Life of Fuller*, 172.

10. Wightman, *Life of Capers*, 121; Basil Manly, "Church Journal of B. Manly from May 6, 1826 to Dec. 29, 1829" (MS in Manly, Jr., Papers); Thomas Smyth, *Autobiographical Notes, Letters and Reflections*, ed. Louisa Cheves Stoney (Charleston, 1914), 534, 534n.

If lack of time prevented some evangelicals from carrying out the duty of visitation, feelings of shyness or inadequacy inhibited others. As a new pastor John Holt Rice at first felt ill at ease while visiting members of his Cub Creek congregation, and worried over his "poor talent for talking." William Winans confessed that pastoral visitation was something "I never could perform with even tolerable respectability. . . . From a foolish timidity of disposition, I am unable to lead a reluctant companion in any course of conversation, whether secular or religious; and an invincible repugnance to being troublesome renders it, next to impossible for me to propose prayers in a family out of the regular routine of family devotion."[11]

But the main difficulty in the way of regular and frequent pastoral visitation was the dispersal of the southern population and the lack of ministers. Ministers who had charge of more than one church could visit only one or two families each time they made a stop. On a day when Abner Clopton had an appointment to preach, he would ride to the place, deliver the sermon, "ride again several miles to dinner, present a subscription for some benevolent object to the family, discuss the merits of the temperance reform, have a conversation with every accessible person on the subject of religion, engage in social prayer, and then ride many miles to attend a night meeting, or be near his next appointment." Methodist itinerants could depend to some extent on local preachers and class leaders to help with pastoral duties. But the Baptists had no such auxiliaries. Many of their ministers not only served two or more churches on weekends, but also engaged in secular employment during the week. The editor of the *Religious Herald* observed that under such a system, pastoral duties "can be very inadequately, if at all discharged."[12]

Discipline was a duty which the southern minister shared with lay members of the church. He was responsible, along with the appropriate disciplinary body of the church, for supervising the admission of persons into church membership and for seeing that they obeyed the standards of conduct set forth in the Scriptures. In the Methodist church, the society and the class were the most important disciplinary bodies as far as laymen were concerned. Each society was divided into classes of between twelve and fifteen members, which met weekly under the direction of a class leader. The class and its leader, who was appointed by and responsible to the circuit preacher, inquired into and supervised closely the spiritual progress

11. Maxwell, *Memoir of Rice*, 37–38; William Winans to the Reverend W. Hamilton Watkins, February 6, 1851, in Winans Collection.
12. Jeter, *Memoir of Clopton*, 260; *Religious Herald*, March 8, 1854, p. 34.

and the outward conduct of each member, offering encouragement and administering reproofs when necessary. If a member's misconduct were such that a formal trial became necessary, he was brought before the society to which he belonged, or a committee drawn from its membership, with the minister usually presiding. In the Presbyterian church, the session administered discipline. It was made up of the minister, who usually served as moderator, and the ruling elders of the church. Among the Baptists, the church as a whole heard and judged cases of discipline at the monthly business meetings. As with the Methodists and Presbyterians, the minister played an important role on such occasions, frequently by serving as moderator.[13]

Perhaps no other duty required as much tact, courage, and wisdom of the minister as discipline. Although he shared with other church members the responsibility for meting out punishment, the minister often bore the brunt of hard feelings on the part of those disciplined, their families and friends. Divisions and discord in the congregation were frequent byproducts of disciplinary action. It is not surprising that ministers regarded discipline as a painful and unpleasant, though necessary, duty, and that many of them suffered periods of "anxious meditation" over it. Sometimes the minister and the session (or society or church) entertained very different notions regarding the extent to which discipline should be applied. Or a new minister might find, as Peter Cartwright did on one occasion, that his "predecessors had for several years held the reins of discipline with a very loose hand." In such a situation, the preacher who determined to exercise firm discipline was likely to find a "war" on his hands. He had to be careful not to be too rigid. What one Baptist elder called a "dignified prudence" was necessary if the preacher were not to drive members out of his own church and into another.[14]

For southern ministers, as for virtually all nineteenth century evangelicals, preaching was the most important duty. *"You must preach the gospel,"*

13. For information on the disciplinary standards and procedures of Presbyterians, Methodists, and Baptists in the Old South, see Thompson, *Presbyterians in the South*, I, 77, 312–14, 314n, 317–19; Richard M. Cameron, *Methodism and Society in Historical Perspective* (New York, 1961), 128–30; William W. Sweet, "The Churches as Moral Courts of the Frontier," *Church History*, II (March, 1933), 11–13, 17; Posey, *Baptist Church in the Lower Mississippi Valley*, 38–40, 48–49.

14. Wightman, *Life of Capers*, 103; John Early Diary (typed copy in Southern Historical Collection, University of North Carolina Library), September 27, 1807, July 17, August 6, 1812; Basil Manly, Jr., to parents, January 1, 1851, in Manly Family Papers, Special Collections, Furman University Library; Thomas Cary Johnson, *Life and Letters of Palmer*, 93–97; Cartwright, *Autobiography*, 182; *Religious Herald*, October 19, 1843, p. 165.

Jeremiah Jeter insisted. "The ordinances of the gospel, and the discipline of the church must, in due season, receive your attention. . . . But preaching is your great work." The importance assigned to preaching is clearly seen in the schedules of southern ministers, who spent the greater part of their time preparing and delivering sermons. Ministers who had charge of one church preached at least two sermons a week (one on Sabbath morning and another in the afternoon), in addition to holding prayer meetings and Bible classes and giving lectures. Occasionally they might preach to a group outside the church, such as a local temperance society, or deliver a sermon on the Fourth of July or a similar occasion. As pastor of the First Baptist Church in Richmond, Basil Manly, Jr., prepared three sermons a week, as did Moses Drury Hoge of the Second Presbyterian Church. Each sermon had to be different, for some members of the congregation attended more than one service. Preachers who served more than one church had an easier task in this regard, for they could utilize the same sermon before different congregations. But the time they spent delivering sermons was equal to, if not greater than that expended by ministers who had charge of only one congregation. Abner Clopton's churches were scattered over an extensive territory, which required him to preach on an average of four or five times a week. Writing in his diary at the close of 1826, Clopton estimated that he had ridden about four thousand miles during the year and had preached two hundred ninety times. Methodist itinerants also spent most of their time preaching. During the four years that he was assigned to the Yadkin District, Peter Doub traversed the circuit about twenty times, preaching an average of fifty times each round, besides delivering many exhortations and addresses.[15]

Preaching was the preeminent duty because the evangelical denominations regarded it as a principal means of grace. God used preaching to convert sinners. The minister's task was to present God's plan of salvation, to warn sinners of the danger they were in, and to persuade them of their duty to accept salvation. According to Basil Manly, Jr., the minister must preach the gospel "in such a way that men shall have *no excuse* of not receivg it, & not only deprive them of excuse, but actually *enchain* their unwillg ears and *force* them to hear the lifegivg words so disagreeable to the unconverted mind—so that they may have to bear the responsib. of havg

15. *Religious Herald*, November 14, 1839, p. 181; Thomas Cary Johnson, *Life and Letters of Palmer*, 92, 183; Cuthbert, *Life of Fuller*, 80; Wightman, *Life of Capers*, 119; Cox, "Life and Work of Basil Manly, Jr.," 95; Jeter, *Memoir of Clopton*, 95; Plyler, "Peter Doub, Itinerant of Heroic Days," 40. The average sermon lasted between an hour and an hour and a half.

heard & known the truth and rejecd it." Like other southern evangelicals, Manly did not claim that the minister could actually convert an individual. "More than this, the preacher cannot do," he declared; for "the H[oly] S[pirit] alone can apply this truth thus heard & intellectually apprehendd." But, he added, "less than this he shd not be satisfied w."[16]

How to enchain unwilling ears was a question southern evangelicals discussed and debated throughout the nineteenth century. Most agreed that extemporaneous preaching—as opposed to reading sermons or reciting them from memory, as was done in the Episcopal, Congregational, and northern Presbyterian churches—was best calculated to awaken impenitent sinners and backsliding Christians. In the 1840s and 1850s some southern ministers took up the practice of reading their sermons, but the reaction to this was generally unfavorable. "The feelings and judgment of the masses" were said to be decidedly against it. Consequently, extemporaneous preaching remained the preferred method of delivery in all three denominations. Some preachers, mostly Presbyterians, wrote the sermon out in full or made an extensive outline and brought the manuscript into the pulpit, glancing at it occasionally during the sermon. Others made the same sort of preparation but appeared in the pulpit without notes of any kind. Baptists and Methodists were less likely to write out sermons or to use notes during preaching.[17]

The principal argument advanced in favor of extemporaneous preaching was its effectiveness in awakening sinners. After preaching his first sermon, Robert Lewis Dabney wrote his mother that he was convinced that "*extempore* preaching" rather than reading sermons was the better way. "I could notice the difference plainly between the paragraphs I threw in, although not expressed with half as much propriety of language as that which was on the paper," he wrote. Dabney concluded that "it is much more important that sinners should be excited to listen to the truth than that I should have the reputation of a pretty writer." Similarly, when Benjamin Morgan Palmer stopped writing his sermons and preaching from a manuscript, he found that his sermonizing was much more acceptable to his congregation. One advantage of extemporaneous preaching

16. Basil Manly, Jr., to his parents, February 24, 1847, in Manly, Jr., Papers.

17. "The Pastor.—No. I," *Virginia Evangelical and Literary Magazine*, XI (October, 1828), 538; Thompson, *Presbyterians in the South*, I, 220–21, 461–62; David Benedict, *Fifty Years Among the Baptists* (New York, 1860; rpr., Glen Rose, Tex., 1913), 43; *Christian Index*, April 17, 1851, p. 62; *Central Presbyterian*, March 21, 1857, p. 46; *Southern Christian Advocate*, June 30, 1854, p. 13; *Religious Herald*, February 19, 1857, p. 26.

was that the minister was able to adapt his message to his audience. As Basil Manly, Jr., observed, "A man has a much fairer chance of lookg around . . . when he is speakg off hand than when he has notes before him even if he is not closely confined to them." Many ministers developed a facility for making members of the congregation feel that the sermon was addressed to them personally, even though, in fact, no direct application was made to particular individuals or groups.[18]

Extemporaneous preaching was also valued for its effect on the minister himself. Palmer found that extemporaneous preaching made for more "mental excitement" in the pulpit. The effort of finding suitable words and phrases to clothe the skeleton sermon he had in mind produced a certain exhilaration in him. Ministers who spoke of enjoying "light and liberty" or of being "transported" while preaching, seemed to be describing a similar kind of excitement, which came from giving themselves up to the inspiration of the moment and relying on the aid of the Holy Spirit in delivering their message. That such feelings contributed to the distinctiveness of southern preaching is suggested in a letter Moses Drury Hoge wrote to his uncle, Drury Lacy. Hoge wrote that he was looking forward to hearing Dr. William Plumer preach again. "I am hungry to hear him roar once more. I want to see his eyes glare and his hair stand up on end. It will refresh me to see him foam at the mouth again." Plumer's successor, a northerner, was a man with a good and highly cultivated mind, whose sermons instructed and pleased, but they were not "Southern sermons," according to Hoge. "No bursts of passion, no involuntary emotion, no sudden and splendid inspiration, bearing a man away from his manuscript and from his commonplaces as in a chariot of fire. Yankees seem to say good things because they have studied them, calculated them out and know it to be a duty to say them. Southern men say good things as if they could not help it."[19]

18. Robert Lewis Dabney to his mother, July 8, 1845, in Thomas Cary Johnson, *Life and Letters of Dabney*, 87; Thomas Cary Johnson, *Life and Letters of Palmer*, 81; Basil Manly, Jr., to his parents, March 28, 1847, in Manly, Jr., Papers; Jeter, *Life of Witt*, 274; Peyton Harrison Hoge, *Moses Drury Hoge*, 93; Maxwell, *Memoir of Rice*, 35; Broaddus, *Sermons and Other Writings*, 545.

19. Thomas Cary Johnson, *Life and Letters of Palmer*, 81; Bumpas Autobiography and Journal, February 28, September 1, 1842; Jeter, *Memoir of Clopton*, 93, 96–97; Adolphus W. Mangum Diary (in Mangum Family Papers, Southern Historical Collection, University of North Carolina Library), October 13, 1855; Joseph B. Stratton Diary (typed copy in Joseph B. Stratton Papers, Louisiana State University Archives), April 21, 1850, June 24, 1855; Moses Drury Hoge to Drury Lacy, November 12, 1847, in Wyndham B. Blanton, *The Making of a Downtown Church: The History of the Second Presbyterian Church, Richmond, Virginia, 1845–1945* (Richmond, 1945), 132.

Southern evangelicals exhibited great variety of diction and expression, ranging from the "holy whine" of the early Baptist preachers to the "noble and poetic language" of Benjamin Morgan Palmer.[20] Baptists and Methodists favored plain and simple language as best adapted to the humble ranks of society, and their sermons tended to be informal and discursive. Depending on the level of education and sophistication of their congregations, the preaching of Presbyterian ministers could be quite plain and simple or more learned and elaborate. But whatever the style, southern preaching was full of "unction" and "pathos," to use the words evangelicals themselves frequently employed. It was "warm, animating, lively . . . full of fire," but above all "breathing love and compassion." Most ministers followed the advice offered in the *Christian Index*: "When you have occasion to speak of the character or prospects of sinners, let it appear to be done, (and to appear natural it must be real,) not from delight in their misery, or from exultation at being raised above them, or from a propensity to threaten and arraign, but from necessity and love: and make manifest from your compassionate looks, and softened tones that the description gives you pain."[21]

As for content, sermons were overwhelmingly biblical, abounding in scriptural phrases and references. Evangelicals believed, with Jeremiah Jeter, that they were "called . . . to preach, not human philosophy, nor your own speculations, but the truth—evangelic truth—God's truth—the whole system of revealed truth." Benjamin Morgan Palmer echoed the widely accepted notion of the minister as "a messenger from God" whose duty was "to speak only the word that is put into his mouth." He was not to invent or add anything to the message, Palmer insisted. "His sole care must be to inquire what God the Lord will say." He was "to study God's Book, to expound its doctrines, to enforce its precepts, to urge its motives, to present its promises, to recite its warnings, to declare its judgments."[22]

Most preachers combined doctrinal and practical preaching in varying

20. On the "holy whine" (also referred to as the "heavenly tone") see Posey, *Baptist Church in the Lower Mississippi Valley*, 28–29; Jeter, *Recollections*, 23. A writer in the *Christian Index*, June 13, 1860, n.p., described it as "a measured sing-song tone in preaching and reading hymns, which would be amusing to the present race of worshippers." The description of Palmer is in Thomas Cary Johnson, *Life and Letters of Palmer*, 662.

21. Jeter, *Recollections*, 315–16; Broaddus, *Sermons and Other Writings*, 542; Humphrey and Cleland, *Memoirs of Cleland*, 186; Wightman, *Life of Capers*, 497; Jeremiah B. Jeter to James B. Taylor, November 7, 1826, in Virginia Baptist Historical Society Collection; William M. Baker, *Life of Baker*, 61; *Christian Index*, October 20, 1836, p. 649.

22. *Religious Herald*, November 14, 1839, p. 181; Thomas Cary Johnson, *Life and Letters of Palmer*, 89.

amounts. Presbyterians were more likely to emphasize doctrinal preaching—expounding the doctrines of sin and grace, justification by faith, the atonement, the sovereignty of God, etc. All evangelicals were aware, however, of the popular preference for practical preaching and of its effectiveness in converting sinners. Therefore virtually every sermon, whether Presbyterian, Methodist, or Baptist, preached both doctrines and duties and was addressed not only to the understandings but to the hearts and consciences of the congregation. After instructing their audience in the fundamental truths of religion, evangelicals invariably moved on to the application, stressing the necessity of repentance and faith.

Few doubted the effectiveness of southern preaching in accomplishing its objective of converting sinners. Most ministers could point to hundreds, even thousands, of individuals who had found grace under their ministrations. Increasingly, effectiveness in converting sinners became the principal criterion by which ministers were judged as to usefulness and by which they judged themselves. The minister whose record of conversions was unimpressive—whether as a result of his "incautious severity" in rebuking sinners, or his awkward mannerisms in the pulpit, or his too great fondness for doctrinal as opposed to practical preaching—was pointed to as an example of how not to preach.[23] The principal duty of evangelicals was, without a doubt, preaching—a certain kind of preaching that was calculated to enlarge the ranks of professing Christians.

While the duties of Southern ministers remained fairly constant throughout the first half of the nineteenth century, the context in which they carried them out varied considerably. In the first decade or so of the nineteenth century, when churches were few in number, many preachers held religious meetings in groves, school houses, court houses, barns, or private houses. By the 1840s and 1850s many of the larger towns and cities could boast of rather imposing edifices, such as the one built by the Baptists in Mobile. It was described as "one of the most beautiful and commodious churches in our city" with "a fine Ionic portico" and "a lofty steeple and spire, 'pointing like a finger of faith into Heaven.'" Some city churches featured rented pews, expensive organs, chandeliers, and tinted glass, but in the country more modest buildings were the rule, usually frame or per-

23. Jeter, *Life of Witt*, 167; Plyler, "Peter Doub, Itinerant of Heroic Days," 40; Smyth, *Autobiographical Notes*, 739; Bumpas Autobiography and Journal, February 28, March 18, 1842; Jeter, *Memoir of Clopton*, 102; George G. Smith, *The Life and Letters of James Osgood Andrew, Bishop of the Methodist Episcopal Church, South* (Nashville, 1883), 108, 168–70; Broaddus, *Sermons and Other Writings*, 33–34.

haps brick or stone, about fifty feet long and forty feet wide. Even these were a vast improvement over the meeting houses of the early nineteenth century, which were frequently made of logs, with unplastered walls and ceiling, pews of pine plank or slabs usually without backs, and no stove or even fireplace. Traveling through Virginia in 1848, Joseph S. Baker was impressed with the improvements the Baptists had made in their church buildings. Seventeen years ago, he recalled, "neat and comfortable houses of worship in the country were . . . 'few and far between.' The greater portion of our meeting houses, in the country, looked like old deserted barns. Many of them, too, had only port holes for windows. Their interior corresponded well with their exterior; broken benches, a thick flooring of dust and tobacco juice, a quantum sufficit of leaves, and trash of various kinds, were often to be met with within doors." Now the scene was changed. Baker wrote that Baptist meeting houses in Virginia presented "a neat exterior" and were plastered within; many had "fair proportioned windows, with sashes in good order, and are furnished with stoves." Yet as late as the 1850s, in the newer, less settled areas of the South "cheap and indifferent houses" of worship were still being built, and some congregations were too poor to build even the humblest church, meeting instead in the court house, school house or Masonic hall.[24]

Throughout the first half of the nineteenth century, and especially in the early years, large portions of the South were destitute of religion. The manners of the people who met for worship in these areas were as crude as the buildings in which they assembled. Whispering, sleeping, and even laughing during services were not unusual. People came and went during the meeting, distracting the rest of the congregation, and were often disrespectful, even hostile, to the minister. No wonder that religious newspapers often published articles advising readers on proper conduct in church. The conditions of life in such areas were equally unattractive. "Hardship and privation" were the lot of evangelicals who served the destitute areas. William Winans remembered what courage and resolution it took to volunteer as an itinerant preacher in the Natchez country (embracing Louisiana, Mississippi, and parts of Alabama and Florida) at the end of the first decade of the nineteenth century. "The inhabitants were generally supposed to be a mongrel race, compounded of French, Spanish and Negro,

---

24. Watkin, "Forming of the Southern Presbyterian Minister," 314, 416; Thompson, *Presbyterians in the South*, I, 71, 114–15, 215, 459–60; *Christian Index*, January 25, 1849, p. 29, August 31, 1848, p. 277; *Religious Herald*, April 25, 1850, p. 67, June 20, 1850, pp. 98–99, July 19, 1855, p. 111; *Southern Christian Advocate*, August 11, 1854, p. 39, May 15, 1856, p. 198, March 19, 1857, p. 167.

with a slight sprinkling of Anglo-Saxon ruffians and outlaws, and that [*sic*] they were illiterate and profligate," he wrote. "And the climate was understood to be so noxious, that there was scarcely a chance for a man, under its influence, 'To live out half his days.'"[25] By the 1820s and 1830s religion had become more familiar and respected and manners had improved, but destitute regions remained a challenge up to the time of the Civil War. The difficulties they presented were many: the sickliness of the climate; congregations too small, too poor, or too stingy to support a church and pastor adequately; the lack of sociable and cultivated neighbors; and the difficulty of obtaining the aid of brethren in the ministry. Only the prospect of additions to the church offered encouragement.

Most ministers agreed that there were distinct differences between a country and a city charge. People in the country, being less educated and less sophisticated, were less likely to demand polished sermons. Thus, country pastors did not have to prepare for the pulpit so laboriously. On the other hand, visiting took more time and was more expected than in the city. Perhaps the most striking feature of the country pastor's life was its lack of variety. "The history of a long rural pastorate," explained Jeremiah Jeter, "must, like the life itself, be monotonous. . . . There is from year to year the same incessant round of studies, labors, and perplexities, occasionally varied by health, weather, seasons, disappointments, successes, and other circumstances." Speaking of Daniel Witt, who served as pastor of Sharon Church at Sandy River in Prince Edward County, Virginia, for forty-five years, Jeter wrote:

For almost half a century he dwelt in the same house; travelled over the same roads; preached at the same places; labored among the same people, or their descendants; proclaimed, not indeed the same sermons, but the same gospel; pursued the same wearisome round of toil; and was subject to the same anxious cares. This uniformity was sometimes broken by a revival in his churches, a visit of a strange minister, a preaching tour in a contiguous county, a trip to the Springs for his health, and once by a journey of several months in the West.[26]

The chief problem evangelicals encountered in the country was that posed by the dispersal of the population. The Methodist system of itiner-

25. Watkin, "Forming of the Southern Presbyterian Minister," 318; Finley, *Autobiography*, 196; Jeter, *Recollections*, 313; Early Diary, December 14, 1808, September 20, 1811; *Religious Herald*, July 4, 1844, p. 107; Winans Autobiography, 56–57.

26. Jeter, *Life of Witt*, 159–60. See also *The Old Pine Farm: Or, The Southern Side. Comprising Loose Sketches From the Experience of a Southern Country Minister, S.C.* (Nashville, 1860), which was termed "a true picture of a Southern Baptist ministerial country life" by the editor of the *Christian Index*, January 4, 1860.

ancy proved the most effective solution, enabling that denomination to cover a wide field and reach even the most remote and thinly settled areas with a relatively small number of circuit preachers. Under the highly centralized system, traveling preachers had no choice of circuit, nor could congregations request a particular individual as their preacher. Itinerants were appointed to circuits by their bishops for a period of no more than two years, as established by the General Conference of 1804. A few might be stationed in cities, but most of them served large circuits with numerous preaching points (as many as fifteen to twenty-five). In newly settled regions, circuits were especially large, sometimes necessitating five to six weeks to make the rounds. The advantages which accrued from the itinerant system have been described by William Warren Sweet as follows:

The large circuits required constant activity and movement on the part of the preachers, which tended to develop a zealous, energetic ministry. The time limit . . . made it impossible for a man to settle down comfortably in one place; and if results were to be obtained on a given circuit, it had to be done quickly. This kept the preachers constantly on the alert. Another factor, contributing to the success of the circuit system, was the fact that a young preacher was not under the compulsion of preparing many new sermons, since on large circuits he constantly preached at different localities and, therefore, could use the same sermon again and again. This made for the development of effective oratorical preaching, the type particularly well adapted to the frontier.

But such advantages were obtained at considerable cost. The life of the traveling preachers was one of hardship and privation. The low level of financial support, the necessity of being in continual movement on circuit, and the time limit on appointments meant that few were able to marry and support families. Although some men spent their entire adult lives as itinerants, many more located after a few years in order to marry and settle down to raising a family. The contribution of these local preachers should not be underestimated. They preached in the vicinity in which they lived, and often, in outlying regions, they were the ones who organized the first Methodist classes in an area, even before a regular circuit preacher had been appointed to it.[27]

Like the Methodists, the Baptists tended to concentrate their efforts in the country rather than in towns and cities. They made some use of itinerants but generally they adopted what was known as the once-a-month sys-

27. William Warren Sweet, *Methodism in American History* (Rev. ed.; New York, 1954), 146–48; Bucke (ed.), *History of American Methodism*, I, 469, 471–72.

tem of preaching.[28] Under this plan a church had no settled pastor, but was supplied by a minister from a distance, who came to preach once or twice a month.

The systems of itinerancy and once-a-month preaching were attempts to solve the problem posed by a dispersed population and a scarcity of ministers. Neither system was entirely satisfactory. W. F. Cook, a Methodist traveling preacher assigned to Culloden Circuit (Georgia Conference) which consisted of ten appointments, two of them village churches and eight in the country, complained that the plan of preaching in the villages on alternate Sundays and supplying the country appointments during the week was unworkable. After six months he had become convinced "that week-day preaching in this section of Georgia is almost a complete *nullity* —utterly useless and inefficient, and that a change in our plan of operation, in this regard, is most imperatively demanded." Cook found that "the people do not, cannot, will not be induced to attend church in the week," and he insisted that "the very existence of Methodism and Methodist churches in many portions of these old counties, where we formerly flourished, depends upon a change." Baptists expressed similar dissatisfaction with the once-a-month plan of preaching. Under this "ruinous policy" the minister spent time riding from place to place which might better have been spent studying and improving himself. It was "impossible for the minister to pursue any regular course of preaching for the instruction and edification of the Church." He could not plan out a series of sermons on one topic or doctrine, because he could not expect that his hearers would be able to retain the whole chain of reasoning, hearing the sermons at intervals of four weeks. The preacher who supplied several churches could spend little if any time in pastoral visitation and personal instruction. It was equally difficult to sustain Sabbath schools, Bible classes, and prayer meetings. For these reasons Baptists waged a concerted, if only partially successful, campaign against once-a-month preaching in the 1840s and 1850s.[29]

Presbyterians were the least successful of the three denominations in reaching the thinly populated, more remote areas of the South. This was partly because Presbyterian ministers tended to favor a settled as opposed to an itinerant ministry, partly because they tended to locate themselves in cities and towns rather than in the countryside, and partly because Pres-

28. Newman, *History of the Baptist Churches*, 382–83, 387; Posey, *Baptist Church in the Lower Mississippi Valley*, 29; Benedict, *Fifty Years Among the Baptists*, 48.

29. *Southern Christian Advocate*, September 2, 1858, pp. 54–55; *Christian Index*, April 29, 1842, p. 265, December 21, 1837, pp. 815–16, November 15, 1838, pp. 708–709.

byterians had fewer ministers in proportion to the population than did Baptists and Methodists. However, Presbyterians did make some effort to extend their range, usually by employing itinerants of various sorts. Sometimes these were licentiates assigned to a particular region by a presbytery prior to ordination, and it was not unusual for pastors occasionally to take a short leave of absence from their congregations in order to make preaching excursions in destitute areas. In some cases synods and presbyteries employed missionaries or evangelists to carry the Gospel to the "neglected and waste places" of the South and to establish new congregations and churches there. Perhaps the most famous and successful of these was Daniel Baker, whose preaching tour through the southern states in the early 1830s resulted in a wave of revivals at which some three thousand persons were converted.[30]

The city pastorate sharply contrasted with the small town or country pastorate. Some ministers preferred the variety, activity, and intellectual challenge of city life just as others preferred the comparative serenity and uniformity of rural pastorates. James Henley Thornwell summarized the advantages of a city pastorate in remarking to one of his seminary students, "that if a man had the love for study which would lead him to redeem the time, the country church was best. But there are few men who still study except under pressure. Rubbing against people keeps one alive; less time is required for pastoral visiting in town, and when a visitor calls, you can excuse yourself; whereas in the country, you have to sit with him and eat your thumbs a whole day, even if bored to death."[31]

City congregations were generally believed to be better educated, wealthier, more refined, and, consequently, more demanding as to sermons than country congregations. The greater wealth of a city congregation promised a higher salary for the minister and more liberal contributions to church and benevolent projects, but sometimes the wealth that was to be found in the cities and large towns distracted people from religion. "Splendid living" in the form of "magnificent houses, grand equipages, [and] splendid dress" became "the grand object" of many city dwellers, while others devoted themselves to the pursuit of various amusements: "the theatre—the card-table—the dance—the midnight revel, and every form of dissipation." Nor was such activity limited to those outside the church. Even many

30. Thompson, *Presbyterians in the South*, I, 187–88, 417; Watkin, "Forming of the Southern Presbyterian Minister," 202, 308–10; William M. Baker, *Life of Baker*, 158–60, 167, 187–88, 295–96, 516; *Religious Herald*, July 27, 1848, p. 118.
31. Quoted in Palmer, *Life and Letters of Thornwell*, 556.

Christians exhibited a grievous "conformity . . . to the world, . . . imbibing its spirit of avarice and ambition, and . . . engaging in the pursuit of business, pleasure and fashion." One evangelical warned that "there is no class of persons more difficult to be approached and impressed by a Minister of Christ than your genteel, decent worshippers of luxury and fashion." The minister was invariably tempted "to soften or keep back the truth. . . . to avoid dwelling on those great practical, Gospel doctrines" which many of his hearers were likely to find "grating and offensive," and the danger did not end there. "It will be well if, besides softening or keeping back the truth, he be not gradually and insensibly drawn to adopt in his own person and family, those very worldly habits against which he was bound to have lifted up both his voice and his example." The city minister was faced with a most difficult task—he must "mingle continually with the members of a wealthy, polished, and fashionable congregation, and at the same time . . . *keep himself unspotted from the world.*"[32]

The emphasis which city congregations placed on elaborate and learned sermons also presented a temptation. "Polished and fashionable society" was likely to demand "SMOOTH and SUPERFICIAL PREACHING." Though such preaching was "greatly admired by people of the world," it failed to alarm unbelievers and the impenitent and allowed them "to slumber in secularity." The minister who offered such preaching abdicated his responsibility to save sinners. Another temptation which the city pastor was likely to fall into was to spend too much time preparing sermons to satisfy the demands of his congregation and too little in performing his other duties, especially those that promised little in the way of popularity and acclaim. Writing in 1858, James O. Andrew contended that the cause of Methodism in New Orleans had suffered because some pastors "have neglected the duties of the pastorate all the week, in order that they might be the better prepared to attract admiring crowds to their churches on the Sabbath; and have regarded the proper delivery on the Sabbath, of a well composed sermon, as covering to a great extent the whole ground of their ministerial responsibility."[33]

Another characteristic of the urban population complicated the city pastor's task. This was the large "public-house population," as James Furman called it—transient persons who came to the city in search of health, wealth, or pleasure, but who took little interest in its institutions, including

32. "Theology-Practical," *Virginia Evangelical and Literary Magazine*, III (November, 1820), 500–13.
33. *Ibid.; Southern Christian Advocate*, August 6, 1847, p. 34.

its churches. Even the permanent residents of some southern cities re-
sided there only a part of the time, leaving during the summer months to
avoid the ravages of yellow fever or to vacation at popular watering places.
Basil Manly cited the sickly climate and its attendant problems in explaining his decision to leave his Charleston pastorate. Throughout the South,
he noted, the months of June to November constituted "the great period
of Baptist work"—the time of protracted meetings and revivals. But because of the yellow fever, "the minister who resides in Charleston can do
no public work during that period." He could not leave the city to participate in a protracted meeting and "*return again*, without risk to life," but,
observed Manly, "if he goes out, *& stays*, he alienates himself from the
place & people." Nor were conditions in the city propitious for religion:

If he stays at home, he can do little out of his study, & not much there. The heat &
the mosquitos are unfavorable to study, together with a general lassitude & disani-
mation. And the people, who *can* get away, whether by hook or crook, . . . have
gone; he sees them no more till frost. That is not the worst,—they leave neither
energy nor life nor hope behind. No one that stays attempts or expects any thing
more than just to provide for a mere vegetative life—a general & quiet snooze—
hybernation in summer.

When vacationers returned to the city in the fall, Manly continued, the re-
sumption of business was uppermost in their minds. "The entire business
of the year being thrown upon the 5 months between the first of November & the first of April,—it is useless to try to get the ear of any *man*, during that period; except once on a Sunday when he is half distracted & half
asleep. And what can you do with him, then? This little fragment of time,
including April & May, is all that a minister has to work in. As for the
women,—they do not 'gee up' much, unless the men are with them."[34]
    Although the cities presented great difficulties, evangelicals agreed that
ministers must go there, "or else," as Basil Manly, Jr., put it, "they must be
given over indeed, deliberately & confessedly, to the Devil." Indeed, the
minister who was able to overcome the obstacles which the city placed in
his way and who had the attainments city congregations demanded was
rewarded with a wider influence than he could ever hope for in the country. This was not only because his congregation was apt to be larger and
more influential, but because city life offered the minister more opportunities to speak outside the church—on civic occasions such as the Fourth
of July, or before the various voluntary associations and institutions which

34. James C. Furman to Thomas P. Sides, September 12, 1838, in James Furman Papers;
Basil Manly to Basil Manly, Jr., August 20, 1858, in Manly Family Papers.

had their headquarters in the city. Regarding the cities as the centers of business and wealth, of "taste, fashion and learning," evangelicals believed that an influence exerted in them would ultimately extend in every direction, thereby affecting "the character, and destiny of millions."[35] To men who conceived of themselves as ambassadors of God, committed to the task of converting the world, this was no insignificant thing.

In 1848 a writer for the *Southern Presbyterian Review* expressed dismay at "the view which many have taken of the nature and warrant of a call to the ministry." He was referring "to the notion that a man should decide the question of his duty to preach the Gospel, on the same rules and principles on which he would decide to enter the profession of law or follow the trade of a blacksmith," that is, by considering his "abilities, . . . means and opportunities." People no longer seemed to believe in "the necessity of an inward, direct, special and supernatural operation of the Spirit of God" calling a man to the work of the ministry. According to their way of thinking, "a call to preach the Gospel, and an obligation to plant cotton, are exactly of the same nature, and to be determined in exactly the same way."[36]
Other evangelicals offered additional proof of the degeneration of the ministry. Ministers, no less than other Americans of the period, seemed preoccupied with self-aggrandizement. Increasingly, they shunned pastorates among "the *poor, needy* and *destitute*" and with "*little,* poor churches, particularly in the country." The editor of the *Christian Index* contrasted the secularized ministry of the day with "the ministry in the days of our fathers." Not a "self-denying spirit of devotion" but a desire for "offices of honor and emolument" motivated present-day ministers. They would not think of "laboring for a bare support." If they failed to secure a city pastorate, or a college professorship, or the secretaryship of some benevolent society, or "some other lucrative and honorable post in the Church," they were ready to abandon the ministry for "any secular pursuit that seems to promise ease and affluence." The frequency with which ministers changed pastorates in order to obtain greater prestige and higher salaries was additional proof that they were motivated by "personal ambition and self-interest." As a result, one evangelical observed, "the practical impression prevails, generally, profoundly, fatally, that the ministry are actuated in their labors, by the same motives with the other honorable professions,

35. Basil Manly, Jr., to Charles Manly, August 21, 1858, in Manly, Jr., Papers; Charleston *Observer*, September 20, 1828, p. 150.
36. "The Power of the Pulpit," 273–74.

viz: the desire to make an honest living, to provide for a family, to acquire wealth, or to achieve a prominent position in the world."[37]

Sermons, too, revealed the degeneration of the ministry. William Winans noted the great change that had occurred in preaching since the early nineteenth century. "There is far more *pretension*, far more *flourish*, far more conformity to worldly taste, in style and language—more learning, *perhaps*; but far less simplicity, solemnity, directness, and earnestness than there used to be thirty or forty years ago," he wrote in 1852. According to a writer in the *Christian Index*, education was being exalted above piety and a literary reputation was valued more highly than "the successful *labors* of those who have never enjoyed the advantages of a collegiate or regular Theological education." In many cases, he noted, "an educated minister of talents and good address, even if his piety is very questionable, is looked up to as an oracle, and his words weigh more with many than the words of divine inspiration!" Another evangelical contended that preaching was being "turned into a mere instrument of popular entertainment." Instead of admonishing sinners and declaring "the *whole* counsel of God," ministers tempered their remarks; or couched them in "such high flown, rhetorical, or metaphysical style" as to make them unintelligible to their hearers; or dwelt on secular themes drawn from literature, philosophy, history, or even politics. "The pulpit," Thomas Smyth wrote in 1839, "might now be considered as dedicated to man, not to God, inasmuch as it displays more man than God and seeks the honor that cometh from man, more than the honour that cometh from God.—The Pulpit is now the theatre for man's performance, the stage for man's wisdom and eloquence and display—the concentration of human ingenuity and device, instead of the simplicity that is in Christ Jesus. It is the people's desk and not God's throne. A minister must now be popular *first*, and *then* Godly. He must please men and gratify itching ears, and then keep a good conscience and preach sound doctrine *as he can*." Smyth concluded that the pulpit had "been transformed . . . from a giant into a dwarf."[38]

These comments by Smyth and other evangelicals point to an important change that was taking place in the ministry of the Old South. They be-

---

37. *Christian Index*, February 13, 1851, p. 26, July 25, 1845, n.p.; *Central Presbyterian*, April 3, 1858, p. 53.

38. William Winans to the Reverend D. DeVinne, March 31, 1852, in Winans Collection; *Christian Index*, August 26, 1847, p. 278, February 18, 1836, p. 89; *Southern Christian Advocate*, May 14, 1841, p. 190; *Southern Baptist and General Intelligencer*, April 10, 1853, p. 229; *Central Presbyterian*, April 3, 1856, p. 70; *Religious Herald*, May 18, 1854, p. 73; Smyth, *Autobiographical Notes*, 125–26.

lieved that the ministry was degenerating. In fact, what was happening was that the traditional notion of the ministry as a calling was giving way to a newer notion of the ministry as a profession. To be sure, evangelicals did not completely abandon the traditional notion. They continued to emphasize the uniqueness of the ministry in comparison with other occupations—the fact that one did not simply choose the ministry but was divinely called to it, and that the minister, unlike other men, labored "for duty, and not for emoluments."[39] At the same time, it is clear that evangelicals were coming to regard the ministry as a profession similar, in many ways, to that of, say, law or medicine. By examining their views on such matters as recruitment, education, support, and influence, we can better understand this new perspective.

The lack of a sufficient number of ministers was a pressing problem for all three denominations. Methodists, for example, worried about the increasing number of traveling preachers who located after serving only a few years in the itinerancy. In the early 1850s the editor of the *Southern Christian Advocate* also noted "an alarming decline in the number of candidates for the ministry." Baptists were similarly concerned. Older ministers were retiring or passing away, others were emigrating to "the richer and more fertile portions" of the west and southwest, and fewer young men were entering the ministry. Of the last group, one Baptist wrote, "We see them entering by hundreds the bar, the practice of medicine, the professorial chair, the counting room, and yet so few seem willing to devote their lives to the work of preaching." His lament was echoed by a Presbyterian writing to the editor of the *Watchman and Observer*. "Why is it," he asked, "that while annually hundreds of our young men enter upon the professions of Law and Medicine so few turn their attention to the ministry?"[40]

To remedy the lack of ministers, evangelicals urged churches and individuals to pray that God would raise up young men for the ministry. "The Scriptures teach us that for nothing are we more entirely dependent on God, than for Christian ministers," observed a writer in the *Southern Presbyterian*. "The Church, cannot, of itself, produce them." Indeed, he declared, "a ministry of purely human origin would be a curse to the Church and the world." Nevertheless, few evangelicals went so far as to claim that the notion of dependence on God ruled out human effort entirely. Did

39. *Central Presbyterian*, February 9, 1856, p. 21.
40. James O. Andrew to John Andrew, December 20, 1816, in George G. Smith, *Life and Letters of Andrew*, 78; William Winans to the Reverend C. K. Marshall, October 18, 1852, in Winans Collection; *Southern Christian Advocate*, October 27, 1854, p. 82; *Religious Herald*, April 21, 1859, p. 61; *Watchman and Observer*, October 8, 1846, p. 29.

not God work through the use of means? Assuming that "the Lord furnishes materials out of which to make as many Ministers as the Church may need," evangelicals argued that churches and individuals could and should engage in efforts to increase the number of ministers. Besides prayer, they urged recruiting efforts to increase the supply of ministers. Parents, for example, were asked whether they were doing their duty in the matter: "Are their children brought up to respect the office of the gospel minister, and to consider that it would be a great privilege conferred on them if they were permitted to preach the unsearchable riches of the gospel to their dying fellow men?" Brethren of the church were urged to do their part by encouraging young men to cultivate religious gifts and by seeing that they gave serious consideration to the question of whether they had a call to preach the gospel. Pastors in particular not only had an obligation to preach on the subject but to talk about it with all young men who had made a profession of religion. As a writer in the *Watchman and Observer* noted, "Many a young man thinks on this subject, but he has taken up erroneous views of a call to the ministry; a few words from his Pastor might set this matter right, and enable him to see the way opened before him." Daniel Baker was only doing his duty in making a practice, whenever he saw "a promising young man in the Lord," of tapping him on the shoulder and saying, "Young man, are you sure it is not your duty to preach the gospel?"[41]

Sabbath schools were also looked upon as agencies of recruitment. Writing in 1837 in the *Southern Watchman and General Intelligencer*, "Benevolence" noted that more than two thousand Baptist ministers were needed to supply destitute churches and to engage in foreign missionary work. The task of Sabbath schools was clear: "They should seek, not only the early conversion of their scholars, but turn the attention of those in the male department toward the service of the church in the ministry; converse with them on this subject; show them the importance of it; instruct them in view of it." Anticipating the objections of those who might say that "this is making ministers, ourselves, whereas, 'no man should take this honor upon himself but that he is called of God,'" "Benevolence" argued that just as the "special divine influence to bring a sinner to Christ does not supersede the necessity of educating a youth in view of his coming to

41. *Southern Presbyterian*, October 5, 1854, p. 203; *Watchman of the South*, October 22, 1840, p. 33; *Religious Herald*, October 22, 1830, p. 165, April 21, 1859, p. 61; *Watchman and Observer*, October 8, 1846, p. 29; Watkin, "Forming of the Southern Presbyterian Minister," 377–78.

Christ, so neither does the special divine call to the ministry render needless or inconsistent an education in direct reference to the ministry."[42] In his view the use of various means of recruitment was not inconsistent with a belief in the divine calling to the ministry.

The recruitment of ministers was particularly problematical for Presbyterians in view of their high educational requirements. In the eighteenth century, such requirements had had the effect of limiting the ministry to those young men who could afford a college education. In the nineteenth century, in an effort to recruit candidates from a broader segment of the population, Presbyterians offered financial aid to pious but indigent youths who desired to study for the ministry. Even before the Board of Education was founded in 1819, a number of local and voluntary societies were dispensing such aid in the South. The American Education Society, an interdenominational enterprise, also provided support. As a result, Presbyterians no longer limited the ministry to a particular class, but, like the Methodists and Baptists (and no doubt influenced by them), drew candidates from all levels of society. The tendency to identify the ministry with gentility persisted, but most Presbyterians recognized that the need for ministers must override such exclusivism. Their attitude is suggested in Robert Lewis Dabney's description of his fellow students (about eighteen in number) at Union Seminary. He reported to his mother that "a few of them [are] of good families, and of pretty high character, as to acquirement and manners." The rest he found "very kind and quiet and very uninteresting." He continued:

All of them, I believe, are young men in limited circumstances. . . . Some of them are sons of mechanics, and are supported partly by charity, or by school teaching, and so forth. When I consider the way in which ministers are generally received into the best society of the country in which they live, and the power they have of giving a tone to manners and feeling in the community, there often arises a feeling of repulsion against this class of candidates for the responsible duties of the office. But, upon the whole, it is right, I am convinced, to employ such materials unless better can be found. . . . These sorts of preachers generally find their level, after a little fluctuating, and either learn the air and deportment of gentlemen, if they have quick parts, or else find their proper place in some plain neighborhood, and work to advantage among people of their own class. There is much ministe-rial work for which the refinement and sensibilities of gentlemen would almost disqualify them, which these sorts of men can do without repugnance; and it should be said, too, that they are generally very exemplary and correct in their characters. . . . It is quite surprising to what an extent they do shed their native rudeness.

42. *Southern Watchman and General Intelligencer*, September 22, 1837, p. 150.

The strict morals, the literary pursuits, and self-denying manners, which they are obliged to cultivate, does as much toward making them real gentlemen as anything could.

Presbyterians also broadened their search for ministerial candidates by appealing to mature men already engaged in other employment. As a writer in the *Southern Presbyterian* admitted, the main reason for turning to this group was that "accessions to the ministry may be more speedily secured" from it. Youths and young men would require long years of preparation "ere their labours can be enjoyed," whereas "the matured male members of the Church" could be fitted for the ministry after "comparatively brief preparation."[43]

The traditional notion of the ministry emphasized self-denial. Ministers were called upon to sacrifice worldly (especially monetary) considerations for the higher goal of serving God. However, many evangelicals recognized that young men were often deterred from choosing the ministry because they believed it would mean a life of hardship and privation. "What inducements do our Churches hold out to their young and promising sons to engage in the christian ministry?" asked the editor of the *Christian Index*. He knew of some individuals who had "abandoned the lucrative professions of Law and Medicine for the pleasure of winning souls to Christ" only to be forced to return to those employments because of "the indifference and stinginess of the people amongst whom they labored." J. L. Kirkpatrick urged a realistic view of the matter. He agreed that young men ought to rise above worldly considerations. "They ought to put their trust in God, go forward, and look for their reward in another world." But he insisted that they were not likely to do so living in the present age, among a "money-loving, ambitious people." It would require a piety which he thought was now probably "beyond our reach." "The truth is, brethren, we must take things as they are, until they are mended. We must have ministers; and if we cannot get them of the greatest possible spirituality of mind and purity of motives, we must take them of less, though always of sincere and genuine piety." He emphasized the necessity of adequate financial support from the churches. This would encourage young men to "come out from the world, abandon other professions and pursuits, and give themselves wholly to the ministry of the word."[44]

43. Thompson, *Presbyterians in the South*, I, 257, 295; Robert Lewis Dabney to his mother, November 22, 1844, in Thomas Cary Johnson, *Life and Letters of Dabney*, 84; *Southern Presbyterian*, October 5, 1854, p. 203.

44. *Christian Index*, June 25, 1840, pp. 413–14; *Southern Presbyterian*, February 24, 1853, p. 73.

Evangelicals' discussion of educational requirements reveals the tension between the traditional and the newer notions of the ministry. The Methodist William Winans criticized such requirements on the ground that they contradicted the notion that "the ministry was purely of Divine selection." Setting up educational requirements implied that, although God calls men to the ministry, they are not qualified to obey the call "till men shall have qualified them for the work to which the Divine vocation has assigned them." In Winans' view, men were usurping the divine function. "Is there not something shockingly insolent in a Conference or Church to say to a man, 'We believe that God has called you to the work of the ministry; but *we* will not permit you to labor with us in that ministry till we have had you prepared for the work, for which you are now unfit?'" he asked. Winans argued that if God called a man to preach, "he intends he should go to the work assigned him *at once* with the qualifications which he has; and that it is wrong, wholly wrong to set him down to the acquisition of elementary Knowledge, whether Literary, Scientific, Theological or Biblical. Let him go to his work, and, in it 'study to show himself approved unto God.'" Winans' attitude is not surprising in view of the fact that the Methodists generally scorned formal ministerial training. Presbyterians, of course, had no such animus, and, as we have seen, Baptists gradually came to support the notion of an educated ministry. However, evangelicals in both these denominations were careful to point out that "even the most splendid talents, and the most extensive literary requirements, are, of themselves, insufficient qualifications for an Ambassador of God." On the other hand, they also insisted that education was a useful auxiliary which enabled a man "more worthily to proclaim the truth." A minister might "be respected for his piety and character," observed a Baptist, "but his influence over his fellow-men will be in proportion to his ability and attainments."[45]

In discussing the matter of support, evangelicals appealed to both notions of the ministry. They sought salaries that would not only be commensurate with their exalted position as ambassadors of God, but would also compare favorably with those of other professions. While they continued to stress the self-denying character of the ministry, they also asserted their claim to a competent support.

45. William Winans to Rev. C. K. Marshall, October 18, 1852, in Winans Collection; Winans Autobiography, 28; Charleston *Observer*, February 16, 1828, p. 26; *Southern Evangelical Intelligencer*, November 10, 1821, p. 249; *Religious Herald*, March 21, 1850, p. 46, April 6, 1854, p. 51.

Of the three denominations, the Methodists ranked lowest in the amount of support provided to their ministers. The General Conference of 1800 set the annual salaries of traveling preachers at $80 plus traveling expenses. In 1816 salaries were raised to $100, and in 1855 to $150. Among Baptists and Presbyterians there was a considerable difference between the salaries of country pastors and those who lived in cities and towns. During the first half of the nineteenth century, the salaries of Baptist country pastors averaged little more than $100 a year, while their Presbyterian counterparts averaged between $400 and $600. In the urban areas, however, the salaries of Baptist ministers ranged between $1000 and $1500. Basil Manly, for example, was receiving about $1000 a year as a preacher in Edgefield Court House, South Carolina, in the mid-1820s. Some thirty years later his son, Basil Manly, Jr., was receiving $1500 in Richmond. The salaries of Presbyterians in the cities and towns ranged slightly higher, averaging between $1200 and $2000. When Moses Drury Hoge became minister of the new Second Presbyterian Church in Richmond, in 1845, his salary was set at $1000 a year. Benjamin Morgan Palmer was probably the highest paid southern minister prior to the Civil War; the New Orleans church offered him $6,000 in 1856.[46]

Evangelicals complained that in most cases salaries were inadequate to meet the minimum needs of a minister and his family.[47] The majority of southern preachers found themselves almost continually beset with financial worries. According to his biographer, William Capers never received more than "a bare subsistence" from the Methodist church, which had to be "eked out . . . by the sale of his patrimonial property" and supplemented by gifts and donations. A writer in the *Central Presbyterian* in January 1856 doubted that there were "six pastors in Virginia and North Carolina with families, whose expenses have not exceeded their salaries during the past year." He noted that while some ministers bore such a situation cheerfully,

46. Sweet, *Methodism in American History*, 139, 140; *The Doctrines and Discipline of the Methodist Episcopal Church, South* (Nashville, 1855), 226–27; *Religious Herald*, November 17, 1837, p. 183; Thompson, *Presbyterians in the South*, I, 461, 461n; John Holt Rice to the Reverend Archibald Alexander, October 16, 1825, in Maxwell, *Memoir of Rice*, 289; Daniel Gillette to Walter Gillette, May 1844, in Gillette, *Memoir of Gillette*, 167–68; Basil Manly, Jr., to his parents, November 15, 1853, February 15, 1854, March 18, 1855, in Manly Family Papers; Abner W. Clopton to Mr. John Whitehead, March 2, 1825, in Virginia Baptist Historical Society Collection; Blanton, *Making of a Downtown Church*, 53.

47. Articles and editorials expressing this view appeared frequently in the religious newspapers and journals. See, for example, *Watchman and Observer*, February 24, 1853, p. 115; *Religious Herald*, March 23, 1854, p. 41.

others "look forward with some anxiety to the future, and feel disquieted with the prospect." Throughout the first half of the nineteenth century inadequate support was cited as the major reason why so many Methodist traveling preachers were forced to locate; among Baptist and Presbyterian ministers, it was said to be a more frequent reason than any other for removal to another church.[48]

Evangelicals also complained that inadequate support prevented them from devoting themselves completely to the ministry. In order to supplement their salaries, they engaged in various secular employments, of which farming and teaching were the most widely practiced. This limited the amount of time a minister might spend on pastoral visiting, preparing sermons, and preaching. Moses Drury Hoge complained to William Plumer that the double work of teaching and preaching "is killing me. . . . I have a growing estimate of what a sermon should be, and am more and more unwilling to enter the pulpit with imperfect preparation," he wrote. "But to make three sermons a week, even such sermons as I preach, and to teach six hours a day, is more than I can stand." Another objection to secular employment was that it vitiated the minister's spirituality. When William Capers located in 1814, after having served as a traveling preacher for six years, and became "involved in the cares of this life," he noted the effect on his spiritual life:

I preached every Sabbath, and heard of no fault-finding, though I was conscious in myself that there may have been cause for it. . . . I had become too much engrossed with secular things through the week to be very spiritual on Sunday. . . . Temporal things were stealthily gaining in importance, if things spiritual were not declining; and the duties of husband and father for this life were getting to be considered too much apart from their indispensable connection with the life to come, and God's blessing for both worlds.

William F. Broaddus characterized his own situation in much the same way. "I am so much divided between the work of the Ministry & my worldly engagements that I am rendered in a great measure unfit for either," he wrote. Yet he felt that he could not give up one for the other. "Merchandising cannot be given up because it has created debts which merchandising must discharge. Teaching cannot be given up because my own children must be educated, and I have no other means of accomplishing their

48. Wightman, *Life of Capers*, 510; *Central Presbyterian*, January 19, 1856, p. 10; *Wesleyan Journal*, February 10, 1827, p. 2; *Religious Herald*, March 10, 1837, p. 39, January 9, 1840, p. 5.

education. And above all, preaching cannot be given up, because souls are perishing, and 'a dispensation of the Gospel is committed unto me.' 'Wo is me, if I preach not the Gospel'!"[49]

As evangelicals themselves realized, the problem of support was not so much a matter of money as of attitude. It was not just poor country churches that failed to maintain their ministers adequately. Too many "people who live in affluence," according to a writer in the *Central Presbyterian*, "expect to secure the services of able ministers on starvation salaries." But evangelicals could not lay all of the blame for inadequate salaries on "the miserable parsimony of church members." Part of the problem was the traditional notion of the self-denying character of the ministry, which meant that church members were bound to look askance at almost any demand for greater support. This was particularly the case with the Baptists and Methodists, whose animus against a "hireling ministry" dated back to colonial times. William Capers, remembering his early days as a preacher, recalled that "it had been reiterated from the beginning that we were eighty-dollar men, (not money-lovers, as some others were suspected of being,) till it got to be considered that for Methodist preachers to be made comfortable, would deprive them of their glorying, and tarnish the lustre of their Methodistic reputation."[50]

Evangelicals devoted considerable effort to removing the popular prejudice against ministerial support. Without entirely giving up the notion of self-denial, they attempted to convince church members of their duty to provide ministers with a competent support. Thus a writer in the *Religious Herald* emphasized the distinction between the payment of hirelings whose sole object was money, and the support of men who entered the ministry out of a love for souls and a desire for the glory of God. The latter group, agreed "Coromis" in the *Virginia Evangelical and Literary Magazine*, sought no private end, but undertook their work "with holy disinterestedness." By their ordination they were "set apart from the ordinary, secular concerns of life, to the special vocation of the ministry," and while they were thus employed, they could not attend to their own private affairs and provide for themselves and their household. Therefore, he declared, "ministers have a scriptural and reasonable claim to a maintenance from the people among whom they are called to labour."[51]

---

49. Moses Drury Hoge to William Plumer, March 21, 1850, in Peyton Harrison Hoge, *Moses Drury Hoge*, 107; Wightman, *Life of Capers*, 180, 183; William F. Broaddus to Reuben Slaughter, December 7, 1838, in Virginia Baptist Historical Society Collection.

50. *Central Presbyterian*, August 28, 1858, p. 138; Wightman, *Life of Capers*, 203.

51. *Religious Herald*, January 18, 1828, p. 7; "On Ministerial Support," *Virginia Evangeli-*

In defining what they meant by a "competent support," some evangelicals began by saying what it was not. It was "not a charity, but a debt." Church members should support their minister because they owed him payment for work done. "Having had the time of your minister, you can no more deprive him of his wages without sin, than you could 'the reaper of your fields.'" "What man," asked J. D. in the *Southern Watchman and General Intelligencer*, "does not feel bound to remunerate those whom he has employed, and for whose *sole* benefit they are laboring from day to day?"[52]

Viewing support as payment for services rendered, evangelicals could not fail to note the discrepancy between ministerial salaries and those paid other professionals. A writer in the *Southern Christian Advocate* in 1855 offered $1,500 as "a very low average of what educated men can command" in the United States. The estimate was based on a survey of the salaries of various professionals: "School Teachers, $500; Lieutenant in the Navy, $1,500; Captain in the Army, $1,500; Clerk in a Department, (U. S. Government) $1,500; Surgeon in the Navy, $2,700; (First class) Engineer, $3,000; Physician (First class) $10,000; Lawyer (First class) $10,000." Rural clergymen fell far short of the average; the writer estimated their salary at $500. Evangelicals believed that they deserved as much remuneration as other educated men. The fact that they generally received less was particularly galling given the exalted nature of the ministry. "Does the professor of religion . . . feel that the services of his lawyer and physician are so much more important than those of his minister?" asked the junior editor of the *Christian Index*. "The lawyer and the physician have to do with the world and the body—the *preacher* labors with reference to the interests of the soul, the nobler part," he declared. "Yet the former get a rich pay, the latter often gets nothing."[53]

Southern evangelicals did not completely abandon the notion of self-denial. Indeed, most of them were compelled to live a life of comparative self-denial by the unwillingness or inability of churches to offer them more than a minimum level of support. But, as the remarks on a competent support suggest, the meaning of self-denial was undergoing a subtle but significant alteration. For many evangelicals it no longer meant accepting

---

cal and Literary Magazine, VIII (July, 1825), 358, 360.

52. *Southern Baptist and General Intelligencer*, May 29, 1835, p. 339; *Southern Watchman and General Intelligencer*, May 5, 1837, p. 71.

53. *Southern Christian Advocate*, March 30, 1855, p. 170; *Christian Index*, February 28, 1839, pp. 132–33.

a subsistence level salary and trusting in God for the future of oneself and one's family. A writer in the *General Presbyterian* declared that "what is barely sufficient with rigid economy to keep the pastor and his family in the necessaries of life from year to year, with no possibility of laying by anything for old age, or for his family when he is taken from them, is not a proper support." Church members were not justified in acting, as they so often did, "upon the principle that a preacher must not lay up anything, forgetting that he must provide for his own, and his families [*sic*] wants as well as others—that he has a future before him as well as they." It is significant that the writer sought to make his point by stressing the similarity between the preacher and his people. In pressing for greater support, evangelicals inevitably diminished their distinctiveness as men who were supposed "to covet no man's silver, or gold, or goodly apparel." The outcome could be ironic, as in the case of William F. Broaddus who encountered some criticism (unjustified, he thought) from his parishioners on that score. He wrote that "if I persuade men against an undue anxiety after worldly good, I am sometimes sneered at as one who would preach one thing, and practise another. 'He preaches (says one) against the love of the world, and behold how anxious he is for riches.'"[54]

In addition to recruitment, ministerial education, and support, there was another matter which received considerable attention from southern evangelicals and which reveals the way in which the notion of the ministry was changing. This was the matter of influence, on which, perhaps more than anything else, the accomplishment of the evangelical task seemed to depend, for without influence on their congregations and the community at large, evangelicals could not hope to convert sinners and promote Christian morality. When the ministry was viewed in the traditional way—as a sacred office to which an individual was divinely called—influence was a function of the office itself. But in a democratic age, evangelicals saw the necessity of abandoning the notion that the minister was entitled to respect simply by virtue of his office. "To our countrymen," one evangelical noted, "generally, there is something peculiarly offensive in assertions of official dignity, and in claims of official respect. What they voluntarily and cheerfully yield to acknowledged merit or superior attainments, they indignantly withold [*sic*] from any one who claims it as a right, or who at-

54. *Central Presbyterian*, February 28, 1857, p. 34; "On Ministerial Support," *Virginia Evangelical and Literary Magazine*, VIII (July, 1825), 358; William F. Broaddus to Reuben Slaughter, December 7, 1838, in Virginia Baptist Historical Society Collection.

tempts to extort it."[55] Therefore evangelicals sought the kind of influence which professional men exerted. It derived not from the office but from the reputation and abilities of the man who filled it. Given the democratizing impulses at work in American society, it was defined largely in terms of popular expectations.

In describing the sort of minister most likely to have influence in society, evangelicals attempted to reconcile the two notions of the ministry. To the qualities associated with the traditional notion they added those most likely to appeal to the common man. Thus the exemplary minister should be "a man of unquestioned piety and active zeal," as well as "good pulpit talents" and "amiableness." On the one hand, he should exhibit a higher standard of behavior than other men, even professing Christians. As the editor of the *Religious Herald* pointed out, "his fellow-members as well as the community look for a greater degree of holiness, circumspection, and consistency of character in him than in the private members of the church. They expect him to be an example in all holiness and godliness." On the other hand, he should not be distant or aloof. He should be a man of "easy manners and address in his intercourse with Society." Evangelicals stressed the latter quality because they wanted the minister to have an influence that extended into the community at large, beyond his own pulpit and congregation. For this purpose, qualities other than the purely spiritual ones associated with the traditional view of the ministry were important. The editor of the *Christian Index* urged ministers "to acquire *moral power* out of the pulpit," and suggested the way in which it might be done: "by dignity of manner, as opposed to frivolity and trifling; by punctuality in the discharge of public duties, as opposed to tardiness and indolence; by a prompt and exact discharge of business obligations, as opposed to indifferent and slow payments; by civility and kindness to all, as opposed to austerity and partiality."[56] The fact that such qualities were appropriate to any profession, not just the ministry, suggests the extent to which evangelicals were adopting secular standards of behavior.

55. "Observations on the Manner of Educating Young Men for the Ministry of the Gospel," *Virginia Evangelical and Literary Magazine*, V (September, 1822), 474.

56. John Holt Rice to William Maxwell, September 16, 1819, in Maxwell, *Memoir of Rice*, 170–71; John N. Waddel to James Thornwell, March 26, 1859, in James Henley Thornwell, Sr., Materials, Historical Foundation of the Presbyterian and Reformed Churches; *Southern Evangelical Intelligencer*, June 19, 1819, p. 102; *Southern Watchman and General Intelligencer*, February 10, 1837, p. 23; M. M. Smith to Mrs. Williana Lacy, July 8, 1834, in Drury Lacy Papers, Southern Historical Collection, University of North Carolina Library; *Religious Herald*, January 9, 1840, p. 6; *Christian Index*, April 14, 1858, n.p.

Evangelicals put special emphasis on the way a minister conducted himself in his relations with other people. A writer in the *Southern Evangelical Review*, who used the pen name "Holem," offered the following recommendations which he claimed were based on twenty years' experience. First, as to "official demeanor," the minister ought to display "a frank, easy, polite and affectionate manner." He should maintain "a decent and dignified gravity," but he should not "look sour" or "be morose." A "soft and winning air of christian love" was more likely to be effective than "harsh stateliness." In the pulpit, though the preacher was obliged to warn his hearers of "the wrath of God and the perdition of the soul," he should beware of giving the impression of coldness, harshness, and hardheartedness. Otherwise, "hearers are very apt, instead of having their fears alarmed and taking the warning given by heaven, to feel resentment towards the preacher, who, as they imagine, takes pleasure in denouncing their destruction." The minister should show compassion. He should convince his hearers that he "gives the warning in love," and thereby win their goodwill. His success as a preacher depended on this, for "if a man is made angry, or his prejudices are excited, it is utterly vain and useless to attempt to reason with him or persuade him."

Finally, the minister should see to it that his dealings with his people were not exclusively ministerial, comprising only pastoral visiting and catechetical instruction. He should take an interest in their everyday life. For "if the people find that their daily labours and cares do not excite any sympathy in the bosom of their minister, they certainly will feel in a great degree separated from him. They will be apt to think of him as a man pursuing his calling, apart from them, yet supported by them—And, certainly, in this case the prospect of usefulness is greatly lessened."[57]

Holem's recommendations suggest the extent to which the traditional notion of the ministry was being undermined in the antebellum period. Perhaps, in a democratic age, it was almost inevitable that the "ambassador of God" should also become a servant of the people. Indeed, except for critics like Thomas Smyth, most evangelicals believed that it was possible to be both, and that in doing so, they were enchancing rather than diminishing their usefulness as ministers of God.

---

57. "Observations on the Manner of Educating Young Men for the Ministry of the Gospel," *Virginia Evangelical and Literary Magazine*, V (September, 1822), 474–75, 478.

CHAPTER THREE
Revivalism

In August, 1831, Daniel Baker, pastor of the Independent Presbyterian Church of Savannah, wrote a letter to the editor of the Charleston *Observer* describing the revival that had occurred in his church during a "four days' meeting" at which ministers of the Methodist, Baptist, and Lutheran churches had united with the Presbyterians. There was preaching in the church three times each day, along with meetings of various kinds in other places, including a prayer meeting at six in the morning and meetings for professors, inquirers, mothers, youths, and other classes of people. All of the churches added members as a result; the number for the Presbyterians was 20. Even after the meeting, religious interest continued for the next year, during which time 100 persons joined Baker's church. He estimated that, including those who had joined other churches in the city, the total number of converts was about 250.[1]

Although in the letter Baker portrayed the revival as the result of the four-day meeting, it seems clear from his journal that it was also an outgrowth of a change in his own attitudes and activities that had occurred about a year earlier. Reading *Payson's Memoirs* one day in August, 1830, Baker said he became conscious of his own "dead state" and saw how "unblessed" his labors had been. He resolved, "by the grace of God, to turn over a new leaf, and in preaching and pastoral visitations to be more faithful and diligent than I had ever been." He also decided, after reading "an account of a prayer-meeting for the special purpose of praying for those for whom prayer might be specially desired," to have such a meeting in his

1. Charleston *Observer*, August 13, 1831, p. 129; William M. Baker, *Life of Baker*, 141.

own church. The special meeting proved "delightful." Forty-six persons requested prayers for themselves or others by placing notes in a box in the church the day before. Baker himself put in a note "requesting the prayers of my people for me; that the Lord would give me a more intense love for souls; would give signal success to my labours, and would cause me to have a richer and sweeter experience of the grace of God in my own heart." He also held a meeting exclusively for members of the church and set another to which he invited "all who had the candour to admit they were not converted." When he went to the lecture room for the latter meeting, he found it crowded. "It was a solemn time, a melting time," he wrote. Six or eight persons were "much wrought upon" and soon after gave evidence of "a real change of heart." Besides holding various types of special meetings, Baker seems to have altered his preaching. It became "so plain and pointed" that some church members expressed disapproval, fearing that young people would not join the church and that some of the pewholders would give up their pews.[2]

Once the news of the Savannah revival spread, Baker was invited to nearby towns in South Carolina. He participated in protracted meetings in Gillisonville, in which 60 persons were converted, and in Grahamsville, where 145 were awakened, but it was the meeting in Beaufort that proved most remarkable. Baker was invited there by a resident who had been converted during the Gillisonville meeting. Since there was no Presbyterian church in the town, Baker held meetings alternately in the Baptist and Episcopal churches. He preached three times a day to large crowds, extended the meetings several days beyond the original closing date, and counted about 80 persons "hopefully converted." Among them were many young men, 8 of whom subsequently decided to preach the Gospel. One of them was a prominent lawyer, Richard Fuller. Shortly after the Beaufort revival, Baker, who had a "hankering after a missionary life," resigned his charge in Savannah and became an evangelist for the Synod of South Carolina and Georgia. His field was extensive, taking him into Georgia, Alabama, Florida, South Carolina, and parts of North Carolina. During the two years of his missionary tour he participated in some fifty protracted meetings, preached, on the average, two sermons a day, and converted about 2,500 individuals.[3]

2. William M. Baker, *Life of Baker*, 125–26, 132–36, 138.
3. *Ibid.*, 145–80.

Baker's tour of 1831–1832 was only one of several seasons of revival that occurred in the southern states in the first half of the nineteenth century. In 1822–1823 numerous Baptist churches in Virginia, South Carolina, and North Carolina had experienced revivals. During the one that began in Bedford County, Virginia, Daniel Witt and Jeremiah Jeter were converted and began preaching. Another general awakening among Baptists began in 1827 with a revival at the church in Eatonton, Georgia. It ultimately spread over the entire state and penetrated South Carolina, involving Presbyterians and Methodists as well as Baptists. The latter are supposed to have added 16,000 new converts in Georgia during the two years of the revival. Daniel Baker's efforts coincided with yet another season of refreshing among Baptists in Virginia, North and South Carolina, and Georgia between 1831 and 1833.[4]

From 1837 to 1839 revivals were widespread among Baptists and Methodists in the Deep South, and Presbyterian churches in south Alabama also shared in the refreshings. The early 1840s saw numerous revivals in all three denominations. In 1841 the Baptist *Christian Index* reported an "outpouring of God's Spirit upon the people . . . in every direction." The result, according to the *Religious Herald*, was that not less than 5,000 persons were baptized in Virginia alone. In Georgia, Alabama, Louisiana, and Mississippi baptisms were estimated at around 9,000; additions to Baptist churches in North and South Carolina were proportionately less numerous, but nevertheless considerable. The Methodists also reported numerous accessions to their churches, especially in the Virginia and South Carolina Conferences during 1841–1843. In 1844 the *Southern Christian Advocate* reported that cheering accounts continued to come in from those conferences, as well as from the Mississippi, Georgia and Alabama Conferences. During the early forties, in the Presbyterian churches in Virginia there were numerous revivals, of which the most noteworthy was the one that began in 1842 in the First Presbyterian Church in Richmond, where William Plumer was pastor. That revival eventually spread among all the evangelical denominations in the city. Jeremiah Jeter, who contrib-

---

4. "Revivals of Religion," *Roanoke Religious Correspondent*, I (May, 1822), 155, 157–59; Monroe Geer, "The Temperance Movement in Georgia in the Middle Period" (M.A. thesis, Emory University, 1936), 35; Charleston *Observer*, September 15, 1827, p. 146; "Religious Intelligence," *Virginia Evangelical and Literary Magazine*, XI (January, 1828), 46, 48; Jeter, *Memoir of Clopton*, 111–14, 135, 198, 200–203; *Christian Index*, December 30, 1834, n.p., April 8, 1857, p. 53; *Religious Herald*, May 20, 1831, p. 75, May 27, 1831, p. 78, February 3, 1832, p. 14, January 18, 1833, p. 7; Jeter, *Recollections*, 153; Basil Manly to the Reverend W. B. Johnson, October 14, 1831, in Manly, Jr., Papers.

uted to the movement by holding a protracted meeting in the First Baptist Church, estimated the number of converts in the city at about 1,500, out of a population of about 30,000. The years 1846–1849 marked another wave of revivals among Methodists and Baptists throughout the South. A final season of refreshing among Methodists, Presbyterians, and, to a lesser extent, Baptists, occurred in the early and mid-1850s, culminating in the Great Revival of 1857–1858.[5]

The forerunner of these later seasons of revival was the Great Revival of 1800–1805. As described by John Boles, the Great Revival developed out of a feeling of crisis in the 1790s over religious coldness and infidelity, along with a growing expectation of "providential deliverance." Beginning in the Cumberland region of Kentucky among the Presbyterians and the Methodists, it ultimately spread over the entire South and involved most other denominations, resulting in a spectacular rise in church membership, especially among Baptists and Methodists. The camp meeting was the principal vehicle of the revival. Although Presbyterians and Baptists began to dissociate themselves from the camp meeting around 1803 and 1804 (so that it became a Methodist institution), in the early years of the revival they used it extensively and with considerable success. Another characteristic of the revival, which eventually caused the Baptists and Presbyterians to withdraw from it, was a tendency toward emotionalism, disorder, and extravagance. At most of the camp meetings, physical responses such as shouting, crying, and falling down were common, though only a few of the meetings, such as the one at Cane Ridge, displayed the extreme "exercises" which critics cited to discredit the revival. Ministers of the Great Revival aimed their sermons at the emotions of their hearers, "juxtaposing . . . fear and anxiety with love and security" in order to arouse sinners to a realization of the need for salvation. The "theology of individualism" which

5. *Christian Index*, November 23, 1837, p. 749, September 13, 1838, p. 565, November 7, 1839, p. 709, October 8, 1841, p. 649, October 14, 1847, p. 334; *Religious Herald*, November 24, 1837, p. 186, June 29, 1838, p. 102, February 10, 1842, p. 23, May 12, 1842, n.p., December 31, 1846, p. 211, December 13, 1849, p. 198, May 9, 1850, p. 74, August 21, 1856, p. 130; *Southern Christian Advocate*, September 2, 1837, p. 42, October 7, 1837, p. 62, October 19, 1838, p. 70, January 11, 1839, p. 118, September 27, 1844, p. 62, September 25, 1846, p. 62, October 30, 1846, p. 83, November 3, 1848, p. 86, September 20, 1855, p. 62, October 8, 1857, p. 74; *Watchman of the South*, January 3, 1839, p. 74, January 2, 1840, p. 74, April 14, 1842, p. 134; Jeter, *Recollections*, 238–41; Richmond *Christian Advocate*, October 29, 1846, p. 138, October 4, 1849, p. 158; Margaret Burr DesChamps, "The Presbyterian Church in the South Atlantic States, 1801–1861," (Ph.D. dissertation, Emory University, 1952), 6n; William M. Baker, *Life of Baker*, 449–60, 464, 478ff, 500, 502, 508; *Central Presbyterian*, October 18, 1856, p. 166 (misnumbered 156); *Southern Presbyterian*, September 22, 1853, p. 194, March 22, 1856, n.p.

Presbyterians, Methodists, and Baptists shared stressed that grace was the gift of God, but also emphasized the elements of human decision and ministerial persuasion. As a result, Boles writes, "the minister's role had become primarily one of activism, more concerned with gaining new converts than counseling old ones."[6]

To some extent the Great Revival of 1800–1805 was the progenitor of later southern revivals. But in the four decades preceding the Civil War the revival theories and practices of southern evangelicals changed and evolved, with the result that southern revivalism in the 1850s was markedly different in many respects from the turn-of-the-century movement. One aspect of revival theory remained constant, however—the notion, which all southern evangelicals accepted, of the providential nature of revivals. A revival of religion was the work of the Holy Spirit converting multitudes to God. Just as the conversion of one individual occurred through God's grace, so was the conversion of many individuals at one time effected by divine power. But while stressing "divine efficiency," southern evangelicals also emphasized the role of "human agency" in bringing about a revival. Thus a correspondent of the Charleston *Observer* noted that revivals, "though properly accorded to the Spirit of God as their efficient cause, depend nevertheless upon human instrumentality," and the editor of the *Religious Herald* pointed out that instead of spreading His gospel "by direct and immediate agency from heaven," God "has condescended to employ man to carry the glad tidings of salvation to his fellow man."[7] Although there was some disagreement among evangelicals as to what constituted the proper sort of human instrumentality, there was no disagreement about the necessity of some kind of human effort in producing a revival.

The doctrine of human instrumentality not only enabled evangelicals to explain how revivals came about, it also helped to explain a lack of revivals. The causes of spiritual declension included worldliness; religious controversy; political excitement; prosperity; neglect of worship, prayer, and other religious duties; and defective preaching. "Nothing is more common than to hear christians attribute the cold state of religion in their hearts, and in the churches, to *the withdrawal of the influence of the Holy Spirit*," observed a writer in the *Southern Watchman and General Intelligencer*. "O how ready we are to throw off responsibility! . . . these influences are *never*

6. Boles, *Great Revival*, 12–13, 19, 26, 47–50, 68, 88–89, 91, 99, 114, 124, and *passim*.
7. *Religious Herald*, August 11, 1837, p. 125, August 12, 1831, p. 122; Charleston *Observer*, April 17, 1830, p. 62.

withheld, without some existing cause *in us.*" Just as the cause of spiritual declension lay with man, so did the remedy. Southern evangelicals insisted that God had promised that prayer and personal exertions for a revival would not be in vain. "The use of *appointed means,* in the *appointed way,* warrants the expectation of the divine blessing," declared Minimus in the *Virginia Evangelical and Literary Magazine.* Similarly, the editor of the Charleston *Observer,* recalling the revivals of previous years, explained that the cause of the present state of declension was not "that God has forgotten to be gracious, but that the Church is in a deep and profound slumber." He was confident that "were the same means used as formerly, with the same degree of faith, the same results might certainly be expected. And this necessarily follows from the fact that we have to do with that God who is not slack concerning his promises—who has said 'Ask and ye shall receive, seek and ye shall find, knock and it shall be opened unto you.'" It was this kind of reasoning that lay behind the Dover Association's setting aside a "day of humiliation, fasting and prayer to God, for the outpouring of his Spirit, and for a revival of religion." In the 1830s a number of Baptist churches and associations took similar action, while Presbyterians and Methodists also gave such measures their approval.[8]

The doctrine of human instrumentality assigned an important role to the minister in bringing about a revival. He could not convert sinners— only the Holy Spirit could do that—but his duty was to address the unconverted, urging them to repent and seek salvation. Some Presbyterians and Baptists, in carrying out this duty, shifted toward the Arminianism of the Methodists, soft-pedaling notions of inability, election, and predestination, and accentuating man's role in the business of salvation. An individual who participated in a revival in the Second Presbyterian Church in Alexandria, Virginia, wrote that "the duty of immediate repentance has been much insisted upon. Sinners have been urged to forsake their sins and to commence the practice of every known duty immediately." He was impressed with the effectiveness of the preaching that held the sinner responsible for a decision, as opposed to the doctrine "which tells the awakened sinner that he cannot do anything and that he must quietly await the

8. *Southern Watchman and General Intelligencer,* February 18, 1847, p. 30, March 10, 1837, p. 38; "Desultory Reflections at the Close of the Year," *Virginia Evangelical and Literary Magazine,* IX (December, 1826), 644; Charleston *Observer,* October 16, 1830, p. 166; *Religious Herald,* October 7, 1836, p. 156, August 31, 1838, p. 138; *Christian Index,* May 7, 1840, p. 295; *Watchman and Observer,* November 13, 1845, p. 50; *Central Presbyterian,* August 28, 1858, p. 138; *Southern Christian Advocate,* October 7, 1837, p. 62.

Lord's time."⁹ But others, including Daniel Baker, preached fairly ortho-
dox Calvinist doctrines with success. A Baptist described the preaching at
revival meetings he attended as "of the plain kind . . . nothing but Christ
and him crucified. No armenianism [*sic*], nor any of Alexander Campbell's new fangled notions. . . . The entire depravity of the human heart
and salvation through the merits of a crucified Saviour, were the theme of
the ministers." The Synod of Virginia, characterizing the kind of preaching which had produced revivals in some of its churches, noted that "it has
consisted chiefly in plain, direct, and earnest addresses to the understanding and heart: the doctrines mostly insisted on, were the total depravity of
mankind by nature, the guilt and danger of their unregenerate state, the
necessity of the efficient operation of the Holy Spirit to convert & sanc-
tify the soul, & of a simple reliance upon the merits of the crucified & Divine Saviour for justification."

Perhaps, as a correspondent of the *Religious Herald* pointed out, what
made preaching effective in converting sinners had less to do with the
doctrines that were presented and more to do with the way they were presented. Whether Calvinist or Arminian, southern revivalists preached
mainly to the heart and conscience, not to the head. They stressed practical rather than doctrinal preaching. In the meetings that produced the revival of 1831–1832, the *Herald* writer observed, "there has been no new
doctrine advanced, but the old doctrine has been urged home upon the
heart with pathos. Repentance and faith have been explained as formerly,
but they have been urged upon sinners as their immediate duty. The
atoning Saviour has been presented in the same light in which he has always been exhibited; but the sinner has been urged with an eloquence all
divine to go to him immediately for salvation. Sovereign grace has been
displayed in all its glory, but not so as to leave the sinner uninterested." He
concluded that what was "termed Revival Preaching, is nothing more nor
less than preaching the truth plainly, and bringing that truth home to a
personal and practical application."¹⁰

Preaching was regarded as one of the ordinary means of grace. Of the
special or "extraordinary" means employed by southern evangelicals in
bringing about a revival, camp meetings and protracted meetings were

9. Thompson, *Presbyterians in the South*, I, 231–32; Jeter, *Memoir of Clopton*, 269.
10. William M. Baker, *Life of Baker*, 460, 463; *Christian Index*, October 10, 1839, p. 644;
"A Narrative of the State of Religion," *Virginia Evangelical and Literary Magazine*, V (November, 1822), 603; *Religious Herald*, March 9, 1832, p. 33.

the most important.[11] Camp meetings originated in the Great Revival of 1800–1805 and were utilized by all three denominations, often working in concert. Although Baptists and Presbyterians repudiated them around 1803–1804, they took them up again after the War of 1812, having become convinced that they could be conducted without the disorder and extravagances that had characterized them during the Great Revival. Methodists, who became virtually the sole proponents of camp meetings toward the end of the Great Revival, continued to view them as a necessary and useful revival method. Annual encampments were held in most of the circuits in the southern states throughout the first half of the nineteenth century.[12]

Evangelicals who favored camp meetings cited the fact that they were not only a way of accommodating congregations larger than could fit into a church, but also a way of attracting persons who would be unlikely to come to church but who would attend a camp meeting out of curiosity or a desire for novelty or in order to hear new preachers. Moreover, camp meetings, by calling persons away from worldly matters for several days of uninterrupted religious exercises, afforded a peculiar opportunity both for the conversion of sinners and the spiritual growth of professors. Finally, camp meetings proved a particularly appropriate means of spreading religion in sections of the country where ministers were few and churches widely scattered. As the editor of the *Southern Presbyterian* observed, "an occasional gathering for a few days of the families of these churches, with four or five ministers to preach to them, often results in rich spiritual blessings."[13]

Even proponents, however, recognized the dangers inherent in camp meetings. Jeremiah Jeter, who was largely responsible for convincing Baptists in the Northern Neck of Virginia to hold their first camp meeting in 1831, admitted that camp meetings "may be adopted wisely or unwisely, according to circumstances. In a sparsely settled country, under good religious influence, where the grounds and its surroundings are controlled by

11. Two treatments of the camp meeting, both of which view it as a frontier phenomenon, are Charles A. Johnson, *The Frontier Camp Meeting: Religion's Harvest Time* (Dallas, 1955), and Dickson D. Bruce, Jr., *And They All Sang Hallelujah: Plain-Folk Camp-Meeting Religion, 1800–1845* (Knoxville, 1974).

12. On the three denominations' use of camp meetings, see, for example, Jeter, *Recollections*, 153–56, 159, *Religious Herald*, October 10, 1850, p. 162, *Central Presbyterian*, September 3, 1859, p. 142, and *Wesleyan Journal*, October 29, 1825, p. 3.

13. *Southern Presbyterian*, June 29, 1849, p. 178. See also *Religious Herald*, November 18, 1831, p. 178, *Christian Index*, April 13, 1837, p. 231, August 30, 1849, p. 274, *Southern Christian Advocate*, August 6, 1847, p. 34.

the friends of good order, where comfortable arrangements are made for the entertainment of an assembly, where public sentiment is sufficiently strong for the suppression of disorder, and where the ministers have gifts and influence for properly conducting such a meeting, it may, by God's blessing, be eminently useful." But he noted that there was a great danger that camp meetings would be "perverted to evil," and cited the "strong tendency to make them occasions of social pleasure, festivity, and even of frivolity, dissipation, and vice." Many Baptists continued to frown on the misconduct which attended such meetings and some, like a correspondent in the *Christian Index*, feared they would "prove a snare . . . if employed as substitutes for the ordinary and regular ministrations of the sanctuary." The editor of the Charleston *Observer* probably expressed the view of a majority of Presbyterians in criticizing camp meetings for arousing an artificial excitement by preaching to the passions rather than the understanding and the conscience. He admitted that such efforts might have an "electrical effect" but questioned whether they led to genuine repentance.[14]

The earliest camp meetings were held in clearings in the woods. People came in wagons with provisions for several days. Usually they camped in tents, but William Winans remembered that at the first meeting he attended, around 1804, "there was neither camp nor Tent on the ground; nor do I recollect that there was anything like a table for eating purposes. Those who had wagons or carts, occupied them as dormitories—those who had not wagons or carts, as most had not, bivouacked, under perhaps a sheet or blanket." Gradually, accommodations improved. Later campgrounds featured log houses for regular attendants and rather complex pulpit and altar arrangements, with benches to accommodate thousands of people and a lighting system for night services.[15] James B. Taylor described the Baptist campground in the Northern Neck of Virginia in 1834 as follows:

Imagine to yourself an area something like one hundred yards square, enclosed by comfortable log houses, occupied by the whites; each of these houses having another in the rear, in which the coloured people lodge.—Within this area is a beautiful grove, under which the congregation meet for worship. The seats are made of logs, and will accommodate some thousands of people. . . . Six or eight scaffolds about eight feet high and four square, are placed at equal distances from each other within the area, and on them fires are built of pine filled with turpentine;

14. Jeter, *Recollections*, 162; *Christian Index*, November 12, 1833, p. 71; Charleston *Observer*, September 11, 1830, p. 146.
15. Winans Autobiography, 10; *Southern Christian Advocate*, October 27, 1859, p. 295.

besides which, a number of lamps are suspended from the trees, whilst through the foliage are to be seen a thousand twinkling stars, which add to the grandeur of the scene.

Taylor estimated the number of houses on the campground at about one hundred. The number of persons who remained overnight varied between five hundred and one thousand. The size of the congregation during the day was "usually very large, amounting, I think, to five or six thousand." The Northern Neck camp meeting lasted a week. (Usually, such meetings went on for only four days.) Activities began at sun rise, wrote Taylor. "The trumpet is blown, and in every direction, the worshippers of the living God are seen coming from their tents, to what might be called family worship. A chapter is read, a hymn sung, and prayer made." After "a plain morning meal," the congregation attended a prayer meeting at 8:00. This exercise, which was "intermingled with exhortation and singing," was followed by an hour recess. At 11:00 a sermon was preached, again at 3:30, and at 8:00 P.M. Taylor explained that "the intervals of public worship are usually employed in conversation and devotional exercises in the tent." He noted approvingly that "the most perfect good order" prevailed throughout the meeting.[16]

Although Methodists remained loyal to camp meetings up to the Civil War, some of them expressed doubts as to their efficacy and pointed to abuses in the way they were conducted. In the late 1840s and 1850s the *Southern Christian Advocate* featured numerous articles and letters discussing the merits and defects of camp meetings. The discussion is doubly revealing, for it not only illuminates changing Methodist attitudes toward the camp meeting, but also reveals the way in which the institution itself was changing. Perhaps the most frequent criticism of camp meetings was that they had become places where religious devotion was subordinated to worldly matters. They had "been turned from their primitive simplicity into places of popular resort, gatherings for the young of both sexes, where belles display their fine feathers to the eyes of admiring beaux;—social reunions where luxurious tables, worldly chit-chat, political discussions, and the like, occupy more of the thoughts of the people than the matters of their everlasting salvation." Critics also noted the different context in which meetings were being held—Methodists now had enough preachers and churches to accommodate the people whom they had once been able to reach only through camp meetings. Some suggested that camp meetings

16. *Religious Herald*, September 12, 1834, p. 142.

were producing fewer converts and exhibiting more abuses because they were too numerous and too frequent. A correspondent who signed himself "A Long Observer and Well Wisher to Camp-Meetings" thought that Methodists had "injured" camp meetings *"by holding too many of them."* What was "only intended as [an] *extraordinary* means of grace" had now "become too common." On the other hand the editor of the *Advocate* believed that one of the reasons why camp meetings failed to convert was because they were too short. They ought to begin Friday evening and last at least until Wednesday morning, he declared. Many could profitably be continued "a week or more." He explained:

In general, but little development of feeling is seen among the unconverted until after the Sabbath services are past. The sermons on Sunday ought to be powerful efforts, addressed to the immense and motley crowd in attendance on that day. These efforts will produce effect, but it will not be so visible until the unwounded 'herd' have left the ground. Those who have felt the arrows of the Almighty will remain, or return on the next day, to seek relief for their bleeding hearts. Then comes the time for the display of converting and saving power: in a few hours scores of persons may be brought into the glorious liberty of the children of God and into the communion of the household of faith. But when the meeting adjourns on Sunday night, or Monday morning, a vast amount of our labor is in vain. Many of the awakened persons return to the business and pleasures of life, and lose their convictions; and many who would have been awakened and converted too had they remained a day or two longer under the continuous and powerful preachings of the Camp-meeting, go away and are never saved.[17]

Most of the writers in the *Advocate*, including the editor, were not really opposed to camp meetings. They pointed to abuses and problems in the hope that they could be remedied and the meetings continued. Like most other Methodists, they still believed that such meetings were the best means of converting large numbers of people and that despite the intrusion of worldly matters, they continued to offer an opportunity for the "separation from secular cares" that was conducive to conviction and conversion. The fact that camp meetings were one of the "aggressive agencies, which marked the zeal of our fathers in the ministry" also reinforced the view that they ought to be continued, especially at a time of considerable discussion of the alleged departure from "'Old Fashioned' Methodism."[18]

It is significant, however, that a few writers who favored the continuance of camp meetings were beginning to assign them less importance or at

17. *Southern Christian Advocate*, September 26, 1851, p. 66, August 14, 1840, pp. 34–35; September 30, 1853, p. 70.
18. *Ibid.*, August 6, 1847, p. 34, May 2, 1851, p. 190, June 26, 1856, p. 13.

least a different function. A writer who signed himself "Onward" began a
letter to the editor by noting that the circumstances which originated camp
meetings no longer existed. Nevertheless, he argued, "every circuit needs
an *annual* meeting of some kind, and a Camp-meeting is the most convenient." Such meetings brought the people of the circuit together and gave
them a sense of having "*one* pastorate." "Onward" also maintained that
camp meetings had a good effect upon "religious communion, for they
are eminently social . . . [and] tend to the refinement and christianizing of
the social habits of the people." He declared that "they should be kept up
on this account, if there was no other reason." He added, almost as an af-
terthought, that they were occasions of religious revival and usually attended with "*unusual* success." (In a second letter to the editor, however,
"Onward" observed that as a result of changed circumstances, camp meetings should now be considered "efficient auxiliaries" in the business of
conversion. "The work is generally started at them," he noted, and urged
that after the close of a meeting the churches of the circuit should hold
services for several days to finish it.) Finally, "Onward" suggested that the
church had arrived at a point where camp meetings could and should perform yet another function: "The Bible, Missionary, Tract, and Sunday-
school interests, must have their festive occasions, and we propose to make
the circuit Camp-meeting the anniversary of them all."[19]

Like "Onward," the editor of the *Advocate* also noted the social function
of camp meetings, and defended them on that ground. "Irrespective of
the religious profit that accrues from them, their social benefit is great,"
he declared. On the one hand, camp meetings enabled people to socialize
in an atmosphere governed by "a high tone of moral feeling." (This was
assured by the rules and regulations governing the meeting and the people's "respect for the object of the meeting.") If their pleasures were not
religious, they were "at least, innocent social pleasures." Neighbors enjoyed "closer than usual fellowship," church members came to know and
appreciate one another better, and strangers found friends for life. Moreover, the editor insisted, camp meetings were a means of socialization and
even social mobility. "Those whose retired homes, or social position, or
disadvantages in other regards, enable them to see or know very little of
what the great world is, or how it lives, or what is decorous in its intercourse, learn more of it here in a few days, than in all the year besides," he
wrote. "A desire to improve themselves, and to deserve the consideration

19. *Ibid.*, September 20, 1855, p. 62, April 13, 1855, p. 179.

of those whom they can but respect, is waked up in many a young heart, that would have remained at rest in ignorance and obscurity, and in the lowest social position, but for the knowledge here obtained." This kind of improvement was not to be taken lightly. "Where we cannot improve the morals of the people, by bringing them to be decidedly religious," he wrote, "we gain much by improving their tastes and their manners. They may be no less sinners against God; but their sins against society are not so gross, and, generally, not of that character that deeply and inevitably involves others besides themselves in the consequences of their crimes."[20]

From the 1830s until the Civil War, the primary revival method used by Presbyterians and Baptists was the protracted meeting. Methodists later adopted it also and were using it extensively by the 1850s. Protracted meetings differed from camp meetings in that they were held indoors, usually in a church, sometimes in another available building. James O. Andrew held the first protracted meeting in Atlanta in 1846 in a large vacant warehouse. Protracted meetings were better adapted to towns and cities, though country churches also conducted them with success. Originally they were four-day meetings, but soon they were being protracted when circumstances—especially the spiritual state of the congregation—warranted it. Meetings of eight or nine days were not uncommon and some were protracted to as many as fifteen or sixteen days. Often they involved cooperation of the denominations, with ministers preaching in each other's churches in sequence or even simultaneously. Like camp meetings, protracted meetings also usually depended on ministerial help from the outside. When a church decided to schedule a meeting, its pastor often wrote to neighboring preachers inviting them to assist in the meeting. Meetings featured preaching (usually practical rather than doctrinal), singing, inquiry meetings, and prayer, with an emphasis on the latter. For example, during a protracted meeting in the Presbyterian Church in Athens, Georgia in 1831, there were three sermons and nine prayer meetings per day. The minister, Nathan Hoyt, believed that "no means was more blessed" than the prayer meetings, which were conducted by private Christians as well as clergymen. The main purpose of the protracted meeting was the conversion of sinners, but the promotion of vital piety among professing Christians was also recognized as an important objective.[21]

As with camp meetings, the primary argument advanced in favor of

20. *Ibid.*, November 6, 1856, p. 90.
21. George G. Smith, *Life and Letters of Andrew*, 388; Charleston *Observer*, June 25, 1831, pp. 102–103; *Religious Herald*, May 11, 1832, p. 71.

protracted meetings was their effectiveness in producing conviction and conversion. That they accomplished this without arousing "animal excitement" was an additional mark in their favor, especially among Presbyterians and Baptists. In describing meetings which they had conducted, ministers of those denominations were always careful to point out that no "noisy excitement," "no ranting, no running up and down the aisles of the church," had been exhibited, but the most perfect order reigned throughout. Perhaps one of the reasons for the decorum of the protracted as compared with the camp meeting was that the minister exercised much more control in the former. Rufus W. Bailey, reporting on a revival in his church in Cheraw, South Carolina, said that "the particular oversight and management of all the measures in every part of the work was never permitted to pass from the hands of the acting pastor." He observed that "a neglect of this precaution has been the fruitful source of many evils, which have prejudiced the labors and diminished the influence of some zealous and meritorious evangelists in our church."[22]

Evangelicals maintained that protracted meetings were more efficacious than regular Sabbath preaching because they provided for extended, virtually uninterrupted religious instruction. "The instructions of the Sabbath, however solemn and pointed, are soon effaced by worldly cares," the editor of the Charleston *Observer* pointed out, noting that "it demands something more than ordinary to abstract the mind from earthly objects, and fix it intently upon the great concern." The protracted meeting did just that. As "A Layman" explained, in such a meeting "all the powers of the mind have been absorbed with, and concentrated upon, one subject. Nothing has been permitted to divert it. . . . The true secret, therefore, of the astonishing results in many instances of the protracted meetings, so far as they depend upon human agency, arises from the fact that they are calculated to induce reflection and to urge it forward when commenced." This type of meeting also shortened the conversion process. In the course of hearing twenty or thirty sermons during a meeting of several days, the sinner received impressions, examined arguments, and reached conclusions in the same way that others might take a period of months to do.[23]

Ironically, the very success of protracted meetings seemed to some evangelicals to pose a danger. They feared that too many individuals, ministers included, would come to rely solely on the meetings for bringing sinners

22. *Religious Herald*, November 2, 1839, p. 174, August 28, 1856, p. 134, July 31, 1835, p. 118; *Watchman of the South*, January 2, 1840, p. 74.
23. Charleston *Observer*, December 31, 1831, p. 210, December 15, 1832, pp. 198–99.

to repentance, forgetting ordinary and more common means. The Presbytery of Georgia deplored the *"disesteem of the ordinary ministrations of the Sanctuary"* which they seemed to encourage. "There is an impression apparent in the Churches," it observed, "that the peculiar and favorable period for conversion is the period of a *Protracted Meeting*. They seem not to pray and act as if conversions should take place on the Sabbath day under the ordinary preaching of the word." It is possible that evangelicals themselves encouraged such thinking, albeit unwittingly, by de-emphasizing preaching as compared with other activities at protracted meetings. Presbyterians probably had more sermonizing at their meetings than did Baptists and Methodists, but they too stressed the greater importance and efficacy of prayer and inquiry meetings. Wm. J., writing in the *Southern Baptist and General Intelligencer,* was even more adamant. He cautioned that too much preaching at protracted meetings resulted in "the introduction into the church of many 'stony-ground hearers,' [and] an increased hardness of heart among the unconverted." Preaching one sermon after another did not allow enough time for the reflection and private prayer that ought to engage a man who is "called upon to 'consider his ways.'" Given the "stimulant" afforded by too much preaching, it was not surprising that there should be "many deceived souls" who requested and gained admission to church, only to have their conversion found spurious. Besides reflection and private prayer, Wm. J. particularly recommended inquiry meetings, which he suggested might be profitably continued even after the close of the protracted meeting if ministers were willing and able to remain in the vicinity.[24]

Protracted meetings, some evangelicals worried, seemed to encourage an increased reliance on "human instrumentality," on means and ministers. There was a danger that people would "forget their dependence on God."[25] Ultimately, as will be seen, southern evangelicals turned against what they saw as an excessive use of means and measures for bringing about a revival. But even in the 1830s it would appear that they had some basis for their fears. Revival meetings were becoming more and more calculated and contrived, as various techniques were developed and applied. As the amount of management increased, meetings became more orderly and decorous (a cause for thanksgiving among evangelicals who remembered or had heard about the excesses of the early camp meetings). They also became much less spontaneous and much more predictable, some-

24. *Ibid.*, May 25, 1833, p. 81; *Christian Index*, July 28, 1835, n.p.
25. Charleston *Observer*, August 27, 1831, p. 137.

thing that did not seem to worry evangelicals at the time, perhaps because they tended to associate spontaneity with "animal excitement" and extravagant behavior.

One way of illustrating this increase in management and the consequent decline of spontaneity is to compare the revival among Virginia Baptists in 1821 with revivals of later decades. The 1821 revival was the one in the Northern Neck of Virginia at which Jeremiah Jeter and Daniel Witt were converted. As Jeter remembered, there were signs of its approach early in the summer. "Congregations were larger, preaching was more searching and earnest, and was heard with greater attention and solemnity; tears furnished proof of more tender feeling, and prayers for the conversion of sinners were more importunate than in years past." Nevertheless, when the revival did come, at a meeting of several days at Hatcher's meetinghouse, there was something inexplicable about it. "The ministers had preached the same doctrine to the same people, under similar circumstances, many a time without any apparent effect. Now there seemed to be a mysterious, pervasive, and subduing influence attending their ministrations. The thoughtless became attentive; the frivolous were awed into solemnity; eyes unused to weeping poured out rivers of water, and not a few persons gave utterance to sobs, sighs, and lamentations." If the means by which the revival had come about were unaccountable, those by which it spread were haphazard and uncalculated. Rather than directing the revival, men found themselves swept up in a movement which seemed to have a life and direction of its own. Protracted meetings, as they later developed, were unknown then, Jeter recalled, but after the awakening at Hatcher's, "religious meetings were greatly multiplied." They were held at night in private houses or in the afternoon in arbors in the forest. Sometimes at these meetings "inquirers were invited to kneel for prayer, and sometimes to occupy special seats for receiving private instruction."

The revival spread "from neighborhood to neighborhood, from church to church" and eventually to nearby counties. "In a remarkable degree," Jeter wrote, "the revival was promoted by agents created by itself." Young men like himself and Witt, converted during the revival, felt impelled to spread its blessings. Although, as Jeter admitted, "they were very imperfectly equipped for their work," nevertheless, "their labors were crowned with success." They knew little of the means and instrumentalities for promoting a revival, but they had an appealing—perhaps even contagious—enthusiasm which proved equally efficacious. Jeter explained,

If these young evangelists could not present a logical argument for the truth of the gospel, they believed it with all their hearts, and preached because they did believe. They were unacquainted with many scriptural doctrines, and especially with the proofs of their divinity, but they understood the way of salvation. If they could not contend with astute sceptics, they could guide the honest, earnest inquirer to life eternal.

The young men knew little doctrine but a great deal about experience— they knew "the corruption of their own hearts and the fearfulness of their own guilt, and could testify [to] . . . the power and freeness of redeeming grace." Indeed, this was the substance of their preaching. Jeter said that when he and Witt began their labors they had "a common sermon" which was based on their own recent experience and "which we diversified with different texts, and with fresh arguments and illustrations as we could find them." At first the two confined their preaching to their native county, Bedford, but as the revival spread into adjoining counties, they followed. The prevailing interest in religion, along with the youthfulness of the two men (young preachers were "a great rarity" at that time) virtually guaranteed success. "Our fame . . . preceded us," Jeter recalled. "It was represented that two Bedford plowboys had suddenly entered the ministry and were turning the world upside down." Often they attracted congregations too large for any house to hold, and were compelled to preach out of doors in groves or arbors. Such large, attentive, responsive congregations were apparently as much of a surprise to Jeter and Witt as the two youths were to the people of the Northern Neck.[26]

Later revivals contrasted sharply with that of 1821. By the early 1830s the promotion of revivals had become a matter of calculation and contrivance, with various measures being utilized before as well as during the protracted meeting. Considerable emphasis was now being placed on preparation for a protracted meeting. The church ought to secure "a positive promise of attendance" from outside ministers; members of the church should pray for a blessing on the meeting; "a tone of elevated piety and devotion," without which no meeting could succeed, should be generated, perhaps by setting aside a day for fasting and prayer and also by "warm, searching, pungent" preaching. Unlike the improvised preaching of Jeter and Witt during the revival of 1821, the sermons delivered in later revivals were carefully calculated to lead the congregation through the various phases of the conversion process. Basil Manly, Jr., described the preach-

26. Jeter, *Recollections*, 38–41, 62–63, 65. See also Jeter, *Life of Witt*, 56–57, 107–110.

ing which he and several other ministers employed during a series of meetings in the First Baptist Church in Richmond in 1856:

The topics were at first mainly doctrinal, such as the necessity for an atonement, the sufficiency & adaptedness of Christ's mediation, the nature & necessity of faith, & of repentance. Having laid the foundation by as clear an explanation of the great facts & duties of the gospel, as we could give, we have dwelt during the remainder of the meeting more especially on the necessity for decision, the unreasonableness of the excuses urged, & the sinfulness & danger of neglecting Christ, —recurring of course frequently to enforce & illustrate the fundamental views urged at the commencement of our efforts.[27]

Besides preaching, there were other measures used during a protracted meeting to promote a revival of religion. Various types of prayer meetings were conducted—sunrise, afternoon, and evening meetings; union meetings (attended by members of different denominations); meetings in private homes as well as churches; meetings for different groups within the church such as young men, male professors, and young ladies. Inquiry meetings, in which individuals engaged in conversation and prayer with the ministers, were held in the vestry or adjoining rooms of the church. At some protracted meetings, the "anxious seat" was used. The minister invited individuals concerned about their spiritual state (sometimes referred to as "mourners") to come forward and occupy certain seats, usually in front of the pulpit, so that special prayers might be offered in their behalf. Another measure that was widely used during protracted meetings was house-to-house visiting by ministers and church members for the purpose of engaging in religious conversation and prayer. Finally, some ministers found that the distribution of tracts among the congregation during a protracted meeting also aided the cause of revival. During the meetings at the First Baptist Church in Richmond, a specially prepared tract "pointing out various *Scriptural Tests of Genuine Conversion*" was circulated extensively throughout the congregation, along with books such as *James' Anxious Enquirer* and *The Great Change*.[28]

Beginning in the late 1830s there were signs of a reaction against reviv-

27. *Religious Herald*, August 10, 1832, p. 122; Basil Manly, Jr., "The Revival in the First Church, Richmond" (MS dated May 19, 1856, in Manly Family Papers).

28. Basil Manly, Jr., "The Revival in the First Church, Richmond" (MS dated May 19, 1856, in Manly Family Papers). For accounts of revivals in which the various measures described were used, see, for example, *Watchman of the South*, May 18, 1843, p. 157; *Christian Index*, July 26, 1838, pp. 465–66; and *Southern Christian Advocate*, August 19, 1837, p. 34. The "anxious seat" has been attributed to Charles Grandison Finney, but Thompson, *Presbyterians in the South*, I, 230–31, argues that southern Presbyterians had been using it extensively several years before Finney employed it in the Rochester revival of 1830–31.

alism among southern evangelicals. The reaction did not lead to a complete repudiation of revivalism. Baptists, Methodists, and Presbyterians continued to use many of the methods that had proved so effective in the 1820s and early 1830s. But some evangelicals became increasingly concerned about certain abuses connected with revivalism, and others were led to abandon some or all of the extraordinary means that had been developed for promoting revivals. One of the abuses was what evangelicals termed "periodical revivals" or "periodical religion." They recognized that late summer and fall were auspicious times for religious meetings, mainly because of the mild weather, which was as important a consideration for protracted meetings as for camp meetings since many churches in the South were less than comfortable in the winter. But the evangelicals lamented the fact that people had come to think that conversions could occur only in revivals and that revivals could take place only during certain times of the year. This resulted in "the neglect of the ordinary means of grace." Moreover, it was "contrary to the teachings of God's word." God was not to be confined to any particular time or season in the manifestation of his grace. "We should be 'instant in season and out of season,'" declared Melancthon, writing in the *Southern Christian Advocate*. "We should always be ready—always abound in the work of the Lord." Another consequence of periodical religion was noted by a writer in the *Christian Index*: "Many there are, who, during the seasons in which we usually experience revivals of religion, are very zealous in the cause of their Master, but as soon as these seasons are past, seem to think that there is nothing more for them to do, *so they provide to go into winter quarters at once*. The market places are *crowded*, and the house of God deserted."[29]

The Methodist Williams Winan placed some of the blame for the post-revival apathy of church members on itinerant revivalists. Such men (Winans was thinking in particular of John Newland Maffit) often produced numerous conversions, but Winans believed that "the comparatively noiseless ministry of the regular Pastor will be found to have accomplished more substantial good than that of the irregular 'Revivalist.'" He explained why:

When the services of the *irregular* Preacher are withdrawn, a large portion of those, who have yielded to the influence of his ministration, are not in a condition to profit by the labors of the *Pastor* to whose care they are left, from want of congeniality of feeling, habits of thought &c. and from the absence of the strong sympa-

29. *Watchman and Observer*, September 6, 1849, pp. 14–15; *Southern Christian Advocate*, April 5, 1850, p. 173; *Christian Index*, January 2, 1851, p. 2.

thy, which they have with the minister by whom they were arroused [*sic*], and, of that dependent confidence which they had placed in his prayers and his teachings. Hence as they have, but just entered upon a religious course, the impulse which placed them in it being withdrawn, they, for the most part, soon halt, go back, conclude that the whole is a delusion, and become seven times as hard to move as they were before.[30]

Methodists were not alone in complaining about the effect of itinerant revivalists. David Benedict, in *Fifty Years Among the Baptists*, pointed to the jealousy with which settled ministers regarded these "new men," the preference they received from church members, and the ill effects which often accompanied their "new measures." The Presbyterian Robert Lewis Dabney also found fault with "brother ministers" who virtually ignored a pastor "during all the wearisome months and years" he was working "to bring the people up to the proper state of spirituality and zeal," but who, when "the harvest season" finally arrived, came "flocking in uninvited, or on the least pretext of an invitation." Besides the fact that the people were likely to draw "most unfavorable comparisons" between the outsiders, whom they associated with their awakening, and their own pastor, Dabney admitted another reason for his complaint. The time when a revival was beginning was "just the time I don't want them," he declared. "Now it is a delightful indulgence to preach. The congregations are full, the listening intent and solemn, one's own mind roused and elevated, and the people catching up any portion of divine truth, as if it were most powerful eloquence . . . , it is no effort to preach and no trouble. I don't want help. It is like taking the bread out of a hungry man's mouth, just when he had been toiling a whole year to get it ready." Dabney added, in further justification of his viewpoint, that the outside ministers, coming as they did from "other congregations in a cold state," were not "up to the mark of our feeling." Preaching from "old, time-yellowed manuscripts," they offered "their cut-and-dried orthodoxy in so chilling a style that it ruins the whole affair."[31]

The hasty reception of converts into the church was another abuse of revivalism which worried southern evangelicals, particularly in the 1840s

30. William Winans to the Reverend C. K. Marshall, October 18, 1852, in Winans Collection.

31. Benedict, *Fifty Years among the Baptists*, 150–51; Robert Lewis Dabney to his mother, June 8, 1850, in Thomas Cary Johnson, *Life and Letters of Dabney*, 112–13, and see also 114. Joseph Benson Cottrell took the opposite view. He recalled that during a revival in his town another minister came and "arrived just at a time when it seemed that a new man was needed." Joseph Benson Cottrell Diary (MS in Joseph Benson Cottrell Papers, Southern Historical Collection, University of North Carolina Library), December 31, 1863.

and 1850s. To be sure, many southern ministers carefully scrutinized persons who requested church membership, and many of them, like Basil Manly, Jr., were not disposed "to *string* the fish—as soon as caught, & be a little indiscriminate about it." But there were others who were willing to relax requirements in times of revival. Some were said to be motivated by "an ambitious desire to report every year large accessions, to the glory, not so much of God, as of the Pastor as a great and successful preacher." Others, it was suggested, subordinated religious and moral qualifications to social positions and wealth. Whatever the reason, southern evangelicals agreed that the hasty admission of persons to church membership had a deleterious effect. The church was not strengthened but weakened as a result of acquiring members who failed to fulfill their religious duties and obligations. The problem was compounded—and the responsibility of the minister increased—by the fact that, as Manly observed, "so few who enter the ch[urch] unconvtd. ever find out their mistake."[32]

A related abuse of revivalism was the failure of churches and ministers to see to the spiritual improvement of the newly converted, especially young persons. Such instruction was necessary if the results of a revival were to be permanent. Thus, the editor of the *Southern Christian Advocate* declared that "the training [of] young converts after their connection with the church, is little less important than their conversion itself." Conversion, he noted, "is but the starting point in the divine life, . . . only the beginning of a process of inward, spiritual, growth." Instruction was necessary if converts were "to repudiate the notion of that sort of religion which moves spasmodically, once or twice a year, when the electrical current of a Campmeeting or some other great occasion rouses up one's emotionality." Otherwise they were likely "to resume the old mode of worldly living," to refuse to aid the Sabbath school and the missionary and Bible cause, to "half-starve" the minister, and to be "as keen as ever in securing the pelf of earth."[33]

The reaction against the use of certain means and measures to promote revivals is most apparent and most easily documented among Presbyterians.[34] It was partly a result of the controversy between the Old and New

32. Basil Manly, Jr., to Charles Manly, September 19, 1857, in Manly, Jr., Papers; *Christian Index*, September 11, 1856, p. 146, January 14, 1857, p. 6.

33. *Southern Christian Advocate*, October 21, 1853, p. 82, November 3, 1848, p. 86.

34. There is some evidence of a similar reaction among Baptists and Methodists. For criticism of "ultra measures" used to produce religious excitement, and of a tendency to depend more on "feeling" than on "principle," see *Southern Baptist and General Intelligencer*, August 19, 1836, p. 134; *Southern Christian Advocate*, August 26, 1837, p. 38; W. W. Childers to James C.

Schools over the New England Theology, which emphasized freedom of the will, and the "new measures" of Charles Grandison Finney, which included protracted meetings, the anxious seat, sermons that appealed to the emotions, praying for individuals by name, and allowing women to testify in public meetings. The fact that the New School was linked with abolitionism and other "ultra" reform movements in the North also was a factor.[35] But the reaction against revivalism should also be seen as the outgrowth of a tendency which had all along been latent in southern Presbyterianism and which may have been brought to the fore by the controversy within the church. Even though southern Presbyterians employed some of the "new measures" in the 1830s and 1840s (and even, to some extent, in the 1850s), they seem to have done so reluctantly, always fearful that they would produce the extravagance and disorder which they associated with the Great Revival of 1800–1805. Indeed, as Walter Brownlow Posey and Robert Watkin have pointed out, though Presbyterians held revivals and protracted meetings in the antebellum period, the church officially gave them only a cautious endorsement. A pastoral letter issued by the General Assembly in 1832 warned ministers and churches against undue excitement, "bodily agitations," "noisy outcries," and "every species of indecorum." Presbyterians were "not to listen to self-sent or irregular preachers, or to any preaching inconsistent with their doctrinal standards." The assembly also urged restraint in admitting apparent converts to church membership. Something of the same distrust of revival methods can be seen in the comments of the *Southern Presbyterian Review* regarding a volume of Daniel Baker's revival sermons. The editor admitted, begrudgingly, that the sermons when first delivered, "were blessed . . . to men of all descriptions," and he conceded that "the vivid moral painting, the fervid impassioned appeal, and the rhetorical mode of presenting argument, are infinitely more likely to move an audience, than a style more rigidly

---

Furman, October 12, 1839, in James Furman Papers; Basil Manly, Jr., "Jottings Down, August 21, 1844" (MS in Manly Family Papers); Cox, "Life and Work of Basil Manly, Jr.," 43–44. For objections to the notion of "getting up a revival" see *Christian Index*, October 3, 1839, p. 628; *Southern Christian Advocate*, October 25, 1839, p. 74.

35. Thompson, *Presbyterians in the South*, I, 350–63, 373–412; C. Bruce Staiger, "Abolitionism and the Presbyterian Schism of 1837–1838," *Mississippi Valley Historical Review*, XXXVI (December, 1949), 391–414. For criticism of the New England Theology and the "new measures" by southern Presbyterians, see, for example, John Holt Rice to the Reverend Archibald Alexander, March 4, 1828, in Maxwell, *Memoir of Rice*, 338–39; William M. Baker, *Life of Baker*, 208; Thomas Erskine Clarke, "Thomas Smyth: Moderate of the Old South" (Th.D. dissertation, Union Theological Seminary, 1970), 36–38; and Abram David Pollock Diary (typed copy in Abram David Pollock Papers, Southern Historical Collection, University of North Carolina Library), [October, 1832], p. 13.

correct, and reasoning more technical and abstract." Nevertheless, he declared, "our ideas of what belongs to good taste are not met by these discourses. They abound more in anecdote, in exclamations, and free colloquialisms, than suit our views. . . . Apostrophe, and other strong figures of rhetoric, are too freely used, and carried beyond the bounds of propriety."[36]

Given the existence of such attitudes among southern Presbyterians, one is not surprised at the feeling of relief expressed in an editorial in the *Watchman of the South* regarding the revivals of 1841. Noting that they had "been marked by great sobriety," the editor added that "new measures and new doctrines have been alike eschewed." Similarly, the editor of the *Watchman and Observer*, commenting on a revival in the Second Presbyterian Church in Charleston, South Carolina, noted approvingly that "in the progress of this work, the instrumentality employed has consisted chiefly, if not altogether, in preaching the Word, in prayer, and in mutual conversation—to the exclusion of all those mechanical means to which fanatics are accustomed to resort in getting up spurious revivals." Inquiry meetings were not used, though the minister did visit and pray with inquirers in private. Nor were "additional services" introduced. The revival occurred during "the ordinary time of worship" and under "the services of the regular Pastor."[37]

One of the "new measures" that was generally abandoned in the 1840s and 1850s was the anxious seat. Daniel Baker, who had used that device in the early 1830s, seems to have given it up by the late 1830s, relying on inquiry meetings instead. When Presbyterians in southwest Georgia held a protracted meeting in 1852, the propriety of using the anxious seat was the subject of much discussion. Many of the brethren were afraid of it because it "had been generally attended with great extravagances and abuses." Finally they agreed to employ it, not because they considered it essential to a revival but because the people were accustomed to it and it was thought that "a sudden and violent change might not work well." One of the ministers who conducted the meeting noted that the anxious seat was used "in a very guarded manner, mainly to serve as an entering wedge to the inquiry meeting." He explained that the invitation to occupy the anxious seat was

36. Pastoral letter quoted in Watkin, "Forming of the Southern Presbyterian Minister," 443, and Walter Brownlow Posey, *The Presbyterian Church in the Old Southwest, 1778–1838* (Richmond, 1952), 26; *Southern Presbyterian Review*, I (June, 1947), quoted in Thompson, *Presbyterians in the South*, I, 429.

37. *Watchman of the South*, February 10, 1842, p. 98; *Watchman and Observer*, April 30, 1846, p. 146.

"not pressed as an imperative duty," and "no urgency was used." Inquirers were "told that this action was NOT *coming to Christ*," but was simply asking the brethren for their prayers. They "came quietly forward, without noise or outcry." Prayer was offered for them but "personal conversation with the anxious was deferred to the inquiry meeting, or to other fitting opportunities."[38]

Paradoxically, the Presbyterian reaction against revivalism explains the high praise accorded the Revival of 1857–1858. Not only were Presbyterians gratified that the revival was exhibiting much of its saving power in cities and towns such as Richmond, Charleston, Columbus, and Montgomery, but they also rejoiced because a great proportion of the converts were young men. Here was a possible remedy for the paucity of ministerial candidates. That laymen were taking a more active part than was customary in earlier revivals was also noted. However, the most important consideration—what one evangelical termed "the great lesson"—was the way in which the revival had come about. As "Athenian" pointed out in the *Southern Presbyterian*, "no unusual agency" had been relied on. "The people seem to depend more on prayer than preaching; and that preaching has been most effective, which presents the truth in the plainest, most earnest, and affectionate way. Pulpit eloquence, or any attempt at it, is utterly ignored." Similarly, J. O. Lindsay observed in the *Southern Presbyterian Review* that the revival "was not gotten up by 'revival preachers;' it was not brought about by any one man or class of men. It is not the result of protracted meetings, or pre-concerted measures." The diminished role of preaching as compared with prayer—the outcome of a tendency that had manifested itself in earlier revivals—and of preachers as compared with laymen (who often conducted the prayer meetings) was cited as the most distinctive feature of the revival. Presbyterians declared it emphatically "a great work of the Spirit of God," which was, in turn, the result of prayer rather than other, extraordinary measures. The "order," "stillness" and "solemnity" which marked the proceedings of the revival were cited both as proof of the genuineness of the revival and of the possibility of having the right kind of revival without resorting to extraordinary measures.[39]

Thus, the Revival of 1857–1858 seemed, to Presbyterians, to vindicate their reaction against revivalism. It was no "periodical excitement," "artifi-

38. William M. Baker, *Life of Baker*, 147, 163, 165, 180, 213; *Southern Presbyterian*, August 26, 1852, p. 207.

39. J. O. Lindsay, "The Religious Awakening of 1858," *Southern Presbyterian Review*, XI (July, 1858), 256; *Southern Presbyterian*, May 8. 1858, n.p., May 15, 1858, n.p.; *Central Presbyterian*, May 8, 1858, p. 74, April 24, 1858, p. 66, April 3, 1858, p. 54.

cial and temporary." It seemed to be exactly the kind of revival which a writer in the *Central Presbyterian* had called for—"a revival more natural and spontaneous, more in the regular course of divine institutions, attended with the blessing of God, having in it more of the element of durability and progressive advancement."[40] Above all, the revival seemed to Presbyterians to have restored the proper balance, so long deranged, between "divine efficiency" and "human instrumentality." That it did so by diminishing the role of the minister and of preaching was something that seems to have troubled them not at all.

Even among Presbyterians, the reaction against revivalism and revival methods was never total. As Elwyn Smith has noted, Old School Presbyterians (who were the majority of Presbyterians in the South) "never surrendered [their] claim on the tradition of Edwards, Tennent, and Whitefield, whose names they repeatedly invoked." In the 1840s and 1850s Presbyterians continued to hold protracted meetings and to look for revivals of religion. Some even defended religious "excitement" and the use of certain measures to promote it.[41]

Despite its abuses and problems, southern evangelicals, including Presbyterians, regarded revivalism as too valuable to be discarded. Throughout the antebellum period they looked to revivals as an important source of ministerial candidates. They also credited revivals with raising the level of piety among church members and awakening interest in benevolent enterprises such as missionary, Bible, and Sunday school societies, and in reform movements such as temperance, Sabbatarianism, and the religious instruction of the Negroes. In addition, revivals were said to improve the "moral aspect" of communities in which they occurred. Reporting the good effects of a recent revival in Richmond, the editor of the *Watchman of the South* included the following: "a marked change for the better in the observance of the Sabbath—the theatre is less resorted to by any class of people—fashionable parties, producing dissipation of mind, seem to be far less common—the weekly lecture is much better attended—a friendly and kind spirit between professors of religion is . . . decidedly growing." Finally, evangelicals viewed revivals as the chief means of adding members to the churches. Between 1830 and 1854, for example, Presbyterians nearly doubled and Methodists and Baptists more than doubled the num-

40. *Central Presbyterian*, April 25, 1857, p. 65.
41. Elwyn Allen Smith, *The Presbyterian Ministry in American Culture: A Study in Changing Concepts, 1700–1900* (Philadelphia, 1962), 90n, 214–15; *Watchman and Observer*, January 20, 1853, p. 94, June 8, 1854, p. 176.

ber of members in Virginia, North and South Carolina, and Georgia. To be sure, church members remained a minority in the southern population as a whole (as did church members in the United States generally). Nevertheless, by 1860 they constituted a larger and more influential minority than ever before, partly as a result of the fact that many of those converted during revivals were heads of families and persons of standing in the community.[42]

Basil Manly, Jr.'s view of revivalism is typical of that of most southern evangelicals. Manly took a position somewhere between outright hostility and unqualified approval. He recognized the "abuses" and "errors" connected with revivals, but at the same time, looking at the religious situation of the country, he believed that "we should all desire to be revival ministers, able to excite, with the blessing of God great and anxious attention to religion." "To affect people," he insisted, "you must make them listen to you." A man might preach "good sound doctrine" Sunday after Sunday, but if the people did not hear him his efforts would be of little avail. What was required was that "undefinable spiciness which makes people open their ears and hold up their heads to hear you." Besides, he noted, to oppose revivalism would mean challenging "the current of the times, the ruling spirit of the age, the bent & tendency of the multitude in wh. we move." Ministers should therefore take "care not to mistake the dispensation we are fallen under, and not to strive foolishly against it."[43]

---

42. *Watchman of the South*, December 15, 1842, p. 66; Sydnor, *Development of Southern Sectionalism*, 54, 294; Thompson, *Presbyterians in the South*, I, 420n. Bruce, *They All Sang Hallelujah*, 45, estimates that about 20 percent of southerners were church members in 1860. This was a significant rise over the proportion of church members in the first two decades of the nineteenth century.

43. Basil Manly, Jr., "Jottings Down, Newton Theological Seminary" (MS dated November 21 and December 1, 1844) and Manly to parents, November 4, 1846, both in Manly, Jr., Papers.

CHAPTER FOUR

The Church and the World

In 1817, having left the itinerancy, William Capers was living in George-town, South Carolina, where he kept a school. During the summer he lived on Du Bordieu's Island, which, along with North Island, served the planters and inhabitants of Georgetown as a healthful summer retreat. There Capers continued the school and preached on the Sabbath. The school was well attended, his health was good, he had friends and loved ones about him, and he "enjoyed public respect and confidence." Nevertheless, he was unhappy. He explained why in his autobiography:

During the time at the island, when surrounded by men of the world only, and in such near neighborhood with them as to hear and see continually what the world afforded for the happiness of its people, it was as if the mysterious words, "MENE, MENE, TEKEL, UPHARSIN," had been written on the wall of every parlor. I loathed it all, though I loved its victims. I loathed it, and yet I was haunted with spectres of apostates who for the world had abjured religion. Shall I ever be one? . . . I heard the voice of preaching, but it was my own voice that I heard; of prayer, but it was I who prayed. I heard, perchance, the notes of some song of Zion, but the singers were my wife and myself alone. I would contrast my loneliness with the times gone by, when in the woods which had never known an axe I felt not to be alone, because I had left a Christian brother's house and was going to meet a company at the house of God. The prayer-meeting, the class-meeting, the love-feast, I had none; but the world, the world was ever about me, and turn which way I might it still pursued me.

Returning from Du Bordieu's to Georgetown in the fall, Capers experienced a great sense of relief. Now he was able to renew his friendship with a fellow minister and to enjoy "the society of brethren," the class meeting, the sermon, and the Lord's Supper. He now realized that on the island "I had been out of my place, and therefore could not be at ease. God had not meant for me to serve tables, but to preach; nor to keep a school for so much a quarter, but to feed his flock, his sheep and his lambs." The thought of passing another summer on Du Bordieu's, excluded from "the privileges of the Church of Christ," was repugnant. There was but one way of "escape," and Capers decided he must take it. "I must reenter the itinerancy, and I must do so at once." In January, 1818, he was again a traveling preacher, with an appointment in Columbia. "It was a small concern, and poor," but in Capers' view, "poverty itself had a charm when it stood in an open renunciation of the world for the Master's sake."[1]

Capers' dislike for "the world" was a trait he shared with other southern evangelicals. Drury Lacy, for example, expressed feelings similar to Capers' when he described a Sunday evening spent in the company of people whose "principal topic of conversation is horse-racing, cock-fighting, betting and abusing Methodism—Baptism—Presbeterianism [sic] . . . ; and all sorts of *isms* but Deism." He admitted that he had "a sort of unaccountable attachment to the old way of living through the week and going [to church] on Sunday as I always have done. . . . Having once tasted of the honey of old forms & customs I have yet a hankering for the hive from whence it is procured." To some extent, perhaps, the otherworldliness of Capers and Lacy was simply a function of their personalities. They, and southern evangelicals generally, seem to have been particularly introspective, less inclined to socialize than their contemporaries, less comfortable in the world of business and politics, more inclined to see the vanity and impermanence of life on earth. We have seen too that many of them found in the conversion experience and church membership a sense of identity and belonging that the outside world did not provide. Here was an instance where a personality trait corresponded with what were regarded as the duties of the Christian life. Otherworldliness, along with personal piety, was the hallmark of the "eminent Christian."[2]

Southern evangelicals viewed themselves and other Christians as a "peculiar people" set apart by their profession of religion. "A public profes-

1. Wightman, *Life of Capers*, 196–99.
2. Drury Lacy to Williana Wilkinson, June 22, 1823, in Lacy Papers; Basil Manly, Jr., to Charles Manly, March 27, 1853, in Manly, Jr., Papers. For the otherworldliness of other evangelicals see, for example, Stratton Diary, June 21, 1852, October 24, 1855, Robert Hall Morrison to James Morrison, March 17 and September 1, 1851, both in Morrison Papers, and Moses Drury Hoge to Mrs. Drury Lacy, July 7, 1838, in Lacy Papers.

sion of Christianity," declared the editor of the *Religious Herald*, "is an avowal of our separation from the world, as regards its maxims, pursuits, and pleasures. We pledge ourselves to God and to our fellow-men, that we are henceforth separated from it in heart and feeling—being no longer conformed thereto, but transformed by the renewing of our minds, to the love of holiness and hatred of sin. Abstaining from fleshly lusts which war against the soul, we view ourselves as strangers and pilgrims on earth, looking for a better, even a heavenly country. Idle amusements, idle conversation, and whatever will affect our communion with God, are inconsistent with our Christian profession." Membership in the church and faithful attendance on the duties it entailed were some of the principal means by which Christians were enabled to maintain their detachment from the world. Church members, or "professors" as they were sometimes called, were expected to attend Sabbath and weekly religious services regularly and to contribute to the various benevolent enterprises of the church. They were required to submit to church discipline in order that the purity of the membership might be maintained. Church members also owed duties to each other. Though they could not cut off all intercourse with nonprofessors, they were expected to associate mainly with other Christians. Indeed, religious society—as contrasted with worldly society—afforded a welcome and even necessary "retreat to those who are sneered at by the world because they begin to think of the things which belong to their peace." It functioned as a preferable substitute for "ceremonious visits and worldly intercourse" and led to "true friendship" instead of mere "fashionable politeness, and well bred coldness." Religious society—or "Christian fellowship"—also enabled church members to nurture and sustain personal holiness in each other. To this end they were urged to exhibit brotherly love and to avoid contention. They were expected to have sympathy for one another in affliction and to aid one another in distress. They should settle "matters of dispute concerning worldly things" among themselves or through the arbitration of other Christians, rather than appealing to the civil law. Finally, and perhaps most importantly, professors were expected to reprove each other's sins "personally and affectionately."[3] All of these duties were inculcated by southern evangelicals to insure both

3. *Watchman of the South*, October 10, 1839, p. 26; *Southern Christian Advocate*, June 18, 1847, p. 6; *Christian Index*, June 1, 1859, n.p.; *Religious Herald*, May 5, 1837, p. 71; *Southern Evangelical Intelligencer*, September 1, 1821, p. 173, September 15, 1821, p. 189, September 22, 1821, p. 196; "The Friendly Guide, Shewing the Duties of Christians to Each Other . . . ," *Virginia Evangelical and Literary Magazine*, VI (July, 1823), 370–75; "Church Membership," *Virginia Evangelical and Literary Magazine*, VII (January, 1824), 8–10.

the cohesiveness and the distinctiveness of the Christian community.

In describing the state of warfare that existed between the church and the world, evangelicals noted first of all the division of men into two different camps. They were professors and worldlings, or, as Thomas Markham termed them, "the friends of God & the enemies of God." As a result of the "radical change" induced by the conversion experience, professors had abandoned their old objects of desire and founds their "chief good" in God. Worldly men, by contrast, found their objects "in themselves, in other men, or in things about them." They were "lovers of pleasure" and "hunters of Mammon." Whereas professors looked for future, eternal rewards, worldlings sought present, temporal ones; and whereas professors were animated by "spirituality," worldlings were mere "moralists." Their "earthly integrity" and "worldly uprightness" might earn them the respect of other men, but they would "not avail where he who possesses them is an unbeliever." Such men might be "good parents[,] honest friends[,] kind neighbors"; they might have "generous hearts and liberal hands." Nevertheless, Markham declared, "they wrong God. Engrossed with earth and their duties toward men they rob him of his due."[4]

Although Christians were expected to avoid conformity to the world, they were not to withdraw from it entirely. In an editorial entitled "The Church and the World," the editor of the *Southern Christian Advocate* declared that Christians should be "in the world, but not *of* the world." Christianity, he pointed out, was not "an ascetic pietism which shuts up its votaries in monastic seclusion from all society"; the "precepts and spirit alike, of the gospel look to the world of living busy men as the proper theatre for the development of the principles and graces of christian character." As a peculiar people, Christians were "not to seclude themselves from the world; and under the plea of giving themselves entirely to the performance of the duties of piety, renounce all part in the employments growing out of human society." The editor of the *Watchman and Observer* reminded Christians that they were placed in the world for a purpose:

Christ has said that his Church is the salt of the earth. That its savor may be felt in all human concerns, his people are to form a part of human society. But that the salt may not lose its savor, God requires that his people shall carry out into action,

4. Thomas Railey Markham, "Matt. 5:13. Earth corrupt, needs purifying & Preserving" (MS sermon dated February 17, 1856), "Matt. 12:30. He that is not with me is against me" (MS sermon dated April 6, 1856), "Rom. 12:2. Be not conformed to this World" (MS sermon dated June 1, 1856), "My meat is to do the will of him that sent me, & to finish his work" (MS sermon dated August 12, 1860), all in Thomas Railey Markham Papers, Louisiana State University Archives.

in all the relations of life, in their business, and in their relaxations from business, in all their intercourse with men, the principles of that holy religion which they profess. Where this is not done, either from dislike to the course enjoined, or out of defference [*sic*] to the wishes and tastes of those whose only pleasure is in the things of the world, as distinguished from the things of religion; then is such conduct, on the part of God's professing people, sinful conformity to the world.[5]

Throughout the antebellum period, southern evangelicals worried about worldly conformity among their people. Their first concern, as we might expect, was worldliness in the church. Methodists, for example, decried the departure from "primitive Methodism" which they claimed was taking place. Once distinguished by their plain dress and manners and by their appeal to the poor and uneducated, Methodists were now straying from "the old paths." William Winans charged his brethren with having "forgone, for worldly considerations, the distinctive characteristics of Methodism, in our tempers, conversation, association and appearance." In particular, he cited "unmethodistic dress" and neglect of class meetings. Such things had "gone far so to secularize the Methodist Church" that in many cases it was difficult "to show . . . in what she differs from the *decent* world around her."[6]

Other Methodists were apprehensive lest the pew system be introduced into southern Methodist churches, as it had been in some northern ones. Proponents of the system were criticized for having "greater regard for worldly advantages, than . . . to please God." They had "become weary of being a peculiar people" and wished to attract persons of wealth and social position to the church. If "this innovation upon primitive usage" were adopted, its critics charged, the poor—"the most spiritual portion" of the church—would be driven away. The church would come under the influence of the rich, of "a set of men, who are not thorough Methodists, and whose example and influence will inevitably tend to a relaxation of the discipline of the Church, and to a low standard of piety." Methodists would cease looking to "Divine agency" for success, and would look more to "human machinery, [and] church paraphernalia, as the principal means, to secure patronage and advancement." Nor would the evil effects of the pew system stop there. A writer who called himself "Melancthon" warned

5. *Southern Christian Advocate*, July 25, 1851, p. 30; *Watchman and Observer*, January 28, 1847, p. 96.
6. *Southern Christian Advocate*, April 25, 1845, p. 182, August 26, 1837, pp. 38–39; William Winans to the Reverend C. K. Marshall, July 10, 1839, and to Mrs. M. O. Huston, February 28, 1851, both in Winans Collection.

that people who paid pew rent would not wish to "do their own singing in true Methodist style." With their "refined ears," they would find it "especially unpleasant . . . for the preacher to interrupt the concert of sweet sounds, by giving out the hymn, two lines at a time, so that the negroes . . . might join in singing praises to God." "Melancthon" predicted the result: "a choir of singers (paid for the purpose, selected indiscriminately from the world, and, perhaps as in some instances, from the orchestra of a theatre), inducted into the gallery to do the services of the whole congregation in hymning praises to God." Pew holders would probably also demand that an organ be purchased, and they might also decide that instead of having a preacher sent to them, they should choose their own. That would introduce "the still greater evil of a standing ministry, who shall read their sermons in a cold, spiritless manner, and see no fruit of their labor from year to year." If any doubted that all of these things would result from the introduction of the pew system, "Melancthon" urged them to look at the Methodist churches in the northern states.[7]

Although Baptists and Presbyterians were not opposed to the pew system, they too worried about worldliness in the church. Baptists were critical of those who would introduce choir singing, and they agreed with Presbyterians in opposing the intrusion of instrumental music into the worship service. Evangelicals criticized such innovations not only on the ground that they were unscriptural—substituting "the inventions of men for the precepts of divine truth"—but also because they debased "a devotional exercise" into "a mere performance" or "entertainment." Evangelicals in all three denominations also worried that in preparing their sermons, ministers were responding to the worldly notions of their congregations and sacrificing "the God-inspired gospel" to "rounded periods and polished dictum." "Fine houses, splendid organs, fashionable congregations,—these seem to be the rage," James Henley Thornwell complained. "It is not asked, *what* a man preaches; but *where* he preaches, and to *whom*. If he has an imposing building, adorned with sofas for the rich to lounge on, where they are lulled into repose by an equally imposing orchestra, that is the place for a gentleman; and to go there twice on Sunday, is to worship God."[8]

7. *Southern Christian Advocate*, June 12, 1856, p. 5, June 18, 1847, pp. 5–6, December 31, 1841, p. 114, June 25, 1847, p. 9.

8. *Religious Herald*, January 12, 1838, p. 7; *Watchman and Observer*, February 17, 1848, p. 105; James Henley Thornwell to the Reverend Thomas E. Peck, July 1, 1851, in Palmer, *Life and Letters of Thornwell*, 352.

Thornwell's stand on the "board question" in the Presbyterian church and his concept of the spirituality of the church also reflected his concern with worldliness. He regarded voluntary associations and ecclesiastical boards as human inventions. They were not the "institutions which Christ has established for the legitimate action of the Church." In employing such instrumentalities the church compromised itself. It became "secular." The church, Thornwell declared, had "degenerated from a spiritual body into a mere petty corporation," and "the principles of this world" presided in her councils. "When we meet in our ecclesiastical courts," he observed, "instead of attending to the spiritual interests of God's kingdom, we scarcely do anything more than examine and audit accounts, and devise ways and means for raising money." This was "doing God's work by human wisdom and human policy."[9]

To southern evangelicals, the most striking evidence of worldliness in the church was the decline of discipline, the means by which the purity of the church was supposed to be maintained. Both ministers and their people were blamed—the ministers for lax enforcement of discipline, the people for disobeying church standards of conduct and, in some cases, refusing to testify against wrongdoers. Much of the discussion of discipline in the antebellum period centered on what were referred to as "worldly" or "fashionable amusements," which included such things as card-playing, novel-reading, dancing, and attending the circus and the theater. Of these, the theater and dancing at parties and balls drew the greatest amount of criticism.[10]

Although evangelicals denounced worldly amusements throughout the first half of the nineteenth century, their attack increased in volume and intensity in the 1840s and 1850s. By then cities and towns, and even some rural areas, offered a variety of amusements. Moreover, an increasing number of Christians were indulging in them. The editor of the *Central Presbyterian* observed in 1857 "that the indulgence in what are properly

9. James Henley Thornwell to the Reverend John Douglas, August 4, 1840, to Dr. R. J. Breckinridge, January 27, 1841, January 17, 1842, all in Palmer, *Life and Letters of Thornwell*, 223–25, 229.
10. The religious journals devoted considerable space to denunciations of worldly amusements. For representative articles see the following: (on novel reading) *Religious Herald*, January 31, 1856, p. 14; *Central Presbyterian*, February 28, 1857, p. 33; (on gambling) Charleston *Observer*, February 25, 1832, pp. 30–31; (on lotteries) *Religious Herald*, April 5, 1849, p. 54; (on dancing) *Southern Christian Advocate*, September 15, 1848, p. 58; *Watchman of the South*, November 12, 1840, p. 46; (on circuses) *Central Presbyterian*, July 25, 1857, p. 118; (on theater) Charleston *Observer*, November 27, 1830, p. 190; *Southern Christian Advocate*, February 9, 1838, p. 136; (on parties) *Religious Herald*, February 18, 1847, p. 25.

called 'worldly amusements,' is on the increase in the Church. Professors of religion, who once shrank from certain things, as inconsistent with their profession, are now practicing them freely, with the firm belief that they are perfectly innocent." Methodists and Baptists also pointed to a greater disposition on the part of church members to participate in certain pastimes and amusements. "On the subject of *amusements* . . . the church seems to be capitulating," declared the editor of the *Religious Herald*. "We do not stand where our fathers stood—where we once stood ourselves—in this particular."[11]

Enforcing the prohibition against worldly amusements presented certain problems. One was the matter of definition. Evangelicals defined worldly amusements as "those exercises of the mind and body, which have no natural connection with religion; and which are generally pursued by those persons whose thoughts and actions are of an earthly character." Evangelicals argued that when professors indulged in worldly amusements the result was a "blurring, or blotting out, [of] the line of separation between those who serve God and those who serve him not." To the extent Christians participated in such amusements, they were no longer a peculiar people distinguished by their nonconformity to the world. Evangelicals also argued that participation in amusements was inimical to the piety and holiness which were supposed to characterize the Christian. "No man can become worldly-minded, without losing the life and power of religion in his soul," declared the editor of the *Religious Herald*; "and in proportion as he engages in worldly pursuits and amusements, will he lose his spirituality and religious enjoyment. One will eventually impair and destroy the other, if the practice is continued."[12]

It was one thing to condemn amusements in these rather general terms; it was quite another to define them as sinful in themselves and to claim that they were specifically prohibited by Scripture. In fact, evangelicals admitted that some amusements were innocent and harmless in themselves, but they contended that "circumstances" rendered them sinful and injurious in tendency. The editor of the *Christian Index* noted that chess, backgammon, whist, cards, billiards, dancing, and going to balls were not evil in the abstract, but he claimed that "in practice, these acts are inseparably connected with other things that are evil. They lead us into temptation—often into idle and evil company—they tend to generate habits of

11. *Central Presbyterian* quoted in Thompson, *Presbyterians in the South*, I, 322; *Religious Herald*, May 28, 1857, p. 82.
12. *Religious Herald*, April 18, 1850, p. 61, May 28, 1857, p. 82, April 5, 1855, p. 50.

idleness and dissipation; they exclude the thoughts of God, . . . fill the mind with vanity, . . . produce indisposition for religious duties; and, what should be sufficient, of itself, to lead the christian to avoid them, they impair our moral influence over our fellowmen." Regarding the theater and the racecourse, the editor of the *Religious Herald* said, "no express prohibition exists in the word of God against Christians frequenting these places of amusement," but he justified the churches' excluding members who resorted to them on the grounds that such amusements were dangerous to the temporal and spiritual interests of mankind.[13]

How was the faithful Christian to determine whether an amusement was sinful per se, or merely sinful in tendency, or perfectly innocent? The *Herald* editor offered an answer: "As a safe guide, we ought to refrain from every thing which lessens our love to God, our zeal in his cause, which will produce leanness and barrenness in our souls, which is opposed to holiness of heart and purity of life, on which we cannot with a clear conscience invoke God's blessing, and which may furnish any pretext to gainsayers, to regard us as inconsistent professors and dishonored disciples."[14] This guide was meant to be comprehensive, but it was also rather vague. Church members who tried to follow it might come to conclusions different from those of the *Herald* editor about what was permissible. Therefore, professors tended to resist attempts to prohibit worldly amusements in which they saw no harm. At a time when lay power and influence was increasing, only a strong and stouthearted minister was likely to be able to enforce discipline.

Even Benjamin Morgan Palmer encountered resistance when members of his session disagreed with his stand on dancing. The controversy occured in 1847 when Palmer was pastor of the Presbyterian Church in Columbia, South Carolina. General James Shields, a hero of the Mexican War, visited the city and was feted at a public ball. Four members of Palmer's church attended it, along with the children of several other members. When the matter was brought to the attention of the session, a meeting was called to determine the best method of dealing with "this comparatively new tide of evil influence settling in upon the church." At the meeting, according to sessional records, "considerable diversity of opinion prevailed among the members as to the impropriety of dancing and the sin under

13. *Christian Index*, April 19, 1844, n.p.; *Religious Herald* quoted in Henry Smith Stroupe, "The Religious Press in the South Atlantic States, 1802–1865" (Ph.D. dissertation, Duke University, 1942), 123.
14. *Religious Herald*, April 5, 1855, p. 50.

certain circumstances, of attending public balls." The session therefore decided it would be "inexpedient" to discipline the four church members. Palmer then submitted a paper which he suggested should be read from the pulpit and which proposed a course of discipline to be followed in the future by the session in regard to dancing and other amusements. The reaction of the session was adverse: "The document being a stringent one, binding the session, hereafter, to a definite procedure, after a long conversation, it was thought best to postpone a decision upon it till Friday night, or in order to allow for due reflection on the part of the session." Palmer responded by resigning, "giving as his reason that his conscience would not permit him to be the pastor of a dancing church." A few days later the session met again and the members agreed, after modifying the paper, to allow Palmer to read it from the pulpit on Sunday. In the paper the session delivered its testimony "against fashionable worldly amusements, such as dancing parties, balls, the theater, the race course and such like." It admitted the difficulty of drawing "the line of demarcation between the lawful and unlawful pleasures of the Christian." But it argued that Christians were not justified in participating in the forbidden amusements, and it declared that such participation would "be regarded as serious offenses against the order and purity of the church, which require the exercise in some one of its forms of a wholesome discipline." Although Palmer and the session had eventually worked out a compromise, some church members reacted unfavorably to the stand that was taken. Session minutes of July 1, 1848, noted some absences from the Lord's Supper because of disagreement with the statement on dancing. A sermon on dancing which Palmer preached about a year later also had a mixed reception. The session had the sermon published, but some young people expressed opposition to the views contained in it.[15]

It seems likely that Palmer's session was not unique in its unwillingness to adopt the "stringent" course of discipline he recommended. This would explain the discrepancy between the amount of time and effort evangelicals expended in denouncing worldly amusements and the number of cases of corrective church discipline involving them. For example, in a study of corrective church discipline in sixty-one Presbyterian churches, William Davidson Blanks found that sessions were generally reluctant to

15. Thomas Cary Johnson, *Life and Letters of Palmer*, 93–97, 93n. See also Doralyn Joanne Hickey, "Benjamin Morgan Palmer: Churchman of the Old South" (Ph.D. dissertation, Duke University, 1962), 45–47. Palmer's sermon, "Social Dancing Inconsistent with a Christian profession and Baptismal vows," was published serially in the *Watchman and Observer*, beginning October 25 and concluding November 22, 1849.

6096 0

censure worldly amusements such as dancing, gambling, and card playing since they were not specifically condemned in the Westminster Standards or the Decalogue. "Only if the practice was especially flagrant, or involving other offenses such as drunkenness or fighting, did sessions usually instigate action," Blanks concluded.[16]

Evangelicals had little trouble explaining the growth of worldliness in the church. They pointed to fashion and wealth as the sources of the evil. By *fashion* was meant the opinions and values of the world, which Christians deferred to instead of looking to the Scriptures as their "guide and directory." It was "this slavish deference to the world" that induced them to participate in "fashionable amusements" and to adopt extravagant modes of dress, equipage, and manners. According to the evangelicals, the same deference to the world was responsible for lowering the standard of morality in the church. Instead of adhering to the morality of the Gospel, Christians followed that of the world, which substituted "love of self" for love of God. The morality of the Gospel required the Christians to "condemn every species of folly and iniquity; to discountenance vice in every shape; whether in the garb of pleasure or amusement," but the "fashionable Christian" was careful "not to be too rigidly moral or over-nice, to wink or connive at many of the lesser follies practiced by his acquaintances." Even if he did not pursue fashionable amusements himself, he would not condemn or discountenance them. In making moral judgments, the fashionable Christian was guided by human, rather than divine laws. Human laws, according to the editor of the *Religious Herald*, were "based not simply on wright [*sic*] or wrong, virtue or vice in the abstract, but on principles of self-interest." Consequently, "crimes which affect the interests of society, are not only considered disreputable, but are rigidly punished. Others which affect only the interests of the offender himself or those connected with him are overlooked, and the individual may still preserve his standing in society." The editor cited dissipation, licentiousness, and drunkenness as crimes of the latter type. Although condoned by human law, they were "offences against the Majesty of Heaven" when judged by the moral code of the Gospel.[17]

16. William Davidson Blanks, "Ideal and Practice; A Study of the Conception of the Christian Life Prevailing in the Presbyterian Churches of the South During the Nineteenth Century" (Th.D. dissertation, Union Theological Seminary, 1960), 102–103, 232–33, 320–21.

17. *Religious Herald*, May 24, 1833, p. 79, May 17, 1833, p. 75. See also Charleston *Observer*, November 13, 1830, pp. 182–83; *Southern Christian Advocate*, February 16, 1849, p. 46.

Wealth was the other source of worldliness. Methodists were particularly concerned about the way in which it threatened the purity of the church. During the 1840s and 1850s, when they were feeling nostalgic for the "ancient glory of Methodism" with "its simplicity, moral energy, lofty superiority to the frivolities of fashion" and "its strength of piety and restless activities of zeal," Methodists sought to explain why worldliness was making inroads in the denomination. The answer they gave was similar to that of modern day historians: as their economic and social status improved, the editor of the *Southern Christian Advocate* observed, Methodists were "exposed to a class of dangers to which a poor and illiterate body of people are not much liable." Now they were more likely "to profess religion upon a low order of motives, and with many special reservations in favour of self-indulgence, pride and ambition." They were more likely to be distracted from religion by the pursuit of wealth and pleasure. They were less likely to accept the discipline of the church. A writer in the *Advocate* declared unequivocally "that a church or congregation which is composed mainly of rich men, has more of worldly-mindedness and the pomp and show of earth about it, and less of the vital energy of christianity within it, than societies which are not so wealthy, and who possess but little of the luxuries of life." Wealth was also said to engender an "aristocratical feeling" in church members. Affluent church members were likely to share the view of the world that "one man [is] better than another, simply because he possesses more of the pelf of this world." If this view were to predominate, another writer pointed out, "wealth and social position, rather than piety," would gain "precedence and superior influence in the house of God." [18]

Throughout the first half of the nineteenth century, evangelicals of all three denominations denounced covetousness as the besetting sin of the church as well as society. In 1812, Moses Hoge declared that "the love of gain is the predominant vice of the present age." Some forty years later the editor of the *Southern Presbyterian* pronounced avarice "the great and damning sin of the age, the loathsome and lying delusion, which now so degrades the mass of the people in church and State." Evangelicals delivered such denunciations in boom times as well as panics; indeed, they pointed

18. *Southern Christian Advocate*, April 25, 1845, p. 182, February 16, 1849, p. 46, August 26, 1837, pp. 38–39, June 5, 1856, p. 1. The idea that wealth was inimical to piety was not peculiar to Methodists. The editor of the Charleston *Observer* agreed that "great success in worldly pursuits is unfavorable to the growth of vital piety." Charleston *Observer*, October 24, 1835, p. 170.

to the latter as proof of the "uncertainty" of riches and of their contention that God was angry with his people because of their covetousness.[19]

Covetousness was a prime example of conformity to the world. What religion condemned as "a crime of the first magnitude" was seen as a virtue in "fashion's code of morals." Like other kinds of worldliness, covetousness made something other than God the chief good of man. It was idolatry—the worship of Mammon rather than God. Covetous Christians were so immersed in the "hot pursuit of riches" that they neglected personal piety and the cause of Christianity. In 1807 the Presbytery of Hanover lamented the fact that "the minds of multitudes [are turned] to the ardent pursuit of wealth, so that the whole object of their life seems to be, to buy and sell, and get gain. Instead of seeking the pearl of great price, earthly merchandize claims their attention: instead of laying up for themselves treasures in Heaven, they are seeking for the good things of this world."[20] In later decades evangelicals continued to characterize the American people, including professing Christians, in much the same way.

Evangelicals agreed that dealing with the sin of covetousness was complicated by the fact that it was so widespread and that it was difficult to define precisely. The editor of the *Religious Herald* had no doubt that covetousness was a sin and a proper subject for church discipline. Yet there were no cases of discipline for that sin in the Baptist churches, and it was not for lack of "proper subjects." Indeed, the very prevalence of the sin was "one cause for the laxity of discipline." He believed that churches were "afraid to commence the work, as so many are involved." A further problem was "deciding what is covetousness." There was no agreement among the churches here:

When [covetousness] influences a professor to overreach or defraud his fellow-man, though the impelling cause, another name is employed. A man may have the character of making hard bargains, or of giving untruthful statements in his dealings, from love of gain, yet so as not to present any definite grounds for discipline by the church. He may exhibit other concomitants of covetousness, as penuriousness, avariciousness, so as to mar his influence as a member of the church, and

19. Moses Hoge, "The Controversy with Christendom," in *Sermons Selected from the Manuscripts of the Late Moses Hoge, D.D.* (Richmond, 1821), 383; *Southern Presbyterian*, February 9, 1856, n.p.; *Christian Index*, May 9, 1839, p. 296, January 21, 1842, p. 41, October 14, 1857, p. 162; *Southern Watchman and General Intelligencer*, September 8, 1837, p. 142; "Thoughts on the 'Times,'" *Virginia Evangelical and Literary Magazine*, II (October, 1819), 470; *Religious Herald*, April 28, 1837, p. 67.

20. *Christian Index*, March 11, 1852, p. 42; Moses Hoge, "Controversy with Christendom," 383; "An Address From the Presbytery of Hanover . . . ," *Virginia Religious Magazine*, III (May, June, 1807), 154–55.

render him liable to the charge of inconsistency by the world, and yet not bring himself under church censure.

When covetousness leads to injustice, to unfair dealing, or gross cupidity, to degrading avarice, discipline may be, and is generally promptly exercised; but in those numberless cases where the charge is equally injurious, the difficulty of action is so seriously felt, as to lead to an indecisive course.

Usury presented a similar problem of definition. Evangelicals agreed that it was a sin, but since the Bible offered no specific guidelines as to proper rates of interest, they believed that they should be regulated by the Golden Rule and "common usage." By such a standard John Witherspoon condemned 18 percent as usury, but the editor of the Richmond *Christian Advocate* was able to "imagine cases in which it would be wisdom to give ten or twenty per cent for money."[21]

In dealing with the sin of covetousness, evangelicals did not counsel withdrawal from the world and "secular affairs." Their view of Christianity did not allow such a course of action. The Christian, observed a writer in the *Christian Index*, "is placed in a world with which he must necessarily have much to do. He must labor and take care; he must buy and sell; he must advance his interest in some way, if he maintain a reputable stand in society." The problem was, how "to do this and *sin not*." Evangelicals urged Christians to look to the Bible. They argued against the notion that the Bible pertained only to man's "spiritual and everlasting interests." It was "adapted to man's present condition and duties" as well, teaching "what purposes christians ought to have in view in following their worldly avocations, as well as by what principles they ought to be animated and governed." Thomas Smyth admitted that piety "is *essentially* a hidden life of spiritual communion with God," but, he contended, "it is not, as some would represent it, a mere matter of spiritual feeling that shrinks from contact with human affairs. It is a robust and masculine sentiment that guides and regulates our secular everyday occupations by sound Bible principles." Smyth and other evangelicals also argued that following the Bible did not prevent one from being successful in worldly business. "Adherence to the principles we advocate, would increase the aggregate of wealth, and deprive no individual, except of dishonorable gain," declared Henry Keeling. "The gospel not only justifies but requires the pursuit of

21. *Religious Herald*, August 4, 1853, p. 122; *Christian Index*, April 11, 1839, p. 229; John Witherspoon to his daughter, July 9, 1846, in Witherspoon and McDowall Family Papers, Southern Historical Collection, University of North Carolina Library; Richmond *Christian Advocate*, August 5, 1847, p. 122.

wealth. It is not the possession, nor the proper appropriation; but the 'love' of money, that the Apostle pronounced 'the root of all evil.' . . . The world becomes the rival of its Creator, only when sought and possessed not as a means, but an end—when it either destroys or abridges love to HIM."[22]

The Christian, then, should be "diligent in business," not as an end in itself and not for the purpose of self-gratification, but for the benefit of mankind and the glory of God. "No man . . . can pursue his daily business in a *christian* spirit who does not work diligently in order that he may have what he can distribute to the destitute," declared Smyth. "Another and even a weightier motive which aught [*sic*] to animate the christian to industry in his calling is that he may be able to bear an honorable part in the maintenance and extension of the gospel." Other evangelicals agreed with Smyth's notion of Christian stewardship. "Benevolent and religious enterprises are impossible without wealth," observed Keeling. The editor of the *Southern Christian Advocate* believed that "there is no nobler example of a christian than the righteous steward of God's bounty, to whom large wealth has been entrusted—the man, who, with every resource for worldly and sensual enjoyment at command, and who may go on aggrandizing himself and enlarging his possessions, but who denying himself, and living economically and simply, lays up his treasure in heaven by laying out his treasure on earth for the benefit of the race and the glory of God."[23]

Wealth might endanger personal holiness and the purity of the church, but if honestly acquired and properly used, it was a blessing rather than a danger. The rich might have "more temptations to worldliness" than the poor, but few southern evangelicals went so far as to declare that none should be rich. Smyth branded as "extravagant" the "opinion prevalent among some circles of piety according to which it is unscriptural and wrong for any man to be an holder of any considerable monies." Such a view, though certainly preferable to the notion that accumulation of wealth was "the grand object of life," led to the unsound conclusion "that among christians there should be none poor, none rich—a sort of equality in regard to wealth that does not exist in regard to any thing else." There were differences among Christians "in regard to their physical, intellectual and spiri-

22. *Christian Index*, March 10, 1836, p. 129; Thomas Smyth, "The Design and Motive of Worldly Business as Exhibited in the Bible. Two Sermons. . . . October, 1847," in *Complete Works of Rev. Thomas Smyth*, ed. J. William Flinn (10 vols.; Columbia, S.C., 1908–12), X, 465; *Religious Herald*, October 5, 1832, p. 153.

23. Smyth, "Design and Motive of Worldly Business," 474–75; *Religious Herald*, October 5, 1832, p. 153; *Southern Christian Advocate*, May 25, 1855, p. 202.

tual energies;—and why, then, should we not expect differences in regard to their outward worldly condition." He was even willing to give qualified support to the notion that wealth was an indication of God's blessing: "far from looking upon it as a scandal for a christian to be rich, riches honourably acquired and in the exercise of a proper liberality are to be regarded by him on whom they are bestowed, as a blessing, and the acquisition of such riches, therefore, together with the position and influence and power to do good which they give, ought to be one motive in prompting him to diligence and energy in his worldly calling." A writer in the *Watchman and Observer* seconded the notion of wealth as a blessing from God. Like other evangelicals he admitted that "temporal prosperity" endangered "spiritual health." Gain stimulated the desire for gain and money was spent "in living, dressing, building more expensively." But he contended that a benevolent God gave men prosperity "not to be a trap and a curse," but "primarily, that we might find our safe and innocent enjoyment in it, by using it for his glory." Liberality and beneficence functioned as a "safety valve," enabling men to escape the "benumbing effects" of wealth. By using their wealth to support missionary and benevolent enterprises, men might "consecrate it, and render it harmless."[24]

The principles which evangelicals inculcated as a guide to worldly business included integrity, diligence, and moderation. Smyth sketched a portrait of the man who conducted himself according to such principles: "[He] would maintain a strict integrity in all his concerns, making his engagements with caution and fulfilling them with scrupulous fidelity. He would take no mean advantage of any favourable circumstances in which he might be placed; but while he would call his skill into exercise to take every *honest* advantage of their occurrence, he would remember the claims of *equity* and *honour*." He would be guided by the Golden Rule in his "treatment of others." He would work at his business with "unremitting assiduity," but he would be careful to pay attention to other duties such as "the improvement of his mind, the enlargement of his knowledge, the pleasure of social intercourse and benevolent exertion," and, of course, "the duties of religion." A writer in the *North Carolina Presbyterian* offered a more homely application of religion to worldly business. The morality of the Gospel, he declared, "banishes all small measures from the counters, small baskets from the stalls, pebbles from cotton bags, and from sugar, chickory [*sic*] from coffee, alum from bread, lard from butter, strychnine from wine,

24. *Southern Christian Advocate*, May 25, 1855, p. 202; Smyth, "Design and Motive of Worldly Business," 478–80; *Watchman and Observer*, December 15, 1853, p. 73.

and water from milk cans," and the man who adhered to the Bible code would "not put all the big strawberries and peaches on the top and all the bad ones on the bottom."[25]

Evangelicals preached against, and some churches disciplined members for, fraud and dishonesty in business dealings. There was considerable emphasis placed on avoiding debts and paying those that were incurred. This was partly because evangelicals were generally suspicious of the credit system and partly because they viewed nonpayment of debts as theft, a violation of the Decalogue. Evangelicals also pointed to "the uncertainty of life" as a reason why the Christian should "live unencumbered with debt." They contended that although bankruptcy released a man from payment of his debts as far as human law was concerned, under divine law he was still responsible to pay them if ever he were able. In a pastoral address issued in 1843, when the South was still experiencing the effects of the Panic of 1837, James O. Andrew warned the people of the Georgia Conference "to guard against the deceitful influences of a corrupt public opinion. Remember that civil law is not the measure of moral right,—that an obligation once assumed is perpetually binding, whether expressed in the technicalities of law or otherwise. Be not deceived; legal bankruptcy cannot cancel moral obligation, nor the decision of courts release from duty." The speculative fever that gripped many Americans in the antebellum period also drew fire from evangelicals. "The desire to grow rich in a short time," the "feverish anxiety . . . to amass wealth by other than ordinary commercial, mechanical, and agricultural pursuits," "the careless exposure of borrowed capital"—however it was described, speculation was denounced as an evil which not only corrupted religion but produced widespread suffering in the form of periodic panics. Individuals, business firms, whole communities "lost credit, and character, and conscience, and property," noted the editor of the *Watchman of the South*; "and all because men were unwilling to act on the safe, moderate, and sober plans of acquiring gain, which are not condemned in Scripture."[26]

Economic matters did not bulk large in the social thought of southern evangelicals. Politics, as will be seen, occasioned considerably more com-

25. Thomas Smyth, "The Commercial Benefit of Christianity in Producing Integrity, Diligence and Moderation. A Discourse. . . . August, 1847," in *Complete Works*, X, 451, 456–57; *North Carolina Presbyterian* quoted in Blanks, "Ideal and Practice," 255.

26. *Christian Index*, January 5, 1854, p. 2; *Southern Christian Advocate*, March 3, 1843, p. 148; "Thoughts on the 'Times,'" *Virginia Evangelical and Literary Magazine*, II (October, 1819), 470; *Religious Herald*, April 28, 1837, p. 67; Smyth, "Commercial Benefit of Christianity," 455 and see also 454, 456; *Watchman of the South*, August 8, 1839, p. 198.

mentary. Their thinking on economic questions was generally superficial and even naïve. Moral exhortation substituted for informed analysis. Like many of their contemporaries, they felt ill at ease in the national market economy that had emerged in the United States since the War of 1812. To be fair, however, it must be pointed out that evangelicals made no pretense of being able to deal with what one of them called "the curious or hard questions" of trade, finance, and government. They were chiefly concerned, when speaking of the relation between religion and worldly business, with the conduct of individuals, rather than entities like corporations or government. Believing that the Bible offered a set of principles by which worldly business should be conducted, they felt it was their duty to show the application of those principles; to urge individuals, especially church members, to follow them; and, where possible, to enforce them through the administration of church discipline. Henry Keeling summarized the evangelical viewpoint in declaring that "the contrast which has been drawn between temporal and spiritual duties and interests, is anti-scriptural and destructive to the souls of men. . . . Every act of every man's life stands connected with the retributions of the last day. . . . God must be acknowledged, and the power of moral excellence must be seen and felt, in the Workshop, and on the Farm; in the Bank, and at the Custom House; in the Counting-Room, and on board the Ship; on the Bench of Justice, at the Bar, in Legislative Assemblies:—in all the offices of practical life."[27]

As Keeling's statement suggests, evangelicals applied religious principles to political life as well as business practices. This was because they viewed civil government as no "mere invention of man," but an institution ordained by God in order to secure peace and order among sinful men. Therefore both magistrates and citizens were under an obligation to carry out their political duties "in accordance with those laws of eternal righteousness which God has given to regulate our individual and social deportment." Thomas Smyth declared that "Christianity prescribes for citizenship, as well as for domestic or industrial life, and its ethics should be taught in the former department as freely as in either of the latter." One of the functions of the pulpit was to be "the means of instructing Christians in the Christianity of their political relations."[28]

27. Charleston *Observer*, May 13, 1837, p. 74; *Watchman of the South*, August 8, 1839, p. 198; *Religious Herald*, October 5, 1832, p. 153.
28. Thomas Smyth, "National Righteousness," *Southern Presbyterian Review*, XII (April, 1859), 25–26.

At the same time that they argued for the application of religious principles to politics, evangelicals supported the separation of church and state. None of the three denominations had any quarrel with disestablishment or the voluntary system. The evangelical view of the relation between church and state was summarized by Smyth in a discourse entitled "The Relations of Christianity to Civil Polity." He began by noting the existence of two contrasting opinions regarding the proper relation between church and state. "Some maintain that religion has no concern whatever with human politics—that the entire domain of civil polity, in all its bearings, lies beyond the possible reach of christianity and can in no way be directly influenced by it, and that all the affairs of society are therefore to be directed solely by the principles of common sense and political expediency." Others argued "with equal assurance that religion must necessarily interfere with all political concerns, all things being subject to its direction and control." In Smyth's view, both opinions were incorrect and, if adopted, would endanger the interests of both society and religion, the one leading to "atheistic and ungodly infidelity," the other to "persecution and intolerance." Smyth found the correct theory of the relation between church and state in the Scriptures. The "political principles of the Bible" taught that there were two governments, civil and ecclesiastical, both divinely instituted, each "independent and distinct" in its duties and field of operations. The duty of civil government (the state) was to secure order and promote justice among men; the duty of the ecclesiastical government (the church) was to promote holiness. The state used coercion to enforce its measures, whereas the church was confined to spiritual methods. Though "independent and distinct," church and state enjoyed a reciprocal relationship. The state protected the church in the free exercise of its rights, powers, and authority. The church, for its part, upheld the rights, powers, and authority of the civil government, counseling the Christian duty of obedience to "the powers that be." Smyth maintained that church and state were "coordinate and conducive to the common good of the whole community; so that while they can never commingle, they can never be safely disjoined." Here was the basis for his contention that Christianity was "the grand requisite in civil government." He and other evangelicals contended that religion was vital to the preservation of the American republic. They insisted that the United States had been founded as a Christian nation, and they argued that the virtue and intelligence, the prosperity, peace and liberty of the American people depended on the spread of the Gospel and its institutions throughout the land. Indeed, evangelicals appear to have put more faith in religion than in government as the guarantor of order and happiness. T. V. Moore, writing in the *Methodist Quarterly Review*, cited the earthly blessings which religion conferred:

As an agency in the prevention of crime, in fostering habits of temperance, indus-try, honesty, and peace, and thus increasing at once the wealth of a country, and that which wealth cannot buy, the happiness of its homes, and as a great educa-tional institute which trains men to be good members of society and of the family, by the only process, and supported by the only motives that can be efficient on the masses, it is at once the cheapest and the best conservator of a nation's welfare. The pulpit is cheaper than the prison; the Church and the Sabbath school less costly than the police and the standing army that would otherwise be needed to prevent the lawless passions of one class in society from bursting out against an-other.

Similarly, Smyth declared that "it is not by the wisdom of statesmen and legislators; it is not by civil institutions, by the checks and balances of the powers of government, by laws and courts, by armies and navies, that the peace, and order, and happiness of mankind can be secured, and crime and suffering banished from the world." The "true and only panacea for all social and moral ills—the only palladium of all social and political bless-ings—and the only guarantee for honesty, industry and prosperity" was the Gospel of Christ.[29]

As Elwyn A. Smith has observed, the theory of church and state which evangelicals supported provided for what amounted to a "voluntary estab-lishment" of religion. The evangelical theory "accepted the American com-mitment to freedom and the voluntary principle in church-state relations without making sacrifice of the precious conception that religion was the essential ingredient of the public weal." Southern evangelicals defined the political role of the church and her ministers within the framework of this "voluntary establishment." The task of the church, according to Benjamin Morgan Palmer, was to "leaven the whole mass of society with religious principles." The church did this by promoting godliness, using such means as revivals of religion; Sabbath schools; tract, missionary, and Bible soci-eties; and religious newspapers. Through them "a sound religious public opinion" would be produced, which would in turn "constrain public offi-

29. Thomas Smyth, "The Relations of Christianity to Civil Polity. A Discourse. . . . Octo-ber, 1848," in *Complete Works*, X, 485–88; Smyth, "National Righteousness," 29, 35; Rev. T. V. Moore, "God's Method of Saving the World," *Methodist Quarterly Review*, IX (January, 1855), 85.

cers into at least a decent demeanour to the religion of Christ, and to the
hearty recognition of it as the greatest of all the elements which go into
the character of the nation." In other words, legislators and governors
would be constrained to insure that the laws they promulgated were appropriate to "a Christian nation."[30]

As officers of the church, ministers also played an important role in
producing "a sound religious opinion." One way—the most important
way—was by converting people to Christ. As for engaging directly in politics, evangelicals frowned on ministers seeking or holding political office
or mixing in party politics. If ministers engaged in such activities, they argued, religion would be sullied and its authority diminished. The *Christian Index* printed an editorial from another Baptist newspaper which declared that if ministers offered themselves as candidates for political office
"all the party slang in vogue at every election would be directed against
them. Not only would their own minds and character suffer from con-
tamination by the base breath of party zeal, but a large part of their hearers would loose [*sic*] all respect for their teachings as coming from political
opponents.—Party politics would be introduced into the churches, and
rents and divisions, heart-burnings, and enmities of the worst description
would be engendered."[31]

On the other hand, although evangelicals maintained that ministers
should respect constituted authority and preach obedience to the laws
of the land, they also justified ministers speaking out on political questions
that involved moral and religious principles. Because of their conviction
that Christianity was vital to the preservation of the American republic,
evangelicals argued that ministers should show the application of religious principles to the political and social order, reproving magistrates
and citizens when necessary. In answer to "those who seem to think we
have no business to express any opinion, relative to any thing appertain-
ing to the political interests of our country," the editor of the *Christian Index* declared, "We claim the right, and shall exercise it, of expressing our
opinion on any subject that involves the religious interests of our country,
whenever we think proper to do so, let who will take offence thereat. We
believe the political and moral interests of our country are inseparably

30. Elwyn A. Smith, "The Voluntary Establishment of Religion," in Elwyn A. Smith (ed.),
The Religion of the Republic (Philadelphia, 1971), 155; [Benjamin Morgan Palmer], "Church
and State," *Southern Presbyterian Review*, III (April, 1850), 606.
31. *Christian Index*, April 7, 1843, p. 219.

connected; and we feel just as free to censure what we believe to be injurious in its tendency, in the judge upon the bench or the representative in the council halls of the nation, as in the humblest mendicant."[32]

It was not because they were uninterested in political affairs that most evangelicals assigned themselves a rather limited political role, although it is true that some ministers disdained politics. According to Jeremiah Jeter, Daniel Witt "sometimes went to the polls, but never participated in any political party meeting." On one occasion he gave as his reason for not voting that "I have been so disgusted with the *preaching politicians* and the *politicating-preachers* that I eschewed the whole thing." William Capers "held himself aloof from all parties and politics; [and] never attended public dinners, or made after-dinner speeches." He voted but once, at age 25, "for an Alderman, in Savannah, when the object was to put down Sunday markets." As with Witt, Capers' not voting was less a result of disinterest than of contempt for the candidates running for office. In a letter which was published in the *Southern Christian Advocate*, Capers said, only half facetiously, "I might avail myself of an opportunity of voting, when a candidate should be presented possessing full intellectual capacity, and who had not disqualified himself by duelling, gambling, debauchery, secret fees for public service, or any similar enormities which should make a Christian man ashamed of him."[33] Other evangelicals manifested considerable interest in politics, though they too were often repulsed by certain aspects. They read political newspapers, voted regularly, and some even attended political meetings. In their diaries or in correspondence with fellow ministers and laymen they commented freely on political questions of the day, endorsed candidates and gloated over their victories, and pronounced judgment on presidential and gubernatorial messages as well as political speeches and legislative enactments. Some visited conventions or legislative assemblies for the purpose of observing their proceedings.[34] All of these activities, evangelicals agreed, were within the bounds of the proper ministerial role. They were activities which ministers were entitled

32. *Ibid.*, March 9, 1848, p. 77.

33. Jeter, *Life of Witt*, 198–99; Wightman, *Life of Capers*, 514; *Southern Christian Advocate*, September 15, 1843, p. 55.

34. See, for example, Peyton Harrison Hoge, *Moses Drury Hoge*, 55, 92–93, 137–38, Richard Furman to Wood Furman, February 12, 1808, in Richard Furman Papers, Special Collections, Furman University Library, James Smylie to Amelia and Joseph Montgomery, February 12, 1845, in Joseph A. Montgomery and Family Papers, Louisiana State University Archives, Adolphus Williamson Mangum to his father, September 2, 1851, in Mangum Family Papers, Thomas Cary Johnson, *Life and Letters of Dabney*, 24, 65–67, and John McLees Diary (MS in John McLees Papers, South Caroliniana Library), July 24, October 9, 1848.

to engage in by virtue of their being citizens as well as clergymen. They were legitimate so long as they did not distract ministers from their principal duty of converting sinners.

Although southern evangelicals generally frowned upon ministers running for office and mixing in party politics, there were a few who did so. William Winans of Centreville, Mississippi, was one of the most politically active ministers in the Old South. Indeed, Winans engaged in virtually every practice condemned by his fellow evangelicals. He stood for office twice, once in 1817 when he was a candidate for the state constitutional convention, and again in 1849 when he accepted the Whig nomination to run for Congress. He was defeated both times, primarily, as he himself admitted, because of "a determination on the part of the people not to confer political office upon a Minister of the Gospel." In both instances, recognizing the popular view regarding ministers seeking public office, Winans refused to campaign in his own behalf, but his prudence neither won him election nor saved him from being attacked by the opposition. In the 1849 campaign the Democratic press not only accused him of being an abolitionist but also criticized him for forgetting "his high calling." "There is nothing we detest more than a reverend politician," declared the Natchez *Free-Trader*.[35]

Winans' other political activities met with an equally hostile reception. He had no compunction about publicly endorsing candidates and campaigning in their behalf. He claimed that he never used the pulpit for such purposes, but on at least two occasions he was accused of doing so. For example, in the 1822 congressional election, Winans opposed George Poindexter, mainly because he had authored a provision in the Mississippi constitution which restricted religious meetings of blacks. As Presiding Elder, Winans decided to be "conspicuous" in his opposition to Poindexter and his "iniquitous legislation," though he said he "was careful to shun everything like electioneering in my pulpit or other official performances." Nevertheless, on the day before the election he preached at a camp meeting on the increase of vice in the county and gave as an example the rise of drunkenness, which, he said, "is so encreased [*sic*] that of all classes from those who are lowest to those in high official stations, men are to be found who are not ashamed of being seen wallowing in the filth of this debauch in the very streets." When he came down from the stand, someone said to

35. Winans Autobiography, 129–30; Rex Paxton Kyker, "William Winans: Minister and Politician of the Old South" (Ph.D. dissertation, University of Florida, 1957), 259, 277, and see also 252–54, 275–76, 278–80.

him, "You meant that for Poindexter." Winans said that he had not, "at least with any reference to his election," but he admitted that given the fact that Poindexter's "addictedness to drunkenness, and his having often been picked up in the streets were matters of general notoriety . . . it was very natural to suppose that my reference to the matter, though entirely in general terms, was designed to prevent his election."[36]

In 1840 Winans campaigned for William Henry Harrison. He gave a Fourth of July address at the Midway Church which some people interpreted as a denunciation of the Van Buren administration, and he wrote two letters which were read as political speeches at Whig rallies. In one of them, which was published in the Liberty *Advocate*, Winans declined an invitation to attend a Whig barbecue because of the opposition of *"public opinion* . . . to Ministers of the Gospel engaging, actively and prominently, in electioneering movements." But he went on in the letter to declare that the election was a contest between "political *salvation* and political ruin." Denouncing the administration of the last eleven years as "subversive to our institutions," he charged that Jackson and Van Buren had "forged a chain, whose weight, unless we promptly break it, will weigh us down to the dust of political bondage." Harrison he praised as a "steady and confidential votary of Jefferson and Madison," a "venerable and well-tried patriot." The Galatin *Galaxy*, a Democratic paper, declared that Winans' letter had "inflicted a deep wound upon the cause of Christianity" and predicted that it would prevent him from "exercising a salutary effect over his fellow men." Winans had "said enough to cause his expulsion not only from the church but from all moral society," the paper charged. "And if every other person should regard him in the future as we shall, he would never again address a congregation from the pulpit." Undaunted, Winans campaigned for Henry Clay in 1844, and met with similar criticism.[37]

The most clear-cut example of a political sermon was one that Winans preached at a camp meeting in 1847. Entitled "The Citizen of Zion," it elaborated the theme that "Man, neither now [n]or hereafter, ever can enjoy the Divine presence and favor, unless he acquit himself, as a moral agent, to Divine approbation." In the course of the sermon, Winans denounced falsehood and cited *"party-politics"* as an example. "Men who would shrink with horror from a slanderous lie in other departments of social in-

36. Winans Autobiography, 166–67. For the other occasion on which Winans was accused of endorsing candidates from the pulpit, see William Winans to G. C. Brandon, Esq., September 7, 1827, in Winans Collection.
37. Kyker, "William Winans," 265–68, 272.

tercourse have no difficulty in bringing themselves to slander the characters of candidates to whom they are opposed," he declared. Winans' principal argument against "political falsehood" was that it prevented voters from acquiring "a knowledge of the political principles, the ability, and moral virtue" of candidates for office. Thus, it endangered the very form of government. "To the wickedness and baseness of lying, the political slanderer adds Treason to his country by corrupting the very fountain of power," Winans charged. He believed that "he who will deliberately slander or misrepresent an opposing candidate, or ascribe to the candidate whom he supports estimable qualities which he believes do not belong to him, deserves to be disfranchised, and to be detested by every sincere patriot in the community." He urged the people to withhold public office from those who were "undermining the firmest pillars of the social edifice, at the same time that they are doing their utmost to blast the good name of worthy men, and showing themselves to be unworthy of all confidence and respect." Winans also cited Mississippi as an example of dishonesty. Referring to the state's repudiation of bonded indebtedness after having overextended herself in a bank chartering venture, he asserted that such action had destroyed Mississippi's credit and made her name "a reproach throughout the civilized world." Lest some charge that he was "preaching politics," Winans declared, "We hold that political morality lies as properly within the range of pulpit discussion, as morality between man and man; and that he who, in the exercise of political power, violates moral obligations, is equally guilty as he who violates moral obligation in transactions with an individual neighbor. . . . Hence, *the duty of the preacher* to 'cry aloud and spare not,' in showing them their sin." In 1856 Winans sought to have the sermon published but the Book and Tract Society of the Mississippi Conference refused to circulate it because of its statements on political dishonesty and its criticism of the state government. "The Citizen of Zion" was finally published in pamphlet form by the Natchez *Daily Courier*, a Whig paper, thereby lending credence to charges that it was more of a political tract than a sermon.[38]

Very few other southern evangelicals engaged in politics to the extent that Winans did. Why did most of them choose a more limited political role than he was willing to accept? Part of the explanation may be found by looking at the way in which Winans defended his activities. He believed it was his duty, both as a citizen and a clergyman, to promote the welfare

38. *Ibid.*, 221–25.

of his country. "After God," he said, "my Country is entitled to my best services." Replying to the Vicksburg *Sentinel's* criticism of his campaigning for Clay in 1844, Winans declared that he had been motivated by patriotism, that he had felt it his "duty to labor for the overthrow of a Party, the uniform tendency of whose measures has been, in his judgment, to corrupt, impoverish and finally to ruin the country in which are his home, his family, his all." On several occasions he criticized clergymen and pious laymen who "left politics to the world." The result was a loss of the religious and moral influence needed to counteract the "pernicious tendency" of selfish and corrupt politicians. Winans said that he found nothing in the Scriptures to suggest the "impropriety" of ministers "using their best efforts to secure the appointment to office of the men best qualified to promote the well-being of the country in which they live." Indeed, he implied that ministers who thought themselves "elevated above the level of politics" and who left politics to "the world" in order to engage in theology, science, and literature "sacrificed the well-being of their country" to their own selfish interests. The same concern that the United States should be a Christian commonwealth underlay his justification of offering prayers at Whig political rallies. Winans agreed that it would be improper for a minister to "use the pulpit as a political rostrum," or to offer "prayer in relation to political affairs in . . . associations for *religious* worship." But, he asserted, "as nothing should be done without prayer for Divine direction and aid, it is entirely proper that those who have met to further an enterprise the object of which is the overthrow of an injurious party, should invoke the Divine blessing on their well-meant efforts." To reinforce his argument he pointed to the example of "our Fathers, of Revolutionary times." Unlike many at the present day, "they did not deem the human machinery which they were able to employ of sufficient efficiency, to dispense with Divine counsel and divine aid." [39]

Winans was positively scornful of those who criticized his and other ministers' political activities on the ground that the spirituality of the church was being compromised. Most of the people who offered such arguments he condemned as hypocrites. He was particularly incensed by the provision in the Mississippi constitution disqualifying ministers from political office. He remembered that at the time it was enacted "the exclusion was predicated on a concern for the religious efficiency of the Clergy," but he contended that that was something "for which nine in ten of the members

39. William Winans to Editor, Vicksburg *Sentinel*, December 5, 1844, in Winans Collection.

of the Convention had not the least solicitude." Though he admitted that there was some plausibility in the argument that "political office would deteriorate the piety of a clerical incumbent," he observed that "if there be any force in this objection, no Christian ought, and no judicious Christian would, accept political office: for, it is inconceivable that the holding of political office would deteriorate the piety of the Clergyman, and at the same time be innoxious to the piety of the Layman." Of course to admit such an objection would mean the end of any religious or moral influence in government and, thereby, the demise of the Christian commonwealth. But even if the objection were true, Winans contended that a convention to form a state constitution was not justified in excluding ministers from political office. "A Convention is not charged with the guardianship of Ministerial piety or integrity," he noted. The church might have a right so to restrain its ministers, but for a convention to do it was "to perpetrate outrage upon the rights not of the Clergy only, but of all such citizens as might deem it to be their interest to elect Clergymen to offices in their gift and for their service."[40]

Winans' defense of his involvement in politics reveals that while he shared the evangelical notion of a "voluntary establishment" of religion, he tended to place more emphasis on the importance of religion in preserving the American republic than he did on the separation of church and state and the spirituality of the church. He seemed to believe that clergymen could infuse politics with religious and moral principles. In contrast, the great majority of evangelicals emphasized the ways in which political activity was likely to corrupt the minister and compromise the church. Thus "Paul" in the *Southern Christian Advocate* cited the temptations, which were likely to confront a "preacher politician," " 'to return evil for evil;' to say hard, and unkind, and uncharitable things" about his opponents. "The effect of success in political life, [was] even more dangerous still," as was "passion for worldly honor, . . . which is even more calculating, more selfish, and more absorbing than avarice." In the heat of the campaign, the "preacher politician" would have little time for his ministerial duties. "When not in

40. Winans Autobiography, 130–31. Although most evangelicals disapproved of ministers running for political office, they seem to have agreed with Winans in opposing constitutional provisions disqualifying ministers from public office. See, for example, [Wood Furman], *A Biography of Richard Furman*, ed. and sup. Harvey T. Cook (Greenville, S.C., 1913), 21, *Watchman and Observer*, August 29, 1850, pp. 10–11, John Leland, "The Virginia Chronicle" (1790), in *The Writings of the Late Elder John Leland, Including Some Events in His Life, Written by Himself, With Additional Sketches, &c. by Miss L. F. Greene, Lanesboro, Mass.* (New York, 1845), 122, and *Religious Herald*, September 25, 1851, p. 155, October 9, 1851, p. 163.

the pulpit, he is on the stump, for all who can speak, 'stump it'. . . . To-be-sure he never omits to preach on *every* Sabbath. But in what condition is he to preach, coming into the sacred desk, covered with the dust and dirt of the scramble on the stump, the very day preceding?" Given the dangers involved in political activity, most evangelicals were disposed to agree with the Richmond *Christian Advocate* that ministers ought to be willing to sacri-fice—if indeed it could be called that—the exercise of a political right in order better to perform the duties of their high office. Indeed, the ten-dency among some evangelicals so to emphasize religious duties could lead to a positive devaluation of any kind of political activity. The *Central Presbyterian* printed an excerpt from the *Princeton Repertory* which declared that "it is no part of the preacher's commission to make the promotion of men's worldly interests any prominent object of his inculcations. . . . Preachers who spend their strength in efforts at worldly amelioration, usually spend their strength for nought. Those who spend it in promoting godliness, usually build up every interest of man, temporal, spiritual, eter-nal, individual, and social."[41]

Another difference between Winans and other evangelicals was that they did not think that the argument about the deleterious effect of politi-cal activity on "ministerial efficiency" was unfounded. Although evangeli-cals distinguished between the political role of the minister as citizen and his political role as an "ambassador of Christ," they found it difficult to persuade church members of the distinction. Even though a minister were careful to avoid any mention of political issues in the pulpit, if, as a citizen, he publicly supported a particular candidate or took a stand on a contro-versial question, some members of the church who disagreed with him were bound to take umbrage and perhaps even to accuse him of overstep-ping the bounds of proper ministerial conduct. Just voting could elicit criticism, because in parts of the South, even late in the antebellum pe-riod, voting was oral and public. In this regard, the nullification contro-versy of the early 1830s provided the great object lesson for many south-ern evangelicals. As Margaret Burr DesChamps has pointed out, many ministers believed that the crisis was so grave that they must take a stand, despite their disapproval of ministers engaging in political activity. Inevi-tably, in a time of great political excitement, church members were antag-onized. Basil Manly was said to have displeased many in his Charleston

41. *Southern Christian Advocate*, August 3, 1849, p. 33; Richmond *Christian Advocate* ex-cerpted in *Christian Index*, March 15, 1844, n.p.; *Central Presbyterian*, November 18, 1856, p. 167.

church. A writer in the Charleston *Observer* noted in 1833 that ministers who had entered into the controversy had suffered as a result. "As *Ministers*," he wrote, "their influence is unfavorably affected with *their own party* —with the *opposing party*, it is destroyed." Even when ministers stayed out of the conflict, they found that the excitement it generated interfered with revivals they were holding, curtailed contributions to missions and other benevolent enterprises, divided churches into political factions, and generally distracted attention from religious matters.[42]

Another difference between Winans and other evangelicals was that most of them were not undaunted by criticism from the outside. The fact that a number of southern states had disqualified ministers from holding public office was one indication of public sentiment. Editorials and letters to the editor in secular and religious newspapers provided another. Throughout the antebellum period, a time of intense party conflict as well as excitement over the slavery question, ministers were often criticized on the ground that they were "meddling in politics." Even the most innocent actions were liable to bring censure. In 1840 the *Christian Index* published an article about a humble man living in a log cabin whose Bible was his bosom companion. Two readers complained to the editor of his "mixing politics with religion," and he felt compelled to declare that he had had no "political design" in printing the piece. In 1856 when the clergy of Richmond appealed to their fellow citizens to avert the danger of civil war by repenting of their sins and praying to God for guidance, the *Virginia Semi-Weekly Examiner* accused them of copying "the pulpit tactics of Parker, Beecher, Rev. Mrs. Antoinette Brown, *et id omne genus*." Although the *Examiner*'s main objection was that the clergy were mixing religion and politics in commenting on the sectional controversy, it is clear from the editorial that the paper found their appeal irritating for another reason:

We were entitled to expect that if these gentlemen, living in a Southern city, could no longer keep their garments "unspotted from the world," but must of necessity draggle them in the mire of politics, they would at least have uttered some vindications of those who are now engaged in a struggle for the Constitution; that if they did not do this, they would discriminate in their clerical censure between the people of the South and the national and conservative citizens elsewhere now

42. DesChamps, "Presbyterian Church in the South Atlantic States," 190–91; Rev. James P. Boyce, *Life and Death the Christian's Portion. A Discourse Occasioned by the Funeral Services of the Rev. Basil Manly, D.D. At Greenville, S.C., Dec 22, 1868* (New York, 1869), 48; Charleston *Observer*, November 9, 1833, p. 178; Margaret Burr DesChamps, "Union or Division? South Atlantic Presbyterians and Southern Nationalism, 1820–1861," *Journal of Southern History*, XX (November, 1954), 490–91.

acting with them in defence of Constitutional rights—and the mad fanatics of the North banded together in an unholy alliance, assaulting the Constitution and the Union, because under the Constitution the rights of the South are acknowledged and guaranteed.

On the one hand the *Examiner* criticized the clergy for meddling in politics. On the other it accused them of not being sufficiently partisan. Given the existence of attitudes like this, it is no wonder that ministers throughout the South generally avoided political involvement. The fact that they were being compared with northern ministers and abolitionists must have been particularly disconcerting, for southern evangelicals were quite outspoken in condemning "clerical agitators" who prostituted "the high and holy office of the Gospel ministry . . . to the malign work of creating and fostering the fanatical mania which is spreading in the Northern section of this country."[43] This, along with the hypersensitivity of their parishioners on slavery and other issues, combined to persuade southern evangelicals of the wisdom of a limited political role.

Some of the same assumptions that governed evangelicals' thinking about their own political role informed their view of the political duties of Christian citizens. Christianity, they declared, did not counsel evasion of civic responsibilities any more than it sanctioned abstention from worldly business. Living *in* the world, the Christian must take an interest in the welfare of his country and seek to understand the nature of the government under which he lived and the duties he owed to it. This was especially true in a republic, "in which the will of the people is the law of the land." The very existence of republican government—and the political and religious liberty it provided—depended on citizens responsibly and disinterestedly exercising the power entrusted to them.[44]

Evangelicals insisted that citizens were accountable to God for the faithful discharge of their political duties. This was not only because government was a divine ordinance, but because the particular government of the United States was "a government created by christian men,—framed in accordance with christian principles,—founded upon and presupposing christian institutions as existing in the land—and looking to the influ-

43. In 1850, according to the *Watchman and Observer*, August 29, 1850, p. 10, nine states had constitutional provisions disqualifying ministers from holding public office: Virginia, North and South Carolina, Florida, Texas, Louisiana, Missouri, Kentucky, and Tennessee. *Southern Christian Advocate*, July 31, 1840, p. 26, December 13, 1850, p. 110, June 23, 1854, p. 10; Charleston *Observer*, October 6, 1832, p. 158; *Christian Index*, August 13, 1840, p. 525; *Virginia Semi-Weekly Examiner*, June 27, 1856, n.p.; Richmond *Whig and Public Advertiser*, June 27, 1856, n.p.

44. *Religious Herald*, January 18, 1828, p. 7.

ence and power of christian principles for its growth, stability and permanency." Worldlings might act as though they were bound only to obey the laws framed by men for the purpose of regulating society. Christians realized that they held citizenship in two governments, one earthly, the other divine, and that, therefore, they were bound to obey not only civil laws but the laws of God as well. True patriotism consisted in performing one's civil duties in accordance with religious principles.[45]

One of the duties of a Christian citizen was obedience to constituted authority. Since government was ordained by God, resistance to government was resistance to God. The editor of the *Southern Christian Advocate* noted that "a Christian . . . from the very terms of his religion, is under obligation to yield obedience to the magistrate as the representative of CONSTITUTIONAL LAW. This submission is to be unreserved, on principle, and for conscience sake, even though it might cost something.—So long as the officer of the law keeps within the bounds prescribed by the constitution of the country, he claims our obedience." Another duty was that of voting in elections. In a Fourth of July discourse entitled "The Christian's Principle and Motive in Voting," Thomas Smyth urged his hearers to regard voting as "a most weighty and serious duty." It was "no light and trifling matter to be considered and settled in a tavern or in the street caucus." The Christian citizen should pray to God for guidance. In exercising his prerogative he should "act deliberately, disinterestedly in the fear of God, and with a single eye to the best interests of the commonwealth." Though they did not proscribe it completely, evangelicals had strong reservations about Christians running for office. In a pastoral address of 1843 the ministers of the Georgia Annual Conference declared,

We would not dissuade you from the exercise of your right as citizens, of giving your votes, nor would we have you in every case refuse appointments or public offices when freely offered to you; yet we are assured that such is the deplorable state of things, that whoever engages warmly in politics, if he hopes for success, must join himself to a faction where honesty and uprightness are lost sight of in the struggle for power.—Few of our people that have been active politicians, have failed to be stained by the moral pollution with which they have come in contact. We are therefore convinced that the less you have to do with politics, the better will it be for your growth in grace, and your religious peace.[46]

45. Thomas Smyth, "The Christian's Principle and Motive in Voting. A Discourse," in *Complete Works*, X, 504–505; *Watchman and Observer*, January 28, 1849, p. 96; *Watchman of the South*, July 23, 1840, p. 190.

46. *Southern Christian Advocate*, January 8, 1841, p. 118; Smyth, "Christian's Principle and Motive in Voting," 502, 507, 508; *Christian Index*, April 14, 1843, p. 232.

As the pastoral address indicates, southern evangelicals took a generally negative view of parties and party spirit, at a time when, as Richard Hofstadter has shown, many Americans were coming to see them as a positive good. Evangelicals deplored the "political excitement" fomented by parties and their leaders during elections. Indeed, they were as fearful of political as of religious enthusiasm. They repeatedly urged their people against being swept up into "the whirlwind of party warfare." In 1840 the Dan River Baptist Association, fearing that the brethren were "in danger of being brought, in too great a degree, under the influence of party politics," went so far as to pass a resolution urging them to "keep aloof from all improper electioneering measures of every party." Nevertheless, in almost every election, Christians were drawn into the "Maelstrom" and the result was coldness in the churches and controversy among the brethren. Although citizens were partly responsible—since they succumbed to "partizanship"—evangelicals placed most of the blame on party politicians. Thus the editor of the Charleston *Observer* denounced politicians "whose chief business appears to be, to excite the public mind and keep it constantly in a fermented state." They declared that they were contending for principles on which the preservation of the republic depended. "But," sneered the editor, "who does not know that the same principles are put on and put off by political men, with wonderful facility? . . . in most cases the clamour about principle is to secure a popular election, promote some private interest, or gratify some personal pique." Evangelicals also condemned the electioneering measures commonly employed by politicians —"bribery, drunkenness, perjury, violence, fraud, falsehood." As temperance advocates, most ministers especially deplored the practice of "treating." They also upbraided candidates for using abusive and slanderous language in attacking each other, for being motivated by ambition and avarice, and for appealing to the passions and self-interest of the voters instead of to their reason and concern for the general welfare.[47]

But the worst evil of party politics—the one that seemed to pose the greatest threat not only to republican government but to religion as well— was the stress laid on party loyalty. Because of it bad men were elected to office, and voters, even Christian voters, allowed themselves to be gov-

47. Richard Hofstadter, *The Idea of a Party System: The Rise of Legitimate Opposition in the United States, 1780–1840* (Berkeley, 1970); *Southern Christian Advocate*, February 18, 1848, p. 145, July 14, 1848, p. 22, October 23, 1856, p. 83; *Religious Herald*, October 15, 1840, p. 167; Charleston *Observer*, May 8, 1830, p. 74, September 8, 1832, p. 142, October 16, 1830, pp. 166–67; Basil Manly, "National Stability" (MS sermon delivered June 21, 1844, Tuskaloosa, Alabama, in Manly, Jr., Papers); *Watchman and Observer*, August 19, 1852, p. 8.

erned by party considerations rather than religious principles in exercising the right of suffrage. All evangelicals condemned the doctrine of party loyalty but none was more caustic than Bishop James O. Andrew, who stated his views in an article entitled "A Christian Man's Politics" which appeared in the *Southern Christian Advocate* of February 11, 1858. He began his indictment by stating as a fundamental premise that "a christian man will make the will and honor of God, the paramount law of his conduct. . . . acting on this principle, the first aim of every christian citizen should be, to have the country governed by the principles of Bible truth, to have its legislation accord as nearly as possible to the great principles enunciated by Jehovah, which embody the only safe rules for the conduct of nations as well as of individuals." It followed that "christian patriots, in exercising the important right of suffrage, will first regard their relations and obligations to God, and let partly [party] considerations be a secondary matter," but, Andrew observed, generally the rule was reversed. It was "party first, and God and religion secondly or thirdly." Nothing more clearly reveals the profound skepticism and contempt with which Andrew and other evangelicals viewed the political process than his description of the way in which candidates for public office were nominated and elected:

Say there is an election about coming off for a legislator, either state or national, and in accordance with the established usages of all parties, a convention meet to select suitable candidates to present to the people for their suffrages. When the august assemblage proceeds to the performance of its weighty and responsible task, there are but two questions to be answered—is he sound in the faith of the party? and is he the most available man? If to these questions there be a satisfactory response, the case is settled. He may be a drunkard. . . . He may be a notorious libertine . . . a gambler . . . ; or sum up all in one word he may be an infidel, a scoffer at christianity, a bold and senseless blasphemer. . . . It matters not—the party sages assembled, who claim to represent the wisdom and respectability of the party, after due deliberation and possibly a prayer to God, select this embodiment of moral leprosy as their standard bearer, and straightway all the organs of the party announce the glorious news. . . . Now, many members of this nominating convention were perhaps professedly the followers of Christ—possibly all the churches of the country were represented, and yet the nomination was *unanimous*, and then christian men go out . . . and seek earnestly to secure the election of a man, whose whole course is an outrage on all the proprieties of common morality, and thousands of christian men throughout the district will, on election day, march to the polls and cast votes for the party nominee, although they have so repeatedly witnessed his utter moral degradation.

Acting thus, Christian men violated the fundamental precepts of their religion and conducted themselves as mere worldlings would. They "utterly ignored God and his government," Andrew declared. "Religion has scarcely been allowed to breathe a whisper in this whole business—the god of party alone has been invoked and the God of heaven and earth has been boldly dishonored."[48]

Instead of "party preferences" evangelicals urged the Christian voter to make "moral worth" the chief criterion. In other words, he should judge candidates in accordance with "the precepts of religion," not "the maxims of the world." Thus, the editor of the *Religious Herald* declared that "no vicious or immoral man ought to be supported for any office, by the disciples of the Redeemer, however well fitted he may be for the station, or however great may be his talents, or acquirements." Only if Christians followed this rule of action would "virtuous and upright statesmen" be elected, who would "preserve our institutions free and unimpaired." Although evangelicals urged the principle of Christians voting for Christians throughout the antebellum period, they never made any concerted effort to implement or enforce it. They did not endorse particular candidates, for example, or attempt to weld church members into an effective voting bloc or even a third party. Their aversion to engaging in politics, as well as popular sensitivity to anything that suggested a religious establishment, precluded such action. However, editors of religious newspapers often urged the principle on their readers, and a few religious bodies and voluntary societies recommended it to their members. For example, the Savannah River Baptist Association, after expressing its alarm at "the shameful and demoralizing extent, to which electioneering is carried within our bounds," resolved "that we do individually and collectively determine to withhold our vote and influence from any, and every man, who, may hereafter directly or indirectly, in his own person, or by his friends attempt to introduce himself into office by such means, as have been so perniciously pursued; namely, by going from place to place, collecting together the idle and vicious, the young and inexperienced, and dealing out to them copious draughts of ardent spirits; thereby inflaming their senses, destroying their reason, and preparing them to answer any purpose, that designing men may desire."[49] As will be seen in the next chapter, the principle of

48. *Southern Baptist and General Intelligencer*, February 12, 1836, p. 26; *Southern Christian Advocate*, February 11, 1858, p. 145.
49. *Southern Christian Advocate*, May 10, 1844, p. 190; *Religious Herald*, September 10, 1830, p. 143, June 3, 1836, p. 87; *Wesleyan Journal*, December 30, 1826, p. 3.

Christians voting for Christians had its greatest appeal and its most extensive implementation among temperance groups.

Taken as a whole, the political and social commentary of southern evangelicals reveals how alienated they were from the society in which they lived, and how far they were from accepting the dominant American ideology of self-reliance, democracy, and progress. The same distrust of "human instrumentality" that influenced their attitudes toward revivals of religion underlay much of their criticism of American political life. It was not just that Christians were distracted from religion by "political excitement," or that they were guided by worldly maxims such as self-interest or party loyalty rather than religious precepts. Evangelicals were also concerned that Christians—indeed all Americans—placed too much faith in human institutions and efforts (government, political parties, banks, internal improvements, mechanical contrivances) as the means of securing peace, order and prosperity.[50] Bishop Andrew, in his criticism of the doctrine of party loyalty, charged Christians with "adopting party politics as the gospel of their salvation," and "A Baptist," writing in the *Religious Herald*, criticized his brethren for exerting themselves during a campaign "as if the salvation of souls, as well as that of the country, depended on the triumph of party, or the elevation of a partisan to office." Christians ought to take an interest in their country, "but," he asked, "is it right to manifest that deep anxiety which would seem to argue no superintending providence?" Evangelicals agreed that too often Christians acted as if they were self-sufficient, as if they had forgotten that "there is a God that ruleth on earth as well as in heaven." The "true patriot" was "conscious that human wisdom and human power are inadequate to the government and protection of his country," declared the editor of the Charleston *Observer*. Therefore, "he implores the blessings of Heaven upon our councils, and reposes his confidence in the permanency of our institutions, solely upon the continuance of the divine favor." Yet most Christians, instead of attributing their earthly blessings to "divine favor," viewed them as the result of human effort. As a prime example of this kind of thinking, evangelicals cited the way in which the Fourth of July was observed. Instead of being an

50. See, for example, *Southern Christian Advocate*, April 18, 1840, p. 174, *Southern Presbyterian*, July 3, 1858, n.p., "Address, To the friends of Religion . . . ," *Georgia Analytical Repository*, I (September–October, 1802), 98–99, and Basil Manly, "Sermon on the occasion of a publick Fast. September 25, 1830. Baptist Church, Charleston" (MS in Manly, Jr., Papers).

occasion for thanksgiving and prayer to God for a continuation of his blessing, the anniversary of independence was desecrated by "revelry and drunkenness" and "the envenomed harrangues [*sic*] of opposing political parties." Orators describing the great events of the Revolution ignored Providence and gave honor exclusively to men. Throughout the antebellum period evangelicals sought to make the Fourth of July an occasion for signifying that sense of dependence on God which they believed was lacking in the American people. They urged Christians to celebrate the day "as a political Sabbath, which neither strife, nor intemperance, nor vice in any form should be suffered to profane." As a result of their efforts, in many communities churches held services and Sabbath schools conducted exercises on the Fourth. Ministers frequently participated in the processions and offered prayers, benedictions, and addresses at the civic celebrations. Evangelicals also supported the proclamation of days of thanksgiving by church bodies or civil authorities, and often delivered sermons or discourses on such occasions.[51]

Evangelicals' opposition to the popular notion of self-reliance contributed to their skeptical view of democracy. They had little confidence in people, whether politicians or otherwise. We have already seen the contempt with which men like William Capers and James Andrew viewed politicians. Other evangelicals generally characterized them as men of dubious integrity, motivated chiefly by self-interest, utterly lacking in piety— in sum, worldlings through and through.[52] The people who elected them to office were little better. They were easily "gulled" by demagogues, and "party spirit . . . not conscientious political views" usually determined the way they voted. Most evangelicals doubted that the "multitude" had the wisdom and virtue necessary to the proper exercise of self-government. Thinking thus, evangelicals like James Henley Thornwell were horrified at the democratic tendencies of the age. What Thornwell labeled "the deifi-

---

51. *Southern Christian Advocate*, February 11, 1858, p. 145; *Religious Herald*, September 26, 1844, p. 153; Charleston *Observer*, June 28, 1828, p. 102, June 12, 1827, p. 94; "National Anniversary," *Virginia Evangelical and Literary Magazine*, VII (July, 1824), 337; *Wesleyan Journal*, June 3, 1826, p. 3; *Watchman and Observer*, June 27, 1850, p. 182, July 11, 1850, p. 190. For accounts of Fourth of July celebrations which evangelicals organized or participated in, see, for example, *Southern Watchman and General Intelligencer*, July 14, 1837, p. 110, *Watchman and Observer*, July 27, 1848, p. 198, Frances Bumpas Journal (typed copy in Bumpas Family Papers), July 4, 1843, p. 24, and Mangum Diary, July 3, 1852. For days of thanksgiving, see, for example, *Wesleyan Journal*, November 19, 1825, p. 3, *Religious Herald*, November 14, 1829, p. 182, and *Southern Christian Advocate*, November 25, 1858, p. 102.

52. See, for example, *Watchman of the South*, August 3, 1843, p. 200 (misnumbered 100), *Christian Index*, January 20, 1848, p. 22, and *Southern Christian Advocate*, August 16, 1850, p. 42.

cation of the people" was but one more indication of the tendency to rely on "human instrumentality" rather than God. The people, Thornwell explained, "are frequently represented as the source of all political power and rights; the very fountain head of sovereignty. . . . A supremacy is ascribed to [their] will which he who reads the Bible and recognizes a God that has dominion over the children of men, must feel to be shocking. They are really treated as a species of Deity upon the earth." In Thornwell's view, "the true and legitimate end of government" was not to do the people's will, "but to do and enforce what reason, conscience and truth pronounce to be right." Because government was a divine ordinance it had "great moral purposes to subserve." It was a means by which the laws of God were applied "to the countless exigencies of social and individual life." Therefore, "the will of the people should be done only when the people will what is right, and then primarily not because they will it, but because it is right." To argue otherwise, Thornwell asserted, was to oppose religion and "the true conception of our government," which Thornwell believed supported a "representative system," not "pure democracy."[53]

What Thornwell viewed as the corruption of "a *representative* into a *democratic* government" was but one symptom of the general declension which he and other evangelicals believed was the dominant tendency of the age. While their contemporaries celebrated progress, evangelicals cited the evidence of degeneration: "widespread, practical infidelity" which resulted in a "loosening of the ties of moral restraint" and an increase in crime, the "spirit of insubordination and lawless violence" which manifested itself in mob action and challenges to the Constitution and its laws, the corruption at the polls, and the rising tide of worldliness, avarice, dissipation, and extravagance. The rage for speed and novelty which other Americans offered as proof of the progressive spirit of the age, evangelicals viewed with alarm. Commenting on the increasing number of railroad and steamship accidents, Robert Morrison denounced "the reckless growing & insatiable thirst to drive every thing at *Steam Speed*. . . . This *Go ahead* mania is the bane of our Country, and I often fear it will drive us to ruin," he continued. "Cautious men, moderate measures, wise counsel, prudent forethought, and Common Sense are commodities too old for consideration &

53. Robert Hall Morrison to James Morrison, January 1, 1852, in Robert Hall Morrison Papers, Southern Historical Collection, University of North Carolina Library; Mangum Diary, August 5, 1852; John Holt Rice to the Reverend B. B. Wisner, November 22, 1828, in Maxwell, *Memoir of Rice*, 381; James H. Thornwell, *Judgments, A Call to Repentance. A Sermon Preached by Appointment of the Legislature in the Hall of the House of Representatives, . . . Saturday, Dec. 9, 1854* (Columbia, S.C., 1854), 17–19.

too contracted for this expanding age—Already one part of our Citizens, can look with complacency only on enlargement, conquest, land stealing, & fillibustering and I fear they will soon become the majority. . . . In this *very wise* age too that old Revelation we call the Bible has to many become *stale*—Something newer is wanted. Hence Spirits are called, *not from God*, to tell us amazing things in a foolish way—Old tables & Empty walls are looked to for messages from the invisible world. . . . Truly this is a time of progress, and the *manifest* destiny of multitudes is to leave behind them wisdom & safety & peace & life and to sail amid the reefs of fanaticism and anarchy and blasphemy—Very exciting sailing it may be; but the end of these things is death."[54]

Like Morrison, most evangelicals had no doubt that Americans would be punished for their sins. Indeed, they pointed to epidemics, drought, panics, steamboat disasters, and other "public calamities" as indications of God's disapproval and warnings of a worse chastisement yet to come. They saw the hand of Providence in all things—in "national afflictions" as well as blessings. Thus, the notion of a social covenant between God and the American people was an integral part of their thinking. Evangelicals believed that so long as Americans followed God's laws, conducting themselves as befitted citizens of a Christian commonwealth, they might expect to be rewarded with peace, well-being, and prosperity. However, if they departed from the path of righteousness—as evangelicals contended they were doing—then they must expect divine punishment. The only remedy, the only way of averting God's wrath and regaining his favor, was through repentance and reformation. Throughout the nineteenth century evangelicals reiterated this message. Each successive judgment visited on the nation—the panics of 1837 and 1857, the death of Presidents Harrison and Taylor, the explosion on the *Princeton*—provided them with an opportunity to point out the "national sins" of the American people, to warn them of divine chastisement, and to exhort them to repentance and reformation.[55] As political and sectional controversy accelerated, as worldly

54. James Henley Thornwell to Matthew J. Williams, July 17, 1848, in Palmer, *Life and Letters of Thornwell*, 310; *Southern Christian Advocate*, May 18, 1849, p. 198; Charleston *Observer*, August 22, 1835, p. 134; Robert Hall Morrison to James Morrison, May 31, 1853, in Morrison Papers.
55. The ideas sketched above appeared frequently in the three denominations' newspapers. See, for example, *Southern Presbyterian*, June 29, 1849, p. 178; *Religious Herald*, October 15, 1857, p. 162; *Southern Christian Advocate*, November 18, 1858, p. 98. See also Basil Manly, "Sermon on the occasion of a publick Fast. September 25, 1830. Baptist Church, Charleston"

conformity increased, as their calls to repentance proved unavailing, evangelicals took an increasingly pessimistic view of the prospects of their country. The crisis of 1860–1861 would come as no surprise to them. They were conditioned to look for divine retribution.

(MS in Manly, Jr., Papers); Thomas Smyth, "Reflections on the Loss of the Steam-Boat Home, October 9, 1837. A Sermon," in *Complete Works*, V; Thornwell, *Judgments*; Thomas Railey Markham, "Isa. 59:19. Enemy Come in like a flood" (MS sermon dated July 4, 1858, in Markham Papers).

CHAPTER FIVE

The Temperance Reformation

The first temperance society in the South was formed at a meeting called by Abner Clopton at the Ash Camp Meeting House in Charlotte County, Virginia, in October, 1826. For three years since coming to the area, Clopton had been preaching against intemperance. He had previously used "ardent spirits" himself, but early in 1826 had resolved to abstain from them. About the same time he conceived the idea of forming a temperance society "as a means of demolishing the kingdom of Satan" and called the meeting for that purpose. Several ministers and a large congregation attended. Eli Ball, another Baptist minister, preached a sermon on temperance. Then a constitution, resolutions and a circular address—all prepared by Clopton—were presented to the group. Despite what Jeremiah Jeter remembered as "a stirring appeal in behalf of the cause," only 10 persons, 8 of them preachers, were willing to sign the pledge "to abstain from the habitual use of spirituous liquors, and use them as a medicine only." Nevertheless, Clopton was sufficiently encouraged to begin employing "tongue, pen and purse" in behalf of the new society. Within a year the Virginia Society for the Promotion of Temperance had increased its membership to 123, including 27 Baptist ministers, and had acquired several auxiliaries. By 1828 the Society boasted 307 members and nine or ten auxiliaries.[1]

When they founded the Virginia Society, Clopton and his associates

1. Jeter, *Memoir of Clopton*, 171–72, 174–82, 186–87; Jeter, *Recollections*, 35; *Religious Herald*, December 19, 1828, p. 199. For statistics on the Virginia Society for later years see Charleston *Observer*, May 15, 1830, p. 78; *Religious Herald*, May 6, 1831, p. 67.

were unaware of the existence of the American Society for the Promotion of Temperance, which had been organized earlier that year. The southern temperance crusade was an indigenous movement which developed simultaneously with, but largely independent of, the northern movement. Shortly after Clopton's group was organized, temperance societies appeared in other southern states. Jesse Hartwell and C. D. Mallary organized the South Carolina Anti-Intemperance Society at the annual meeting of the Charleston Baptist Association in November, 1826. By that date an association for the suppression of intemperance was already operating within the bounds of the Presbytery of Orange in North Carolina. The next year Adiel Sherwood formed the first temperance society in Georgia at a union meeting of the Baptist Church of Eatonton, of which Sherwood was pastor. In Alabama a temperance group connected with the Valley Creek Presbyterian Church in Dallas County was functioning as early as 1828. The number of such organizations multiplied rapidly in the late 1820s and early 1830s. Most were local societies, but county and state associations were also formed, and some of the groups were affiliated with the American Society. The Baptists were generally recognized as the "most forward" of the denominations in promoting the cause of temperance, but Methodists and Presbyterians were becoming increasingly active by the early 1830s.[2]

The reasons why evangelicals promoted the temperance cause varied. In some cases, youthful experiences may have played an important role. Brantley York and Adolphus Williamson Mangum, for example, had been employed in the business of distilling and retailing liquor and had been repulsed by "the wickedness caused by drinking." Similarly, when young William Winans encountered drunk and disorderly persons at the first camp meeting he attended, he reacted with "fear, disgust and horror." Others, like Jeremiah Jeter and Daniel Witt, had resolved to abstain from the use of intoxicating liquors as a beverage even before the temperance movement was underway. Viewing the use of ardent spirits as "a useless habit" which was "fraught with pernicious consequences," they were early supporters of temperance societies, including the one formed by Clopton.[3]

2. Jeter, *Memoir of Clopton*, 173–74; John Allen Krout, *The Origins of Prohibition* (New York, 1925), 130–31; Geer, "Temperance Movement in Georgia," 31, 33–35; *Southern Watchman and General Intelligencer*, May 12, 1837, p. 74; *Christian Index*, July 24, 1856, p. 118; *Wesleyan Journal*, November 18, 1826, p. 1; James Benson Sellers, *The Prohibition Movement in Alabama, 1702 to 1943* (Chapel Hill, 1943), 15; *Religious Herald*, July 9, 1830, p. 105.

3. York, *Autobiography*, 31, and see also 11–12; Mangum Diary, July 15, 1854, October 23, 1855; Winans Autobiography, 12; Jeter, *Recollections*, 33–35; Jeter, *Life of Witt*, 58–61.

Clopton's decision to abandon the use of ardent spirits as a beverage owed something to Witt's influence, but more to Clopton's concern over the extent of drunkenness among members of his churches and his fear that he himself might be "overtaken" by the "ruinous vice." Writing to his father in May, 1824, Clopton said that the "trials" he had recently undergone in disciplining a church member for drunkenness had served "to put me on my guard; and a new case of intemperance (a female) has occurred that makes me almost afraid to drink spirits." He made the decision to abstain when, as he later told a fellow minister, he was sitting at dinner one day and was informed that a woman "of respectable connexions, with whom he had been well acquainted, and for whom he had entertained high esteem, had been carried home from a distillery in a state of beastly intoxication. He was astounded. Dropping his knife and fork he resolved, instantly and solemnly, to use ardent spirits no more." Shortly thereafter he issued the call for the meeting to form the Virginia Temperance Society.[4]

Clopton's account suggests what was probably the main reason why evangelicals became involved in the temperance movement. Beginning in the teens and throughout the 1820s, they were becoming more and more concerned about the increasing prevalence of intemperance, especially among church members. In those years they attempted to arrest its spread by condemning "the crime of Drunkenness" and by urging Christians to refrain from "the intemperate use of ardent spirits," or even to abstain entirely.[5] Such action was in keeping with the stand taken by the three denominations. All three viewed drunkenness as a sin. In its condemnation of drunkenness in the General Rules, the Methodist church also included "drinking spirituous liquors, unless in cases of necessity." The Presbyterian General Assembly in 1818 had recommended that "officers and members of our Church . . . abstain even from the common use of ardent spirits," and in 1829 it urged "that all members of the churches adopt the principle

---

4. Jeter, *Memoir of Clopton*, 171–73. See also Jeter, *Life of Witt*, 60–61. For the reactions of other evangelicals to intemperance see Mangum Diary, July 23, 1852, July 15, 1854, October 23, 1855, February 2, 1857; Early Diary, December 19, 1807, July 27, 1808, December 10, 1811, September 6, 1812; Taylor Diary, June 27, 1855; Stratton Diary, July 31, 1849, February 1, 1850, January 13, 1856.

5. *Christian Monitor*, September 28, 1816, p. 22, August 16, 1817, pp. 399–400; "Description of a Pernicious Disorder," *Roanoke Religious Correspondent*, I (August, 1821), 9; "A Pastoral Letter . . . ," and "The Influence of the Bible in Improving the Moral Character," *Virginia Evangelical and Literary Magazine*, I (July, 1818), 333–34, 450.

of entire abstinence from the use of ardent spirits." Nevertheless, despite such pronouncements and exhortations from the pulpit, cases of drunkenness continued to occur. Moreover, although church courts were willing to mete out punishment in cases of drunkenness, they were reluctant to take disciplinary action against moderate drinking.[6] Yet an increasing number of evangelicals were coming to believe that moderate drinking led to drunkenness. Seeing that church courts were failing to deal with one of the principal causes of drunkenness, they looked for some other agency that would. The temperance society, a voluntary association of individuals pledged to abstain from the use of ardent spirits as a beverage, seemed to provide the answer. Many evangelicals supported such organizations as a means of supplementing churchly efforts to arrest the spread of intemperance.

The temperance societies of the late 1820s and 1830s were of two kinds: either church congregations, which had formed themselves into societies, or organizations unconnected with any church, which offered membership to all without regard to religious sentiment.[7] Evangelicals were active in both types of societies, playing a leading role in organizing them and frequently serving as officers or managers. In addition ministers often delivered addresses at temperance meetings and preached sermons in their churches on the subject of temperance. It was not uncommon for protracted meetings to urge the claims of temperance along with religion. Thus William Snow, a Virginia Baptist, reported holding a protracted meeting at James' Square, following which fifty-three persons signed the temperance pledge.[8] No wonder revivals produced converts to temperance as well as religion and resulted in the formation of temperance societies.

Like the one formed by Clopton, most of the early societies required members to pledge to abstain from ardent (*i.e.* distilled) spirits except when necessary as a medicine and to observe caution and moderation in the use of wines and other intoxicating drink. However, in the mid 1830s some

6. Cameron, *Methodism and Society*, 134; Blanks, "Ideal and Practice," 102, 216, 219, 222–23; Cortland Victor Smith, "Church Organization as an Agency of Social Control: Church Discipline in North Carolina, 1800–1860" (Ph.D. dissertation, University of North Carolina, 1967), 129, 143, 168.

7. See, for example, *Religious Herald*, September 11, 1829, p. 146, October 16, 1829, p. 162, August 3, 1832, p. 118, March 1, 1833, p. 31, December 5, 1834, p. 191, Charleston *Observer*, April 10, 1830, p. 58, and *Christian Index*, October 22, 1833, p. 59.

8. *Religious Herald*, June 5, 1835, p. 86.

societies began to include all intoxicating beverages in the pledge.[9] The shift to a more comprehensive pledge was part of a nationwide trend. Like their counterparts in the North and the West, southern reformers were becoming convinced that the eradication of intemperance depended on "total abstinence." A Virginia reformer, explaining the origins of a total abstinence society in his neighborhood, noted that two cases of discipline for drunkenness in the church had opened many people's eyes to the need for such a society. Both of the disciplined men had belonged to the local temperance society, he observed. One had become "intoxicated by beginning on wine and ending on whiskey, the other began on cider and ended on whiskey." He said that their friends and neighbors had concluded "that both cider and wine tend to form intemperate habits, and that while they are continued to be used as a beverage, intemperance can never be done away."[10]

The disciplinary procedures followed by the temperance and total abstinence societies were often similar to those of the churches. For example, the constitution of the Louisa Goldmine Society for the Promotion of Temperance declared that members were subject to "the penalty of being discountenanced, and disowned by the Society" if they violated the pledge, "except where there is evidence of repentance." The regulations of the Middlesex Temperance Society provided that any member charged with violating the rules of the society should be tried before seven of its members. A member found guilty of any offence except drunkenness was to be privately admonished by the president or vice-president, while anyone "convicted of drunkenness shall cease to be a member of the Society."[11]

While the early southern societies directed most of their efforts toward getting individuals to pledge themselves to temperance or total abstinence and to persuade others to do likewise, they also took additional measures to eradicate intemperance. Some societies denounced the practice of selling liquor to blacks or supplying it to them on plantations and farms. Societies also urged members not to employ professional men and mechanics who were "notorious for intemperance" (and whose services might be ob-

9. See, for example, "Constitution of the upper King Wm. temperance society" (MS dated November, 1829, in Virginia Baptist Historical Society Collection), *Religious Herald*, August 21, 1829, p. 130, September 11, 1829, p. 146, October 16, 1829, p. 162, January 23, 1835, p. 11; *Wesleyan Journal*, November 18, 1826, p. 1, and Charleston *Observer*, July 16, 1836, p. 114, September 3, 1836, p. 142.

10. *Religious Herald*, May 4, 1839, p. 70. See also *Southern Baptist and General Intelligencer*, July 31, 1835, pp. 69–70.

11. *Religious Herald*, September 11, 1829, p. 146; August 21, 1829, p. 130.

tained more cheaply than those of "sober and orderly citizens"), and to withhold their votes from politicians who "treated" or who were habitually intemperate. Some societies denounced the sale and consumption of liquor at militia musters, court sessions, and public sales, and other societies passed resolutions praising local merchants and tavern owners who ceased selling liquor.[12] As will be seen, all of these measures were an outgrowth of evangelical views of intemperance and its remedy. Nor is this surprising, given that the leadership of the early societies came largely from evangelical ranks.

A survey of the writings, sermons, and addresses of southern evangelicals on the subject of temperance reveals that they were in general agreement as to why intemperance was an evil. They contended that it subverted the family, the church, and the social order. Intemperance destroyed "connubial felicity," undermined republican institutions, and "impede[d] the progress of the gospel." It was responsible for much of the poverty, crime, and idleness that afflicted society. Evangelicals were particularly concerned about the "pernicious and demoralizing effect" of ardent spirits on politics. In their view "the constant and habitual use of ardent spirits" threatened to undermine the morality and virtue on which republican government depended. As proof, they cited the practice of "treating" by political candidates during election campaigns. Treating subverted public morality by "leading the young and inconsiderate into habits of intemperance and folly." At the same time, it undermined the "rights of freemen" by reducing politics to bribery—to what the Presbytery of Orange and Stony Creek, North Carolina, called "that corrupt system of bargain and sale, by which a man disposes of his vote to the most liberal bidder in ardent spirits." It exposed "the peace and prosperity" of the country to "the *perfect* caprice of vitiated taste, and to the ambition of aspiring demagogues." Wherever treating was practiced, candidates were placed in office not by the "virtuous people," but by "swinish swill-loving voters." Evangelicals also decried treating on the ground that it destroyed "fair competition." Virtuous and good men were deterred from offering themselves as candidates for political office "because they cannot condescend to gain favour upon such terms; and when they are induced to make the attempt, they must act contrary to their own views of propriety, and go with the multitude; or lose

12. See, for example, *ibid.*, December 19, 1828, pp. 198–99, June 26, 1829, p. 98, September 11, 1829, p. 146, October 16, 1829, p. 162, December 25, 1829, p. 203, March 5, 1830, p. 34, and Charleston *Observer*, September 18, 1830, p. 150, April 16, 1831, p. 62, January 5, 1833, p. 1.

the object of their pursuit." As a result, the Savannah River Baptist Association concluded, "the public are deprived too frequently, of the talents and services of the upright and worthy part of the community."[13]

Evangelicals also voiced concern about intemperance among the black population. It was thought to be most extensive in the cities and towns, but almost as prevalent on the plantations. To combat the evil and the vices associated with it, evangelicals urged various measures. They called for stricter regulation of groceries, whose shopkeepers were said to treat slaves in order to secure their trade and to encourage them to exchange goods they raised or made (or even stole) for ardent spirits. They also called for regulation of grog shops, which were said to derive "their chief support from the corruption of the negroes." Not a few evangelicals pointed out the inconsistency of prohibiting religious assemblies of slaves and yet permitting them to gather at grog shops. Thus the Georgia Conference Missionary Society observed bitterly, "To meet for singing and prayer is an outrage upon order to be severely and promptly punished— . . . but to throng the doors of the *dram seller*, and pollute the purity of the Sabbath morning and evening with blasphemy and intoxication, is no offence— awakens no alarm, and prompts to no attempt at reform!!! Is the morality and subordination of the slave population to be committed to the care of the dram shop, and the vender of ardent spirits, rather than to the Church of God and her authorized teachers?" Evangelicals advised employers and masters to refrain from the customary practice of supplying blacks with liquor, or offering it as a reward, or furnishing it for holiday celebrations. It is significant that in addressing masters on the subject of temperance, evangelicals made the same appeal to "interest" and "philanthropy" that became common in the movement for the religious instruction of the Negroes. Thus the editor of the Charleston *Observer* remarked that "the difficulty of managing servants is increased tenfold by their intemperate habits; and their labor is far less productive than it would be, if this source of their misery and crime were removed." At the same time, noting that "God has made of one blood all that dwell upon the face of the earth, and to bondsmen as well as to freemen, are the unsearchable riches of the Gospel presented," he urged masters to acknowledge the responsibility they owed their servants. Masters should be the "guardians" of their servants, re-

13. Rev. R. B. Cater, *An Address, Delivered Before the Greenville Temperance Society, on the 17th March, 1832* (Greenville, 1832), 5, 7–9, 11; *Wesleyan Journal*, December 30, 1826, p. 3, November 18, 1826, p. 1, September 23, 1826, p. 2.

straining them from evil; they "should not be the instruments of leading them into temptation," he argued. They should give their servants "articles of substantial comfort, of food or of clothing, instead of that *liquid fire* which injures all who use it—which wastes the strength—sears the conscience, and more than anything else, excludes from the kingdom of Heaven." Above all, masters should teach their servants temperance by example.[14]

Besides appealing to masters, evangelicals also encouraged the formation of "African" temperance societies. Most of these societies were formed among Negroes in the larger cities and towns, such as Portsmouth, Manchester, Hampton, and Richmond in Virginia and Charleston in South Carolina. As early as 1830 the Georgia Temperance Society reported that of the more than forty temperance societies in the state, three were composed of blacks, one of them having more than eighty members. Some, perhaps most, of the African societies were organized, at the behest of and under the leadership of whites. However blacks in Charleston were reported to have formed a temperance society "of their own accord," and there were probably other societies formed as a result of black initiative.[15] Whether the result of black or white initiative, the societies were no doubt closely supervised by whites. A correspondent of the Charleston *Observer*, reporting the existence of temperance societies composed exclusively of Negroes, reassured the editor that "they do not meet . . . without having white people present, and their discussions are public." Surveillance was certainly the principal reason for the presence of white persons, though the editor of the *Religious Herald* urged another reason why white members of temperance societies should exhibit "constant watchfulness and attention" with regard to the African societies. If left to themselves, he explained, the black societies soon dwindled away. "They have neither the dispositions nor talent to make a meeting interesting," he declared. This was the "appropriate sphere" of the white temperance society members. They must aid the blacks by "procur[ing] suitable persons to address

14. *Religious Herald*, October 8, 1830, p. 153, August 29, 1834, p. 135, December 7, 1848, p. 195; *Christian Index*, June 26, 1845, n.p.; Charleston *Observer*, April 16, 1831, p. 62; *Southern Christian Advocate*, January 11, 1839, p. 118. For a particularly harsh indictment of retailers of spirituous liquors who sold to Negroes, see *Preamble and Regulations of the Savannah River Anti-Slave Traffick Association. Adopted November, 21st, 1846* (n.p., n.d.), 5–6.

15. *Religious Herald*, September 17, 1830, p. 146, August 22, 1834, p. 131, September 2, 1836, p. 136, April 22, 1841, p. 63, March 24, 1842, p. 47, June 23, 1842, p. 99; Charleston *Observer*, May 8, 1830, p. 75, June 12, 1830, p. 95, March 26, 1831, p. 50.

them, and . . . keep[ing] their minds continually alive and interested in the temperance cause."[16]

Most evangelicals argued that the formation of temperance societies among the slaves on the plantations was "inexpedient." Instead they urged masters to call the slaves together several times a year to talk to them on the subject of temperance or to allow others to address them. Apparently such exhortations did not go entirely unheeded. In Bryan County, Georgia, for example, slaveholders and managers drew up a list of some two hundred slaves who voluntarily promised to abstain from ardent spirits. The Baptist church in the area, to which many of the slaves belonged, seconded their efforts by voting to refuse membership to any person who would not agree to total abstinence.[17]

While not underestimating the corrupting influence of intemperance in the home and in the social order, evangelicals were chiefly concerned about its effect in the church and on the cause of religion. Most shared James Furman's view that intemperance was "one grand hindrance of the success of the gospel." R. B. Cater enumerated the ways in which ardent spirits impeded the progress of religion. First of all, men under serious impressions "by one drink of grog" succeeded in removing them, for, Cater contended, ardent spirits "excited a class of feelings, foreign entirely to the pure and holy principles of the gospel." Secondly, professing Christians, by indulging in ardent spirits, "checked their own growth in grace, and injured their souls." Moreover, Cater argued, moderate drinking by church members and ministers inevitably led to "*drunken professors of religion, and even drunken ministers of the gospel.*" He estimated that nine out of ten cases of discipline in the various denominations had their origin in the use of ardent spirits. He declared that "the use of ardent spirits has done more injury to the cause of Christ, than Tom Paine, Voltaire, Bolingbroke or Rosseau [*sic*], with the host of modern infidels, ever did or ever can do." Thus, most evangelicals argued that drinking Christians not only inhibited the cause of temperance but of religion as well. So long as church members refused to view the drinking of ardent spirits as immoral, declared a writer in the *Religious Herald*, "they act against the great object for which the church was established; for which the Saviour died; for which the gospel is preached; and all the means of grace were appointed. They oppose

16. Charleston *Observer*, September 24, 1831, p. 154; *Religious Herald*, August 29, 1834, p. 135.
17. *Religious Herald*, October 10, 1834, p. 158; Charleston *Observer*, June 16, 1832, p. 95.

the reign of the Redeemer over the minds and hearts of men; and exert a mighty influence to render sinning and suffering eternal."[18]

Although they recognized that intemperance had made serious inroads in the churches, evangelicals nevertheless looked primarily to church members to stop it. They directed their appeals mainly to professing Christians, believing that if Christians were temperate or total abstainers, the rest of society would follow their good example. In describing the duty of Christians in the temperance reformation, evangelicals thus drew on the notion of Christians as a peculiar people. Professors must be willing to live according to religious rather than worldly principles, they emphasized. They must be willing "to set at defiance the laws of fashion" and to challenge a custom which both legislation and public sentiment sanctioned. Until the mid-1840s evangelicals did not seek legislative prohibition. They believed that Christians would be able to eradicate intemperance through moral suasion in the form of individual testimony and example and the "associated influence" of temperance or total abstinence societies.[19]

While they agreed that Christians should play a primary role in the temperance reformation, evangelicals did not always agree on the particular doctrines and methods to be employed. The "wine question" which was agitated in the late 1830s and 1840s exposed significant differences of opinion among southern evangelicals. To be sure, most southern evangelicals saw no need to give up the use of wine in the Lord's Supper and they disagreed with northerners who warned that reformed drunkards might backslide as a result of having drunk communion wine, but they could not easily ignore the questions which the controversy raised regarding the doctrine of total abstinence. If, as most evangelicals maintained, Scripture sanctioned the use of wine in the Lord's Supper, how could temperance societies require members to pledge total abstinence from all intoxicating beverages? Some evangelicals, like James Morrison, believing that the Bi-

18. *Southern Baptist and General Intelligencer*, May 1, 1835, p. 276; Cater, *Address*, 11–12; *Religious Herald*, November 16, 1843, p. 183.

19. *Christian Index*, January 19, 1854, p. 10; A. W. Leland, D.D., *A Discourse Delivered Before the State Temperance Society of South Carolina, at Its First Anniversary, in the Representatives' Hall, Columbia, Nov. 29, 1838, With an Appendix of the Minutes of the Meeting* (Columbia, 1838), 8–11; Rev. Thomas O. Summers, "Philosophy of the Temperance Cause," in Rev. James Young (ed.), *The Lights of Temperance* (Louisville, 1851), 154–55; Rev. J. R. Kendrick, "Address to Christians," in *Course of Lectures on the Claims of Temperance, Delivered Before the Charleston Total Abstinence Society, by Fourteen of Its Members, on Successive Monday Evenings, From the 31st March 1851* (Charleston, 1852), 114–15; *Christian Index*, January 19, 1854, p. 10; Charleston *Observer*, November 26, 1831, p. 190.

ble did not condemn the use of wine as a beverage, refused to join "any society that set itself against wine." To do so, Morrison declared, "would be an impeachment of the character of our blessed Saviour." Other evangelicals, while agreeing to the use of wine in the communion service, argued that it would be best for individuals to give up wine as a beverage. They continued to adhere to the doctrine of total abstinence, though they took care to define it more precisely as "total abstinence from all intoxicating drinks as a *beverage*." They mustered the same arguments against wine drinking that they used against moderate drinking of ardent spirits. Wine drinking, they said, helped to make drunkards. They also contended that wine drinking by persons involved in the temperance reformation undercut the influence they exerted in favor of the cause. Although proponents of total abstinence generally did not claim that the Bible condemned drinking per se, they did contend that there were Scriptural grounds for advocating total abstinence. Thus, J. Hartwell, in a sermon preached to the Welsh Neck Temperance Convention, reminded his hearers of their duty "not only to do what was good to others, but to abstain from every thing which might injure them." He urged this principle, along with the Golden Rule, against Christians drinking and inviting others to drink. Other evangelicals cited Saint Paul's distinction between the lawfulness and expediency of a thing. On this reasoning, they argued, though the moderate use of alcohol might not be unlawful, it was inexpedient, for such indulgence might encourage others "in *habitual*, or even in *occasional*, intoxication." "There are too many instances of *habitual* drunkards sheltering themselves under the *moderate* indulgence of professed christians," declared a writer in the *Southern Watchman and General Intelligencer*.[20]

Another division of opinion among evangelicals concerned the role of the church in the temperance reformation. Some looked to the churches to lead the reformation. Others, pointing to the extent of intemperance within the churches, placed their faith in temperance societies. Still others argued that it was not only unfeasible but undesirable for the churches to become directly involved in the temperance movement. Since the debate over the role of the church took a slightly different form in each of the de-

20. William Winans to the Reverend D. DeVinne, March 31, 1852, in Winans Collection; *Christian Index*, October 19, 1848, p. 333; *Religious Herald*, January 15, 1836, p. 7; *Southern Christian Advocate*, April 15, 1842, p. 175; James Morrison to Francis McFarland, July 8, 1836, in Francis McFarland Collection, Historical Foundation of the Presbyterian and Reformed Churches; Robert Hall Morrison to James Morrison, March 3, 1838, in Morrison Papers; Charleston *Observer*, February 27, 1830, p. 34; *Southern Baptist and General Intelligencer*, July 31, 1835, p. 69; *Southern Watchman and General Intelligencer*, April 7, 1837, p. 55.

nominations, it will be helpful to treat them separately, beginning with the Presbyterians.

In the late 1820s and early 1830s, Presbyterians lent direct support to the temperance cause. Following the example of the General Assembly, which had approved the objectives of the American Society for the Promotion of Temperance, synods and presbyteries in the South passed resolutions recommending that church members abstain from the use of spirituous liquors except as a medicine and either join existing temperance societies or form them in their congregations. A few presbyteries recommended that the churches make total abstinence a term of communion, but although several churches did so, most did not. Ecclesiastical bodies also issued stern censures of Christians manufacturing or selling ardent spirits. By the mid-1830s, however, some Presbyterian evangelicals were beginning to take a more critical view of the temperance movement. They had become particularly concerned about what they regarded as the "ultraism" and extravagance of the movement, as manifested in the controversy over the use of wine in the communion service.[21]

A pamphlet, published in 1836 entitled *Reasons for Not Joining the Temperance Society* by Clement Read, pastor of the Cub Creek Church in Charlotte, Virginia, suggests the doubts and fears which were beginning to disturb some Presbyterian evangelicals. Read began by observing that he had initially viewed temperance societies (meaning societies founded on the principle of total abstinence) as "well intended" but of doubtful efficacy. Now, having examined their principles more fully, he felt compelled to resist their "extravagant claims." He contended, first of all, that the joining of a temperance society was not necessary for him to maintain his own sobriety. In supporting this argument, Read developed the notion used by many critics of temperance societies, that the church itself was a temperance society and that the duties of a professing Christian included temperance. "Does the Temperance Society bring its members under stronger obligations to lead temperate lives, than a professed subjection to Christ?" he asked. The pledge to the society was not more binding than the authority of God, nor did the society have "greater or more awful penalties to inflict on drunkards, or greater rewards to offer to the temperate" than were held out in the Bible. Read concluded that since the organization gave "no

21. For recommendations and actions of church bodies see, for example, Charleston *Observer*, February 2, 1828, p. 18, January 16, 1830, p. 10, February 11, 1832, p. 22. For concern about "ultraism" see Charleston *Observer*, August 22, 1835, p. 134, and *Watchman of the South*, February 24, 1842, p. 106.

better security for the preservation of my temperance, than the obligations under which, as a professed Christian, I am at present placed," there
was no reason for joining it.[22]

Nor was joining a temperance society necessary to insure the sobriety of
others. Read contended that the temperate use of ardent spirits was "not
an example injurious to the sobriety of others." Here he argued that "entire abstinence is no where enjoined in the Bible as a duty incumbent on
all." He also took exception to the common view that moderate use of ardent spirits led inevitably to excessive use and to the notion that the use of
ardent spirits set a bad example to "weak brethren."[23]

Read's third argument against joining a temperance society was that its
"plan of reformation" was dubious. In the first place, it was unnecessary,
since the Gospel offered a plan of reformation which, having been "dictated by infinite wisdom and goodness . . . must consequently be more efficient in reforming men, than any device [such as a temperance society] of
human wisdom." But it was not just that the temperance society's plan of
reformation was unnecessary. In Read's view, it threatened the Gospel.
The temperance plan of reformation "tends to weaken our confidence in
the gospel as a scheme of reformation," he charged. Too many people,
"relying more on the efficacy of a human, than a divine institution, are
giving an undue proportion of their exertions in promoting the Temperance Societies, to the great disparagement and neglect of the Scriptures."
Even worse than the tendency to exalt human as opposed to divine instrumentality was the fact that the temperance society, unlike Bible and
tract societies and the Sunday School Union, did not propose merely to
aid the Gospel plan for reformation, but "distrustful of the efficacy of the
gospel, proposes a new plan of reformation, founded on a principle unknown to the Scriptures, the principle of entire abstinence." Read gravely
noted the implications of this "dangerous tendency": "if men by their own
authority can make the drinking of ardent spirit a sinful act, they can make
as many acts sinful as they please. And thus we may have a new list of sins
as often as occasion requires; and the Bible, the only standard of morals,
would be entirely set aside."[24]

Read's final argument related to "the close alliance" which had been

22. [Rev. Clement Read], *Reasons for Not Joining the Temperance Society. By a Clergyman*
(Richmond, [1836]), 6–8. A handwritten note on the front of the copy in the Virginia State
Library indicates that the author was the Reverend Clement Read of Cub Creek Church,
Charlotte County, Virginia.
    23. *Ibid.*, 8, 13–20.
    24. *Ibid.*, 21–25, 44.

formed between the church and the temperance cause. The church not only "countenanced" temperance societies, but "actually and officially received them into its service," employing them as auxiliaries in the work of reformation. In Read's view, the alliance was unnecessary, since the church was already seeking to promote temperance. More important, the alliance compromised "the purity and simplicity of the Church." Viewing the church as "a divine institution," Read argued that "the annexing to it of any human schemes or institutions, forms an unnatural and an unholy alliance." He also noted the way in which the "peace of the Church" had been injured when attempts were made to introduce temperance societies into it, and he observed that the connection with temperance societies brought "a reproach on Christianity and the Church" because it was "an implied admission on the part of the Church of the insufficiency of Christianity to preserve the temperance of the members of the Church." He reserved his most trenchant language, however, for the argument against making total abstinence a term of communion. "Make the taking of the pledge of entire abstinence a test! A mere human requirement—a standard by which the genuineness of a religious profession is to be tried, by which the qualifications for full membership in the Church below and for Heaven itself, are to be ascertained." Here again was the specter of human instrumentality. Those who made the pledge a term of Christian fellowship added to the word of God and usurped the prerogative of the head of the church. Read warned of the practical consequences of such arrogance: "Let this test be once submitted to by the Church, and others will soon be presented, as many as designing or fanatical men may choose to prescribe." It would not be long, he predicted, before joining a colonization or antislavery society would be required.[25]

In the 1840s and 1850s other, better known and more influential Presbyterians voiced concern similar to that of Read. Thomas Smyth, for example, opposed what he regarded as "the ultra views and fanatical and censorious spirit" of the "Tee Total Enterprise," even though many of his congregation, including his mother-in-law, gave it their warm support. In a series of articles published in the Charleston *Observer* he criticized the doctrine of total abstinence as unscriptural, arguing that the Bible defined temperance as moderation not abstinence, and he contended that for an individual to be temperate "the heart must be reformed, the will changed, and the desires and inclinations of the mind all regulated by the dictates

25. *Ibid.*, 51–55.

of conscience, subject to the supreme regard of the divine will."[26] Thus, Smyth implied that the chief means of advancing the cause of temperance was the conversion of individuals to religion rather than the formation of voluntary associations for reform.

James Henley Thornwell drew on the notion of the church's spirituality in emphasizing the importance of distinguishing between temperance societies and the church. In his view, temperance societies were "secular enterprises, for temporal good, having no connection whatever with the kingdom of Christ." He recommended and encouraged them, believing them to be "of great service to society," but he emphatically disagreed with those who saw them "as . . . helps to the cause of Christ, instruments of building up His kingdom; that is, as a *means* of *grace*." At the General Assembly of 1848, Thornwell was successful in securing unanimous approval of his views regarding the proper relation between the church and temperance societies. Since the church was a spiritual body whose objective was the gathering and perfecting of the saints, he maintained, it should not "league itself to any secular institutions for moral ends, nor be subsidiary to associations founded upon human policy."[27]

Among Methodists, discussion of the role of the church in the temperance reformation focused on discipline. In the late 1830s and early 1840s the denomination debated whether to strengthen the rule regarding intemperance by revising it in accordance with a proposal by the New York Conference. In place of the existing prohibition against "drunkenness, or drinking of spirituous liquors unless in cases of necessity" the New York Conference urged the restoration of Wesley's rule prohibiting "drunkenness, buying or selling spirituous liquors, or drinking them, unless in cases of extreme necessity." William Capers of the *Southern Christian Advocate* waged an extended editorial campaign against this proposal. Whether Capers' views were representative of other southern Methodists is problematic, but it is significant that his reasoning on the subject of the church and temperance was similar to that of Presbyterians such as Read, Smyth, and Thornwell. Like them, Capers was willing to support the temperance movement so long as it operated "within Scriptural limits," but he also expressed concern for "the safety of the church." He objected to the revision

26. Smyth, *Autobiographical Notes*, 142–43; Thomas Smyth, "Bible Temperance," in *Complete Works*, VI, 357, 360–61.
27. James Henley Thornwell to the Reverend John Douglas, August 4, 1840, in Palmer, *Life and Letters of Thornwell*, 226, and see also 303.

of the General Rules on the ground that it would substitute "rules and pledges of human institutions" in place of Biblical rules. To change the Rules of the church, Capers declared, would be to yield to "popular excitement," to look to the temperance cause rather than to the Scriptures as the source of authority, and to compromise the mission of the church. What was the foundation of the New York Conference proposals? he asked.

The Bible? No. Is it so much as one word from the Lord? No, but "The Cause!" "The Cause!" They reverse the order of life, and make "the cause" "vital" to the Church—not the church to "the cause." . . . The church is lowered . . . to the level of "a Cause." Nay, she is put still lower, and the cause,—the good, the great, the glorious cause—is actually made paramount. Why then, should the "whole-souled" friends of the cause, stick at rules and orders of the church? . . . Ought not the church to conform her laws, even *her fundamental laws,* to the cause? . . . What then is the authority of the church more than a cobweb? Leave your circuits and go lecturing for the cause! Turn your prayer-meetings, class-meetings, love-feasts, quarterly conferences, annual conferences, all, into cabals for the cause! And if any one tell you you neglect your work,—call him a fool! that you ought to be saving souls—what are souls! that you ought to be preaching Christ—who is Christ! you are the man of a "cause."

In Capers' view, support for revision of the rule on intemperance indicated the extent to which "partial views of truth" had gained ascendancy over "first principles," and the way in which, as a result, the temperance movement was becoming intemperate. The New York Conference proposals were "of the essence of radicalism and tending to sacrilege." Instead of changing the Rules of the church, Capers urged stricter enforcement of the existing prohibition.

Capers also opposed the New York Conference proposals on the ground that their adoption would pave the way for further, even more dangerous changes in the Rules of the church. Once they substituted human authority for that of Scripture, Methodists would find themselves "wide at sea, with the needle varying unknown degrees, and every man to calculate it as he likes," he warned. "If one arbitrary law, why not another? When you have loosed from the Bible, whither may you not be carried." Like Read, Capers invoked the specter of abolitionism to underscore his point. Nor was he indulging in mere speculation, for at the same time that the revision of the rule on intemperance was being debated, a proposal by the New England Conference to expel slaveholders from the church was under discussion. Capers emphasized that the same principle lay behind the proposals of the two northern conferences: the church was being made subordinate to a cause. Passage of either proposal jeopardized "the temple of Methodism," even "the whole fabric of Christianity."[28]

The General Rules regarding slavery and intemperance were not revised, but Capers' admonitions did not completely vanquish sentiment in favor of strengthening the prohibitions relating to ardent spirits. In the 1850s the southern church debated whether to amend the Discipline so as to exclude retailers and manufacturers from membership, and Methodist evangelicals continued to disagree on the proper role of the church in the temperance reformation and its relation to temperance societies. Some, like a writer in the *Methodist Quarterly Review*, echoed Clement Read in doubting the efficacy of and scriptural warrant for the total abstinence pledge and in contending that the church was a better temperance society than any devised by man. Others, pointing to the drunkards and moderate drinkers in the church and the class leaders and exhorters, even deacons and preachers, who distilled and sold ardent spirits, stressed the need for temperance societies. As one observed, "Where the Church fails to perform its functions properly, in the furtherance of the great principles of Christianity, other and more efficient means will be instituted, under the auspices of God himself, to accomplish what it should have done but failed to do." Still others stressed the way in which the temperance reformation aided the church. In an address entitled "The Connection between Temperance and Religion," W. A. McSwain described the temperance movement as "distinct from the Church in its lines and boundaries, but not in its *spirit* and *object*," which was "to preserve the sober, and reform the fallen." McSwain contended that the movement "prepares *for*, and leads persons *into*, the bosom of the Church." Likening Christianity to "a steam engine," and the cars drawn by it to the denominations, he placed the "temperance effort . . . in front of the great moral engine." It was the sweep, "designed to pick up the unfortunately fallen, save them from being crushed by the engine, and seat them in the cars, and let them ride in moral purity in this life, and into immortality and eternal life hereafter."[29]

The most prolonged debate over the role of the church in the temper-

28. *Southern Christian Advocate*, December 21, 1838, p. 106, October 11, 1839, p. 66, October 18, 1839, p. 70, November 22, 1839, p. 90, November 29, 1839, p. 93, January 3, 1840, p. 114, January 10, 1840, p. 118.

29. E. M. P., "The Church and Temperance Societies," *Methodist Quarterly Review*, IV (July, 1850), 377; Rev. W. A. McSwain, *The Connection Between Temperance and Religion: An Address, Delivered Before Head's Spring Temperance Society, Newberry District, S.C., August 4th, 1855* (Charleston, 1856), 5, 10. On the debate over amending the Discipline, see, for example, *Southern Christian Advocate*, April 19, 1850, p. 181, September 2, 1853, p. 53, January 27, 1854, p. 138, March 31, 1854, p. 175, May 5, 1854, p. 194.

ance reformation occurred among the Baptists. Associations regularly endorsed total abstinence and advised church members to join societies, and ministers offered public testimony in favor of the cause. Nevertheless, Baptists could not agree on the propriety of temperance churches, or "test churches" as they were called, which denied fellowship to persons who drank, manufactured, or sold ardent spirits. Numerous churches of this sort were formed in the 1830s, 1840s, and 1850s, but evangelicals remained divided on them. Throughout the antebellum period the columns of the *Religious Herald*, the *Christian Index*, and other Baptist newspapers reverberated with the debate. Abner Clopton, who maintained that the use of intoxicating beverages was a sin, believed that churches should make total abstinence a test of membership. William Sands, a layman and long time editor of the *Religious Herald*, initially favored test churches, noting, among other things, that Baptist churches already acted on the principle by requiring members to refrain from visiting the theater and the racecourse. In Sands's view, making abstinence from the use, manufacture, and sale of ardent spirits a test of church membership was not only necessary to "the welfare and prosperity" of the church; it was also the only way the church could eradicate intemperance. By the late 1830s, however, having seen the dissension caused by the test principle, Sands was advising that it be applied with great caution. "Friendly remonstrance and the salutary exercise of discipline" might prove as effective, or more effective, he wrote. This was particularly the case with those individuals who had become members of the church when dram-drinking was not disreputable. Such persons should be entreated and admonished to give up drinking, but he doubted the propriety of the church's calling them to account. The church could, however, refuse membership to applicants who were moderate drinkers. By such means it would be "gradually purified," ultimately becoming "what she was designed to be, a temperance church."[30]

Sands's doubts about applying the test principle were shared by a number of prominent Baptist evangelicals, including Jeremiah Jeter, Andrew Broaddus, Jr., and Henry Keeling. Although they were inclined to favor excluding manufacturers and retailers from church membership, they opposed making total abstinence a test of fellowship. Jeter, whose views were representative of this group, voiced the same concern for the au-

---

30. *Religious Herald*, January 31, 1856, p. 14, April 25, 1856, pp. 62–63, March 8, 1833, pp. 34–35, March 1, 1833, p. 31, March 10, 1837, p. 39, January 30, 1840, p. 19. For examples of test churches see *Southern Watchman and General Intelligencer*, January 20, 1837, p. 10, *Religious Herald*, January 28, 1847, p. 15.

thority of Scripture and the integrity of the church as some of the Presbyterians and Methodists we have discussed. The Bible did not condemn moderate drinking, he declared; to make total abstinence a test of church fellowship was not only unscriptural, but antiscriptural. Jeter also argued that making total abstinence a test of fellowship involved "a most mischievous principle of church discipline, that is, that the churches, or the majorities of churches, have the right to ordain terms of fellowship, at their own pleasure." The churches were "merely exponents of the laws of Christ," he asserted. When they established new terms of fellowship they invaded "God's authority." Such efforts at "human legislation" were working much "mischief" in the churches by causing disruption and controversy. Jeter also feared that, rather than diminishing the evil of intemperance, they might actually increase it. Like Sands, he favored efforts on the part of the church to persuade members to voluntarily abstain from drinking intoxicating liquors and the more rigorous enforcement of existing church discipline. In his own First Baptist Church, he noted, there was no rule forbidding the temperate use of ardent spirits, but very few of the two hundred male members used them.[31]

As we have seen, Jeter was not alone in fearing for the unity and integrity of the church. Other evangelicals, Presbyterian and Methodist as well as Baptist, shared his concern. The debates over wine, total abstinence, and the proper role of the church impelled a reconsideration of the relation between religion and the temperance reformation. Wanting to protect the church from the mischief which might result from its direct involvement in the temperance movement, evangelicals in the 1840s became more inclined to view the cause as a secular rather than a religious enterprise, to be prosecuted separately from the church.

Their new perspective did not diminish the evangelicals' enthusiasm for the temperance movement. Church bodies continued to express approbation, and ministers continued to be active in state and local temperance societies, though they seem to have yielded some of the leadership to laymen. Nevertheless, around 1837 the movement began to languish. Societies disbanded, reformed drunkards relapsed, and temperance papers failed for lack of subscribers. Evangelicals lamented the decline but could not agree on its causes. Some blamed ultraism in general and the wine controversy in particular. Others attributed it to a reliance on "half-way principles"—what was needed, they said, was a firm stand in favor of total

31. *Religious Herald*, March 4, 1847, p. 34, March 8, 1833, p. 35, March 15, 1833, p. 39, March 22, 1833, p. 43.

abstinence. Still others cited widespread apathy among the friends of the cause, and a few pointed to factors outside the movement itself such as the Panic of 1837 and the political excitement (and treating) of the campaign of 1840.[32]

Whatever the cause of the decline (probably all of the factors cited played a role), it coincided with the development among evangelicals of the new perspective on the temperance reformation and made them particularly receptive to methods that promised to rejuvenate the cause. It is not surprising, therefore, that they greeted the Washingtonian movement of the early 1840s with considerable enthusiasm. The society of reformed drunkards gave what the editor of the *Religious Herald* called "a new impulse" to the movement. Evangelicals who had once thought it futile to appeal to drunkards now noted the effectiveness of the Washingtonians in doing so. Thousands of individuals, moderate drinkers as well as drunkards, were induced to pledge themselves to total abstinence, new societies were founded, and old ones were revived. Some evangelicals, like Robert J. Breckinridge, complained that too much emphasis was placed on "the wonder-working power of *the pledge*" and too little on "the fact, well known to all the old workers in this field—that all pledges are very slender holds upon an unsanctified conscience." But even Breckinridge conceded that the merits of the movement outweighed its deficiencies. It offered "a new mode of concentrating an overwhelming public sentiment" which the cause badly needed, and he was confident that it would produce "instantaneous and tremendous results."[33]

Southern evangelicals also welcomed the Sons of Temperance when they began organizing in the 1840s, and for many of the same reasons that they supported the Washingtonians. Some ministers joined the organization and a few, like Charles Force Deems, Peter Doub, and John B. McFerrin, held office in it. Many others supported the Sons by attending their celebrations and delivering sermons or addresses on such occasions. No doubt numerous evangelicals found themselves in the position of Samuel S. Frierson, who wrote to James Henley Thornwell that he was considering joining the organization. He admitted that he was not yet completely convinced of its worth or "its power to perform what it promises." But, he observed, the town "was thoroughly under the dominion" of the Sons, and

32. See, for example, *ibid.*, March 3, 1837, pp. 34–35, March 31, 1842, p. 51, *Christian Index*, January 8, 1841, pp. 27–28, and Jeter, *Memoir of Clopton*, 189.
33. *Religious Herald*, March 31, 1842, p. 51; *Watchman of the South*, February 3, 1842, p. 94.

he had received "intimations from various quarters that his influence would be greatly enhanced if he joined them.[34] In such circumstances, if a clergy-man remained aloof, the sincerity of his interest in the temperance cause was likely to be questioned.

Expediency was not the only or even the most important reason why evangelicals supported the Sons of Temperance, though. Many regarded the order as the best and most efficient existing means of promoting temperance. Unlike other, short-lived temperance groups, the Sons endured; they had a "vitality" which others seemed to lack. Some evangelicals were bothered by the fact that the order was a secret society, but others dismissed the criticism as trivial. The editor of the *Christian Index* compared the Sons to the Masons, Odd Fellows, political clubs, and literary societies, all of which, he said, "have their secrets." In his view the Sons of Temperance were "the least objectionable of any of the 'Secret Societies'," because of the good they accomplished. Friends of the order contended that it conformed to "the known principles of the government of Divine Providence" and had "the sanction of the Almighty." The Sons, Charles Force Deems declared, were "co-laborers with Christ in . . . the moral emancipation of the world." Perhaps the most telling argument which evangelicals made in favor of the order was that it was able to do what the church could not. The church was not a sufficient temperance society, Deems insisted. "If it be so, how do you account for the thousands of church members, including some ministers, who manufacture and sell ardent spirits, or die notorious drunkards, in the bosom of the church?" Nor was the church able to reach thousands whom the Sons received as members. If many of them were not "regenerated, and made fit members of the church," at least the order made them "decent members of society." Deems did not doubt that some of those who joined the order actually became "more likely subjects of Gospel grace" once they had given up intoxicating beverages. Reinforcing Deems's argument that the Sons aided the work of regeneration, some of his fellow ministers described them as "the forerunners and harbingers" of revivals. Reporting on a camp meeting held near Campbelton, Georgia,

34. Deems, *Autobiography*, 111, 113–14, 117; Rev. Peter Doub, *Address Delivered Before the Grand Division of North Carolina, Sons of Temperance, at the October Session, 1852* (Raleigh, 1852); Fitzgerald, *John B. McFerrin*, 253; Sereno Taylor Diary (MS in Sereno Taylor Papers, Louisiana State University Archives), June 23 and 30, 1849; Stratton Diary, February 22, 1848, February 26, 1849, April 18, 1849; John Witherspoon to William McDowall, August 5, 1849 and February 20, 1852, in Witherspoon and McDowall Family Papers; *Religious Herald*, October 31, 1850, p. 174; *Southern Presbyterian*, April 26, 1850, p. 138; Samuel S. Frierson to James Henley Thornwell, September 26, 1848, in Thornwell Materials.

W. C. Matthews wrote that much of its success was "traceable to the Order of the Sons of Temperance in their efforts to prepare the way of the Lord; and many who were won to Christ here, were won to Temperance before, and thus placed in a position where the gospel could reach them."[35]

The extent to which evangelicals were willing to adopt new methods of reform is seen not only in their support of organizations like the Washingtonians and the Sons of Temperance but in their efforts to secure legislative action against manufacturers and vendors of intoxicating liquors. The reasons why they turned to "legal suasion" are not obscure. On the one hand, the decline of the temperance cause in the late 1830s convinced many evangelicals that moral suasion was inadequate. At the same time, once they began to view the temperance reformation as a secular enterprise, "worldly methods" seemed more appropriate. Certainly the example provided by prohibitory legislation enacted in some of the northern states also served as a stimulus to southern efforts. Some evangelicals called for stricter enforcement of the existing licensing laws and an end to the indiscriminate granting of licenses for the purpose of retailing liquor. Most went further in seeking the repeal of all license laws in order to stop the retailing of liquor and to eliminate the grog or dram shops, and the passage of a law prohibiting the sale and manufacture of intoxicating liquors. There was some support among evangelicals for an alternative approach in the form of a law giving voters of each county, town, or election district the right to decide whether they wished liquor to be sold in their area.

Evangelicals worked in various ways to secure legislative action. They delivered addresses and sermons in favor of it; they wrote memorials and signed and circulated petitions to the legislatures; they were active in conventions and societies formed to bring about prohibition. Religious newspapers carried editorials and correspondence in favor of ending the retail system and outlawing the manufacture of liquor, and some church bodies passed resolutions supporting such action.[36]

35. *Religious Herald*, August 28, 1851, p. 138; *Christian Index*, March 18, 1848, pp. 85–86; Doub, *Address*, 36; Charles F. Deems, *What It Has Done, and What It Must Do. An Address Delivered Before the Grand Division of the Order of the Sons of Temperance of North Carolina, in the Presbyterian Church, Raleigh, on the Evening of the 19th of October, 1847* (Philadelphia, 1847), 23, 24, 28; *Southern Christian Advocate*, October 25, 1850, p. 79.

36. See, for example, *Southern Christian Advocate*, January 11, 1839, p. 118, *Christian Index*, August 30, 1838, p. 534, April 11, 1839, pp. 232–33, Richmond *Christian Advocate*, May 6, 1847, p. 70, *Southern Presbyterian*, May 18, 1854, pp. 121–22, and *Religious Herald*, June 1, 1838, p. 87, March 1, 1839, p. 35, January 6, 1848, pp. 1–2, January 13, 1853, p. 6, January 26, 1854, p. 11, July 20, 1854, p. 110.

Whatever type of legislative action they sought, evangelicals explained its necessity by arguing that the sale and manufacture of liquor impeded the progress of the temperance cause and injured the community by causing poverty, disease, and death and by subverting religion and morality. Notwithstanding the success of the Washingtonians and Sons of Temperance, evangelicals seemed to feel that legal action was the only way of dealing decisively with drunkards as well as retailers and manufacturers. Moral suasion had been aimed primarily at the moderate drinker; legal suasion seemed to many evangelicals to offer a more comprehensive and therefore more effective means of finally eradicating intemperance from the land.[37]

Replying to those who insisted that temperance was "purely a moral subject," evangelicals observed that the legislature had already brought it within the sphere of its operations by establishing the license system. It had the power to repeal or modify what it had established, and the people had the right to urge such action. In an address delivered in the Baptist Church in Columbia, South Carolina, at the request of the Central Committee of the State Temperance Convention, James Henley Thornwell contended that the matter of temperance fell properly under the jurisdiction of law because the purpose of law was to define and protect the rights of men. Whatever interfered with "the rights of others & with the peace & prosperity of the community at large" fell within the province of legislation. On the basis of this reasoning Thornwell declared that he favored some type of law to punish and suppress drunkenness. John G. Bowman justified legal action on grounds similar to those offered by Thornwell. He began by citing the "cardinal objects" of civil government which were "the protection of men in the enjoyment of life, liberty, and the pursuit of happiness." The traffic in liquor subverted those objects. Therefore, Bowman declared, "it is not only the unquestionable right but the imperative duty of our legislators, as the conservators of public morals, to put an end to a traffic so destructive in its actual results—so dangerous in its tendency!" He assured his listeners that the restraint, even the prohibition of the liquor traffic "would involve no violation of human rights, nor any of the fundamental principles of good government." Bowman did not claim that temperance was purely a legal question, although he did believe that there was "a firm basis" for legal suppression of the liquor traffic "entirely independent of moral considerations." Like most evangelicals, he viewed

37. *Christian Index*, December 2, 1852, p. 194; *Religious Herald*, March 20, 1856, p. 43.

temperance as both a moral and a legal (or civic) question. "It involves considerations affecting our *rights as citizens*, and our *duty as moralists*," he observed. In the matter of temperance, as in certain other matters, "the ends of moral and civil government" coincided. Just as the moral and civil law coincided in outlawing murder and perjury, so they ought to concur in suppressing the liquor traffic.[38]

Some people defended the sale of liquor on the ground that it was not forbidden by the law of the land. To refute this claim, evangelicals resorted to the "higher law" argument. Thus, Wilton H. Broaddus contended that though retailers were "shielded by a human statute, they are not therefore shielded from the guilt of the deed; by no means; the law which grants this privilege may be in itself an immoral law; it was passed when we were under the delusion of supposing the moderate use of ardent spirits beneficial, but this belief is now known to be false." Broaddus concluded, "If a thing be in itself wrong, no human statute or license of man can make it right."[39] His argument was a variation on a theme that evangelicals had used before. During the 1820s and 1830s, they had argued against the notion that, because public opinion sanctioned drinking and because the Bible did not condemn moderate drinking, it was not immoral for Christians to drink. Broaddus' argument was more radical in challenging the civil law and, by extension, the social order.

Southern evangelicals did not invoke the higher law very frequently, probably because they feared its radical implications. (It was a favorite theme of the abolitionists.) But the idea of a higher law was at least implicit in the criticism they directed against the licensing system. The anti-retail campaign constituted a challenge, however mild and indirect, to the existing order. Although they concentrated most of their fire on retailers and manufacturers, by attacking the licensing system evangelicals implicitly criticized the magistrates who maintained it or refused to repeal it. Thus evangelicals were vulnerable to the charge of meddling in politics. Some of them dismissed that charge by claiming that temperance was both a moral and a legal question. Such an argument apparently satisfied a majority of the evangelicals, but it seems likely that many experienced an occasional twinge of uneasiness regarding their venture into the civil sphere. This may be why Thornwell was unwilling to commit himself in his ad-

38. *Christian Index*, December 2, 1852, p. 194; James Henley Thornwell, "Notes of an Address, delivered in the Baptist Church, Columbia, on the 4th July 1854" (MS in Thornwell Materials); [John G. Bowman], *Address to Legislators on Temperance* (Nashville, 1855), 16–17.
39. *Religious Herald*, December 8, 1842, p. 193.

dress to any particular legislative measure. The account of a debate at a meeting of the Georgia Baptist Association reveals even more vividly the way some evangelicals were torn between the desire for legal action and the fear of being charged with improper interference in politics:

> Brother Campbell offered a resolution approving the efforts of our fellow-citizens to abolish the present system of licensing retail grog-shops. . . .
>
> Brother Thornton wished a Committee on Temperance to be appointed. The present temperance movement was assuming a political aspect, and this body should be cautious about meddling with politics.
>
> Brother Mell hoped the resolution would not be passed, for many who would be opposed to any action of this Convention on this point, would dislike, by voting in the negative, to create the impression that they were opposed to the cause of temperance.
>
> Brother Campbell said, this is not a political movement. The members of this body are of different political parties, but they are agreed on this question. He read the minutes of the Convention which met with the Richland Creek Church, and showed that the resolutions then adopted were as strong as those which he now proposed.
>
> Brother Cabaniss was heartily in favor of the present antiliquor movement in this State, but he did not wish this Convention to express an opinion on this subject. The temperance organizations with which he was connected, thought it expedient to keep aloof from this question so far as it is a political matter, and he hoped the Georgia Baptist Convention would take a similar position.
>
> Brother Callaway was not afraid of the political bearing of this resolution. He was willing to press a moralizing influence into politics.
>
> Brother Wilson thought the only question to be considered was, is it right? If so, why need we care what politicians may say? . . .
>
> Brother Stillwell called attention to the difference between the present aspect of the temperance cause, and what it was when the Convention adopted the resolutions referred to by brother Campbell. We are narrowly watched, and we should exercise caution on a subject which may be used for making political capital. He proposed a substitute, expressing our gratitude to God for what had been done in the temperance cause, and for the prospect of further success.
>
> Brother Foster moved to lay this subject on the table, to allow members an opportunity to consider it more maturely. The motion prevailed.

When the matter was taken up later in the convention, Brother Campbell announced his willingness "to express his opinions in the Church conference, in Association, in Convention, at the ballot-box, or any where else, against this retail system." By using our influence against the liquor traffic, he declared, "we are promoting the cause of Christ." Brother Gresham, who called himself "an *ultra* man," said that he favored putting retailers in the penitentiary and urged the brethren to "bear a decided testimony against this evil." Despite such ringing statements in favor of the original motion, the convention did not endorse the antilicense movement. The resolution that was finally adopted simply prayed that God would remove from the land the influence arising from the use and sale of intoxicating drink.

Much of the uneasiness expressed by the delegates to the Georgia Baptist Convention was probably owing to their concern that the convention was acting improperly in attempting, as Brother Cooper put it, "to meddle with secular concerns." He declared that "as an individual he would go as far as any one for the suppression of the evil complained of, but as a Convention we were going beyond our sphere, in dictating to the civil authorities *how* to suppress an evil. We might complain of the evil," Cooper said, "but we ought to leave the Legislature to decide as to the manner of its suppression." Other associations and conferences were not so reluctant as the Georgia Baptist Convention to express their approbation of the anti-retail movement. A resolution passed by the Alabama Conference was representative: "Resolved, That this Conference heartily approve of the doings of the late Temperance Convention held at Selma, in which it was resolved to urge upon our next Legislature to pass a law empowering each county, town, and beat to determine whether ardent spirits shall be sold in them, and that we will use our influence to promote the Temperance Reform through this process."[40]

Beginning in the late 1830s evangelicals were increasingly inclined to merge their efforts in behalf of temperance with "men of the world." In so doing, they set aside their identity as "a peculiar people" and surrendered the exclusiveness that had characterized their activities in the early phase of the movement. For the most part the alliance between Christians and worldlings was harmonious, but by the mid-1840s some evangelicals, especially Presbyterians, began to have second thoughts. The alliance with the men of the world and the tendency to view the temperance reformation as a secular enterprise seemed to be leading Christians away from Christian principles to notions bordering on infidelity. Presbyterians were particularly apprehensive because temperance reformers seemed to place too much reliance on temperance societies, pledges, and legal action to promote moral reformation, instead of relying "solely and wholly on the gospel and the grace of God." Evangelicals of all three denominations worried that temperance organizations, especially the Sons of Temper-

40. *Christian Index*, May 5, 1853, p. 70; *Southern Christian Advocate*, January 14, 1853, p. 134.

ance, were becoming a substitute for and a distraction from religion. Thus, a writer in the *Religious Herald* argued that when a church member joined the Sons of Temperance or a similar order he in some measure rejected his covenant with God for the purpose of making a covenant with man. This was "trusting in an arm of flesh rather than the living God." Moreover, he observed, the Sons tended to draw church members away from their religious duties. The order might be a good one "for the world," but he doubted the propriety of Christians becoming members of such a society and joining "in fellowship with the world."[41]

Evangelicals also expressed apprehension about what one of them termed "the semi-infidelity" of many temperance lecturers and the fact that some of them seemed to go "out of their way to speak disparagingly of the Ministers and Institutions of the Church." Philip T. White, the most notorious of these, seems to have struck a particularly sensitive chord in condemning the churches for continuing to tolerate moderate drinking among members and thereby perpetuating the evils of intemperance.[42]

Besides worrying that the temperance reformation was being corrupted by infidel and antireligious notions, evangelicals were also disturbed by the failure to achieve prohibition and by the apparent increase of intemperance. By the mid-1850s a few of the southern states had passed local option laws, but none of them introduced anything like the Maine Law, which was the prototype of statewide prohibitory legislation. In 1856 the editor of the *Central Presbyterian* warned that intemperance was growing, "in some cases with fearful rapidity," and especially in the towns and cities. "Groggeries are springing up in every street, elegant saloons attract the young with sofas, mirrors, pictures, and glittering rows of decanters and glasses, the bar-rooms of hotels are located where drinking can be performed in the most private manner, and clubs, societies, wine-parties and social drinking in a variety of forms present the most seductive facilities for the formation of this habit." Even the churches were afflicted with "the poisonous malaria." The editor knew of one church that had recently suspended four members for drunkenness and, he observed, "this Church is not peculiar in this melancholy characteristic." He predicted that unless

41. Thomas Smyth, "The Principle of Secrecy and Secret Societies. Two Discourses," in *Complete Works*, V, 403; *Watchman and Observer*, September 25, 1845, p. 22; *Southern Christian Advocate*, December 2, 1858, p. 105; *Religious Herald*, September 5, 1844, p. 141.

42. *Christian Index*, July 4, 1850, p. 106; *Watchman and Observer*, August 25, 1853, p. 9; *Watchman of the South*, August 18, 1842, p. 206. On White see *Watchman and Observer*, February 9, 1854, p. 106, March 9, 1854, p. 122; *Religious Herald*, June 30, 1853, pp. 102–103.

they gave up their present bad habits, many other church members now in good standing would "in a few years fill a drunkard's grave."[43]

Given all these concerns, it is not surprising that some evangelicals in the 1850s began calling for a renewal of the kind of religious impulse and emphasis that had characterized the temperance movement in the 1820s and 1830s. This was the remedy urged by the editor of the *Central Presbyterian*. "Let the Temperance Reform begin again, as it did at first, in the Church, and be carried forward on Christian principles," he wrote. One effort in this direction was made by the ministers of the various denominations and their congregations in Richmond in 1850. They organized a temperance society on the principle of total abstinence and planned a series of sermons and addresses on the subject of temperance to be delivered consecutively in the different churches on Sunday afternoons. The editor of the *Watchman and Observer*, commenting on the new society, assured readers that it was not "prompted by any hostility to, or dissatisfaction with, the 'Sons of Temperance'." Nevertheless, it seems clear that the Richmond society was an attempt to correct what were regarded as deficiencies in the existing temperance movement. It was an effort to arrest the decline of the movement, which in turn was attributed to the loss of religious emphasis. The editor of the *Religious Herald* noted that one of the objects of the ministers in forming the society "was, to bring the influences of the church to bear more directly and forcibly on the Temperance reformation. It had been too much dissociated from religion, and therefore many ministers and members of the church, had for a few years past, manifested less interest in the subject, leaving the control of it measurably to other hands." The Richmond society also indicates a definite reaction against the campaign for legislative prohibition. "No other means are contemplated but such as are *moral*," explained the editor of the *Watchman and Observer*. "And with the blessing of God upon the enterprize, it will do far more to suppress the use and the sale of intoxicating drinks, than any number of statutory regulations however stringent, which the civil authorities may enact."[44]

The 1850s saw a reaction among evangelicals involved in the temper-

43. Ernest H. Cherrington, *The Evolution of Prohibition in the United States of America* (Westerville, Ohio, 1920), 111, 121, 128, 146, 149, 153; *Central Presbyterian*, December 20, 1856, p. 202.

44. *Central Presbyterian*, December 20, 1856, p. 202; *Watchman and Observer*, February 7, 1850, p. 102; *Religious Herald*, February 21, 1850, p. 30.

ance movement similar to the reaction against revivalism that occurred in the same decade. The apparent failure of legal action and the problems raised by secular organizations like the Sons of Temperance made evangelicals increasingly skeptical of the use of purely human means to eliminate intemperance. As with revivalism, so in the temperance movement they became more and more concerned about what they regarded as too great a reliance on "human instrumentality"—on pledges, associations, and legislation rather than on the church and God's grace. Nor is this surprising, considering that man's dependence on God was one of their cardinal beliefs. Evangelicals did not entirely repudiate temperance societies and their paraphernalia in the 1850s, but they emphasized that they were "purely a human work" and therefore capable of but limited success.[45] Intemperance would be eradicated, they insisted, not by human effort alone, but by the grace and power of God.

45. A Georgia Pastor, "The Church a Spiritual Power," *Southern Presbyterian Review*, XII (October, 1859), 488.

CHAPTER SIX

Benevolence and Reform

Southern evangelicals thought that the period in which they lived was unique. It was an era of "unexampled benevolence, when the whole Christian world is alive to the interests of the Redeemer's kingdom." Never before in the history of Christendom, not even in the age of the Apostles, had there been so much effort expended to spread the Gospel. Never before had there been so many charitable institutions, each pursuing a different object, yet all mingling "their streams in an ocean of common and extensive good." No wonder that evangelicals were prompted to call the nineteenth century "the age of benevolence."[1]

In explaining the "unparalleled exertions" that marked their century, southern evangelicals were quick to credit providence. "Doubtless, the hand of God is to be acknowledged in this thing," wrote the editor of the *Southern Evangelical Intelligencer*. He attributed "the liberality of the present age, and the various forms which it assumes, to that divine influence, which disposes the heart to abound in the exercises of benevolence." Moreover, many evangelicals contended that it was through benevolence that God intended "the glorious things foretold in the Bible" to be accomplished. Most did not anticipate the immediate dawning of "the Millennial glory," but they did believe that benevolent efforts would ultimately bring about the Kingdom of God on earth. For the editor of the *Southern Baptist and General Intelligencer*, at least, the kingdom seemed near enough for him to be able to describe it in detail:

1. *Southern Baptist and General Intelligencer*, November 25, 1836, p. 190; *Southern Evangelical Intelligencer*, May 8, 1819, p. 54; Charleston *Observer*, March 3, 1827, n.p.

In such a state there will be no necessity for bolts and bars, no City Guards, no Patrols, no Military array, keys will rust for the want of use, Jails and Court Houses dilapidated by time will not be repaired, or perhaps be fitted up for places of worship. The meaning of such words as stocks, pillory, penitentiary and gallows will be forgotten—larceny, burglary and other such terms may perhaps occasionally be seen on a scrap torn from some old law book, no longer worthy a place on the shelf of a library. Undisturbed by apprehensions of robbery or assassination, men will sleep securely during the hours appointed for rest; and passion and prejudice, unexcited by selfishness, will never interrupt the harmony of Society; and instead of conversing about some ruinous policy, or forming political clubs, each one will attend to the business assigned him and think no evil of his neighbor. Nations, too, unrestricted in their commerce, will be at peace, and governments will no longer tax for the support of standing armies, naval armaments and extensive fortifications. . . . Undivided in their political state or other social relations, they will be united in their religion. No more shall it be thought necessary to support in a small village, several distinct Churches, and though in a large city it may be expedient to have several places of worship, yet a sectarian name will be unknown, and the division of congregations will be a mere matter of convenience.[2]

But the millennium would not come without human effort. It was "to be brought about by the agency of man—by the prayers, labours, and the sacrifices of the Church." As with revivals, evangelicals emphasized that God worked through "means." Referring to the millennium, the editor of the *Southern Baptist and General Intelligencer* declared that "upon us devolves the principal responsibility of its accomplishment. We are the instruments of God to effect this work." To be sure, God could, if he wished, accomplish "this immense moral revolution, this new creation" by "his mere word or nod," but for reasons that remained obscure to man, he chose rather to accomplish it through human instrumentality. This is why evangelicals emphasized the necessity in professing Christians of "earnestness, diligence," and above all "activity." Benevolence was "a desire for the good of others accompanied by deeds suitable to our means and condition." It was both the result and proof of inward piety. Thus, the true Christian was what Jeremiah Jeter called "a useful Christian." His hallmark was not merely "good wishes, kind intentions, or even . . . earnest prayers," but effort. "It is by effort—direct, earnest, well applied effort—that Christian usefulness is secured," Jeter declared. Nor did the useful Christian "waste his sympathies on distant or irremediable woes." He aimed at "present, practicable, substantial usefulness," and the world was such that he

2. *Religious Herald*, May 30, 1828, p. 83; *Southern Evangelical Intelligencer*, May 8, 1819, p. 54; John Holt Rice to Dr. Thomas Chalmers, quoted in Thompson, *Presbyterians in the South*, I, 283; *Southern Baptist and General Intelligencer*, January 24, 1835, p. 54.

would never lack "the means or opportunity of usefulness." Jeter enumerated some of the ways in which the Christian might fulfill his duty to be "a laborer with Christ": "The sick may be visited and relieved. The wants of the poor may be supplied; the ignorant may be instructed in the way of salvation and of duty; the vicious may be reclaimed from their devious and dangerous wanderings; the weak may be strengthened in their combats with the world, the flesh and the devil; and the distressed may have the fountains of Gospel consolation opened to them."[3]

In promoting benevolent efforts, southern evangelicals aimed at what John L. Thomas has termed "moral reform," the reformation of character "through a revival of piety and morals in the individual." They were not primarily concerned with the reformation of society, though they believed that individual reformation would lead to the betterment of society and, eventually, to the millennium. What explains this individualistic orientation? Donald Mathews has argued that the evangelicals' confrontation with slavery was decisive. "The bold, often quixotic confrontation with slavery settled once and for all the problem of whether or not the moral struggle of the Christian would be carried on in the world of power and traditional relationships or within the mind and psychology of the individual believer. Already inclined to individualize the fight with evil, southern Evangelicals were forced by slavery to settle for a personal struggle to gain possible victories, rather than social warfare to achieve impossible dreams." As a result, Mathews observes, evangelicals failed to develop a "mature social ethic," that is, "a social ethic which could affect institutions and power relationships." Another explanation of southern individualism, which is compatible with Mathews' view, may be deduced from Thomas' theory of the origins of antebellum perfectionism. Thomas notes that in the North and Old Northwest, what started out as an impulse to moral reform turned into an impulse to social reform, regeneration of the social order by "immediate action" aimed at liberating individuals "from the restraints of institutions and precedent." Southern evangelicalism never underwent such a metamorphosis. One reason is that it was largely unaffected by the "theological revolution" which Thomas sees as the source of northern reform movements. Religious and secular utopianism, Unitarianism and tran-

3. Charleston *Observer*, May 26, 1827, p. 82; *Southern Baptist and General Intelligencer*, January 24, 1835, p. 54, October 9, 1835, p. 231; *Southern Christian Advocate*, May 7, 1847, p. 190; J. B. Jeter, *The Mirror; or, A Delineation of Different Classes of Christians, in a Series of Lectures. With an Introduction, by Rev. A. M. Poindexter* (New York, 1855), 61–63.

scendentalism, and the "new divinity"—what Thomas terms the "three major fronts" of the revolution—did not find acceptance in the South. Neither did the "romantic perfectionism" which grew out of the theological revolution and which fostered many of the isms and ultraist movements of the 1840s and 1850s in the North. Southern Presbyterians and Baptists remained essentially Calvinist, repudiating Arminian notions that were popular in the North and all that they implied regarding man's duty and ability to reform himself and the social order. Southern Methodists, though Arminian in theology, were no believers in the perfectibility of man and society as that notion was defined in the North. Millennialism also received less emphasis in southern evangelical thinking, for while southern evangelicals looked upon religious revivals and benevolent enterprises as "signs of the times" ushering in the Kingdom of God on earth, they did not infuse that belief with the urgency and optimism that many northern evangelicals did. It is hard to imagine a southern evangelical declaring, as Charles Grandison Finney did, that "if the church will do her duty, the millenium [sic] may come in this country in three years."[4]

Benevolent schemes in which southern evangelicals participated included Bible, tract, Sunday school, and home and foreign missionary societies, as well as efforts on behalf of prisoners, the insane, those who were deaf, dumb, and blind, seamen, the urban poor, and young men. Southern involvement in the "benevolent empire" was extensive and has been adequately treated in the denominational histories and in a recent dissertation.[5] Less attention has been paid to southern efforts on behalf of what were referred to as the "neglected classes," and it is these efforts with which I am concerned. Interestingly, evangelicals who engaged in such efforts sometimes operated on a more expansive conception of benevolence than that represented by the various benevolent societies. Although they did not go so far as to call for a restructuring of the social order, they did concern themselves with the temporal as well as the spiritual welfare of the people they sought to help.

The condition of the insane, deaf, dumb, or blind was not a major con-

4. John L. Thomas, "Romantic Reform in America, 1815–1865," *American Quarterly*, XVII (Winter, 1965), 658, 659; Donald G. Mathews, *Religion in the Old South* (Chicago, 1977), 65, 77–78; Sydney E. Ahlstrom, *A Religious History of the American People* (New Haven, 1972), 321–22, 420n, 438, 441–42; William G. McLoughlin, Jr., *Modern Revivalism: Charles Grandison Finney to Billy Graham* (New York, 1959), 105.

5. Bucke (ed.), *History of American Methodism*, I, 582–600; Thompson, *Presbyterians in the South*, I, 286–304, 453–54; Newman, *History of the Baptist Churches*, 419–42; John Wells Kuykendall, "'Southern Enterprize': The Work of National Evangelical Societies in the Antebellum South" (Ph.D. dissertation, Princeton University, 1975).

cern of southern evangelicals, but it did evoke some discussion and activity in the direction of securing better, more humane treatment for them. Besides urging that they be provided with religious instruction, evangelicals also advocated the establishment, at state expense, of asylums and institutes to provide proper care and education. Religious newspapers such as the *Watchman of the South*, the *Christian Index* and the *Southern Christian Advocate* regularly published reports regarding the various institutions, commended the efforts of reformers such as Dorothea Dix and Thomas Gallaudet, and emphasized the claims of the mentally and physically disabled on their fellow men. William S. Plumer, pastor of the First Presbyterian Church of Richmond and editor of the *Watchman of the South*, was among the most vocal evangelicals on the treatment of these people. He was one of the signers of a memorial to the legislature recommending establishment of an asylum for the education of the blind, deaf, and dumb, and he served as a member of the Board of Visitors for the Deaf, Dumb and Blind School at Staunton, Virginia.[6]

The penal system evoked somewhat more interest among southern evangelicals. On the one hand, they strongly opposed efforts toward the abolition of capital punishment. Such efforts, which were generally regarded as the work of Universalists and sentimentalists, were said to be responsible for the increase of crime. Southern evangelicals contended that the death penalty served as a deterrent and that it was recognized in "the statute book of the only infallible Lawgiver." Those who advocated its abolition were ignoring "divine authority" and allowing "the higher law sympathies [to] rule in its stead." If capital punishment were eliminated, declared the editor of the *Southern Christian Advocate*, "nothing but violence would be heard in our land."[7]

Opposition to the abolition of the death penalty did not preclude interest in other types of penal reform, however. The Baptist Henry Holcombe, for example, was an early and strenuous advocate of penal reform. He waged a concerted campaign to mitigate the severity of the Georgia penal

6. See, for example, "The Deaf and Dumb," *Virginia Evangelical and Literary Magazine*, VIII (April, 1825), 190, 193, *Religious Herald*, July 25, 1828, p. 116, *Southern Christian Advocate*, July 6, 1838, p. 9, June 17, 1842, p. 2, *Southern Presbyterian*, December 21, 1849, p. 66, April 10, 1851, p. 130, *Christian Index*, July 19, 1849, p. 230, and *Watchman of the South*, January 25, 1838, p. 88, October 17, 1839, p. 30, April 1, 1841, p. 126, March 14, 1844, p. 120, March 21, 1844, p. 122.

7. *Watchman of the South*, February 10, 1842, p. 98; *Southern Presbyterian*, May 22, 1851, p. 154; *Southern Christian Advocate*, August 27, 1847, p. 46. See also "The Divine Appointment and Obligation of Capital Punishment," *Southern Presbyterian Review*, I (December, 1847), 1–29.

code and to establish a penitentiary where criminals might be rehabilitated as well as punished. Later evangelicals, while not de-emphasizing the need for punishment, also stressed rehabilitation and reform of criminals. They viewed penitentiaries as places where criminals would not only receive suitable punishment for their crimes, but would also be subjected to appropriate moral and religious influences and would be encouraged to form "habits of industry" which would fit them to return to society. Therefore, they urged that programs of religious instruction and opportunity for religious worship be provided in jails and penitentiaries, and some served as chaplains in such institutions. Some southern evangelicals were outspoken opponents of the system of solitary confinement and labor that many northern evangelicals favored and that was being utilized at such institutions as Auburn Penitentiary in New York and Eastern Penitentiary in Pennsylvania. William Plumer, for example, denounced it as "the greatest monument of barbarism and cruelty" that he knew in America, "and the more likely to be perpetuated and be mischievous, because its friends evidently had very good intentions and were philanthropic in their feelings." Plumer maintained that the solitary system resulted in insanity, ill health, and death, and he expressed satisfaction that the Richmond penitentiary did not utilize it. At the same time, deploring "the cruelty practised on our own prisoners, in denying to them, while in their cells, all heat from fire," he appealed to the legislature to ameliorate their situation.[8]

Benjamin Gildersleeve, editor of the *Watchman and Observer*, was another evangelical who advocated certain types of penal reform, including the establishment of a house of refuge for juvenile offenders. In Gildersleeve's view, such an institution would prevent youths from being incarcerated in the penitentiary with older criminals, by whom they were apt to be corrupted. In a house of refuge, youthful delinquents could be educated in a trade and could be subjected to "healthful moral and religious influences." A further advantage was that youths would be unlikely to escape punishment, as they were presently doing because judges hesitated to impose a severe penalty (the penitentiary) and no lighter penalty (such as a house of refuge) existed. If there were such a place, Gildersleeve pre-

8. John B. Boles, "Henry Holcombe, A Southern Baptist Reformer in the Age of Jefferson," *Georgia Historical Quarterly*, LIV (Fall, 1970), 391–93; Stroupe, "Religious Press in the South Atlantic States," 8, 213, 213n; *Southern Presbyterian*, August 17, 1849, p. 206; Charleston *Observer*, August 23, 1834, p. 133; *Watchman and Observer*, June 5, 1851, p. 170; McIlwaine, *Memories*, 124; Leroy M. Lee, *The Life and Times of the Rev. Jesse Lee* (Richmond, 1848), 482–84; William M. Baker, *Life of Baker*, 201; *Watchman of the South*, December 8, 1842, p. 62.

dicted, "no injudicious sympathy would suffer any juvenile offender to go at large before he should be taught the lessons which such an Institution is designed to impart."[9]

On the eve of the Civil War, one of the editors of the *Central Presbyterian* suggested the formation of a prison association in Richmond similar to ones which existed in New York, Baltimore, and Philadelphia. Its purpose would be to provide religious instruction for inmates of the penitentiary and the jail, to offer advice and assistance to prisoners being detained for trial (some of them "month after month"), and perhaps most significant of all, to provide aid and guidance to discharged convicts. The editor explained the necessity of such assistance by observing that when a prisoner was released from the penitentiary "he is thrown upon the world with a lost character. And as a little money is given him when he is discharged, there are harpies ready to seize him, and lead him again into the same temptations, for yielding to which he has already suffered the penalty of the law." A prison association could act as a friend and adviser of ex-convicts, offering assistance including employment, "and separating them as much as possible, from their old haunts and their old associations." By such means, it "might restore many a one to society as a useful citizen, who would otherwise fall again—and be again returned to the prison from which he has escaped."[10]

Evangelical activities in the direction of prison reform were largely individual in nature. As the remarks of the *Central Presbyterian* editor suggest, southern clergymen were late in applying the principle of association to the subject. Their approach to another social problem, the condition of seamen, was quite different. As early as 1821–1822 Bethel Union Societies, in which evangelicals played an important role, were operating in Richmond and Charleston, and similar societies were formed in other southern port cities during the antebellum period. Religious newspapers regularly reported the proceedings of the American Seamen's Friend Society and urged readers to contribute to it.[11]

Initially, evangelicals concerned themselves with the religious and moral improvement of sailors, holding special prayer and Sabbath meetings,

9. *Watchman and Observer*, March 2, 1854, p. 118.
10. *Central Presbyterian*, March 17, 1860, p. 42.
11. "The Cause of Seamen," *Virginia Evangelical and Literary Magazine*, IV (December, 1821), 701; "Richmond Bethel Union Society," *Virginia Evangelical and Literary Magazine*, V (May, 1822), 277–79; *Southern Intelligencer*, April 20, 1822, p. 63, June 1, 1822, p. 87; *Wesleyan Journal*, January 28, 1826, p. 2; *Southern Christian Advocate*, March 30, 1838, p. 163; *Watchman and Observer*, March 10, 1853, p. 122.

erecting seamen's chapels, and distributing Bibles and tracts. They sought to convert sailors to Christianity, both for the sailors' own good and for the good that they in turn might do for the cause of religion. As the editor of the *Southern Christian Advocate* pointed out, "by the fact of their conversion, seamen become distributors of Bibles and Tracts to the ends of the earth; and preachers—virtually preachers, but without the title—telling in every place of the love of God, and the blessings bestowed by christianity." In urging the claims of these neglected men on their fellow citizens, evangelicals also pointed out that seamen were "an important and useful class of men." Commerce would cease without their labors. Moreover, evangelicals argued, if Christians continued to neglect them, not only commerce but the very safety of the community would be jeopardized. "Will not broils, and riots, and murders be likely to abound in our streets?" asked one Charleston evangelical. "Will not the expences of our City police, and the labors of our Criminal Courts be greatly increased? . . . in a community constituted like this, what evils might not a large body of abandoned seamen collected in a mob, and excited to phrenzy, accomplish?" He concluded his warning by noting "that sailors usually constitute a very material part of mobs in large commercial cities." To eliminate such a threat, seamen must be brought "under the mild, pure, and peaceable influence of the gospel. Human laws, a vigilant police, an inflexible magistracy, stocks and prisons, will not do it," he asserted. Only the religion of Jesus Christ could make seamen pious, temperate, and orderly.[12]

But even the Charleston minister conceded, and most evangelicals agreed, that religious instruction alone, however effective it might prove in comparison with laws and magistrates, was not enough to improve the lot of the seamen. No general and lasting reformation could be accomplished unless the various agencies of oppression, vice, and fraud which preyed upon them were eliminated. Therefore evangelicals waged unrelenting warfare against the "landsharks" who operated "those dens of intemperance and pollution, into which sailors are decoyed as soon as they reach the dock, and where . . . they are stupefied and intoxicated with liquor mingled with drugs, till they are fleeced and robbed of every cent of their hard earned wages, and then kicked out into the streets." Evangelicals also sought, through the Bethel and Seamen's Friend Societies, to have established special boarding houses, hospitals, savings banks, schools, and temperance societies for seamen. Such institutions were viewed as a

12. *Southern Christian Advocate*, July 1, 1837, p. 6, May 18, 1838, p. 191; *Southern Evangelical Intelligencer*, January 13, 1821, p. 334.

means of separating sailors from corrupting places and people and thereby making their regeneration possible. The emphasis on special churches, boarding houses, hospitals, and other facilities for sailors is significant. Evangelicals did not believe it necessary—or even desirable—to integrate seamen into the larger Christian community. As the editor of the *Central Presbyterian* explained, "It requires but a slight acquaintance with this class of men to learn that their habits and customs unfit them for mingling freely with the citizens of the ports they visit: and if they are to receive any benefit from religious teaching, it must be in assemblies of their own, and in houses of worship set apart especially for them."[13]

Another "neglected class" with which evangelicals were involved was the urban poor. In a variety of ways they sought to supplement the tax-financed relief for the needy that was administered by municipal authorities. Some churches dispensed aid to indigent members. Evangelicals frequently cooperated with or assisted charitable societies which aimed to supply the temporal needs of the poor. Many such societies were formed and administered by women, for example the Juvenile Female Benevolent Society of Columbia, South Carolina, which aided destitute female children by supplying clothing and education; the Fragment Society of Charleston, which provided clothing and Sunday school education to children of the poor; and the Dorcas Association of Richmond, which supplied clothing to poor children and sick persons. The last named society was an auxiliary of the Union Benevolent Society which was organized in 1836 by a group of women belonging to the several Protestant churches in the city. Its stated objective was "To ascertain the habits and circumstances of the poor, the causes of their poverty, to devise means for the improvement of their situation, to suggest plans of calling into existence their own endeavors to improve their condition, and afford the means of giving them increased effect." To accomplish this, it set up a system of visitation to poor families, established a depository of work for indigent females and sewing schools for young girls, and supplied money, fuel, blankets, and clothing to poor persons. Support for these projects came from collections taken in several churches, as well as donations by private individuals and money from the sale of clothing and work done at the depository. Each year the

13. *Southern Christian Advocate*, March 23, 1838, p. 159; *Southern Evangelical Intelligencer*, December 8, 1821, p. 285; *Southern Intelligencer*, February 16, 1822, p. 26, April 20, 1822, p. 63; Charleston *Observer*, March 15, 1828, p. 42; *Southern Christian Advocate*, September 9, 1837, p. 46, March 22, 1839, p. 159, May 18, 1838, p. 191; *Watchman and Observer*, January 6, 1853, p. 86; *Central Presbyterian*, November 27, 1858, p. 190 (misnumbered 180), August 27, 1859, p. 138.

society held a meeting at one of the Richmond churches, at which time an annual report was offered. Usually two or three ministers presided over the meeting and delivered addresses, though all the officers of the society were women. At the 1838 meeting, for example, William Plumer opened the session with prayer and he and Jeremiah Jeter were among four evangelicals who addressed the group.[14] No doubt clergymen rendered other, similar services to the society throughout the year.

Evangelicals justified the giving of aid to the poor on several gounds. First of all, they argued, charity was in accordance with Biblical pronouncements such as: "He that hath mercy on the poor, happy is he"; "Blessed is he that considereth the poor; the Lord will deliver him in time of trouble"; and "He, that hath pity upon the poor, lendeth unto the Lord; and that which he hath given, will he pay him again." Second, aiding the poor was an act of benevolence which was in turn a means by which God saw to the "care-taking of his people in things temporal." Thomas Markham explained the relation between providence and benevolence in a sermon delivered in the Presbyterian Church in Vicksburg, Mississippi. "Each man who with singleness of eye & earnestness of heart seeks first God's kingdom & righteousness is promised a due share of those things which are to support his life. His necessities will be cared for," Markham declared. Moreover, he continued, "the dependent & the destitute of Gods [*sic*] people have the promise of especial care. . . . God will raise up earthly helpers to relieve the destitute & distressed." Invoking the doctrine of stewardship, Markham exhorted the members of his congregation to "look around them & see if there are not those among them toward whom they may become God's helpers?" Reminding them of the hardships of an especially severe winter, he urged them "not [to] forget the needy & the poor," and to "go to them good Samaritans with food & coal & clothing."[15]

Although he argued that providence would ensure that men's "necessities" would be cared for, Markham was careful to point out that men's necessities differed as widely as men themselves differed, being determined by "education, association and position." The Bible was "no

14. "A Sketch of the Baptist Church in Savannah," *Georgia Analytical Repository*, I (November–December, 1802), 182–83; *Wesleyan Journal*, January 7, 1826, p. 3; *Southern Evangelical Intelligencer*, June 19, 1819, pp. 98–99, November 3, 1821, p. 215; *Watchman of the South*, November 16, 1837, p. 48, December 20, 1838, p. 67, November 21, 1839, p. 52, January 23, 1840, p. 86, January 7, 1841, p. 78, December 12, 1841, p. 58.

15. *Central Presbyterian*, January 10, 1857, p. 5; Thomas Railey Markham, "Matt. 6:33. God's Temporal Care of His People," (MS sermon dated Vicksburg, January 27, 1856, in Markham Papers).

agrarian no leveller no socialist." In common with other evangelicals, Markham did not believe that the Christian doctrine of benevolence threatened existing social and economic differences among men, which were, after all, ordained by God. Moreover, Markham also maintained (and without any apparent sense of contradiction) that benevolence fostered brotherhood among men of different classes and conditions. How it did so was explained by a writer in the *Presbyterial Critic* who observed that "God has made individuals dependent upon one another in the same political community; and by this mutual dependence maintains the feeling of brotherhood." The benevolent relationship was one expression of the mutual dependence of men. It fostered brotherhood by strengthening feelings of compassion and sympathy in the giver and of gratitude and humility in the recipient, "and, on the part of both, . . . the feeling of dependence upon God, and of thankfulness for His mercies." [16]

The theory of the *Critic* writer points to a third ground on which evangelicals justified relief to the poor. "The systematic relief of the poor diminishes the danger of revolution and agrarian violence," he declared. Benevolence, in exciting feelings of gratitude and humility in the poor, inhibited their "feelings of envy, jealousy, and even hostility" toward the rich. Antipathy toward the rich was likely to be especially strong in large cities where the contrast between the two classes was more striking, where the poor were more conscious of their strength and numbers, and where the "social affections" were weaker, "being thwarted by the selfish passions commonly vigorous in commercial places." [17]

While justifying the giving of relief to the poor, evangelicals insisted on the importance of distinguishing between the deserving and the nondeserving, the "virtuous" and the "vicious poor." The latter were the idle, dissolute, and improvident. To aid them was to encourage their vices as well as to waste benevolent funds. The former were "such as have been reduced by the unavoidable force of circumstances; such as have been the victims of misfortune; such as strive to the utmost of their ability, to render themselves independent of charity." Evangelicals agreed that Christians ought to be willing to help these persons who were trying to help themselves. Among this group of worthy poor were orphans, children of needy parents, and women. Evangelicals seem to have been especially concerned to help the latter, particularly those who attempted to make a liv-

16. Markham, "Matt. 6:33. God's Temporal Care of His People"; "The Relief of the Poor," *Presbyterial Critic*, II (January, 1856), p. 19.
17. "The Relief of the Poor," 18.

ing by sewing. Indeed, the plight of the needlewomen so moved the editors of the *Southern Christian Advocate* and the *Watchman of the South* that they not only recommended that aid be given them but also condemned their employers for not paying them sufficient compensation and suggested that some sort of legislative or municipal action to regulate their wages might be in order. Evangelicals also supported efforts of charitable societies (such as the Union Benevolent Society) which provided work for the needlewomen. Such programs to encourage industry, thrift and self-reliance were regarded by evangelicals as the most significant type of temporal relief that could be administered to the poor.[18]

"True charity," declared the editor of the *Central Presbyterian*, "is that which relieves genuine poverty, and discourages and removes the causes that lead to vicious poverty."[19] While evangelicals supported efforts to relieve poverty, they were even more concerned to prevent it in the first place, and they believed that mere temporal relief could not do this. (Indeed, indiscriminate, impulsive charity often seemed to encourage poverty.) What was needed, they said, was not just relief but regeneration of the poor. Their spiritual as well as their temporal needs must be addressed.

How to meet the spiritual needs of the poor was the subject of some debate among evangelicals. Some contended that pastors of existing churches should do more to encourage the poor to come to church (and to send their children to Sunday school), but most agreed that these ministers were already fully employed with their regular charges. Some advocated making churches more accessible to the poor, but the majority doubted the value of such an approach. As James O. Andrew pointed out, the vicious among the poor preferred to spend their Sabbaths in riot and dissipation, while those "who still maintain their hold on virtue . . . feel their poverty and degradation in a worldly point of view too sensibly to permit them readily to mingle with the people who are well dressed, and associate freely with respectable society." For these reasons, most evangelicals agreed that what was needed was a special ministry and special places of worship for the poor. As one evangelical declared, "The Gospel must be taken to them. They will not come to it." Therefore, "free churches" which charged no pew rent were erected. Bethel Church, for example, was built by the Methodists in the early nineteenth century for the poor, both black and white,

---

18. *Central Presbyterian*, January 10, 1857, p. 5; *Southern Christian Advocate*, February 7, 1840, p. 134, February 14, 1840, p. 138; *Watchman of the South*, August 29, 1839, p. 2; *Southern Evangelical Intelligencer*, November 18, 1820, p. 271.
19. *Central Presbyterian*, February 14, 1857, p. 26.

of Charleston; Bethel Presbyterian Church was established in the mid-1830s in the Rocketts section of Richmond; and the Medium Street Chapel was built in Columbia in 1856 to minister to "the poor, the abandoned, and the reckless." Also, "city missionaries" were employed by charitable, interdenominational, and church missionary societies to evangelize the poor. They visited families, the poorhouse, hospitals, and the jail, distributed tracts and Bibles, collected children into Sabbath schools, held prayer meetings and worship services. As early as the 1820s a city missionary was laboring in Charleston, supported by the Female Domestic Missionary Society of that city. In the 1830s the Richmond City Mission Society supported two missionaries; and the City Mission Sewing-Circle of the First Baptist Church also supported a city missionary in Richmond at various times during the antebellum period.[20]

By such means evangelicals sought to eliminate the causes of poverty as wells as to carry the Gospel to the poor. For they believed, as "Amicus" declared in the *Southern Evangelical Intelligencer*, that much of the poverty and distress among the lower orders of society was the result of "dissolute habits, intemperate living, idleness and vice." A large part of the work of the city missionary was to preach thrift and industry, to wage war on tippling houses and intemperance, and generally to inculcate middle class standards in the poor. "Amicus" was typical of evangelicals in predicting the results of such efforts. "If half the sums that are annually expended on poverty and disease, were laid out in the erection and support of a place or places of worship for the destitute, and in the establishment and maintenance of Sabbath schools, . . . the number of Paupers would be vastly diminished—poorhouses, and hospitals, and dispensaries would be far less necessary," he predicted.[21]

Another group of city people besides seamen and the poor attracted the attention of evangelicals. These were the young men of the city, especially those who had recently arrived in search of employment. Evangelicals,

20. *Southern Christian Advocate*, July 22, 1837, p. 18, July 16, 1847, p. 22; *Central Presbyterian*, May 17, 1856, p. 78. On Bethel Church and the Medium Street Chapel see *Southern Christian Advocate*, January 28, 1853, p. 143. August 28, 1856, p. 51; on Bethel Presbyterian Church see Blanton, *Making of a Downtown Church*, 34–35. On city missionaries see, for example, *Southern Evangelical Intelligencer*, August 11, 1821, pp. 146–47, *Religious Herald*, June 29, 1832, p. 99, December 18, 1856, p. 198, *Southern Christian Advocate*, April 20, 1855, p. 183, Joseph B. Stratton, *Memorial of a Quarter-Century's Pastorate. A Sermon Preached on the Sabbaths, Jan. 3d and 17th, 1869, in the Presbyterian Church, Natchez, Miss.* (Philadelphia, 1869), 40–41. Similar to the city missions were the "factory missions" established by Methodists in Georgia in the late 1840s and 1850s. See, for example, *Southern Christian Advocate*, May 4, 1849, p. 190, May 2, 1851, p. 190, June 12, 1856, p. 7.

21. *Southern Evangelical Intelligencer*, October 30, 1819, pp. 252–53.

who regarded cities as places of worldliness and temptation, worried that inexperienced youths who came to live in them, having left "the salutary restraints of the domestic circle," would be led astray. "Large cities are dangerous abodes for young men," declared the editor of the *Religious Herald.* "The theatre, the gambling-house, the saloons, restoratives and oyster-houses, not to speak of more disreputable haunts, are ever ready, seconded by the enticements of evil associates, to allure them within their precincts and cause them to err." Other evangelicals, such as Moses Drury Hoge, were equally concerned about the apparent purposelessness of many city youths. "The majority of young men in Richmond seem to have no aim in life," he wrote; "they do nothing, aspire to nothing. They saunter about in the most miserable vacuity, and actually seem too lazy to serve the devil with any briskness or spirit." The fact that young men were generally looked upon as the "rising generation" and "the chief hope of the country" only reinforced evangelicals' concern for their spiritual and moral condition.[22]

When, in the 1850s, Young Men's Christian Associations were formed in numerous southern cities and large towns, evangelicals gave them their enthusiastic support.[23] They had nothing but praise for the associations' programs, which included such things as libraries, reading rooms, literary societies, lectures, aid to youths in finding good boarding houses and situations in business, as well as Bible classes and prayer meetings. Such programs were admirably designed, evangelicals thought, to preserve young men from temptation by throwing around them "a salutary and christian influence." They not only afforded young men with a means of moral, religious, and intellectual improvement, but offered the opportunity for "usefully employing those hours which might otherwise be devoted to trifling, if not demoralizing pursuits." The fact that many YMCA members engaged in evangelistic and benevolent activities was an additional mark in their favor. Evangelicals helped to form associations and they also joined in their activities, teaching Bible classes, leading prayer meetings, or offering lectures. At an anniversary meeting of the YMCA in Richmond, in 1857, to cite just one example, at least five of the "reverend gentlemen" of the city participated, including Basil Manly, Jr., (Baptist) who

22. *Southern Presbyterian,* January 12, 1848, p. 82; *Religious Herald,* December 29, 1853, p. 207; Moses Drury Hoge to William Plumer, March 21, 1850, in Peyton Harrison Hoge, *Moses Drury Hoge,* 108.
23. For the history of the YMCA in the United States prior to the Civil War see C. Howard Hopkins, *History of the Y.M.C.A. in North America* (New York, 1951), 11–103.

opened the meeting with prayer, and John Edwards (Methodist) and Moses Drury Hoge (Presbyterian) who delivered impromptu addresses.[24]

The involvement of southern evangelicals in benevolent activities increased steadily throughout the antebellum period. By the 1840s such activities constituted a prominent part of the minister's schedule. Thus Moses Drury Hoge observed to his brother that the longer he lived in Richmond "the more engagements multiply around me." He had "so much business to transact for various boards, societies, etc.," that he had "scarcely any opportunity for the prosecution of those branches of knowledge which a minister should be well versed in." Like many other evangelicals, especially those residing in cities and large towns where benevolent activity was concentrated, Hoge felt compelled to choose "efficient action"—what Jeremiah Jeter called "usefulness"—over "the acquisition of profound and various learning."[25]

If some evangelicals complained that benevolent activity distracted ministers from certain endeavors, others worried that laymen were coming to think that benevolence was the whole of religion. Too many Christians, declared a writer in the *Christian Index*, mistook "the bustle of religious effort for the reality of religious character." "Zeal and liberality," rather than piety, were coming to be regarded as the test of true religion. Some evangelicals feared that the increasing emphasis on benevolent activity was fostering a "censorious" and self-righteous spirit on the part of Christians who were members of one or another benevolent society. They were too ready to condemn other Christians, including ministers, who were not as zealous as they in a particular cause. When this happened congregations divided, church members were alienated from their pastors, and the welfare of the church was impaired. Still other evangelicals warned that benevolent societies, which had originally been informed by a religious spirit, were becoming more worldly. This was so not only because worldlings were permitted to join them, but also because the societies were adopting worldly methods to advance their cause. What was once a "noble system of pious benevolence" was "degenerating into a low system of finance," charged "Timothy" writing in the *Wesleyan Journal*. Not the salva-

24. *Religious Herald*, December 29, 1853, p. 207, April 3, 1856, p. 50, December 25, 1856, p. 202; *Watchman and Observer*, August 23, 1855, n.p.; *Southern Presbyterian*, November 2, 1854, p. 10; Stratton Diary, April 24, November 27, December 18, 1854; *Central Presbyterian*, December 12, 1857, p. 198.

25. Moses Drury Hoge to his brother, 1848, in Peyton Harrison Hoge, *Moses Drury Hoge*, 79.

tion of souls but "money and devices for getting it" were becoming the primary concern. The editor of the *Southern Christian Advocate* expressed a similar view. Benevolence, he said, was becoming fashionable. "Fairs and Concerts, and Readings and Balls, for charitable purposes are the rage of the season." Not only New York, but "even our own conservative city of Charleston" was "infected by the mania." As proof he pointed to the forthcoming ball of the Ladies' Charitable Association. Churches were using similar means to raise money for their benevolent enterprises, including "Fancy Fairs where, very often, lotteries and raffles which encourage gambling are held." In the editor's opinion, benevolent societies and the church had "come too near to the world."[26]

The criticisms which evangelicals made regarding benevolent activities bear a certain resemblance to their criticisms of revivals and the temperance movement. Just as with revivalism and temperance, evangelicals worried that benevolence was coming to be regarded as the whole of religion, that it was being corrupted by "the world." Despite these criticisms, no general reaction against benevolence occurred among southern evangelicals. The criticisms which they made of benevolent activities were sporadic and infrequent. They never constituted a definite trend, and they never were sufficient to deter evangelicals from promoting benevolences of various kinds. Even the emergence of abolitionism and other types of radical reform did not cause southern evangelicals to abandon benevolence, though they did make a point of distinguishing between enterprises they regarded as worthy and those they regarded as foolish or evil. Included in the latter category were schemes which aimed at "supplant[ing] the church and subvert[ing] the government."[27] Southern evangelicals' involvement in local and regional benevolent activities actually increased during the antebellum period, and they continued to support many of the national benevolent societies headquartered in the North.

Just as southern evangelicals' benevolent schemes aimed primarily at a reformation of individual character, so did the reform movements which they championed. This is as true of the temperance movement, which has already been examined, as of other reform movements, such as Sabbatarianism and the antidueling crusade.

26. *Christian Index*, April 15, 1834, p. 58; *Watchman of the South*, February 4, 1839, p. 99; *Wesleyan Journal*, August 5, 1826, p. 2; *Southern Christian Advocate*, January 22, 1857, p. 134.
27. *Watchman of the South*, May 9, 1839, p. 146; Rev. Samuel J. Cassels, "The Relation of Justice to Benevolence in the Conduct of Society," *Southern Presbyterian Review*, VII (July, 1853), 91, 92, 94.

The desecration of the Sabbath was a problem which occupied southern evangelicals throughout the nineteenth century. Although the Bible enjoined "abstinence from all secular concern, and the due worship of God on the Sabbath day," evangelicals complained that too many Christians came to church only when it was convenient or when the weather was nice. Others attended church services but spent the rest of the day occupied with secular activities, indulging in "worldly conversation" or in "visiting and idle-gossiping." There was too much "travelling, loading of waggons, writing of letters on business, &c. &c." The conduct of young people was especially deplorable. A writer in the *Christian Monitor* described the way many of them spent Sunday afternoon:

In the first place, they make parties, either beforehand, or at church, to go somewhere else than home. . . . The party, having set off at a brisk, dashing gait, employ themselves either in a kind of soft, half-way courting chit-chat, or in criticising the sermon they have heard. . . . Next comes, either on the road, or at the place of rendezvous, a vast uproar of remarks on every body's appearance at church. . . . The discussion runs upon hats, cravats, coats, pantaloons, boots, canes, bonnets, corsetts, capes, veils, combs, curls, ear-bobs, and a hundred other things of equal importance. And here are materials sufficient, especially with the aid of some separate corner amusements, such as tender sheep-eye glances, wooing intreaties, and squeezing of hands, to pass away the longest Sunday afternoon that was ever seen in our climate.

The "old folks" shared some of the blame for this, he added. "Instead of reproving the giddy profaneness of God's Holy day, they retire to another room with all becoming gravity, either to pore over a chapter in the bible, or to lie down and go to sleep."[28]

While they criticized the Sabbath-day conduct of individual Christians, evangelicals were equally concerned about what they called "the more public violations" in which the community as a whole participated. Sunday markets operated in many towns and cities, and some newspapers published Sunday editions. The solemnity and quiet of the Sabbath were increasingly violated by funeral parades involving military or fire companies, or orders and lodges of various kinds. Some evangelicals pointed with alarm to efforts to introduce "Sunday entertainments" in their cities similar to those that were beginning to appear in certain northern cities and that had long disgraced New Orleans. Other evangelicals joined northern

28. *Religious Herald*, February 24, 1832, p. 26; *Southern Baptist and General Intelligencer*, October 21, 1835, p. 215; *Christian Index*, March 23, 1837, p. 180; *Christian Monitor*, December 21, 1816, p. 114.

Sabbatarians in protesting the transportation and processing of mail on Sunday.[29]

More than anything, however, the railroads drew the fire of evangelicals. They regularly condemned stockholders and managers of railroad companies for permitting cars to run on Sunday. Companies, the editor of the *Southern Presbyterian* declared, were no more exempt from the law of God than individuals. Investors and company officials who allowed cars to run on Sunday were setting the influence of their companies "against that righteousness which exalts a nation," and were fathering "that sin which is the reproach and ruin of any people." The editor observed that while many of the stockholders would scorn to labor on Sunday on their plantations or in their stores or shops, in "their corporate capacity" they did "that which is a far more public, and consequently vastly more flagrant violation of [the] sacred day." The editor of the *Southern Christian Advocate* agreed as to the "demoralizing tendencies" of railroads and other corporations. He termed them "bodies without souls" and declared that "railroads and steamboats (conducted as they are,) do more to corrupt the morals of the people, than could be done by all the deists, blacklegs and drunkards in the country, working by individual means. . . . If corporations, and the body politic, may perpetrate, by wholesale, the most shocking immoralities in the face of the sun, what shall restrain individuals from following their example?" If something were not done to prevent such "crying abuses," it would not be long before "men will come to consider religion and good morals as things of the gone-by time, drivelings of the nursery, idle superstitions, pitiful prejudices—things unfit for the age of improvement, the epoch of steam, the glorious reign of the gold-headed god." In the editor's mind at least, the demoralizing influence of the railroads raised questions about the wisdom of multiplying the number of corporations and extending internal improvements. "It is melancholy in the extreme," he wrote, "to think that we cannot advance in our schemes of profit and convenience, without retrograding as respects good morals."[30]

29. *Southern Watchman and General Intelligencer*, December 6, 1837, p. 196; *Watchman of the South*, July 24, 1845, pp. 194–95; *Southern Christian Advocate*, July 7, 1848, p. 19; *Central Presbyterian*, February 16, 1856, p. 26, January 16, 1858, p. 10; *Religious Herald*, January 8, 1830, p. 3. For a summary of the Sunday mails controversy see Anson Phelps Stokes, *Church and State in the United States* (3 vols.; New York, 1950), II, 12–20.

30. *Southern Presbyterian*, January 18, 1850, p. 82; *Southern Christian Advocate*, November 29, 1839, p. 94. See also "Sabbath Rail-Way Trains—To the Presbyterian Stockholders and Directors in Railway Companies," *Presbyterial Critic*, I (March, 1855), pp. 134–140; Charleston *Observer*, October 5, 1833, p. 157; *Watchman and Observer*, July 19, 1855, p. 202; *Southern Christian Advocate*, February 16, 1855, p. 145.

Evangelicals contended for the proper observance of the Sabbath on the ground that it was a "divine institution"—"a day consecrated by God to holy purposes"—and also on the ground that it was vital to the Republic. A republican government could be sustained only as long as the people were virtuous, but without religion there could be no morality. The editor of the *Southern Christian Advocate* explained the connection between perpetuation of the Republic and observance of the Sabbath as follows:

Without faith in Christ and the public worship of God, giving vigor and vitality to public morals, how could your laws be sustained? In the wide-sweeping ungodliness of your population how long would it require to bring up a rampant rowdyism, which would bid defiance to municipal rule, and fill the streets with violence and blood? A standing army with a dictator or emperor at its head, would soon be required to keep down the insolence of popular misrule. And thus would end the chapter of representative government.[31]

To promote the observance of the Sabbath, evangelicals used means similar to those employed in the temperance crusade. On the one hand, churches and church courts disciplined members for Sabbath-breaking, though church discipline on this matter, as on other matters, seems to have become increasingly less effective and more difficult to administer as the nineteenth century progressed. Church bodies also issued pastoral letters and passed resolutions condemning the desecration of the Sabbath and urged ministers to preach sermons on the subject. These means offered a way of dealing with individual church members who profaned the Lord's Day. However, many evangelicals came to feel that the root cause of Sabbath-breaking was a corrupt public opinion. To reform public opinion— and to persuade worldlings as well as professing Christians of the necessity of keeping the Sabbath holy—something more than churchly efforts was required. The answer lay in the voluntary association. Just as they advocated the formation of temperance, Bible, tract, and Sunday school societies, evangelicals supported the formation of special societies to promote the observance of the Sabbath. Some of these were auxiliaries of national organizations such as the General Union for Promoting the Observance of the Christian Sabbath or the American and Foreign Sabbath Union. Others, probably the great majority, were state or local societies. Ministers played a prominent if not a chief role in them. In the Charleston Society for the Due Observance of the Lord's Day, for example, although

31. *Southern Evangelical Intelligencer*, November 13, 1819, p. 270; *Southern Christian Advocate*, March 11, 1853, p. 166.

the president and vice-president were laymen, a number of clergymen held lesser offices. All of the societies solicited the cooperation of ministers, urging them to deliver sermons on the subject and to enlist the aid of church members in promoting observance of the Sabbath.[32]

Some of the societies relied on moral suasion to achieve their objective. They sought by exhortation and the good example of the members to persuade citizens, government officials, educators, and parents of the evil of Sabbath desecration and the need for reform. Other societies advocated legal suasion as well. The Charleston Society in 1843 sent a petition to the city council calling for the abolition of Sunday markets. Not all evangelicals favored such efforts to secure legislative action. They seemed to feel that a reformation of public opinion through moral suasion was a more legitimate enterprise and would be sufficient "to rescue the Sabbath from profanation and oblivion." Whether or not they favored direct efforts such as petitions to influence the civil authority, though, evangelicals generally agreed that the civil authority had a responsibility to see that the Sabbath was properly observed. A nation covenanted with God, as the United States was, was bound to obey his laws. Civil government, itself a divine institution, was bound to enforce them. Evangelicals believed in "the retributive justice of God toward communities as well as individuals," and they warned that if Americans persisted in profaning the Lord's Day, and if the government continued to permit it, God's wrath would soon be visited upon the nation.[33]

Because they placed considerable importance on the role of the civil authority in prohibiting desecration of the Sabbath and in promoting its proper observance, evangelicals were sharply critical of government officials who failed in this regard. In 1849 the Presbyterian General Assembly set aside a day of fasting and prayer "in view of the great desecration of the Sabbath by our National Legislature, and men high in political place and favor." In a sermon delivered on that day a Presbyterian minister pointed to the fact of Congress meeting on Sunday and accused the legislators of perverting "the christian purposes" of the founding fathers so "as to

32. Thompson, *Presbyterians in the South*, I, 307, 319; *Southern Intelligencer*, April 13, 1822, p. 58; Charleston *Observer*, March 15, 1828, p. 42, August 9, 1828, p. 126; *Christian Index*, April 14, 1836, p. 210; *Southern Watchman and General Intelligencer*, February 10, 1837, p. 21; *Southern Christian Advocate*, April 7, 1843, p. 168, April 14, 1843, p. 173.

33. *Religious Herald*, April 15, 1831, p. 58; *Southern Christian Advocate*, August 18, 1843, p. 38; *Southern Presbyterian*, January 18, 1850, p. 82, February 22, 1850, p. 102, March 24, 1860, n.p.; *Wesleyan Journal*, September 2, 1826, p. 3, June 17, 1826, p. 3, July 29, 1826, p. 2; *Southern Intelligencer*, June 29, 1822, p. 3; Charleston *Observer*, July 26, 1828, p. 118.

destroy our character as a christian nation, and make us but little better so far as religion is concerned, than pagans!" Though some people defended the legislature on the ground of religious liberty, the minister contended that "there is no principle of our constitution, framed as it was for a christian nation, which can, if properly understood, and rightly exercised, cause a violation of the requirements of the christian religion." Not the principles of government but "unchristian men who pervert our freedom" were responsible for the desecration of the Sabbath. "It is because men 'high in political place and favor' have not the christian principles which would lead them in private life, to observe our holy day, that their public legislation is not more conformed to the demands of our religion. O that our rulers were more God-fearing men!" Having reprimanded the Congress, the same minister went on to reproach President Taylor for having traveled on Sunday, "disturbing the religious assemblages" of two cities by arriving "amid the roar of cannon, the sound of martial music, and the parade and firing of the soldiery!" Significantly, the minister lamented the actions of the President and Congress for much the same reason that other evangelicals criticized the railroad companies—because, in violating the Sabbath, they exercised an evil influence on the community. If "public men" provided such an example, the minister asked, what could be expected of private citizens?[34]

The results of evangelical efforts to insure proper observance of the Lord's Day were inconclusive. Here and there Sabbatarians were successful in obtaining legislation prohibiting desecration of the Sabbath, and they influenced some newspapers and railroad and steamboat companies to cease operations on Sunday, though never for long. On the other hand, the movement to stop Sunday mails was a failure, and Sabbath-breaking by individual Christians seems to have increased or at least assumed new forms. In 1857, for example, the editor of the *Presbyterian Herald* noticed an increasing tendency on the part of church members to absent themselves from the second Sunday worship service.[35] By the late 1850s, while the number of church members was increasing, so were the number and

---

34. *Southern Presbyterian*, July 6, 1849, p. 182. For other criticism of "public men" by evangelicals see *Wesleyan Journal*, December 3, 1825, p. 3, December 9, 1826, p. 2, *Religious Herald*, April 15, 1831, p. 58, July 13, 1838, p. 110, *Southern Christian Advocate*, February 16, 1844, p. 141, Stroupe, "Religious Press in the South Atlantic States," 131.

35. See, for example, *Watchman of the South*, February 3, 1842, p. 94, *Southern Christian Advocate*, August 18, 1843, p. 38, *Christian Index*, August 9, 1855, p. 124, *Southern Presbyterian*, February 23, 1856, n.p., *Presbyterian Herald* quoted in Thompson, *Presbyterians in the South*, I, 461.

variety of activities and entertainments which distracted even professing Christians from strict observance of the Sabbath. Despite all efforts to eliminate them, violations of the Sabbath continued, proof of the ineluctable advance of worldliness and secularization in the Old South.

Like Sabbath-breaking, dueling was condemned by evangelicals as a violation of the law of God and therefore "a sin, a crime." It was also deemed a violation of human laws prohibiting murder. "Killing in a duel . . . is murder," declared a writer in the *Watchman of the South*, and "intent to kill in a duel is intent to commit murder, and it ought not to be allowed to bear any other name among all good men." Besides these fundamental arguments, evangelicals advanced others. Thomas Smyth, in a series of articles published in the *Southern Presbyterian*, defined dueling as "treason against . . . the State" because it represented "the assumption by private citizens of the supreme authority of the State, against the express prohibition of the State," in order to execute "the highest penalty of the State, not by public authority or for the public good, but for the gratification of private revenge or retaliation." In Smyth's view, dueling represented "the very *principle* of anarchy," for if it were lawful for one citizen to redress his wrongs in defiance of the law, then it was lawful for all citizens to do so. The result of such thinking, according to Smyth, was the prostration of all law and authority; society became "a band of desperadoes, and the bowie knife, the pistol and the sword, the only standards of right and wrong."[36]

Evangelicals employed a good deal of argumentation in an effort to discredit the code of honor which sustained dueling in the Old South.[37] They pronounced the code not only "immoral" but "false and vicious in its principles." Duelists claimed that the code was "necessary to the vindication of individual character and the maintenance of personal respect," but evangelicals contended that in fact duelists were slaves of the code, submitting to its "cruel" demands "no matter what obligations of prior and more sacred authority may be violated, nor what injury others may suffer, nor what guilt they themselves contract." The code of honor required its adherents to "surrender . . . the rights of private judgment, of the genial and truly ennobling sentiments of the human heart, and of even the legitimate means of self-defence." Even worse, it required men "to plant them-

36. *Southern Presbyterian*, January 3, 1857, n.p.; *Watchman of the South*, September 27, 1838, p. 18; Thomas Smyth, "Series of Articles on Duelling," [published in the *Southern Presbyterian*, January-May, 1857], in *Complete Works*, VII, 443–45.
37. The classic statement of the code as it applied to dueling is John Lyde Wilson, *The Code of Honor; or Rules for the Government of Principals and Seconds in Duelling* (Charleston, 1858).

selves in avowed hostility to the law of God, and in defiance of His displeasure." Evangelicals also criticized the code as "a higher law," a law above the constitution and statutes of the government. Those who upheld the code condemned William H. Seward and the abolitionists for invoking the "heresy" of the higher law, but they were no better than those they condemned, according to evangelicals. Disregard for the law, whether by abolitionists or duelists, set a bad example and weakened the force of all law.[38]

Another way that evangelicals attempted to discredit the code of honor was by disputing the notion that the duel was a test of courage and that to refuse a challenge branded one as a coward. A writer in the *Watchman and Observer* declared that participation in a duel did not prove a man "fearless of his fellows," but the contrary, for in most cases it was "fear of men"— "an indefinable dread of averted looks and cold salutations"—which drove the duelist to the field. Thus the duel proved cowardice, not courage. In a somewhat similar vein, Benjamin Mosby Smith contended that the code represented "false honor" rather than "true honor." True honor was the reward of "true virtue," of obedience to the laws of God and man. "Into the composition of true honor all qualities enter, which ally our nature with the divine," Smith asserted, but the qualities which composed false honor "ally us with devils." He insisted that, whereas "true honor cultivates the noble and ennobling elements of human character; false, degrades man to the savage in revenge, and the ruffian in malice."[39]

All of these arguments implied that dueling did not maintain or raise a man's stature, but degraded him—to the level of a slave, a coward, a savage, and a ruffian. There was a special pointedness to the evangelical contention that dueling degraded a man, for dueling was an activity which was generally regarded as the prerogative of the upper or gentry class in the Old South. In attacking dueling and the code of honor, evangelicals were criticizing the class of men associated with them. Thus, the editor of the *Southern Christian Advocate* lamented the fact that good Christian men should fear to call the crime of dueling "by its right name, because the false and imperious 'code of honor,' dictated by wealth and fashion and high blood, sanctions it."[40]

38. *Watchman of the South*, October 4, 1838, p. 22; *Southern Presbyterian*, January 3, 1857, n.p.; *Central Presbyterian*, November 8, 1856, p. 178, January 10, 1857, p. 5.
39. *Watchman and Observer*, February 3, 1848, p. 97; *Central Presbyterian*, July 4, 1857, p. 106. Smith, a professor at Union Theological Seminary, made the remarks in a sermon occasioned by the death of a young man in a duel at Hampden-Sydney College.
40. *Southern Christian Advocate*, October 9, 1856, p. 74.

Evangelicals especially protested the double standard which public opinion and even the courts enforced. Why should a "silken scoundrel" be allowed to commit murder, when a common villain was not? queried one. "Is the crime redeemed of its ignominious wickedness, because it is introduced with all the punctilios of etiquette, and perpetrated according to all the rules of polished gentility? Is the malice less bitter or the hate less rancorous, because enveloped in the observances of a well-bred society? Is the wound inflicted on the welfare of society by the destruction of its members, less dangerous because inflicted with a smile, and accompanied by a bow?" The editor of the *Central Presbyterian* voiced the same opinion, observing that the reason why laws against dueling were not enforced was because "the duel is patronized by the class whose wealth, influence, and position in society, enable them to escape conviction." If the code of honor were "adopted in theory and practice by those who are not 'gentlemen' in the technical sense, in which the *par excellence* men of honor use the word," they would doubtless be convicted. "But should *gentlemen* be the only men who can violate the laws with impunity?" he asked. He believed that dueling was especially reprehensible precisely because it was an activity of the upper class and set a "pernicious" example to the rest of society, especially the young.[41]

As with Sabbath-breaking, intemperance, and other evils, evangelicals believed that the root cause of dueling was a corrupt public opinion. Dueling occurred, the editor of the *Watchman and Observer* declared, because of "the false principles of honor which enter deeply into the whole structure of public sentiment." Not only the combatants but the whole community shared in "the blood guiltiness of such transactions." On the subject of dueling, he insisted, "the whole tone of public sentiment is radically subversive of the principles which the gospel of Christ inculcates." Because public opinion was corrupt, laws against dueling were not enforced. Officers of justice, following the views of the community, "wink[ed] at the offense," and juries, "intimidated by the frown of society," refused to convict. Thus, in the case of dueling, in contrast to Sabbath-breaking and intemperance, evangelicals did not think that the evil stemmed from a lack of prohibitory legislation. Indeed, most of the southern states had laws against dueling, but, evangelicals complained, they were "utterly unavailing," because they were nullified by a corrupt public sentiment. They noted, too, that "the direct tendency of such a state of affairs is to bring the laws into

41. *Watchman and Observer*, January 27, 1848, p. 95; *Central Presbyterian*, September 25, 1858, p. 154.

contempt and sully the purity of justice." Violation of dueling laws presaged the breakdown of all law. "If one law can be despised with impunity," explained G. C. in the *Watchman and Observer*, "others will soon be despised, and at length every restraint will become obsolete and useless, but that of a sentiment, mutable as caprice and easily corrupted."[42]

To reform public opinion on the subject of dueling, evangelicals prescribed the familiar remedies of moral suasion and voluntary association. Next to intemperance, according to Henry Smith Stroupe, the religious press gave most space to dueling. Evangelicals also urged secular newspapers to take a firm stand against the evil. Church bodies passed resolutions, and ministers preached sermons and wrote articles against it. Sometimes, as in Charleston in 1857, the ministers of various denominations within the city agreed to deliver antidueling sermons in each of their churches on the same Sunday, so as to speak "as with one voice against [the] murderous practice" and thereby exert a greater influence on the community as a whole. Evangelicals had no doubts about their duty in regard to dueling. As the editor of the *Southern Christian Advocate* declared, "the pulpit and the religious press is bound to protest against this flagrant disregard of God's law—to assert unequivocally the damning guilt of all such personal rencontres—and to ask in the name of righteousness and mercy, how these things can be allowed?"[43]

In cooperation with laymen, evangelicals also supported the formation of antidueling societies. The Charleston Anti-Duelling Society, founded in October, 1826, was perhaps the best known of these associations, but there were others, including one formed in Savannah in December, 1826, in Milledgeville, Georgia, and Natchez, Mississippi, in 1828, in Camden, South Carolina, in 1829, in New Orleans in 1834, and in Grahamville, South Carolina, in the mid-1850s. The object of the Charleston Society was "to lessen the frequency of duelling" in the city and to achieve "the gradual suppression of the practice." To do this, the society sought on the one hand to reform public opinion by publishing essays or papers against dueling, by seeking the cooperation of clergymen in North Carolina and

42. *Watchman and Observer*, June 19, 1851, p. 178; Charleston *Observer*, January 18, 1834, p. 10; *Watchman and Observer*, January 20, 1848, p. 89.
43. Stroupe, "Religious Press in the South Atlantic States," 117, 118, 122; *Watchman and Observer*, February 17, 1848, p. 105; Charleston *Observer*, January 27, 1827, n.p.; Flournoy, *Benjamin Mosby Smith*, 72; Peyton Harrison Hoge, *Moses Drury Hoge*, 94–95; J. R. Kendrick, *Dueling. A Sermon Preached at the First Baptist Church, Charleston, S.C., on Sunday Morning, August 7, 1853* (Charleston, 1853); *Southern Christian Advocate*, January 15, 1857, p. 130, October 9, 1856, p. 74.

Georgia in forming antidueling societies, and by urging educators to impress upon their pupils the evil nature of dueling. The society also sent a memorial to the state legislature "praying them to consider the propriety of further amending the law in relation to slanderous and opprobrious words, making them more extensively actionable than they are at present; or using any other constitutional or legal means which they may deem efficient, for the better removal of the causes which ordinarily lead to duels." Perhaps the most interesting feature of the Charleston Society was its Standing Committee, made up of thirteen members, which was "to endeavor by seasonable interposition, with the aid of the civil magistracy, or otherwise, as may seem to them most expedient, to prevent the occurrence of any contemplated or appointed duel of which they may have information, or well-founded apprehension." The Savannah society had a similar committee of seven. They were to use mediation to bring about an adjustment of differences, but if mediation failed, they were to have recourse to the law to prevent a hostile meeting. Although their interposition was not successful in every case, the Charleston and Savannah societies were credited with preventing several duels.[44]

Because public men, especially politicians, were often involved in duels, evangelicals advocated special measures for dealing with them. Government officials who violated the law deserved "the stern and indignant rebuke of every well-principled and law-abiding man." Some evangelicals favored legislation to prohibit duelists from serving in the state and national legislatures. Others urged Christians not to vote for candidates for public office who countenanced dueling or who had served as a principal or a second in a duel. Here evangelicals advised the same action against dueling politicians as against intemperate ones. "Christians! who believe in a life to come: upon you our Country calls for an interference," exhorted the editor of the *Southern Christian Advocate*. "Speak, and let public opinion

44. On the Charleston and Savannah societies see *Wesleyan Journal*, October 7, 1826, p. 2, October 14, 1826, p. 3, October 21, 1826, p. 3, Thomas Gamble, *Savannah Duels and Duellists, 1733–1877* (Savannah, 1923), 183–86, 190–200; John Hammond Moore (ed.), "The Abiel Abbot Journals: A Yankee Preacher in Charleston Society, 1818–1827," *South Carolina Historical Magazine* (October, 1967), 236. On the other societies see Stroupe, "Religious Press in the South Atlantic States," 120n, 121; John Hope Franklin, *The Militant South, 1800–1861* (Boston, 1968), 60, 274; Jack Kenny Williams, "The Code of Honor in Ante-Bellum South Carolina," *South Carolina Historical Magazine*, LIV (July, 1953), 123. Most evangelicals appear to have approved the formation of antidueling societies. For the view of one who opposed them—and for reasons similar to those which Clement Read and other Presbyterians offered against temperance societies—see "Duelling," *Southern Presbyterian Review*, X (April, 1857), 131–32, 134–36.

know what *Christian opinion* is on this subject. Speak, where your voice will
be most effective—at the *ballot box!*"[45]

The demand for action at the ballot box was especially pronounced during the late 1830s and early 1840s. Perhaps the fact that the temperance
crusade was beginning to move toward legal suasion at this time influenced
evangelicals to urge a political remedy for suppressing dueling. Perhaps,
too, evangelicals were by that time discouraged by the failure of moral
suasion. Indeed, by the mid-1850s, some of them were convinced that
dueling was not declining, but increasing. As political and sectional tensions intensified, so did the incidence of hostile meetings. By the eve of
the Civil War, evangelicals had been no more successful in suppressing
dueling than they had been in eliminating Sabbath-breaking or intemperance.

45. *Religious Herald*, March 18, 1852, p. 46, March 16, 1838, p. 42; *Wesleyan Journal*, October 7, 1826, p. 2, November 18, 1826, p. 3; Charleston *Observer*, July 2, 1836, p. 106; Cortland Victor Smith, "Church Organization as an Agency of Social Control," 90; *Southern Christian Advocate*, December 18, 1840, p. 106.

CHAPTER SEVEN

Slavery

I was born and brought up in the midst of slavery," wrote Jeremiah Jeter in his autobiography. He remembered that his early impressions of the peculiar institution were unfavorable, mainly because he believed that many masters in his part of Virginia treated their slaves with "great severity." As a result, Jeter recalled, "I grew up with a determination never to own a slave. Whether slavery was right or wrong, was a question which I did not consider. The management of slaves was attended with so much responsibility, care and trouble that I was resolved not to be involved in it. They could not be profitably governed without firm authority, and its exercise was uncongenial with my taste and habits." When he grew to manhood and moved to eastern Virginia, Jeter found that slaves in the region "were generally treated with greater care and lenity." This helped to modify his view somewhat, but it did not affect his resolve never to own a slave. Then he married a woman who held slaves, and he thereby became an owner. During their engagement, the couple had agreed that once they were married, in view of Jeter's determination, he could dispose of the slaves in whatever way he thought proper. When faced with "the practical question" of what to do with them, though, the young preacher found it difficult to arrive at an answer.

I could not free them, for the laws of the State forbade it. If they had not forbidden it, the slaves in my possession were in no condition to support themselves. It was simple cruelty to free a mother with dependent children. Observation, too, had satisfied me that the free negroes were, in general, in a worse condition than the slaves. The manumission of my slaves to remain in the State was not to be thought of. Should I send them to Liberia? Some of them were in a condition, but none of them desired, to go. If sent, they must be forced to leave their wives and children, belonging to other masters, to dwell in a strange land. Besides, to send away the men who could support themselves and aid in the support of others, and retain the women and children to be supported by my own labors, was stretching my humanity quite beyond its power of endurance. They could not go to Africa. The same insuperable difficulties lay in the way of sending them North. Parents and children, husbands and wives, must be separated, and many of them sent forth to certain starvation, unless they should find charitable hands to support them.

Jeter decided that the only practicable course of action "was to sell them or give them away." But the slaves themselves protested against this, and, wrote Jeter, "my heart revolted." Finally, "after careful inquiry" as to his duty in the matter, Jeter concluded "that it was not only allowable for me, but my solemn obligation, to hold and rule them, for their interest and for my own, as best I could. I should have been recreant to my duty and guilty of inhumanity if, under the circumstances, I had not assumed the relation of master and endeavored to meet the responsibilities arising from it."

At about the same time that Jeter was abandoning his resolution against slaveholding, the climate of opinion in Virginia regarding slavery was changing. In the 1820s, Jeter remembered, the "prevalent opinion" was "that the system imposed great responsibilities, and was fraught with many evils, economical, social, political, and moral, and should as soon as possible be abolished." But in the late 1820s and early 1830s, slavery became a subject of debate, first in the Virginia Constitutional Convention, then during the more prolonged controversy between abolitionists in the North and proslavery men in the South. "The more the matter was examined," Jeter recalled, "the more insuperable seemed the obstacles to the emancipation of the slaves." Under the impact of the controversy, Jeter wrote, "a marked change in public opinion on the subject of slavery took place at the South. All doubt as to the lawfulness of the institution, under existing circumstances, was banished from the public mind. Many went further still, and maintained that it was not only lawful, but eminently adapted to secure the highest intellectual and social development; and that it afforded the simplest and safest solution of the long-continued and frightful contest between capital and labor."

Jeter observed that his own views were affected by the controversy. He happened upon a pamphlet by the Reverend Thornton Stringfellow, a Virginia Baptist. It was "a plain, logical, and vigorous statement of the scriptural teaching on the subject." Upon reading it, Jeter was persuaded that the Bible was more favorable to slavery than he was. "Up to that time," he wrote, "I had believed that slavery in the South was allowable from the necessity of the case, and that its abolition would be fraught with more mischief than good." Stringfellow's argument "placed the subject in a new light." It suggested that slavery was not a "necessary evil," but was sanctioned by God himself. Moses had established slavery among the Israelites; Christ and the Apostles had not condemned slavery but had pointed out the duties of masters and slaves. Jeter conceded that this did not mean "that all slavery is right, or that it belongs to the most desirable condition of society," but it did prove that it was "allowable." And "under some circumstances," he observed, it might "belong to the best order of society that human, or even divine, wisdom can devise." For Jeter, as for many other antebellum southerners, the scriptural argument offered a "vindication of American slavery," which effectively suppressed any doubts they might have had regarding it.[1]

Jeter's account suggests some of the factors which helped to shape the southern evangelical view of slavery. The impact of the abolitionist crusade and the "discovery" of the scriptural argument in favor of slavery were crucial. Equally important was the experience of living in a slaveholding society and owning slaves. According to William Warren Sweet, by 1844 at least 200 Methodist itinerants owned 1,600 slaves, a thousand local preachers owned 10,000, and at least 25,000 Methodist laymen held more than 200,000 slaves. There are no figures on the number of Baptist and Presbyterian preachers who held slaves, but some idea of the extent of slaveholding among ministers may be gotten from Mary B. Putnam's estimate that in 1837 Baptists held 115,000 slaves and from James Smylie's claim, in 1849, that three-fourths of all Presbyterian church members in the South were slaveholders.[2]

Like Jeter, most evangelicals probably grew up without questioning the morality of slavery. Even those born in the North who later migrated to the South grew up at a time when most northerners were unconcerned about slavery and when even antislavery reformers believed that immediate emancipation would be impossible to effect or that it would be harmful to both blacks and whites alike. For both northern-born and native southern evangelicals, the experience of living among slaveholders and owning slaves had an important influence on their views of slavery. Ed-

---

1. Jeter, *Recollections*, 67–69, 71.
2. Sweet, *Methodism in American History*, 273; Mary Burnham Putnam, *The Baptists and Slavery, 1840–1845* (Ann Arbor, 1913), 13; Posey, *Presbyterian Church in the Old Southwest*, 76.

mund Botsford provides a good illustration of this. He told the Baptist historian, David Benedict, that when he arrived in Charleston in 1776 he had "had every prejudice I could have against slavery." After more than thirty years in the South, he was still "no advocate for it," but he admitted, "it does not appear to me in the same light as it did on my first arrival." Botsford seems to have moderated his view of slavery because he came to believe that most slaves had "no proper idea of the nature of freedom" and because he felt that they were not badly treated by their masters. Botsford himself had acquired a "few slaves," and he explained why. "Providence has cast my lot where slavery is introduced and practiced, under the sanction of the laws of the country," he wrote. "Servants I want; it is lawful for me to have them; but hired ones I cannot obtain, and therefore I have purchased some: I use them as servants; I feed them, clothe them, instruct them, &c;—as I cannot do as I would, I do as I can."[3]

Botsford was not the only southern evangelical who held slaves despite personally feeling that slaveholding was disagreeable. Discouraged by the shiftlessness and disobedience of his slaves, and disliking the task of disciplining them, Benjamin Mosby Smith complained, "Oh what trouble,—running sore, constant pressing weight, perpetual wearing, dripping, is this patriarchal institution!" No abolitionist knew "what a sore evil holding these people is," he declared. Smith was one of several evangelicals, including Sidney Bumpas, Drury Lacy, and John Witherspoon, who talked of leaving the South in order to be free of slavery, but while they remained in the South, they continued to hold slaves. Like Jeter, they did not see any alternative. In 1858, Smith wrote, "I am more and more perplexed about my negroes. I cannot just take them up and sell them though that would be clearly the best I could do for myself. I cannot free them. I cannot keep them with comfort. . . . Oh, that I could know just what is right." Even if they complained of the trouble attending slaveholding, most evangelicals considered themselves good and humane masters. They avoided as much as possible the buying and selling of slaves, and they tried not to separate families. They worked their slaves moderately (indeed, some, like James Henley Thornwell and Moses Waddel, were regarded by other slaveholders as too lenient). They fed and clothed them, and provided them with religious instruction. They believed that in holding slaves they

3. Edmund Botsford quoted in Annie Hughes Mallard, "Religious Work of South Carolina Baptists Among the Slaves From 1781 to 1830" (M.A. thesis, University of South Carolina, 1946), 16–17, and see also Botsford to the Reverend John M. Roberts, February 28, 1812, in Edmund Botsford Letters, Special Collections, Furman University Library, and Winans Autobiography, 122, 124.

were fulfilling a duty. It was for some an unpleasant duty, but a duty none-theless, and one which they felt they could not shirk. Mary Burruss Mc-Gehee, the daughter of a Methodist minister and planter of Wilkinson County, Mississippi, expressed the sense of duty which many evangelicals felt in a letter to her brother, John William F. Burruss. The young college student was debating whether to return home to take over the family plan-tation and had expressed some distaste for the business of slaveholding. She wrote,

Duty plainly calls you to the station of a "Planter" & a planter here, is the *Master of slaves*. God knows I would gladly make them *freemen*, if I could. But in his Provi-dence we are called to their care now & of course, their government. My theory is, as far as possible, treat them as you would *your children*, as such they need *restraint, discipline*; & however *painful*, & painful it is, what judicious parent will withhold *discipline* when its infliction is necessary. The subject of slavery, as it now stands, is the most perplexing that I have ever tried to think on; but to us who own slaves, one duty is clear, to govern them, make them happy if you can, as far as possible mitigate the evils of the lot & yet use every exertion to have the evil removed. . . . Think of this matter as a Man & a Christian. Turn it over in your mind and ask where is the remedy? Shall we groan under an acknowledged evil, while the rem-edy is in our power? Perhaps to you may be the honor of doing, of intigating [*sic*] something to be done in this matter that will bless others & ennoble yourself. Here is work for your philanthropy & a field for the exercise of that usefulness after which you pant. It is better than the fame of the Poet or the politician, for it par-takes of his character "who went about doing good." I wish you were at home now, I wish you were to begin your career *as a Man* to-day. But do not let any sickly sen-timentalism affect your notions of duty, or of life.[4]

It is important to recognize that the evangelicals' sense of duty regard-ing slaveholding was not in conflict with their religious profession. By the third decade of the nineteenth century all three denominations had re-treated from their earlier antislavery stand. The Methodists, for example, had been outspoken opponents of slavery in the 1780s and 1790s. The

4. Flournoy, *Benjamin Mosby Smith*, 59, 74; Bumpas Journal, August 15, 1844, p. 42, No-vember 25, 1844, p. 45; Drury Lacy to his wife, May 24, 1845, in Lacy Papers; John Wither-spoon to his daughter, January 14, 1836, and February 18, 1836, and to William D. Mc-Dowall, February 6, 1836, all in Witherspoon and McDowall Family Papers; Mary Burruss McGehee to John William F. Burruss, March 17, 1836, in John C. Burruss and Family Pa-pers, George M. Lester Collection, Louisiana State University Archives. On some evangeli-cals who owned slaves and the treatment they accorded them, see Robert Manson Myers (ed.), "Prologue," *The Children of Pride: A True Story of Georgia and the Civil War* (New Haven, 1972), 17, Fitzgerald, *John B. McFerrin*, 242, 270, Deems, *Autobiography*, 97–98, 110–11, Palmer, *Life and Letters of Thornwell*, 342–43, Waddel, *Memorials of Academic Life*, 119–20, and Adger, *My Life and Times*, 346–48.

Christmas Conference of 1784 had passed a series of stringent rules designed to eliminate slavery from the church, and in 1796 the General Conference had reiterated its concern regarding "the great evil of the African slavery which still exists in these United States." But the early nineteenth century conferences gradually compromised the church's stand against slavery, and in 1816, in a report that was adopted by the General Conference, the Committee on Slavery admitted that "under the present existing circumstances in relation to slavery, little can be done to abolish a practice so contrary to the principles of moral justice." The committee regarded the evil as "past remedy" because civil authorities in the South and West rendered emancipation "impracticable" and because it was "not in the power of the General Conference" to change the civil code. The next quadrennial conference took essentially the same stand as that adopted in 1816, and the slavery question ceased to be an important issue in General Conference until the renewal of controversy in the mid-1830s.[5]

Baptists had made their peace with slavery more than two decades earlier. South of Virginia, antislavery sentiment among Baptists was "virtually non-existent," even in the late eighteenth century. But in Virginia in 1790 the General Committee (forerunner of the Virginia Baptist State Convention) passed a resolution declaring slavery to be "a violent deprivation of the rights of nature, and inconsistent with a republican government," and recommending the use of "every legal measure, to extirpate the horrid evil from the land." The associations' response to the committee's action was generally unfavorable. As a result, in order to rid itself of the divisive question, in 1793 the General Committee voted to dismiss the subject of slavery on the ground that it belonged to the political rather than the religious authority. By the end of the eighteenth century slavery was firmly established among Virginia Baptists.[6]

The Presbyterian church adopted its strongest antislavery statement in 1818. In that year the General Assembly passed the following resolution by a unanimous vote:

We consider the voluntary enslaving of one part of the human race by another, as a gross violation of the most precious and sacred rights of human nature; as ut-

---

5. H. Shelton Smith, *In His Image, But . . . Racism in Southern Religion, 1780–1910* (Durham, 1972), 38–39, 45; Bucke (ed.), *History of American Methodism*, I, 255–56; Donald G. Mathews, *Slavery and Methodism: A Chapter in American Morality, 1780–1845* (Princeton, 1965), 51.

6. Smith, *In His Image*, 52–53; W. Harrison Daniel, "Virginia Baptists and the Negro in the Early Republic," *Virginia Magazine of History and Biography*, LXXX (January, 1972), 65–67.

terly inconsistent with the law of God . . . and as totally irreconcileable with the spirit and principles of the gospel of Christ. . . . it is manifestly the duty of all Christians who enjoy the light of the present day . . . to use their honest, earnest, and unwearied endeavours . . . as speedily as possible to efface this blot on our holy religion, and to obtain the complete abolition of slavery throughout Christendom, and if possible throughout the world.

In the years following the passage of this resolution, the General Assembly refused to take further action, despite appeals from antislavery elements within the church. In 1835, however, abolitionist delegates were numerous enough to get their petitions and memorials read before the assembly. The entire question of slavery was referred to a committee which was instructed to report at the next General Assembly. When the assembly met in 1836, the committee offered a report that was calculated to appease southern Presbyterians. It acknowledged that slavery was so entangled with state laws that no church body could interfere with it, and it conceded that any action on slavery by the General Assembly would divide the church. Therefore, the committee resolved, "it is not expedient for the Assembly to take any further order in relation to this subject." [7]

The churches' retreat from antislavery would not have been so important a factor in shaping the southern evangelical view had some ministers in the South continued to voice antislavery opinions. But in the early nineteenth century, preachers who opposed slavery either left the South or fell silent. David Barrow, Peter Cartwright, William Williamson, and James Hoge moved west. James Gilleland and George Bourne were disciplined by their presbyteries. Two Methodists who had formerly opposed slavery, Edward Dromgoole and Lewis Myers, became slaveholders themselves. Thus, by the 1820s there were virtually no ministers in the South who might have provided an antislavery example to the younger generation of evangelicals. To be sure, John Holt Rice and Robert Hall Morrison retained their antislavery convictions and held positions that would have enabled them to influence scores of would-be preachers. Rice was the head of Union Theological Seminary and Morrison became president of Davidson College. However, neither man was willing to express his convictions publicly or to use his influence to persuade others to oppose slavery. Morrison justified his silence on the ground that "the public mind of the Southern states" was not prepared for emancipation. Similarly, Rice argued that

7. Thompson, *Presbyterians in the South*, I, 331; Smith, *In His Image*, 81, 93. For a fuller discussion of the denominations' retreat from antislavery see Smith, *In His Image*, chaps. 1 and 2, and Mathews, *Religion in the Old South*, 66–80.

antislavery efforts within the church would "retard the march of public feeling in relation to slavery." More important, he contended that "direct exertions" on the part of the church would have no effect in abolishing slavery and would probably "injure religion." The membership of the church, he explained, was "three-fourths . . . *women and minors*, persons not acknowledged in law. What could they do? Of the remaining fourth, three out of four are people in moderate circumstances, without political influence." Given such a situation, Rice argued, "any direct movement of the church on the subject would . . . inevitably do harm rather than good."[8]

In the early 1830s, when the abolitionist movement was organizing in the North, other southern evangelicals, including many who did not share Rice's antipathy to slavery, echoed his concern regarding the effect of the slavery controversy on the church. The abolitionists, many of whom were members or ministers of evangelical churches and who based their argument against slavery on religious grounds, sought to convince southerners of the sinfulness of holding slaves and the duty of immediate emancipation. To accomplish this work of regeneration, they employed various types of moral suasion, such as sending agents into the southern states to preach the gospel of immediatism, publishing abolitionist newspapers, and mailing antislavery tracts and pamphlets to individuals in the South. Southern evangelicals reacted to the abolitionist campaign in much the same way that their fellow southerners did. They condemned abolitionist efforts as interference in a matter that was the exclusive concern of the South. They contended that emancipation would be ruinous for both blacks and whites. They predicted that if abolitionists persisted in their efforts, the result would be dissolution of the Union.[9]

In addition, evangelicals raised another, and to them more important, objection to the abolitionists. They argued that they endangered the cause of religion in the South. On the one hand, evangelicals maintained that

8. Robert B. Semple, *A History of the Rise and Progress of the Baptists in Virginia* (Richmond, 1894), 466; Peyton Harrison Hoge, *Moses Drury Hoge*, 16; Cartwright, *Autobiography*, 244–45; DesChamps, "Presbyterian Church in the South Atlantic States," 140–42; Mathews, *Slavery and Methodism*, 40, 45, 55–56; George G. Smith, *Life and Letters of Andrew*, 154–55; Robert Hall Morrison to James Morrison, February 12, 1820, in Morrison Papers; John Holt Rice to the Reverend Archibald Alexander, April 14, 1827, and to William Maxwell, February 24, 1827, both in Maxwell, *Memoir of Rice*, 312–13, 306–308.

9. See, for example, *Southern Baptist and General Intelligencer*, August 21, 1835, pp. 119–20, November 13, 1835, p. 324; Charleston *Observer*, October 3, 1835, p. 157, November 14, 1835, p. 180. On the emergence of abolitionism and the nature of its argument against slavery see Anne C. Loveland, "Evangelicalism and 'Immediate Emancipation' in American Antislavery Thought," *Journal of Southern History*, XXXII (May, 1966), 172–88.

the activities of the abolitionists made southerners suspicious of their ministers' views on slavery. While some evangelicals may have exaggerated this effect of abolitionism, their claim, nevertheless, had a basis in fact. Although, as we have seen, the three denominations had retreated from their earlier antislavery position by the 1820s, the Vesey and Turner insurrections of 1822 and 1831 had momentarily revived slaveholders' suspicions as to the subversive influence of religion. Investigations of both insurrections had revealed that many of the participants were church members and that some, notably Nat Turner, had claimed to have acted under religious inspiration. At the time of the proceedings against the Vesey plot, Richard Furman had expressed concern that "an idea of the Bible's teaching the doctrine of emancipation as necessary, and tending to make servants insubordinate to proper authority, has obtained access to any mind." It was to combat this view that Furman had written the *Exposition of the Views of the Baptists Relative to the Coloured Population in the United States*, in which he declared that slaveholding was justified "by the doctrine and example contained in Holy Writ; and is, therefore consistent with Christian uprightness, both in sentiment and conduct." [10]

Although evangelicals were successful in quieting the suspicions excited by the Vesey and Turner insurrections, they were not able to eliminate them completely. In the early 1830s abolitionists became increasingly vocal. Northern religious newspapers such as *Zion's Watchman*, the New York *Evangelist*, and the *Christian Watchman* began printing editorials and articles against slavery. In 1833 the American Anti-Slavery Society was formed and began promoting abolitionism by means of a program that was aimed particularly at the religious community in the North. Antislavery agents were sent out to discuss the sin of slavery and to engage people, especially ministers, in the cause, and auxiliary chapters were organized. The society also sought to infuse abolitionist principles into other evangelical societies, clerical assemblies, and the religious press. Then, in 1835, it began flooding the South with abolitionist pamphlets and newspapers, which were sent to community leaders, including many ministers. Southerners reacted with a vehemence and unanimity that surprised even abolitionists. And the old suspicions of southern ministers' views of slavery were revived. W. F. Broaddus wrote to the editor of the *Religious Herald* that as a

10. Richard Furman, *Exposition of the Views of the Baptists, Relative to the Coloured Population in the United States, in a Communication to the Governor of South Carolina* (Charleston, 1833), 13, 14. See also *Southern Intelligencer*, August 24, 1822, p. 135, Adger, *My Life and Times*, 53–55, and "The *Confessions* of Nat Turner," in Eric Foner (ed.), *Nat Turner* (Englewood Cliffs, 1971), 41–45, and see also 22–23, 26–27, 30, 33.

result of the pamphlet campaign, the impression prevailed in Virginia "that Christians, and especially *Ministers*, are favorable to the doctrines taught in the various abolition papers with which our land is at present inundated." As a result, he observed, "we are viewed with suspicion; and our efforts for the conversion of sinners, especially our labors for the conversion of our coloured population, are very materially hindered." Broaddus suggested that "Christian ministers and Christian communities throughout the South, for the sake of the cause of religion, and for the good of the slaves themselves, should most expressly discountenance [abolition] doctrines . . . and use all prudent measures to avoid being identified, even in appearance, with Northern Abolitionists."[11]

Not only were suspicions revived as a result of the abolitionist pamphlet campaign, but intimidation of ministers also occurred. In Cass County, Georgia, for example, a grand jury investigating the "intermeddling of the fanatics and vicious of the north, with the slave population of the south" expressed the fear that the church was becoming "the medium through which the premeditated mischief is to be accomplished," and recommended that citizens closely watch all missionaries, as well as tract, temperance, and Bible society agents. An antiabolition meeting in Clinton, Mississippi, in the summer of 1835 declared that slavery was not a moral or political evil, but "a blessing both to master and slave" and resolved "that the Clergy of the State of Mississippi be hereby recommended at once to take a stand upon this subject, and that their further silence in relation thereto, at this crisis, will in our opinion, be subject to serious censure."[12]

Evangelicals responded to suspicion and intimidation by protesting their innocence. Thus Andrew Broaddus wrote a letter to the Richmond *Whig*, which was also published in the *Religious Herald*, saying that he had been sent three abolitionist newspapers and that since a number of his acquaintances knew that he had received them, he wanted to make known what he had done with them. He explained that he had returned the papers to the publisher, along with a letter, which the newspapers printed in full, in which he declared that although he was "in principle, opposed to slavery, and consequently . . . in favor of emancipation," he was "utterly opposed to *your scheme of Abolition and Amalgamation*" and to abolitionist efforts to disseminate their publications among blacks in the South. Joseph Rock re-

11. Bertram Wyatt-Brown, *Lewis Tappan and the Evangelical War Against Slavery* (Cleveland, 1969), 113–14; *Religious Herald*, August 28, 1835, p. 135.
12. Donald Blake Touchstone, "Planters and Slave Religion in the Deep South" (Ph.D. dissertation, Tulane University, 1973), 68; [James G. Birney], *The American Churches, the Bulwarks of American Slavery. By an American* (London, 1840), 6–7.

sponded to the charge of being an abolitionist by writing a letter to the
Religious Herald. "I am no abolitionist," he insisted. "There need no suspicions rest on me. I am a native of Virginia, and her interests are mine. I
have never read a sentence in one of the abolition papers, nor do I remember to have seen one, and I protest against all their principles and
proceedings, so far as I know anything about them." Rock charged that
"indefinite allusions," such as the one made about him, were "exceedingly
unjust, yea criminal." Moreover, he observed, they tended "to injure the
character, and consequently, the usefulness of ministers, whose design is
alone, to preach the gospel." [13]

Individual ministers were not the only ones who felt obliged to defend
themselves during the crisis of 1835. In the late summer and fall of that
year various synods, presbyteries, associations, and conferences throughout the South issued statements insisting that the Bible sanctioned slavery,
condemning the interference of "mistaken philanthropists, and deluded
and mischievous fanatics," discountenancing the circulation of incendiary
literature, and deprecating the discussion of abolitionism in the pulpit.
That such statements were intended to neutralize prevailing prejudices
against southern ministers is seen in a statement which the Goshen Association of Louisa County, Virginia, appended to its resolutions: "This Association trusts, fellow citizens, that after this public expression of our sentiments, our ministering brethren will not be viewed with jealousy, and
that the gospel they preach will not be hindered." [14]

Suspicion and intimidation of southern ministers reached a peak in
1835 and then declined. There were isolated incidents in later years, but
evangelicals' readiness to denounce abolitionists seems to have persuaded
most southerners of their innocence.[15] The division of the Presbyterian
church in 1837–1838 and of the Baptist and Methodist churches in 1845
also helped eliminate suspicion by breaking the ecclesiastical link between
southern clergymen and abolitionists.

13. *Religious Herald*, September 11, 1835, p. 143, October 2, 1835, p. 154.
14. *Southern Baptist and General Intelligencer*, November 13, 1835, p. 324, October 30,
1856, p. 203, DesChamps, "Presbyterian Church in the South Atlantic States," 142–43, and
180; Touchstone, "Planters and Slave Religion," 67; Walter B. Posey, "The Baptists and Slavery in the Lower Mississippi Valley," *Journal of Negro History*, XLI (April, 1956), 126; *Religious Herald*, October 2, 1835, p. 154.
15. See, for example, *Southern Christian Advocate*, October 5, 1838, pp. 62–63, *Christian
Index*, August 13, 1840, pp. 527–29, August 9, 1844, n.p., *Religious Herald*, December 24,
1857, p. 203, DesChamps, "Presbyterian Church in the South Atlantic States," 142–43, and
Rev. W. H. Brisbane, *Speech of the Rev. W. H. Brisbane, Lately a Slaveholder in South Carolina:
Delivered Before the Female Anti-Slavery Society of Cincinnati, February 12, 1840* (Cincinnati,
1840), 6–7.

Nevertheless, evangelicals continued to denounce abolitionists. They had other reasons for resenting them, besides the fact that they had rendered their position in the South precarious, if only for a time. William Winans thought that by their "phrensied" actions abolitionists produced the opposite of what they claimed as their objective. "Abolitionists mistake grievously if they suppose they are thwarting the views, or injuring the *recognized* interests of the *Ultra* slave-holders—so far from it such an influence as they exert was nessary [*sic*] to secure those views and interests against the silent but powerful opposition that *was* accumulating in public opinion and in the moral feeling of the Southern community," he wrote to his cousin in Jamestown, Ohio. Winans insisted that the effect of northern abolitionism was "to impose new hardships on the slave, and to rivet more firmly the fetters of his bondage." Most southern evangelicals agreed with Winans in condemning the "misguided, and mistaken zeal" of the abolitionists. They blamed abolitionists for the enactment of prohibitions against teaching slaves to read and of restrictions of their religious privileges. In their view, abolitionists not only jeopardized the cause of religion among southern whites—by making them suspect their ministers—but among the blacks as well.[16]

Evangelicals also criticized abolitionists for creating dissension and strife in the churches. They complained that by denouncing slaveholding as a sin and declaring nonfellowship with slaveholders, and by excluding slaveholding ministers from their pulpits, abolitionists were not only acting in an "unChristian" way, but were impelling southerners in the direction of separation. As early as 1835, the Edgefield Baptist Association of South Carolina charged that northern Baptists were pursuing "a course tending to a dissolution of the connexion which has so happily subsisted between us of common sympathies, common counsels and common labours." The Presbyterian John Witherspoon wrote to a friend in North Carolina, "Why then bind together in one church under one constitution, men who can never agree? Are there not many hundred ministers in our church who will not exchange pulpits? And many more professing christians who think those that differ from them destitute of piety? Does not A. Tappan and others North think that no slaveholder can be a christian? (and is not this a pretty common opinion there—'tho a concealed one on the part of many for the sake of peace?) Now then I say, let these two hetrogenous [*sic*] par-

16. William Winans to the Reverend M. Winans, June 29, 1836, and to Abadiah Winans, November 14, 1835, both in Winans Collection; *Southern Baptist and General Intelligencer*, May 1, 1835, p. 278.

ties separate. . . . Let there be openly what there is secretly, two presbyterian churches in the United States." As Witherspoon's comment suggests, evangelicals came to advocate and work for separation, even though they held abolitionists ultimately responsible for it.[17]

Besides denouncing the conduct of abolitionists, evangelicals also attacked their doctrines. They criticized them for dealing with slavery as an "abstract question" instead of a practical one. Abolitionists talked as if the question were "whether slavery should be introduced, for the first time, into the community or not." If this were the question, Richard Fuller declared, he would "oppose such an act as firmly as any man," but the question was not whether to introduce slavery, but what to do about it as it existed in the southern states. To answer that question, evangelicals insisted, it was necessary to look at slavery "in its actual state, in all its bearings, ramifications, and connections." Its "practical effects," its bearing on "the interests of the community," must be considered. Arguing from this vantage point, evangelicals echoed other southern defenders of slavery in declaring that emancipation would be ruinous both to whites and blacks, especially the latter. Suppose slaveholders should agree to immediate emancipation, what would happen to the slaves? asked the editor of the *Southern Christian Advocate*. "Whither would they go? Who shall provide for the aged among them, and attend upon the sick? Who would be their protector in a country where slavery is recognized and established by law? It is obvious that their liberty would be held by a very precarious tenure; and they who are best acquainted with the negro character can judge what reason the master would have for expecting that they would provide for themselves, when left to their own discretion." To send the slaves north to the nonslaveholding states, the editor continued, would be inhumane. The physical, moral, and political condition of blacks in the free states was deplorable, as anyone who had traveled in the North could testify.[18]

Evangelicals also criticized abolitionists for operating on an abstract def-

17. *Religious Herald*, December 11, 1835, p. 192; *Southern Baptist and General Intelligencer*, October 30, 1835, p. 274; John Witherspoon to Shepard Kollock, July 14, 1832, quoted in Elwyn Allen Smith, "The Role of the South in the Presbyterian Schism of 1837–1838," *Church History*, XXIX (March, 1960), 62n. On the division of the Presbyterian, Methodist, and Baptist churches, see Smith, *In His Image*, chap. 2.

18. *Southern Christian Advocate*, April 14, 1843, p. 172; *Christian Index*, October 8, 1840, pp. 648–49; *Southern Baptist and General Intelligencer*, October 2, 1835, p. 313. For other comments on the deplorable condition of blacks in the North see *Religious Herald*, December 1, 1859, p. 190; *Watchman and Observer*, April 24, 1851, pp. 145–46, August 28, 1851, p. 10, April 21, 1853, p. 146; *Central Presbyterian*, May 22, 1858, p. 82; [Patrick Hues Mell], *Slavery. A Treatise, Showing that Slavery Is Neither a Moral, Political, nor Social Evil. By a Baptist Minister* (Penfield, Ga., 1844), 39–40.

inition of slavery. Moral philosophers in the North, such as William Ellery Channing, William Whewell, and Francis Wayland, defined slavery as "the property of man in man—as the destruction of all human and personal rights, the absorption of the humanity of one individual into the will and power of another." Southern evangelicals denied that this definition accurately described the relation between master and slave in the South. The abolitionist definition of slavery was "a fiction," a "spectre" produced by a "distempered imagination." Citing the Scottish philosopher, William Paley, evangelicals defined slavery as "the obligation to labour for another man . . . independently of the provisions of a contract." Under the terms of this definition, the master had a right, "not to the *man* but to his labour." Abolitionists assume that "the word 'property' involves a degradation to the state of a chattel," Richard Fuller observed. "This, however, is plainly fallacious. Property in my furniture is one thing; property in my horse is a very different thing; and property in a slave entirely distinct still. To treat the brute as I might a chair, would be barbarous; and to use the slave as I might the brute, would justly make me infamous in any society, and draw down the vengeance of laws, human and divine." Fuller concluded that "property in a slave is only a right to his service without his consent or contract." Moreover, he argued, the master's right to the slave's labor did not deprive the slave of the possibility of moral, intellectual, and religious cultivation and, therefore, did not deprive him of his "humanity." A man might be held in bondage, Fuller asserted, "and yet be treated in every respect as an immortal, intelligent, moral, fallen, ransomed being, yea and a Christian brother." He believed that most slaves in the South were treated in this way.[19]

The purpose of the foregoing arguments was to prove that slaveholding in the South was not immoral. They were an attempt to get abolitionists to stop talking about slavery in the abstract and to focus on slavery as it actually existed in the South. When it became clear that abolitionists were unwilling to do this, evangelicals looked for a way to meet them on their own ground, that is, to justify slavery in the abstract. They found it in the Bible.

The scriptural justification of slavery was nothing new in the 1830s. Americans had invoked it in eighteenth century debates and it had been

---

19. [James Henley Thornwell], "Slavery and the Religious Instruction of the Coloured Population," *Southern Presbyterian Review*, IV (July, 1850), 116–17, 121–22; *Religious Herald*, April 15, 1841, p. 57; Richard Fuller and Francis Wayland, *Domestic Slavery Considered as a Scriptural Institution: In a Correspondence Between the Rev. Richard Fuller, of Beaufort, S.C., and the Rev. Francis Wayland, of Providence, R.I.* (rev. ed.; New York, 1845), 9, 146, 163.

employed recently by Richard Furman in his 1823 *Exposition of the Views of the Baptists* and by advocates of slavery during the Virginia debate of 1830–1831. Nevertheless, some southern evangelicals seem to have viewed the scriptural argument as a discovery of the 1830s. A southern minister told David Benedict that the abolitionist attack had impelled evangelicals in the slaveholding states to "set about a new course of study" and to make "new and more thorough examinations of the Bible, to find where we stood; and soon we were surprised to discover from the sacred word how easily we can defend our cause, from the practice of the early Christians, among whom we believe slavery most certainly existed." Perhaps one of the reasons evangelicals viewed the scriptural argument as a discovery was because it seemed admirably suited to meet the specifically religious argument of the abolitionists. If, as evangelicals claimed, the Bible sanctioned slavery, then abolitionists who termed it a sin and who denied fellowship to slaveholders not only were wrong but were guilty of "impiety." Moreover, unlike the arguments of moral philosophers—"the testimony of men"—the scriptural argument came from a higher source. As the revealed word of God, it offered an "infallible rule of faith and practice."[20]

Evangelicals derived the scriptural argument from both the Old and New Testaments. They argued that slavery was divinely sanctioned since God had permitted the Hebrews to hold slaves. The Old Testament text they most often cited was Leviticus 25:44–46, which authorized the buying, selling, holding, and bequeathing of slaves as property. Evangelicals also pointed to the Fourth Commandment which enjoined the authority of the master over the servant, and the Tenth Commandment, in which the servant or slave was named as a type of property. Although the New Testament did not contain texts explicitly sanctioning slavery, evangelicals pointed out that neither Christ nor the Apostles ever condemned slavery and that on occasion they had indicated tacit approval of it. Evangelicals also emphasized that the Apostles had upheld the compatibility of slavery and Christianity by offering specific instructions regarding the duties of

20. David Brion Davis, *The Problem of Slavery in the Age of Revolution, 1770–1823* (Ithaca, 1975), 132, 226n, 531–32; Frederika Teute Schmidt and Barbara Ripel Wilhelm, "Early Proslavery Petitions in Virginia," *William and Mary Quarterly*, XXX (January, 1973), 133–46; Richard Furman, *Exposition of the Views of the Baptists*, 6–11; William Sumner Jenkins, *Pro-Slavery Thought in the Old South* (Chapel Hill, 1935), 73, 87, 105; Benedict, *Fifty Years Among the Baptists*, 55; Fuller and Wayland, *Domestic Slavery*, 146; Rev. James Smylie, *A Review of a Letter, From the Presbytery of Chillicothe, to the Presbytery of Mississippi, on the Subject of Slavery* (Woodville, Miss., 1836), 13–15.

masters and slaves and by allowing slaves and slaveholders to be members of the church. Thus, in the view of southern evangelicals, the Bible revealed conclusively and unequivocally that slavery was not a sin. "WHAT GOD SANCTIONED IN THE OLD TESTAMENT, AND PERMITTED IN THE NEW, CANNOT BE SIN," wrote Richard Fuller.[21]

Evangelicals also relied on Scripture in challenging the natural rights argument against slavery. Some, like Fuller, apparently accepted the notion that liberty was a natural right, but argued that it was no crime to deprive a man of it. Government, Fuller pointed out, was "the ordinance of God," and, "government is restraint; the very idea of government includes an abridgement of that personal freedom which a savage has in the forest, and a modification of it into political freedom, or civil rights and privileges." It followed that it was no crime for government "to discriminate between those whom it controls, in the distribution of civil privileges and political liberty." Every government had a right, according to Fuller, to pass laws and establish regulations to promote the good of the whole population. Slavery, along with other "civil institutions," interfered with the liberty of men, but that did not "make it necessarily and amid all circumstances a crime." Other evangelicals, such as a writer in the *Southern Presbyterian Review*, repudiated the state of nature and natural rights altogether. Describing "the Christian doctrine of the origin of government," he declared that "civil polity is not a device of man, but the institution of God, nor is it the result of a compact between the individuals of a multitude, each of whom was previously the sole master of himself. It is rather the offspring of the nature and providential circumstances which God has assigned to man." The idea of a state of nature was "pure fiction." Mankind had never "existed otherwise than in society and under government." The idea that "all men, simply from the fact of being *men*, have a natural right to an equal amount of property, or an equal share of personal liberty," was also mistaken. The right to property or liberty depended on the circumstances and relations in which men were placed, "under the providence of God." "Some are rulers, some subject; some are rich, some poor; some are fathers, some children; some are bond, some free. And if a man is justly and providentially a ruler, he has the rights of a father; and if a

21. Fuller and Wayland, *Domestic Slavery*, 170; see also *Southern Christian Advocate*, October 13, 1843, p. 71, Clarke, "Thomas Smyth," 116, Jeter, *Life of Witt*, 208. For more detailed accounts of the scriptural argument than I have given see Jenkins, *Pro-Slavery Thought*, 200–207; Smith, *In His Image*, 129–36.

slave, only the rights of a slave." Most evangelicals appear to have agreed with the writer that the rights of individuals differed according to their different circumstances and relations.[22]

If, as southern evangelicals contended, slavery was sanctioned by the word of God, then the role of the church in the slavery controversy was clear. Evangelicals opposed what they regarded as the scriptural view of the church's role to the unscriptural one advocated by the abolitionists. They argued that since slavery was not a sin, the church had no reason to take cognizance of it, and since it was established and protected by civil law, the church had no right to interfere with it. Virginia Baptists had taken this position as early as 1793 when the General Committee resolved that slavery was a political, not a moral or religious matter, and therefore not a proper subject for discussion. Southern Baptists generally adopted this position in the early nineteenth century, and were successful in getting the Baptist Triennial Convention of 1844 to support it by passing a resolution of neutrality on the slavery question. Presbyterian and Methodist evangelicals also insisted that the church had no right to interfere with the question of slavery. Thus the Synod of South Carolina and Georgia resolved in 1838 that it considered "Slavery as a civil institution, with which the General Assembly, has nothing to do, and over which it has no right to legislate." South Carolina Methodists expressed a similar view, as seen in the resolution of the South Carolina Conference of the same year: "Whereas, we hold that the subject of slavery in these U. States is not one proper for the action of the church, but is exclusively appropriate to the civil authorities—Therefore, *Resolved* that this conference will not intermeddle with it in any way, farther than to express our regret that it has ever been introduced in any form into any one of the judicatories of the church." When the first General Conference of the Methodist Episcopal Church, South, met in 1846, it reaffirmed the position most southern Methodists had taken before the schism, declaring, "We wholly disclaim any right, wish or intention to interfere with the civil and political relation between master and slave; we consider the subject as having been put beyond the legislation, by the General Government, as well as the control of ecclesiastical bodies; the only safe, scriptural, and prudent way for us, both as ministers and people, is wholly to refrain from agitating this subject."[23]

---

22. Fuller and Wayland, *Domestic Slavery*, 147–49; "The Christian Doctrine of Human Rights and Slavery," *Southern Presbyterian Review*, II (March, 1849), 569–73; Jenkins, *Pro-Slavery Thought*, 230–32.

23. Daniel, "Virginia Baptists and the Negro in the Early Republic," 67; Newman, *History*

In explaining the reasoning behind the doctrine of noninterference, evangelicals offered a variety of arguments. First, they pointed to the distinction between church and state, between "the things that are God's" and "the things which are Caesar's." The editor of the *Southern Christian Advocate* expressed the view of most evangelicals regarding the relation between church and state: "as a church, we have no authority from heaven or of men, to disturb or change the civil relations which are authorized and established by the State; we claim no right of interference with the duties and obligations which legitimately grow out of these relations. These all belong to the province of Caesar. The responsibility is on the shoulders of Caesar. There we let it rest."[24]

The doctrine of strict separation of church and state had long been a part of the Baptist tradition. But for Presbyterians and even more so for Methodists, adoption of the doctrine and its application to the slavery question involved an important shift in thinking. In the 1820s, for example, Presbyterians like John Holt Rice had opposed the church's interfering with slavery because they thought it would harm the church and retard the progress of abolition. What for Rice was a matter of expediency became, for most southern Presbyterians by the mid-1840s, a matter of principle. Most of them by that time accepted the doctrine of strict separation embodied in James Henley Thornwell's notion of the spirituality of the church.[25]

In the case of the Methodists, the shift of thinking was even more dramatic. As Donald Mathews has pointed out, prior to the 1830s they had not "scrupulously adhered to a strict theory of separation between the secular and the spiritual worlds." They had preached to state legislatures, had served as chaplains to Congress, had petitioned that body regarding the Indian trade, and had memorialized state legislatures for temperance legislation. Methodists had believed "that the Church should help to effect good laws for a better society." But under the impact of the slavery controversy, southern Methodists found it necessary to revise their notion of the relation between church and state. William Capers and William Wight-

of the Baptist Churches, 444–45; *Christian Index*, January 25, 1838, pp. 39–40; *Southern Christian Advocate*, February 2, 1838, pp. 130–31; Eugene Portlette Southall, "The Attitude of the Methodist Episcopal Church, South, Toward the Negro from 1844 to 1870," *Journal of Negro History*, XVI (October, 1931), 361.

24. *Southern Christian Advocate*, April 21, 1843, p. 176.

25. John Holt Rice to William Maxwell, February 24, 1827, and to the Reverend Archibald Alexander, April 14, 1827, both in Maxwell, *Memoir of Rice*, 306–308, 311–13; James Henley Thornwell to his wife, May 19, 1845, in Palmer, *Life and Letters of Thornwell*, 286.

man were the chief architects of the new view which said that the church should not interfere with the civil relations established by the state or "with the duties and obligations which legitimately grow out of these relations." Thus, Capers explained that slavery, "where it may exist as an element of the constitution of the country, an institution guaranteed by the laws—is not a moral evil." Wightman went even further and declared that Christians were obligated to support the civil authority. He contended that Christianity impelled its followers to obey the law for the sake of "social order, public peace, security and happiness." Methodists had always recognized this, Wightman contended. As proof he cited the fact that the early conferences had exempted from the antislavery rules those states where slavery was established by law. "Canon law," Wightman noted approvingly, had bowed "submissively as it ought to do, to civil." By the early 1840s the new view of the relation of church and state and of the church's relation to slavery was generally accepted by southern Methodists. Most of them probably agreed with the sentiment expressed in an article entitled "The Old Methodist Preachers vs. Slavery" in the *Southern Christian Advocate* for 1843. The author (probably Wightman) pointed to "the injudicious course" of the early preachers who had fought against slavery, and declared, "Give us *modern* Methodism . . . in preference a thousand times, to *old* Methodism with its 'itching palm' to touch civil relations, with its imprudent zeal to interfere with Caesar's prerogative." Interestingly enough, however, it was not until the late 1850s that southern Methodists brought the Discipline into line with the doctrine of noninterference. At the time of division, the southern church had taken over the General Rule of the Methodist Episcopal Church forbidding the "buying and selling of men, women, and children with an intention to enslave them." In 1846, 1850, and 1854, attempts were made in the General Conference to eliminate it, but not until 1858 were opponents successful in getting the conference to adopt the following resolution: "Whereas: The rule in the General Rules of the Methodist Episcopal Church, South, forbidding the 'buying and selling of men, women, and children with an intention to enslave them' is ambiguous in its phraseology, and liable to be construed as antagonistic to the institution of slavery, in regards to which the Church has no right to meddle, . . . therefore, the rule is declared expunged from the General Rules of the Church."[26]

26. Mathews, *Slavery and Methodism*, 238–39; *Southern Christian Advocate*, October 27, 1843, p. 78; Southall, "Attitude of the Methodist Episcopal Church, South, Toward the Negro," 367. One of the reasons for the delay in eliminating the rule on slavery was the desire not to alienate the border state conferences. See W. M. Wightman and Whiteford Smith,

Another argument which evangelicals offered to explain the doctrine of noninterference had to do with the nature and office of the church. They contended that "the root of the error of abolitionists" was that they made Christianity "a scheme of revolutions" and the church its agent. They made the chief objective of the church the reform of society rather than the saving of souls. James Henley Thornwell offered the most trenchant indictment of this point of view in a report on slavery to the Synod of South Carolina in 1851. Too many people, he feared, regarded the church as "a moral institute of universal good, whose business it is to wage war upon every form of human ill, whether social, civil, political or moral, and to patronize every expedient which a romantic benevolence may suggest as likely to contribute to human comfort, or to mitigate the inconveniences of life." Thornwell believed that "the healthful operations of the Church, in its own appropriate sphere" affected the interests of man and contributed to the "progress and prosperity of society," but he denied that "under the present dispensation of religion," God intended that "all ill shall be banished from this sublunary state, and earth be converted into a paradise, or that the proper end of the Church is the direct promotion of universal good." The church, Thornwell emphasized, "has no commission to construct society afresh, to adjust its elements in different proportions, to re-arrange the distribution of its classes, or to change the forms of its political constitutions. . . . The problems which the anomalies of our fallen state are continually forcing on philanthropy, the Church has no right directly to solve." This was because of the distinctive nature and office of the church. Its "doctrines, discipline and order" were not "the creatures of human will, deriving their authority and obligation from the consent of its members." Rather, the church had "a fixed and unalterable constitution" which was "the word of God." Thornwell explained:

It [the Church] is the kingdom of the Lord Jesus Christ. He is enthroned in it as a sovereign. It can hear no voice but His; obey no commands but His; pursue no ends but His. Its officers are His servants, bound to execute only His will. Its doctrines are His teachings, which He, as a prophet, has given from God; its discipline His law, which He as king has ordained. The power of the Church, accordingly, is only ministerial and declarative. The Bible, and the Bible alone, is her rule of faith and practice. She can announce only what it teaches; enjoin what it commands; prohibit what it condemns, and enforce her testimonies by spiritual sanctions. Beyond the Bible she can never go, and apart from the Bible she can never speak.[27]

The Discipline of the Methodist E. Church, South, in Regard to Slavery (Charleston, 1849).
27. *Southern Christian Advocate*, December 7, 1838, p. 98; [James Henley Thornwell], "Re-

While evangelicals contended that the church should not interfere with slavery as a civil institution, they did not believe that the church should have nothing at all to do with slavery. Slavery was not only a civil institution, it was also a personal relationship between master and slave. While the church had no right to meddle with the one, it had an obligation to enforce the commandments of the Bible regarding the other. The Bible taught that there were certain duties growing out of the master-slave relationship. Slaves were commanded to "obey in all things your masters," and masters were directed to give their slaves "that which is just and equal." Evangelicals believed that it was their duty, as ministers of the church, to enforce those duties. They did this mainly by exhortation in the form of sermons, essays, and catechisms describing the duties of masters and servants. (Although they insisted that the master-slave relationship was a proper subject for church discipline, what little information is available suggests that few cases involving slavery came before church judicatories.) The chief duty that evangelicals urged on masters was the religious instruction of their slaves. Probably one reason for the emphasis on religious instruction was that it was a duty that was regarded as entirely within the province of the church, as an institution whose "primary purpose [was] the holiness and salvation of the individual." Another reason was that in advocating religious instruction, the church did not deviate from its commission, by acting as an engine of social reform. "Our design in giving them [the slaves] the Gospel, is not to civilize them—not to change their social condition—not to exalt them into citizens or freemen—it is to save them," declared Thornwell. The church contemplates the slaves "only as sinners," he observed. "She sees them as the poor of the land, under the lawful dominion of their masters; and she says to these masters, in the name and by the authority of God, give them what justice, benevolence, humanity would demand even for a stranger, an enemy, a persecutor— give them the Gospel, without which life will be a curse." Thus, in Thornwell's view, and in the view of most evangelicals, the church's advocacy of religious instruction was entirely consistent with the doctrine of noninterference and with the church's commission to enforce the commandments of the Bible.[28]

---

port on Slavery," *Southern Presbyterian Review*, V (January, 1852), 381–82.

28. [Thornwell], "Report on Slavery," 384; *Southern Christian Advocate*, January 5, 1838, p. 114, April 21, 1843, p. 176; "Duties of Masters," *Southern Presbyterian Review*, VIII (October, 1854), 272; Fuller and Wayland, *Domestic Slavery*, 209; DesChamps, "Presbyterian Church

While evangelicals waged a concerted attack on the doctrines and methods of northern abolitionists, most of them were also at odds with fellow southerners who defended slavery as a positive good. Evangelicals contended that the Bible sanctioned slavery, but they did not generally argue that slavery was an ideal state that should be perpetual. Some, like James Henley Thornwell, contended that slavery had been introduced into the world and continued to exist because of man's sin, and that when the millennium arrived, slavery—along with poverty, sickness, disease, and death —would cease to exist. "If Adam had never sinned, and brought death into the world with all our woe, the bondage of man to man would never have been instituted; and when the effects of transgression shall have been purged from the earth, and the new heavens and the new earth, wherein dwelleth righteousness, given to the Saints, all bondage shall be abolished," he wrote. Other evangelicals believed that slavery would be abolished when Christianity had prepared slaves and masters for emancipation, or as a result of the working of divine power. None anticipated its early demise, however. William Winans, for example, thought that it would take fifty or one hundred years to prepare the slaves for "self-dependence and self government." And while Thornwell believed that the coming of the millennium would mean the end of slavery, he did not believe that the millennium was imminent.[29]

Most evangelicals disagreed with the positive good theory which held that slavery was "a great blessing" to both whites and blacks and, as John C. Calhoun argued, "the most safe and stable basis for free institutions in the world." Thornwell declared that the most strenuous defender of slavery should never forget that slavery was "inconsistent with a perfect state— that it is not absolutely good—a blessing." A writer in the *Southern Presbyterian Review* emphasized the difference between Christians and exponents of the positive good theory:

---

in the South Atlantic States," 63–65; Mathews, *Slavery and Methodism*, 82; Cortland Victor Smith, "Church Organization as an Agency of Social Control," 167; Posey, "Baptists and Slavery in the Lower Mississippi Valley," 123–24; Thompson, *Presbyterians in the South*, I, 317–18; [Thornwell], "Slavery and the Religious Instruction of the Coloured Population," 139.

29. Fuller and Wayland, *Domestic Slavery*, 157, 135; Robert Lewis Dabney to G. Woodson Payne, January 22, 1840, in Thomas Cary Johnson, *Life and Letters of Dabney*, 68; [Thornwell], "Slavery and the Religious Instruction of the Coloured Population," 127; Robert Hall Morrison to James Morrison, February 12, 1820, in Morrison Papers; *Southern Christian Advocate*, October 13, 1843, p. 71; Willie Grier Todd, "The Slavery Issue and the Organization of a Southern Baptist Convention," (Ph.D. dissertation, University of North Carolina, 1964), 61; Jenkins, *Pro-Slavery Thought*, 217–18; William Winans to the Reverend D. DeVinne, March 31, 1852, in Winans Collection.

Southern politicians say, "Slavery is a positive blessing." In the fear of God we, and all other Christians that we know of, say the same thing, *absolutely*, as respects the negro. As respects the whole community of whites and blacks, whom an unscrutable [*sic*] but wise Providence has joined here together, we also say the same thing, *as comparing Slavery with Emancipation*. But as comparing the present advantages of our white population with what they might have been, had not the negro been introduced, the Christian people of the South have never yet said that Slavery is a positive blessing, and we know not that they will ever be driven by all the fierceness of the attacks upon them to say so.

Evangelicals insisted that unlike southern ultraists they did not defend slavery in the abstract, but only Negro slavery as it existed in the South. They viewed slavery as the only possible form of social organization for "two distinct races—who can never amalgamate—and one of which must be master." Slavery was "not a beautiful thing, a thing to be espoused and idolized, but the best attainable thing, in this country, for the negro."[30]

Evangelicals also opposed the movement that developed in the 1850s to reopen the African slave trade. Distinguishing between slavery and the slave trade, they argued that while the Bible sanctioned the one, it condemned the other "as sinful in itself, contrary to the law of God." The African trade, declared J. L. Wilson in the *Southern Presbyterian Review*, "never has been, and cannot be, carried on to any considerable extent, except by fraud, by violence, and by perpetual warfare and bloodshed." The South could not support a revival of the trade "without dishonoring herself, and inflicting renewed and incalculable misery and wretchedness upon the inhabitants of Africa." Other evangelicals offered additional and, to them, equally compelling reasons for opposing the reopening of the trade. Some pointed to the dangerous situation that would be created if "a mass of barbarians—vicious, unruly, discontented, accustomed to the rule of force, speaking a different language, and never having learned to regard their master as their friend"—were introduced into the southern states. Others, for example Thornwell, believed that the importation of African slaves would subvert the "domestic and patriarchal" system of slavery that existed in the South and, he implied, thereby undermine the evangelical justification of it. Finally, most evangelicals agreed in condemning the pro-

---

30. John C. Calhoun quoted in Jenkins, *Pro-Slavery Thought*, 80–81; [Thornwell], "Slavery and the Religious Instruction of the Coloured Population," 127; "Christian Doctrine of Human Rights and Slavery," 579; *Central Presbyterian*, May 30, 1857, p. 85; *Religious Herald*, November 19, 1840, p. 187.

posal to reopen the African trade because it divided southerners, thereby weakening their common and rightful cause, the defense of slavery.[31]

One reason why evangelicals did not espouse the positive good theory was because they recognized certain abuses connected with slavery. However, in opposition to the abolitionists, they contended that the abuses were not inseparable from the system of slavery. Like any other lawful institution, slavery was susceptible of abuses. But, evangelicals insisted, the abuses did not make slavery a sin any more than harsh and cruel treatment of apprentices made apprenticeship a sin. Among the various abuses of slavery evangelicals included excessive labor, extreme punishment, withholding of necessary food and clothing, separation of families, and the denial of religious instruction and the opportunity for religious worship. They argued that Christians had a responsibility to eliminate such abuses. Not abolition, therefore, but the "amelioration" of slavery was the proper course of action for southern Christians. Indeed, evangelicals insisted that application of the biblical argument to southern slavery depended on the removal of abuses and the recognition of the slaves' rights as "immortal and domestic beings." Slaveholders, declared Robert Lewis Dabney, "must be willing to recognize and grant in slaves those rights which are a part of our essential humanity, some of which are left without recognition or guarantee by law, and some infringed by law. . . . If we take the ground that the power to neglect and infringe these interests is an essential and necessary part of the institution of slavery; then it cannot be defended." Slaveholders must concede that practices or laws which violated the slaves' rights "are not a part of the scriptural and lawful institution, but abuses."[32]

Evangelicals proposed at least four means by which abuses might be eliminated and the condition of the slaves improved. First, individual masters should fulfill their duties toward their own slaves. Second, church

31. *Central Presbyterian*, January 3, 1857, p. 1, December 26, 1857, p. 206; [J. L. Wilson], "The Foreign Slave Trade.—Can It Be Revived Without Violating the Most Sacred Principles of Honor, Humanity and Religion?" *Southern Presbyterian Review*, XII (October, 1859), 493–94; James Henley Thornwell to John B. Adger, December 10, 1856, in Palmer, *Life and Letters of Thornwell*, 422; *Southern Presbyterian*, December 6, 1856, n.p.; John B. Adger, "The Revival of the Slave Trade," *Southern Presbyterian Review*, XI (April, 1858), 106.

32. Fuller and Wayland, *Domestic Slavery*, 159; Sherman Everett Towell, "The Features of Southern Baptist Thought, 1845–1879" (Th.D. dissertation, Southern Baptist Theological Seminary, 1956), 144; "Duties of Masters," 272–74; "Christian Doctrine of Human Rights and Slavery," 579; *Religious Herald*, August 9, 1849, p. 126; Smylie, *Review of a Letter*, 67; *Southern Christian Advocate*, January 5, 1838, p. 114; Robert Lewis Dabney to G. Woodson Payne, January 22, 1840, and to his brother, January 15, 1851, both in Thomas Cary Johnson, *Life and Letters of Dabney*, 68, 129.

discipline should be administered to members who neglected or violated their duties toward their slaves. Third, southern Christians should exert their "influence to form a just and healthy public sentiment, that will bear down any, who may treat their slaves with indecency, or inhumanity." Finally, Christians should aid the passage of laws to protect slaves from cruel treatment.[33] But what was in theory a comprehensive program for the reform of the slave system in the South was in practice much less than that. Church discipline, as has been noted, was not generally administered in matters relating to slavery. Moreover, the reluctance of evangelicals to become involved in politics and the doctrine that the church had no authority to interfere with slavery as a civil institution hindered evangelicals from pressing for legislation to eliminate abuses. Thus, they were forced to rely principally on exhortation as a means of ameliorating the condition of the slaves.

Among the abuses cited by evangelicals there were two that were of special concern. One of these was denying the Gospel to the slaves, which will be discussed in the following chapter in connection with the religious instruction of the Negroes. The other was denying or violating the marriage relation. Masters either did not permit marriages among their slaves or violated them by separating husbands and wives. Evangelicals urged masters to introduce regular marriages among their slaves and to see that they were solemnized in a formal ceremony, conducted either by a minister or by the master himself. Besides arguing that this was a duty imposed by God's law, evangelicals also offered other, pragmatic considerations in its behalf. If masters enforced a proper regard for the marriage relation, they declared, "the endless brawls and contentions on this subject" among the slaves would cease. "Virtuous and fixed attachments" would take the place of "indefinite polygamy" and licentiousness. Not only would the moral condition of the slaves be improved. Evangelicals assured masters that slaves would also be more contented and therefore less likely to run away. Thus, as James Furman observed, "duty to our fellow men . . . conspires in this case with duty [to] God."[34]

The separation of married slaves posed a greater problem. For one

33. "Duties of Masters," 273.

34. *Southern Presbyterian*, January 3, 1857, n.p.; "Duties of Masters," 268, 274–76; Haven P. Perkins, "Religion for Slaves: Difficulties and Methods," *Church History*, X (September, 1941), 237–38; Touchstone, "Planters and Slave Religion," 159; DesChamps, "Presbyterian Church in the South Atlantic States," 54; *Southern Christian Advocate*, September 2, 1837, p. 42, May 5, 1854, p. 194, April 4, 1845, p. 170; James C. Furman, "Address on Slavery" (undated MS in James Furman Papers).

thing, slave marriages were not recognized in the civil code and the separation of married slaves was not prohibited by law. Some evangelicals thought that legislative action was necessary and appropriate to protect the "family relations" of the slaves, but they did little to obtain such action. Another difficulty was that the Scriptures offered little guidance on the matter. They prohibited divorce, but they said nothing about the degree to which the slaves' civil status qualified the stringency of the law on divorce. Some evangelicals believed that the church should draw up a "code" or "scheme of rule" relating to the marriage relation of slaves, and a number of ecclesiastical conferences were called to discuss the matter. For the most part, however, it was left to individual ministers to devise their own system of rules. Most evangelicals agreed that masters ought not to separate married slaves, and a few, including Richard Fuller, disciplined church members who did so. As slaveholders, evangelicals themselves refrained from separating married slaves, sometimes at considerable inconvenience and monetary loss. At the same time, most ministers and church courts permitted slaves who had been "involuntarily and forever" separated from their spouses to take another husband or wife. When James Davis wrote a letter to the editor of the *Christian Index* asking about this practice and wondering whether church members who separated married slaves ought to be disciplined and excluded from the church, the editor replied: "It is clear the scripture recognizes the relation of master and servant, & commands servants to obey their masters, not only the *good* and *gentle*, but also the froward. Here the *primary* obligation must rest, unless the servant can *alienate* the rights of his master to command, by a voluntary engagement of his own. But who will venture to affirm this? so then it follows that when the absolute commands of his master come in contact with the incidental promises of the servant the latter must yield to the former." In other words, the duty to obey his master, not the marriage relation, was the "paramount obligation" of the servant. Few evangelicals questioned this. To do so, as the *Index* editor noted, was to raise "the question of slavery itself." Admonishing Davis, he concluded his remarks by expressing the "hope that if any thing more should be said on the subject it will be strictly confined to the obligations of masters to their servants, and of servants to their masters in reference to the marriage relation."[35]

35. [Thornwell], "Slavery and the Religious Instruction of the Coloured Population," 138–39; *Religious Herald*, November 19, 1840, p. 187, November 2, 1838, p. 175; *Southern Christian Advocate*, May 5, 1854, p. 194; Palmer, *Life and Letters of Thornwell*, 301, 93; Perkins, "Religion for Slaves," 238–39; Lewis McCarroll Purifoy, Jr., "The Methodist Episcopal Church, South, and Slavery, 1844–1865" (Ph.D. dissertation, University of North Carolina, 1965),

Although they did not regard slavery as a sin, that is, a transgression of God's law, some evangelicals did condemn it as an evil which was harmful or injurious to man. Thus, Basil Manly, Jr., believed that "it was not in itself a sin to be the owner of a slave," but because of "its great liability to abuse," he considered slavery "an *evil*" and wrote that he would be "glad when by proper peaceful & Xtn like means it shall be everywhere abolished."[36]

Different evangelicals had different reasons for viewing slavery as an evil. John Witherspoon feared for the safety of whites. He also believed that slavery might be the cause of disunion. Some evangelicals regarded slaveholding as a crushing responsibility on masters. Others, such as Henry Ruffner of Lexington, Virginia, contended that slavery was a hindrance to southern prosperity. In his *Address to the People of West Virginia*, issued in 1847, Ruffner argued that slavery was less profitable than free labor, that it inhibited the growth of population and of manufacturing, that it exerted "a most pernicious influence on the cause of education," and that, in general, it was "pernicious to the welfare of West Virginia." Not surprisingly, most evangelicals who viewed slavery as an evil were also opposed to abolitionism. Thomas Meredith, editor of the *Biblical Recorder*, was willing to admit that slavery was "a political evil of immense magnitude" and that "the benevolent principles which the gospel enjoins and incites, require the eventual extinction of slavery, as they do the extinction of all other evils both political and moral." But he refused to countenance immediate abolition. Such men as Andrew Broaddus, Basil Manly, Jr., and Henry Ruffner shared his point of view.[37]

208; Thompson, *Presbyterians in the South*, I, 314n, 317; "Report of a Conference by Presbytery, on the Subject of 'The Organization, Instruction and Discipline of the Coloured People,'" *Southern Presbyterian Review*, VII (July, 1854), 15–17; James C. Furman to William E. Bailey, December 18, 1848, in James Furman Papers; Charles Colcock Jones to Charles C. Jones, Jr., January 17, 1856, October 2, 1856, in Myers (ed.), *Children of Pride*, 183–84, 243–44; "Synod of South-Carolina and Georgia," *Virginia Evangelical and Literary Magazine*, IV (December, 1821), 690; Clarke, "Thomas Smyth," 190; *Christian Index*, November 3, 1843, p. 698, July 27, 1859, n.p., April 15, 1834, p. 59.

36. Basil Manly, Jr., "Jottings Down, Newton Theological Seminary" (MS dated March 5, 1845, in Manly, Jr., Papers). A small minority of evangelicals in the South, including J. M. Dickey, John Hersey, Eli Caruthers, and Jonathan Lankford regarded slaveholding as a sin. Patricia P. Hickin, "Antislavery in Virginia, 1831–1861" (Ph.D. dissertation, University of Virginia, 1968), 374–80, 428; John B. Boles, "John Hersey: Dissenting Theologian of Abolitionism, Perfectionism, and Millennialism," *Methodist History*, XIV (July, 1976), 219; George Troxler, "Eli Caruthers: A Silent Dissenter in the Old South," *Journal of Presbyterian History*, XLV (June, 1967), 107–108; W. Harrison Daniel, "Virginia Baptists and the Negro in the Antebellum Era," *Journal of Negro History*, LVI (January, 1971), 6.

37. John Witherspoon to his daughter, January 14, 1836, and February 18, 1836, in Witherspoon and McDowall Family Papers; Flournoy, *Benjamin Mosby Smith*, 74; [Henry

Most southern evangelicals favored colonization. They supported the program of the American Colonization Society in various ways: as members, officers, and agents of the society and its auxiliaries, by publishing their annual reports and appeals in religious newspapers, and by instituting the yearly Fourth of July collection in their churches. They were also responsible for the fact that the Colonization Society received the endorsement of various ecclesiastical bodies, including the Presbyterian General Assembly and a number of presbyteries and synods in the South, the Methodist General Conference, and several Baptist associations.[38]

Some evangelicals, like William Winans, supported colonization because they viewed it as the only feasible means of eliminating slavery. Winans explained his position to the abolitionist Gerrit Smith. He said he had come to Mississippi "with ardent zeal for immediate emancipation." However, once he became aware of "the invincible prejudice of caste, among the whites, and the hopeless depression of the mental energies of the unfortunate Negro, while the object of that prejudice," he decided that immediate emancipation would prove "ruinous" to the slave and would lead to "evils incalculable" in society at large. He did not abandon his "fervent desire for the universal emancipation of the slave," but he now looked to colonization rather than immediate abolition as the best means of achieving that goal. While he admitted that abolition was not one of the stated objectives of the Colonization Society, he insisted that "such is its tendency—such was its original design." More slaves had been emancipated in a month as a result of the influence of the society, he wrote to his cousin Matthias Win-

Ruffner], *Address to the People of West Virginia; Shewing That Slavery Is Injurious to the Public Welfare, and That It May Be Gradually Abolished, Without Detriment to the Rights and Interests of Slaveholders. By a Slaveholder of West Virginia* (Lexington, 1847; rpr. Bridgewater, Va., 1933), 12–30, 4, 8–9; Hickin, "Antislavery in Virginia," 414–17; Drury Lacy to his wife, May 24, 1845, in Lacy Papers; Meredith quoted in Stroupe, "Religious Press in the South Atlantic States," 245; *Religious Herald*, September 11, 1835, p. 143; Basil Manly, Jr., "Jottings Down, Newton Theological Seminary" (MS dated March 5, 1845, in Manly, Jr., Papers).

38. For the activities of evangelicals in behalf of colonization see *Southern Evangelical Intelligencer*, May 29, 1819, pp. 78–79, *Religious Herald*, March 26, 1830, p. 46, June 16, 1837, p. 95, February 22, 1849, p. 31, July 21, 1853, p. 114, Richmond *Christian Advocate*, June 27, 1850, p. 102, *Central Presbyterian*, February 9, 1856, p. 22, William M. Baker, *Life of Baker*, 143, Robert Hall Morrison to James Morrison, February 12, 1820, in Morrison Papers, Taylor Diary, April 11, 1854, Stratton Diary, January 30, December 26, 1851, May 1, 2, 1853, February 8, 1857, Hickin, "Antislavery in Virginia," 270, 310, 313–19, John Lee Eighmy, *Churches in Cultural Captivity: A History of the Social Attitudes of Southern Baptists* (Knoxville, 1972), 7; DesChamps, "Presbyterian Church in the South Atlantic States," 145–46; Mathews, *Slavery and Methodism*, 97–98, 108; Minnie Spencer Grant, "The American Colonization Society in North Carolina" (M.A. thesis, Duke University, 1930), 10, 12, 14, 18–21, 34, 36, 55–73, 98; Todd, "Slavery Issue and the Organization of a Southern Baptist Convention," 42–43, 45.

ans, than the abolition societies had *"ever* freed, or . . . ever will." Winans contended that once the society "afforded evidence that a door was opened through which slaves might reach freedom and happiness, consistently with the safety of whites," many slaveholders were disposed to emancipate their slaves. Indeed, it was for this very reason that the society was "hated, opposed and persecuted by *ultra slave-holders* in the south."[39]

Other evangelicals, who did not share Winans' antipathy to slavery, supported colonization not as a method of abolition but because of the benefits which it promised the Negro, Africa, and the American people. They believed that the objective of the Colonization Society was to send to Africa free blacks who desired to go there. Colonization offered the Negro an opportunity to escape the restrictions imposed by white prejudice, to leave a country where he was doomed to "caste" status and the ignorance and degradation that accompanied it. In Africa he would be able to improve his condition and enjoy the rights of freemen, and in doing so he would "regenerate and reclaim that degraded continent." Many evangelicals also viewed colonization as "the only practical and peaceful solution" of the slavery question and the alternative to disunion. "The elements of danger, the *ignes suppositi* . . . are gathering under our feet," Richard Fuller warned in an address before the Colonization Society in 1851. "Unless something be done, this Union cannot . . . be saved from the agitation of the slavery question, and . . . from civil conflict." If northerners and southerners would only cooperate in supporting the colonization scheme, "the very co-operation would bind the members of this Union together by the closest and most delightful bonds." Like Winans, Fuller saw colonization as an alternative to abolitionism and believed that no true friend of the Negro, whether northerner or southerner, could properly oppose it.[40]

In formulating and expressing their views on slavery, evangelicals were extremely sensitive to public opinion. Their antislavery heritage rendered them vulnerable to criticism and, as we have seen, in the mid 1830s they

39. William Winans to Gerrit Smith, January 27, 1838, quoted in Kyker, "William Winans," 236; Winans to Matthias Winans, December 23, 1836, in Winans Collection. For other evangelicals who viewed colonization as a means of abolishing slavery, see Basil Manly, "On the Emancipation of Slaves" (MS dated April 1821 in Manly, Jr., Papers), *Southern Intelligencer*, November 16, 1822, p. 182, November 23, 1822, p. 187, Robert Hall Morrison to James Morrison, February 12, 1820, in Morrison Papers.

40. *Religious Herald*, June 25, 1830, p. 99, July 6, 1832, p. 102, February 3, 1837, p. 19, June 16, 1837, p. 95, August 3, 1838, pp. 122–23; *Christian Index*, May 5, 1843, p. 279; *Watchman of the South*, March 12, 1840, p. 114, January 11, 1849, p. 86; Smylie, *Review of a Letter*,

were subjected to questioning and intimidation. They were on the defensive at the beginning of the slavery controversy, and for the most part, they remained there throughout the antebellum period, realizing by the late 1830s that any show of support for immediate abolition would not be tolerated. This is why Eli Caruthers never published his four hundred page manuscript, "American Slavery and the Immediate Duty of Southern Slaveholders." Even colonization elicited a hostile response in some parts of the South and proposals for gradual emancipation, such as that offered by Henry Ruffner, were doomed to failure.[41]

The response to Richard Fuller's colonization address of 1851 showed that even the mildest criticism of slavery and the most cautious plan for its removal were likely to meet with an unfavorable reaction. When he delivered the speech, Fuller was a well-known and highly respected Baptist minister who had served a pastorate in Beaufort, South Carolina, for sixteen years before moving to Baltimore in 1846. In 1840 and again in 1845 he had won praise from fellow southerners for replying to abolitionist charges against the South. In the 1851 address Fuller reiterated his strictures of abolitionism and criticized southern extremism as well, noting "a morbid sensitiveness at the South with reference to slavery." Formerly, religious and political bodies had discussed the subject of slavery "freely." Southerners ought still to do so, Fuller declared. "While we repel all impertinent intermeddling, we owe it to ourselves not to allow such impertinence to move us from a calm, generous and conscientious discharge of our duty." He urged northerners to make certain concessions. Instead of denouncing every slaveholder as "a monster of iniquity," they should admit that the South was not responsible for the introduction of slavery, that the Negro had benefitted as a result of his transplantation from Africa to America, that slaves with kind masters were better off than a great portion of the laboring classes in Europe, and, perhaps most important, that slaves enjoyed "religious blessings" in the southern states. Southerners should admit some things too, Fuller declared:

60–62; Cox, "Life and Work of Basil Manly, Jr.," 118–19; Grant, "American Colonization *Address before the American Colonization Society. Delivered at Washington, D.C., January 21, 1851* (Baltimore, 1851), 3–6, 16.

Society in North Carolina," 88; *Central Presbyterian*, October 25, 1856, p. 167; Richard Fuller,

41. Eli Washington Caruthers, Preface to "American Slavery and the Immediate Duty of Southern Slaveholders" (MS in Eli Washington Caruthers Papers, William R. Perkins Library, Duke University); Grant, "American Colonization Society in North Carolina," 17–18, 22–23, 37–38, 97; DesChamps, "Presbyterian Church in the South Atlantic States," 143; Hickin, "Antislavery in Virginia," 417–19.

I shall not dwell on these concessions, as there is only one which bears directly on the subject before us. I know, sir, that man is fallen, and that he would not be fallen, if he at once opened his eyes to unwelcome truths. But, after all, I might confidently ask our statesmen, if they can travel at the North and South, without feeling that, while slavery enriches the individual, it impoverishes and desolates the State, and fosters indolence and luxury, vices which have ever been the bane of nations? I might appeal to every Christian, whether, when God says *"Search the Scriptures,"* the human mind ought to be shut up from reading those Scriptures? Whether, when Jesus says, *"What God hath joined together let not man put asunder,"* the marriage tie ought to be dissolved? I might inquire of every upright man, whether labor ought not to be compensated? . . . I will not insist on those points. The only concession I now urge is one which I made some years ago, when writing to Dr. Wayland, and against which I heard scarcely an objection.—It is, that slavery is not a good thing, and a thing to be perpetuated.

Fuller believed that there were "few at the South who would hesitate about making this concession" and he offered colonization as a "middle ground" on which right-minded southerners and northerners could meet in an effort to resolve the slavery problem. Specifically, he proposed that the Congress appropriate money for the purpose of buying slaves from masters willing to sell them and paying their passage to Liberia. Fuller admitted that such a plan might at first meet with opposition in the South, but just as he believed that most southerners would concede that slavery was not a good thing, he believed that most of them would be "willing to make very great sacrifices, if we can see a way open to enlighten, and elevate, the human beings committed to our care."[42]

When he saw the hostile feelings which his address aroused, especially in South Carolina, Fuller felt compelled to reply in a letter which he published in the *Southern Baptist.* He began by protesting his loyalty to the South. "I am still at the South," he wrote, "and while I never did and never can sympathize with Southern, any more than with Northern, intemperance and fanaticism, yet am I, in all my feelings and actions, as fully as ever identified with the South." He contended that his proposal for compensated emancipation had been misunderstood and expressed "surprise and sorrow" that his address had excited resentment. He was surprised because he thought that his views were well known. "On the subject of slavery I uttered no sentiment which I had not over and over expressed, privately and publicly, before leaving South Carolina," he wrote. He was

42. *Religious Herald*, November 19, 1840, p. 187, April 15, 1841, pp. 57–58; *Christian Index*, October 8, 1840, p. 643; Fuller and Wayland, *Domestic Slavery*; Fuller, *Address*, 7–13.

saddened because the resentment betrayed "a state of feeling most un-propitious to the calm investigation of truth; and, I believe, to the true in-terests of the State and the whole South."[43]

Most evangelicals did not share Fuller's views on slavery. Although he defended it, Fuller had for many years agonized over the slavery ques-tion. Still, his experience must have provided an object lesson for other evangelicals. Basil Manly, Jr., probably expressed the view of many of them when he said that although he did not think Fuller was "altogether right," he was sorry to see "a noble, honest, Christian minded man" ana-thematized for his views.[44]

The pressure of southern opinion was not the only or even the most im-portant factor shaping the evangelical view of slavery. Most evangelicals saw nothing fundamentally wrong with slavery. The "discovery" of the scriptural justification either confirmed preexisting opinions or eliminated vague doubts as to the legitimacy of slavery. Even Richard Fuller did not regard slavery as a sin per se. Their suspicions of human instrumentality also played an important role in shaping southern ministers' views of the slavery question. Evangelicals who criticized the use of "means" in getting up revivals of religion and who worried that temperance reformers placed too much emphasis on societies, pledges, and legal action, instead of on the Gospel and the grace of God, probably shared the view of the Method-ist writer who declared that the problem of slavery would be solved "in due time . . . by the Divine hand" and not by misguided philanthropists and reformers. Indeed, the very complexity of the slavery question en-couraged such a view. The senior editor of the *Christian Index* termed it a question "which admits of no human remedy, except the providence of God should interpose some influence, which would dispose those specially concerned, favorably to it." The abolition of slavery could not be done "without force until all are made willing," he observed, and only divine power could do that. "Let us all wait for the working of that divine power," he wrote.[45]

Thus, many evangelicals placed the ultimate solution of the slavery ques-tion in God's hands. "We must leave it [slavery] for God to remove, when

43. *Religious Herald*, August 7, 1851, pp. 125–26.
44. Cuthbert, *Life of Fuller*, 163; Basil Manly, Jr., to his parents, February 24, 1851, in Manly Family Papers.
45. "Dr. Smith's Philosophy and Practice of Slavery," *Methodist Quarterly Review*, XI (April, 1857), 258; *Christian Index*, August 13, 1840, p. 525.

his time comes," declared a writer in the *Southern Presbyterian Review*. In the meantime, the "*present* duty" of evangelicals—and indeed of all white southerners—was clear. "It is ours to do the duties of intelligent, decided, fearless, conscientious Christian Masters." Evangelicals regarded the religious instruction of the Negroes, not the abolition of slavery, as their most pressing and immediate duty.[46]

46. "Christian Doctrine of Human Rights and Slavery," 584–85; *Report of the Committee to Whom Was Referred the Subject of the Religious Instruction of the Colored Population, of the Synod of South-Carolina and Georgia, at its Late Session in Columbia, (South-Carolina.) December 5th–9th, 1833* (Charleston, 1834), 19.

CHAPTER EIGHT

Religious Instruction of the Negroes

In the fall of 1828 William Capers received a visit from the Honorable Charles Cotesworth Pinckney. The wealthy South Carolina planter, having become interested in providing religious instruction to his slaves, wished to hire a Methodist exhorter as an overseer. He asked Capers, as presiding elder, if he would recommend such a person. Capers demurred and suggested a different approach. He persuaded Pinckney to allow him to make application to the Missionary Society of the South Carolina Conference for a man who would devote his time and efforts exclusively to the religious instruction and spiritual welfare of the slaves.[1]

When the society met in January, 1829, it acted on two petitions for religious instruction, one from Pinckney, the other from Colonel Lewis Morris and his neighbor, Charles Baring, of Pon Pon. Two missionaries were appointed: John Honour to serve the slaves on plantations south of the Ashley River and John Massey to serve those south of the Santee. Capers was appointed superintendent of the missions. In accordance with the wishes of the planters, the missionaries were to limit their meetings to the Negroes of the plantation where they were held. At the time, Capers recalled, "formidable objections were thought to exist to a mission in any form, on the bare suspicion that it might induce negroes of different plan-

1. Wightman, *Life of Capers*, 291–92; J. Carleton Hayden, "Conversion and Control: Dilemma of Episcopalians in Providing for the Religious Instruction of Slaves, Charleston, South Carolina, 1845–1860," *Historical Magazine of the Protestant Episcopal Church*, XL (June, 1971), 143–44; *Southern Christian Advocate*, September 15, 1843, p. 54; Thomas Leonard Williams, "The Methodist Mission to the Slaves" (Ph.D. dissertation, Yale University, 1943), 33.

tations to leave their homes to attend the meetings." He viewed the entire effort as "little more than an experiment." Nevertheless, he could not suppress the hope that the new project marked "the beginning . . . of great and good things for the negroes." With God's help, the experiment might "open the way fully and completely at no distant time to the general dissemination of truth and righteousness among the negroes of the larger estates of the low country who hitherto have been most emphatically 'Sitting in darkness and the shadow of death.'"[2]

The Methodist missions on the Ashley and Santee signaled a new approach to the religious instruction of the Negroes. Prior to the 1830s efforts for the evangelization of the blacks were random, unsystematic, and failed to reach the majority of them. None of the three denominations had any special board or society whose exclusive concern was the religious instruction of the Negroes. Evangelicals emphasized the duty of masters to provide instruction for their slaves, and in some places Sunday schools were established where blacks were given religious instruction and taught to read the Bible. In a few of the larger towns churches were erected for the use of the Negroes. For the most part, however, the matter of religious instruction was left to the initiative of individual ministers. Some held special meetings for blacks, usually following the service for the white congregation, but generally, the blacks attended preaching with the whites—if they attended at all—and most preachers addressed their sermons not to them but to their masters. There were exceptions, of course. William Capers, John Early, James O. Andrew, and John Emory paid special attention to the Negroes on their circuits. John Holt Rice, as pastor of the Cub Creek Church, estimated that he gave one fourth of his time to the slaves, "this unfortunate race of men." The Baptists Edmund Botsford and Abner Clopton also ministered to blacks. Indeed, Botsford was sufficiently concerned about "that class of our poor despised fellow creatures who are too little attended too [sic] by all of us" to write a series of religious dialogues in the Negro dialect for their use. Still, none of these men devoted all or even most of their time to the blacks; instruction of the Negroes was but a small portion of their ministry.[3]

The mid-1820s saw a quickening of interest in the religious instruction

2. W. P. Harrison, *The Gospel Among the Slaves. A Short Account of Missionary Operations Among the African Slaves of the Southern States* (Nashville, 1893), 149, 154–55, 198; Thomas Leonard Williams, "Methodist Mission to the Slaves," 34–37; *Southern Christian Advocate*, September 15, 1843, p. 54.

3. Charles C. Jones, *The Religious Instruction of the Negroes. In the United States* (Savannah,

of the Negroes. In his 1823 *Exposition of the Views of the Baptists*, Richard Furman insisted that masters had a duty to see to the religious interests of the slaves. A number of religious newspapers published articles and correspondence describing the destitution of the blacks and setting forth their claim to the Gospel. The *Virginia Evangelical and Literary Magazine*, edited by John Holt Rice, and the *Wesleyan Journal*, a Methodist paper, were particularly earnest on the subject. In July, 1826, for example, the *Journal* published an article by James O. Andrew, under the pseudonym "Philander," setting forth the duty of "Christian masters, and ministers of the Gospel" regarding the "moral and religious improvement of our slaves." The duty of religious instruction devolved first on slaveowners, Andrew declared. Next to them, ministers had "the strongest obligations to care for the souls of these ignorant, and untutored people." In many parts of the low country, Andrew observed, blacks were more numerous than whites.

And yet, who among our clergy is willing to condescend to the ignorance of his negro hearers, by addressing them in a language from the pulpit, which they understand; or by diligently labouring, as opportunity may offer in private, to impress upon their minds, the subject of their eternal interests? Anxious that their sermons should please their white hearers, too many preachers disdain that simplicity and plainness, which are necessary for the negro; and it is to be feared, that there are some who bear the name of ministers of Christ, who scarcely feel, that the blacks around them, have any claims on their efforts, their sympathies, or their prayers.

Andrew concluded his indictment of the clergy by observing that "there rests much guilt about the altar, in reference to this matter—a guilt which I fear cries loudly to heaven against the priests of our land."[4] Perhaps in-

---

1842; rpr. Freeport, N.Y., 1971), 1–71; "An Address from the Presbytery of Hanover," *Virginia Religious Magazine*, III (May and June, 1807), 159; *Southern Evangelical Intelligencer*, April 15, 1820, p. 18, October 23, 1819, pp. 242–43, August 26, 1820, p. 174; "On Affording Religious Instruction to Slaves," *Virginia Evangelical and Literary Magazine*, V (February, 1822), 67; Thompson, *Presbyterians in the South*, I, 204–206; George G. Smith, *Life and Letters of Andrew*, 180–81, 91; Joe Gray Taylor, *Negro Slavery in Louisiana* (Baton Rouge, 1963), 136, 137; Wightman, *Life of Capers*, 92, 108, 124, 163, 167, 173–74, 215–16; Harrison, *Gospel Among the Slaves*, 136–37, 142–43; Early Diary, August 6, 1808, March 21, 1813; Emory, *Life of Emory*, 62, 63; Maxwell, *Memoir of Rice*, 35–36, 44; Jeter, *Memoir of Clopton*, 116; Edmund Botsford to John N. Roberts, April 24, 1812, and to Richard Furman, May 26, 1812, and October 15, 1808, all in Botsford Letters; [Edmund Botsford], *Sambo & Toney, A Dialogue in Three Parts* (Georgetown, 1808).

4. Richard Furman, *Exposition of the Views of the Baptists*, 13, 15; "On the Moral Condition of Slaves," IV (June, 1821), 309–14; "On Affording Religious Instruction to Slaves," V (February, 1822), 68–70, "On the Improvement of the People," V (December, 1822), 642–45, "The Injury Done to Religion by Ignorant Preachers," VIII (November, 1825), 603–604, all in *Virginia Evangelical and Literary Magazine*; *Wesleyan Journal*, December 16, 1826, p. 3, July 1, 1826, p. 2.

fluenced by appeals like Andrew's, ecclesiastical bodies began to take notice of the religious condition of the Negroes. In 1820 Bishop McKendree
delivered an address to the Methodist General Conference in which he
urged the importance of attending to the spiritual needs of the Negroes.
In 1825 the Presbyterian General Assembly commended efforts by some
of the southern presbyteries to evangelize the slaves and free blacks. Several Baptist churches in South Carolina appointed committees to draw up
plans for the religious instruction of the Negroes, and in 1828, the question was taken up by the Charleston Association.[5]

Evangelicals believed that the increased interest in the religious condition of the Negroes grew out of the missionary impulse generated by the
Second Great Awakening. In the 1820s, Jeremiah Jeter remembered, "the
subject of missions was fresh and inspiring"; a "deep interest" was felt in
the foreign missionary work of the American churches. Many southern
Christians were also awakened to the spiritual needs of the Negroes. As
revivals swept across the southern states, converts were moved to spread
the Gospel to blacks as well as whites. In Beaufort, South Carolina, for example, the revival instigated by Daniel Baker caused a number of planters
to turn their attention to the religious condition of their slaves. Unable to
obtain the services of an Episcopal or Baptist minister, they asked the advice of C. C. Pinckney, who suggested they apply to the South Carolina
Conference for help. The result was the establishment of the Beaufort
Mission in 1832.[6]

In their effort to promote the religious instruction of the blacks, evangelicals sought to capitalize on the prevailing missionary spirit and channel
it in the direction of the Negroes. "We hear it repeated again, and again,
that this is an age of wonderful benevolence; we hear incessantly of mighty
efforts for civilizing and evangelizing Hindoos, Burmese, Hottentots, and
savages in different parts of the world," observed James O. Andrew in
1826, "but what has been said or done toward converting the negroes of
our own plantations?" The church was putting forth "her mightiest efforts" to destroy "pagan idolatry in distant lands . . . while the habitations
of pagan darkness, are before the eyes of every planter, without looking

    5. Thomas Leonard Williams, "Methodist Mission to the Slaves," 26; Thompson, *Presby-
terians in the South*, I, 206; Mallard, "Religious Work of South Carolina Baptists Among the
Slaves," 41–42.
    6. Jeter, *Recollections*, 128; Jones, *Religious Instruction of the Negroes*, 63; Harrison, *Gospel
Among the Slaves*, 203–204. For other instances of revivals stimulating interest in the religious
instruction of the Negroes see Thomas Leonard Williams, "Methodist Mission to the Slaves,"
42, and Charleston *Observer*, September 28, 1833, p. 154.

beyond his own neighbourhood, or perhaps even beyond his own prem-
ises." This theme was reiterated by evangelicals throughout the antebellum period. In 1834 Samuel S. Law and Charles Colcock Jones, while protesting that they did not disparage foreign missions, emphasized that "the
great field of missions for the southern church," which took precedence
over all others, was that presented by the Negroes. They declared it "a
perfect anomoly [*sic*] in the benevolent feelings and efforts of the church,
that this field has so long remained neglected." Ten years later, in an address to a congregation of Baptists, Methodists, and Presbyterians, Basil
Manly also appealed to the "regard for consistency." "Do we sympathize
with the suffering Greeks?" he asked. "Do we desire to [send] the Gospel
to the destitute? Why expend all our charities on distant . . . objects, and
neglect the Heathen of our own homes?"[7]

The blacks constituted a more promising missionary field than other
peoples, Manly insisted. Not only were they numerous enough "to compare with most heathen tribes or nations"; they were also more accessible
and would be easier to convert to Christianity. He explained:

They have not been educated under any prevailing systems of false doctrine or
worship. There are no hoary superstitions, no time-honoured customs or institutions among them to be attacked and destroyed. They present, so far as this is concerned, an open door and a clear stage. Their weak and dependent condition in
the world disposes them for the peculiar doctrines of the gospel which reveal Salvation through the mercies of another, and inclines them to receive with peculiar
alacrity the consolations & aids of Xt. To address them on these high spiritual &
mysterious subjects, we have the advantage of a cultivated & nearly perfect language, well enough understood by themselves. No barbarous dialect is to be mastered by the negro's missionary. Himself & his hearer are in a condition relatively
to each other, the first moment of their meeting, to enter on the great transactions
which have respect to the saving of the soul. There are no ignorant or contemptu-
ous prejudices, as of the Chinese, to contend with. From our acknowledged superior relation, what we say or do attracts their confidence at once and exerts great
power over them. While the Gospel is not wanting in independent authority and
effect, it disdains not the influence which the personal character and relative standing of its propagators exert.[8]

In asserting the claims of the blacks to religious instruction, evangelicals
offered arguments similar to those employed on behalf of missions to other
destitute peoples. Negroes had a right to religious instruction because the

---

7. *Wesleyan Journal*, July 1, 1826, p. 2; *Christian Index*, November 4, 1834, n.p.; Basil Manly,
"National Stability" (MS dated June 21, 1844, in Manly, Jr., Papers).
8. Manly, "National Stability."

Gospel was intended for all men, they declared. This meant "the bond as well as the free," since the offer of salvation was made without regard to the outward condition of men. Whites had a duty to furnish the blacks with the means of salvation because "they are our fellow beings," J. S. Law explained. "Though occupying a different position in life, and though of a different complexion, yet they are members with us of the same great family, involved in the same unholy rebellion against God, and, like us, are destined to unspeakable happiness or insufferable torment." The implication of this argument was spelled out by James O. Andrew: Negroes were slaves, but "Christian slaveholders must be brought to feel that their negroes are *more than mere property*, that they are *fellow-heirs of immortality*." Andrew and other evangelicals also offered pragmatic arguments in favor of religious instruction, as will be seen, but the one based on the humanity of the Negro was preeminent in their thinking.[9]

That the religious instruction of the Negroes was the will of God, evangelicals did not doubt. Indeed, many believed that they had been "signally called" to the "great work" by God himself. Religious instruction was a providential task assigned to the South. Why else did God permit the Africans to be brought to the South, asked members of the Bethel Baptist Association, "if not that we should be to them agents of good, the bearers of the gospel"? Seen in this light, religious instruction was not a matter of choice, but an obligation, and Christians had no excuse for neglecting it. Indeed, Andrew warned that as long as southern Christians neglected their responsibility, "we shall not be well pleasing to God."[10] Viewed in this way, in terms of a covenant with God, the business of religious instruction was invested with awesome significance. Should southerners neglect their duty, they could expect nothing less than divine retribution.

While most evangelicals regarded religious instruction as a duty imposed on Christian slaveholders, some also urged it as repayment of a debt owed to the blacks. Basil Manly, for example, observed that "the labor of our slaves procures for us the luxuries & comforts of life; they constitute a great part of our wealth. They kindly nurse us in infancy, they relieve the fatigue of our journeys, they contribute to the care & hospitality

9. Thomas Leonard Williams, "Methodist Mission to the Slaves," 302–303; "On Affording Religious Instruction to the Slaves," *Virginia Evangelical and Literary Magazine*, V (February, 1822), 67–68; *Religious Herald*, January 20, 1832, p. 6; *Report of the Committee of the Synod of South-Carolina and Georgia*, 11–12; *Christian Index*, October 28, 1834, n.p., March 15, 1855, p. 41; *Southern Christian Advocate*, July 23, 1841, p. 21.

10. Wightman, *Life of Capers*, 405; *Christian Index*, March 28, 1850, p. 50; *Southern Christian Advocate*, July 23, 1841, p. 21.

of our festive houses, they watch & support us in sickness, they risk their lives for us in danger, and when we die, the faithful old servant follows us to our grave, & vents his undissembled grief." Manly believed that the blacks received adequate—even ample—temporal rewards for their services. "But," he said, "it will be more useful to them and acceptable to God, to pay also in spiritual things."[11]

Another impulse behind the evangelicals' advocacy of religious instruction was a concern with the "moral degradation" of the blacks. The movement for religious instruction of the Negroes, like temperance and other reforms, was, in part, an effort at social control. Evangelicals complained that the great mass of blacks seemed to be unacquainted with "moral obligation." J. S. Law listed their "common sins": lying, stealing, drunkenness, gross immorality, and profanation of the Sabbath. Such behavior was not "the necessary result of their condition as slaves," he emphasized, but a consequence of their religious destitution. Religious instruction would be a means of suppressing vice and promoting morality among the black population. Indeed, not only "improved morals" but "more principled and worthy obedience" would be the result. Viewing the Gospel as a system of moral discipline as well as a method of salvation, evangelicals could not but argue that it would make blacks "more orderly and obedient as servants."[12] Although most of them did not regard this as the most important reason for providing religious instruction, they recognized the value of employing it when appealing to slaveholders for support.

Some evangelicals supported the movement for religious instruction as a means of undermining the influence of black preachers. Dismissing black religion as "superstition," they regarded many of the black preachers as "ignorant but cunning" men who "taught . . . the most outrageous antinomian principles, subversive of all morals and ruinous to all correct notions of God and duty." The Nat Turner rebellion of 1831 confirmed their worst suspicions of black preachers. The Southampton insurrection seemed to many of them a fulfillment of the prophecy made by John Holt Rice in 1825, that if ever a slave rebellion occurred, "some *crisp haired* prophet,

---

11. Manly, "National Stability." See also *Christian Index*, November 4, 1834, n.p., March 28, 1850, p. 50; "Duties of Masters," 277; Jones, *Religious Instruction of the Negroes*, 166; *Report of the Committee of the Synod of South-Carolina and Georgia*, 13; Presbytery of Tombeckbee [Mississippi], *The Religious Instruction of Our Colored Population. A Pastoral Letter From the Presbytery of Tombeckbee to the Churches and People Under Its Care* (Columbia, 1859), 10–11.

12. *Southern Evangelical Intelligencer*, April 29, 1820, p. 33; *Watchman and Observer*, May 18, 1848, p. 157; *Christian Index*, April 29, 1842, p. 262; Mathews, *Slavery and Methodism*, 72; *Southern Presbyterian*, July 26, 1856, n.p.

some pretender to inspiration, will be the ringleader as well as the instigator of the plot. By feigning communications from heaven, he will rouse the fanaticism of his brethren, and they will be prepared for any work however desolating and murderous."[13] Evangelicals who thought along these lines were concerned to provide the blacks with "proper" religious instruction and to bring them under the salutary influence of white preachers and missionaries.

In the aftermath of the Turner rebellion and throughout the antebellum period, when rumors of slave revolts circulated throughout the southern states, evangelicals also urged religious instruction as the best preventive of insurrection. They contended that if the Negroes were brought under the influence of the Gospel, they would be "more happy and contented in existing circumstances." "The dissemination of moral truth," Basil Manly declared confidently in 1844, "will always be found at once the cheapest & most effective support of law & order, the most certain check of incendiarism & turbulence."[14]

Evangelicals viewed the religious instruction of the Negroes as part of a larger program which aimed at the regeneration of the entire southern social order. They believed it would not only improve the moral and religious condition of the blacks; it would also *"promote our own morality and religion,"* as Charles Colcock Jones declared. In their present degraded condition, he explained, blacks exerted "a deleterious influence" on whites, especially children and young people. By providing religious instruction to the blacks, whites would be able to counteract that influence. They would also discover, by joining in the benevolent work, the truth of the Gospel promise, "he that waters shall be watered also himself." They would see that "the way to strengthen and increase holiness in the soul is to abound in works of holiness." James O. Andrew noted another way in which religious instruction of the slaves benefitted the masters. "The exemplary conduct of a faithful servant has frequently been the means of leading the thoughtless, Christless master to serious reflection on religious subjects, which has eventuated in his conversion," he observed.[15]

13. *Southern Christian Advocate*, October 30, 1846, p. 82; "The Injury Done to Religion by Ignorant Preachers. A Sermon Delivered Before an Education Society in Sept. 1825," *Virginia Evangelical and Literary Magazine*, VIII (November, 1825), 604; Charleston *Observer*, November 5, 1831, p. 177; William S. Plumer, *Thoughts on the Religious Instruction of the Negroes of This Country* (Savannah, 1848), 20; Jones, *Religious Instruction of the Negroes*, 214–15.
14. Charleston *Observer*, February 4, 1832, p. 17; Manly, "National Stability."
15. Jones, *Religious Instruction of the Negroes*, 217; Andrew quoted in Thomas Leonard Williams, "Methodist Mission to the Slaves," 308.

Missionary zeal and the impulse to moral reform provided the initial impetus behind the movement for the religious instruction of the Negroes, and they continued to serve as its mainspring throughout the antebellum period. In the 1830s an additional impulse was provided by the rise of abolitionism. Evangelicals as well as laymen recognized the utility of the program of religious instruction in answering the critics of slavery. They offered it as evidence that, contrary to the claims of the abolitionists, white southerners did not deny the humanity of the Negro, and as a refutation of the "slanderous" charge that slaves in the South were denied the Gospel. We have seen that evangelicals linked religious instruction to the justification of slavery, insisting that the scriptural defense pertained only if masters fulfilled their moral and religious duties to the slaves. Some also pointed to the Christianization of the Negroes as evidence of the "vast good" accomplished by the peculiar institution. Speaking of the Negroes, S. J. Cassells declared, "But for [their] bondage, they had never been here; but for [their] bondage they had never attained their present *elevation* as Christians and as men." He offered this as proof that "God *intends* the enslaving of the Africans among us for *great good*." As an advocate of colonization, Cassells offered an additional argument in favor of religious instruction—it was part of the providential plan whereby Africa was to be civilized and regenerated "by an exiled and enslaved portion of her long humbled population." [16]

The Methodists were first and foremost in the development of a program of religious instruction. Two men, William Capers and James O. Andrew (elected Bishop in 1832), deserve much of the credit for the development of the Methodist missions to the slaves. Capers, especially, exerted a tremendous influence in favor of evangelizing the slaves, as president of the South Carolina Conference Missionary Society and editor of the *Southern Christian Advocate* and, beginning in 1840, as Secretary of the Church's Southern Department of Missionary Work. He not only built and directed the slave missions in South Carolina and Georgia, but also offered suggestions regarding religious instruction which were adopted by other conferences throughout the South. By 1844, the Methodists had a total of eighty missionaries serving a membership of over twenty thousand slaves. [17]

16. *Southern Baptist and General Intelligencer*, October 23, 1835, p. 258; *Southern Presbyterian*, May 31, 1850, p. 158, June 17, 1852, p. 166; *Watchman of the South*, September 28, 1843, p. 22.
17. Mathews, *Slavery and Methodism*, 69–70.

The division of the Methodist church in 1845 aided the missionary movement by eliminating suspicion as to the trustworthiness of Methodists
among the slaves. In 1846, at its first meeting, the General Conference of
the Methodist Episcopal Church, South, adopted a plan of religious instruction presented by the South Carolina Conference. The plan, which
Capers probably helped to draft and which was to serve the Church until
after the Civil War, was an attempt to establish a uniform system of missionary operations among the blacks. On the one hand it continued the
policy, begun in 1828, of sending missionaries to the slaves in isolated regions of the South, such as the rice plantations of South Carolina and the
sugar plantations of Louisiana. On the other hand, the plan sought to enlarge the scope of missionary operations by enlisting the efforts of the regular ministry, that is circuit and local preachers. Among the recommendations approved by the General Conference were the following: On circuits
and stations where separate accommodations were not provided for the
blacks, they should "be included within the same pastoral charge with the
whites: both classes forming one congregation." Churches should provide
suitable seating arrangements for the Negroes and there should be accommodations and special prayer meetings for them at camp meetings.
Circuit and local preachers, as well as missionaries, were urged to pay particular attention to the catechetical instruction of both adults and children, in addition to the work of preaching the Gospel to them.[18]

The results of Methodist effort among the blacks were impressive. On
the eve of the Civil War the Missionary Society of the Church reported
158 missions among the blacks, with 136 missionaries and 48,582 members
out of a total black membership of 188,041. There were also 74 churches
for Negroes and 19,553 children receiving religious instruction.[19]

Presbyterians were much less successful among the blacks. In 1860 southern Old School presbyteries reported fewer than 8,000 Negro church
members. Many evangelicals attributed the small number to the fact that
the blacks preferred the Baptist and Methodist churches. Equally important was the inadequate number of ministers. The same problem that limited the Presbyterians' missionary endeavors among the whites curtailed
their efforts among the blacks. In 1832 the Synod of Virginia observed
prophetically that "the number of ministers, already too small to supply

18. Thomas Leonard Williams, "Methodist Mission to the Slaves," 177–79, 188–89, 191–
94, 270; Southall, "Attitude of the Methodist Episcopal Church, South, toward the Negro,"
362; *Southern Christian Advocate*, November 6, 1846, p. 86; Purifoy, "Methodist Episcopal
Church, South, and Slavery," 130.
19. *Southern Christian Advocate*, June 16, 1859, p. 218.

adequately our white population, will not, for many years, be so increased as to afford the necessary religious instruction to our slaves and free people of colour."[20]

Lacking a sufficient number of ministers to work with the blacks, Presbyterians put special emphasis on the duty of masters and their families to provide "home instruction" in the principles of religion. Catechetical instruction was especially stressed. Masters were also urged to read the Bible and selected sermons to the blacks, and to teach them hymns. Like the Methodists, the Presbyterians also utilized special missionaries to the blacks, though to a far lesser extent. As early as 1831, B. W. Williams, pastor of the church of Pine Ridge, Mississippi, had two of his assistants serving as missionaries to the blacks on nearby plantations. In the forties and fifties many southern presbyteries either recommended the employment of missionaries or actually sent them out to the Negroes within their bounds. While they emphasized "home instruction" and made some use of special missionaries, Presbyterians believed that the major responsibility for the religious instruction of the blacks rested on the regular ministry. Thus, Charles Colcock Jones agreed that there were some areas where missionaries were required, but he insisted that "our *main reliance* for the general, permanent, and efficient religious instruction of [the Negroes] *is now and ever will be upon the regular and settled ministry of the South.*"[21]

The Presbyterian system of religious instruction was much less centralized than that of the Methodists. Evangelistic efforts among the blacks were generally conducted by presbyteries. In 1835 Charles Colcock Jones proposed the formation of a society to be called "The Southern Evangelical Society." He attempted to get it approved by the Synods of Virginia, South Carolina and Georgia, and North Carolina, but only the last took favorable action. A committee of the Synod of South Carolina and Georgia reported adversely on the plan, citing "the *extent* of the proposed organization; the *excitement* of the times; and the belief that *each synod could of itself* conduct the work more successfully, than when united with the other two." Another effort at centralization was made in 1844 when the Presby-

20. Thompson, *Presbyterians in the South*, I, 207, 443.

21. *Watchman and Observer*, February 12, 1846, p. 101, June 1, 1848, p. 167; *Central Presbyterian*, August 27, 1859, p. 137; DesChamps, "Presbyterian Church in the South Atlantic States," 39, 52–53; "The Baptism of Servants," *Southern Presbyterian Review*, I (June, 1847), 63–102; Harrison, *Gospel Among the Slaves*, 295; James Benson Sellers, *Slavery in Alabama* (University, Ala., 1950), 306; Charles Colcock Jones, *Suggestions on the Religious Instruction of the Negroes in the Southern States: Together With an Appendix Containing Forms of Church Registers, Form of a Constitution, and Plans of Different Denominations of Christians* (Philadelphia, [1847]), 69–70.

tery of Georgia sent a memorial to other southern presbyteries suggesting
that the General Assembly's Board of Domestic Missions include the Negroes in its field of labor and *"endeavor to furnish means and laborers for it as
Providence shall open the way."* Again there were objections, this time from
the Presbytery of Harmony in South Carolina, which declared that it was
"inexpedient to employ any foreign agency in providing for the religious
instruction of the negroes in our midst." Only "the Southern Church" knew
the condition of the Negroes and understood "the peculiar state of public
sentiment" on the subject of slavery. The Harmony Presbytery cited the
danger of accepting "such an arrangement as would throw the burden [of
instruction] mainly upon those who have not enjoyed the means of knowing so fully the operation of the institution of slavery." Unlike the Southern Methodists and Baptists, who formed strictly sectional churches, the
Old School Presbyterian church embraced both North and South, and
some southern Presbyterians feared the consequences of employing other
than a native ministry to instruct the Negroes. They were reassured in
1845 when the General Assembly adopted a statement and resolutions declaring that slaveholding was not a sin according to the Scriptures and that
the church had no authority to legislate on the subject of slavery. Beginning in the mid-1840s, the Board of Domestic Missions began employing
a few missionaries among the blacks, but most of the work of religious instruction continued to be done by southern presbyteries and synods. The
Board not only lacked funds but was also hampered in its operations by
opposition from such southern Presbyterian leaders as Robert J. Breckinridge, James Henley Thornwell, Benjamin Morgan Palmer, and John B.
Adger.[22]

The Baptists had no societies for the express and sole purpose of evangelizing the blacks. Nevertheless, they had more Negro communicants,
more Negro churches, and more ordained Negro preachers than any
other denomination. Indeed, as the editor of the *Religious Herald* noted,
Baptists were frequently "twitted by Presbyterians, as well as members of
other denominations, on account of the large proportion of colored members in their churches." But, he declared, "we have always deemed it a
high honor to our denomination . . . that when all others neglected them,

22. Jones, *Religious Instruction of the Negroes*, 76–77; Charleston *Observer*, May 30, 1835, p.
85, July 11, 1835, p. 110; *Watchman of the South*, August 22, 1844, p. 1; Thompson, *Presbyterians in the South*, I, 436, 531, 510–16, 525, 527; *Watchman and Observer*, June 18, 1846, p.
175.

the early Baptist preachers cared for the souls of the poor blacks, and proclaimed the gospel to them."[23]

Once the movement for religious instruction began, Baptists followed the lead of Methodists and Presbyterians and began considering the blacks as a special missionary field. Baptist newspapers supported the movement and associations created boards and appointed committees to investigate the subject of religious instruction and to make recommendations as to how it might be carried out. A number of associations and churches appointed ministers and missionaries to serve the blacks full time. Regular ministers were urged to devote a portion of their time to preaching and providing religious instruction to them. Like the Methodists and Presbyterians, Baptists also urged the duty of religious instruction on masters. When the Southern Baptist Convention was formed in 1845, it instructed its newly created Board of Domestic Missions to "take all prudent measures for the religious instruction of the colored population." The Board reported annually on the subject but never played a very extensive role in the movement for religious instruction. Many of its missionaries gave a portion of their time to the blacks, but in the period preceding the Civil War the Board appointed only two missionaries for full-time work among them.[24] Thus, the Baptist effort of religious instruction was carried on mainly at the state and local level, by conventions, associations, and churches.

Evangelicals of all three denominations agreed on the type of man needed to preach the Gospel to the blacks. Obviously he should be a man of "unquestionable piety." He should also be humble, dedicated, and self-sacrificing. He must not expect "popular applause." At least at the beginning of the movement for religious instruction, missionaries to the Negroes were often disparaged, not only by laymen but by other ministers as well. Certainly they did not receive the lavish praise accorded the better known foreign missionaries, whose efforts in strange lands among exotic peoples stirred the popular imagination. William Capers wrote of the difficulty of being "a servant of slaves literally—treated as inferior by the proprietors, as hardly equal to the overseers, half starved sometimes, suffocated with smoke, sick with the stench of dirty cabins & as-dirty negroes,

23. Jones, *Religious Instruction of the Negroes*, 94; *Religious Herald*, May 30, 1849, pp. 70–71.
24. *Christian Index*, July 9, 1841, p. 441, August 10, 1854, p. 126; Sellers, *Slavery in Alabama*, 305. On the SBC Board of Domestic Missions see Eighmy, *Churches in Cultural Captivity*, 29; *Religious Herald*, June 25, 1846, p. 102; Torbet, *History of the Baptists*, 382–83.

sleepless for the stings of . . . musquitoes [*sic*] and all in the very centre . . . of the kingdom of disease." It was, as Charles Colcock Jones said, "a laborious & self-denying work." Clearly, none should enter upon it "with worldly motives, or for his own accommodation and ease instead of seeking the glory of God and the salvation of souls."[25]

The evangelist to the blacks should be a southerner, either born and reared in the South or identified with the South, "familiarly acquainted with the structure of society," and with all his interests in the South. The editor of the *Christian Index* added that a missionary's "usefulness" would be greatly enhanced if he were a slaveholder, because it would secure "the confidence of the community" and enable him "to preach to masters by example as well as by precept." Citing Charles Colcock Jones and Josiah S. Law as examples, he expressed the opinion that "the work of preaching to the blacks is peculiarly the work of *slaveholding* ministers. They are best acquainted with the character, the good and evil habits of the slave; and are, consequently, the best qualified to preach to them successfully." Although most evangelicals did not insist that evangelists be slaveholders, they did agree that they should be sympathetic to and knowledgeable about the institution of slavery. Above all, they should be "prudent," confining themselves "to their particular work, carefully abstaining from all intermeddling with the affairs and regulations of the plantations upon which they may preach."[26]

As this last point suggests, evangelicals were very careful to emphasize that religious instruction posed no threat to the peculiar institution. They distinguished between the "moral" and the "civil" condition of the slaves and contended that the one might be attended to without interfering with the other. In its 1841 report, the Board of Managers of the Missionary Society of the South Carolina Conference declared that "this Missionary Society has no ulterior designs beyond our plain and positive present duties. We are working to no secular ends. We have nothing to do with the rights and duties of Caesar. We bow to the authority of the laws; and by the express precepts of the Christianity we preach, we are under obligation to

25. *Christian Index*, July 4, 1845, n.p.; *Southern Christian Advocate*, November 3, 1837, p. 78, July 17, 1856, p. 25; Thomas Leonard Williams, "Methodist Mission to the Slaves," 92; Purifoy, "Methodist Episcopal Church, South, and Slavery," 163; Capers quoted in Mathews, *Slavery and Methodism*, 75; Charles Colcock Jones to John McLees, August 21, 1846, in John McLees Papers, South Caroliniana Library, University of South Carolina, Columbia.
26. *Report of the Committee of the Synod of South-Carolina and Georgia*, 27; Jones, *Religious Instruction of the Negroes*, 196; *Christian Index*, July 4, 1845, n.p., March 22, 1855, p. 45; *Watchman of the South*, July 3, 1845, p. 178.

obey those laws. Our vocation looks to a different end. It contemplates spiritual relations, eternal destinies." Statements such as this, which reflected most evangelicals' views on the slavery question, were designed to eliminate southern suspicions that religious instruction was an "emancipating scheme." Evangelicals also reproached northern abolitionists for endangering the movement of religious instruction by awakening the feeling among slaveholders that evangelists could not be trusted among the slaves.[27]

Bowing "to the authority of the laws" not only meant accepting the system of slavery; it also meant complying with legislation which restricted the religious and educational privileges of the blacks. By the early 1830s, most of the southern states had laws which prohibited teaching slaves to read or write, restricted or outlawed preaching by free Negroes and slaves, and required white supervision of slaves' religious meetings.[28] Evangelical reaction to these laws was mixed. Most blamed their passage on the abolitionists. Some criticized the laws. The Baptist General Association of Virginia went so far as to draft a petition to the legislature seeking a modification of such laws in the state of Virginia. Because Baptists employed a considerable number of Negro preachers, they were especially concerned about laws prohibiting them from preaching, while Presbyterians were more critical of laws prohibiting the teaching of reading. For the most part, though, evangelicals did not challenge the laws. A few gave them their positive approval and the majority assented to them.[29] To teach the blacks the principles of religion they proposed a system of "oral instruction" to be carried out by white ministers and missionaries with the aid and consent of the planters.

Evangelicals divided the work of religious instruction into two main

27. *Report of the Committee of the Synod of South-Carolina and Georgia*, 25; *Southern Christian Advocate*, February 26, 1841, p. 146; *Southern Baptist and General Intelligencer*, March 13, 1835, p. 170, May 1, 1835, p. 278; *Christian Index*, October 7, 1834, n.p.; Charleston *Observer*, August 1, 1835, p. 122, September 17, 1836, p. 152; Wightman, *Life of Capers*, 405.
28. Sellers, *Slavery in Alabama*, 117, 299; John Spencer Bassett, *Slavery in the State of North Carolina* (Baltimore, 1899), 48–49; Charles Sackett Sydnor, *Slavery in Mississippi* (New York, 1933), 53, 55; James Curtis Ballagh, *A History of Slavery in Virginia* (Baltimore, 1902), 95.
29. See, for example, *Christian Index*, September 12, 1845, n.p., June 28, 1855, p. 102, January 28, 1857, p. 14, *Religious Herald*, June 15, 1848, p. 95, May 8, 1835, p. 70, *Southern Baptist and General Intelligencer*, November 13, 1835, p. 324, Manly, "National Stability"; Eighmy, *Churches in Cultural Captivity*, 29, *Central Presbyterian*, November 15, 1856, p. 183, "Duties of Masters," 273, Palmer, *Life and Letters of Thornwell*, 301, Rev. Robert A. Fair, *Our Slaves Should Have the Bible. An Address Delivered Before the Abbeville Bible Society, at its Anniversary, July, 1854* (Due West, S.C., 1854); *Southern Presbyterian*, November 2, 1854, p. 10; Thompson, *Presbyterians in the South*, I, 210.

parts, catechizing and preaching. In the larger towns and villages, catechetical instruction was provided the black children in Sabbath schools.
The First Baptist Church in Charleston, for example, had a Sunday school
attended by 135 black children in 1848; there were 33 teachers, all of them
white, "mostly young gentlemen and ladies." The children in the black
Sabbath schools were not taught to read, but learned passages of scripture, hymns, and catechism by repeating them after their teachers. Children on the plantations were usually catechized on weekdays. A missionary might have as many as several hundred children under his care, with
classes ranging from 10 to 40 or 50. Sometimes adult blacks attended the
classes, either as participants or observers. The method of instruction used
in the plantation classes was similar to that employed in the black Sabbath
schools. William Capers described the procedure that most missionaries
probably followed:

Here then stands the missionary; and before him, in one row or several, the children to be catechized, the smallest standing foremost; behind the children and
around are the grown negroes; who are generally fond to attend, and ought always to be encouraged to do so. They sing, the missionary giving out the lines, and
leading; and the hymn being sung, he prays, concluding solemnly with the Lord's
prayer, all in the house repeating after him. Then commences the catechism. Suppose the lesson to be the ninth chapter. The missionary utters the words of the
first question, "Who will be reckoned righteous in the day of judgment?" and the
answer, "All who believe the Gospel and live by it." He repeats, "Who will be reckoned righteous in the day of judgment?" And they all answer with him, (or rather
following him) in the words, "All who believe the gospel and live by it." Both the
question and answer is repeated by him, perhaps several times; and each time all
join in the answer, (the children with a full distinct voice, and the adults less audi-
bly,) till they seem to have learned it.

Usually a catechism class lasted about an hour and was concluded with
singing and prayer. Evangelicals were generally pleased with the accom-
plishments of their children and praised them in their correspondence.
Nicholas Talley, a Methodist missionary working in the Charleston District, reported that many of the children on the missions "can repeat the
whole of the catechism, including the commandments, the Apostle's creed,
the Lord's prayer, and the hymns attached to the catechism." A Presbyterian minister residing in Mississippi, who devoted full time to teaching
and preaching to the slaves, described the progress of his catechumens:
"*Twenty-one* repeat the Shorter Catechism, verbatim, to the 4th commandment—*nineteen* to the 1st commandment, and *seventeen* to the 26th ques-

tion . . . and the remainder varying from five to twenty questions. More than *fifty* repeat Willison's 'Mother's Catechism' throughout."[30]

Instructors used a variety of catechisms, some of which were published especially for the blacks. The most popular and widely used were the ones written by William Capers and Charles Colcock Jones. Among other evangelicals who authored catechisms for the blacks were the Presbyterians Benjamin Morgan Palmer and John Girardeau, the Baptists Robert Ryland and A. W. Chambliss, and the Methodist Samuel Bryan.[31]

Preaching usually occurred on Sunday. The Sabbath service consisted of singing and prayer, reading the Scriptures, and the preaching of a sermon. Sometimes an inquiry meeting was held either before or after the worship service. Blacks who were under the care of a regular minister heard preaching at a special afternoon service. They might attend the morning service for the white members of the congregation, but the sermon would not be addressed especially to them, and in some cases the churches were not large enough to accommodate large numbers of blacks in addition to the white congregation. Sometimes a regular minister also preached on nearby plantations, either on Sunday or on a weekday or weeknight, but plantation preaching was generally the work of the missionaries. Some of them served as many as fifteen or twenty plantations, where they held services on successive Sabbaths. Those with a large number of appointments preached two or even three times on a Sunday and met the slaves of each plantation once every three or four weeks. Some missionaries were able to obtain preaching appointments on weekdays or weeknights, but many planters refused to allow their slaves to have religious meetings on workdays. Missionaries held their services in whatever place or building was available and capable of holding the congregation (sometimes as many as two or three hundred). A few planters built chapels for their slaves, and occasionally it was possible to use an existing church. Lacking these types of accommodations, missionaries met their congregations in groves or brush arbors, in "sick-houses" (hospitals), barns, cooper shops, or cotton houses.[32]

30. *Religious Herald*, September 21, 1848, p. 150; *Christian Index*, August 29, 1845, n.p.; *Southern Christian Advocate*, July 22, 1837, p. 18; July 28, 1843, p. 26; October 3, 1851, p. 70, December 10, 1852, p. 114, June 30, 1854, p. 14, April 1, 1842, p. 166, August 5, 1837, p. 26; *Watchman of the South*, July 9, 1840, p. 182.

31. The names of these catechisms will be found listed among the primary sources in the Bibliography.

32. *Southern Christian Advocate*, September 15, 1843, p. 54, June 18, 1847, p. 6, August 1, 1851, p. 34, October 3, 1851, p. 70, August 5, 1837, p. 26, September 23, 1853, p. 66; Jones,

Evangelicals agreed that only a special kind of man and a special type of preaching were likely to win the respect, confidence, and affection of the blacks. "There can be no more corrupt notion abroad than that any sort of man can succeed with slaves," declared the editor of the *Watchman and Observer*. The evangelist to the Negroes should be "accessible to all"—ever ready "to meet their calls for his services, in times of sickness, at weddings and at funerals." He should "show them that he is their friend, and is neither ashamed of them nor their service." At the same time, he should be careful to preserve a measure of independence and dignity. Excessive familiarity was as likely as excessive aloofness to compromise his efforts among the blacks. Again, the evangelist was bound to teach the duties of servants to their masters as set forth in the Scripture. But, William Plumer cautioned, "beware of pressing these duties too strongly and frequently, lest you beget the fatal suspicion that you are but executing a selfish scheme of the white man to make them better slaves, rather than to make them Christ's freemen. If they suspect this, you labour in vain." In fact, a black congregation once walked out on Charles Colcock Jones as he was exhorting them to obey their master.[33]

The evangelist to the Negroes must not only have a thorough knowledge of the doctrines and duties of Christianity but the ability to present them plainly and simply, in such a way that the blacks could understand them. Describing the kind of preaching that should be employed, William Capers wrote that "it should be *preaching*, and not dry lecturing on moral duties only; much less should it be a rhapsodical speech paraded full of long meaning words." He and other evangelicals agreed that sermons should be short (Charles Colcock Jones suggested an hour and a quarter as the maximum length) and "pointed in application." The preacher should avoid "abstract propositions and learned arguments" and make his point through the use of illustrative material instead. He should make ample use of parables, religious narratives, biographies, and historical events. If this were done, Jones insisted, even "the most elevated doctrines" might

Religious Instruction of the Negroes, 268; *Christian Index*, July 19, 1849, p. 229; *Central Presbyterian*, March 8, 1856, p. 37; Charleston *Observer*, August 31, 1833, p. 137; Harrison, *Gospel Among the Slaves*, 217; Touchstone, "Planters and Slave Religion," 139, 144–45, 147.
    33. *Watchman and Observer*, June 29, 1848, p. 181; Jones, *Religious Instruction of the Negroes*, 254–55; Charleston *Observer*, August 31, 1833, p. 137; Plumer, *Thoughts on the Religious Instruction of the Negroes*, 26; Donald G. Mathews, "Charles Colcock Jones and the Southern Evangelical Crusade to Form a Biracial Community," *Journal of Southern History*, XLI (August, 1975), 318.

be "profitably exhibited, to ignorant and illiterate people."[34]

Few, if any, of the sermons evangelicals addressed to blacks were recorded, but some idea of their form of expression may be gained from a volume of "plantation sermons" published in 1856. The author, Andrew F. Dickson, had for several years been pastor of a church with a Negro congregation of some four hundred. The sermons were intended to be used by masters or mistresses who desired to provide their slaves with religious instruction, but they probably were similar to those which Dickson had delivered to the blacks under his care. Dickson addressed his hearers in simple, direct, everyday language, using a variety of colloquialisms, figures of speech, and illustrations. For example, in discussing the doctrine of inability (which he did not identify as such), he began by observing that "God earnestly invites sinners to come and be saved," but, he added, God "knows that men never seek him of their own accord. And so, when he invites us to repent and believe, he puts us in mind that there is *something to be done that we can't do*." It is "something so wonderful and mighty that nobody can do it but God. . . . Now there is something very terrible about this. God condemns us for our sins, and our own hearts condemn us, too. God provides a great salvation for us, and invites us to take it; and yet poor, wicked man can't take it! He can look at it, and wish he was safe, and tremble and mourn because of his danger; but he can't stretch out his hand and be saved!" The rest of the sermon aimed at understanding man's situation and finding out "how we can be saved." God has "made it plain that we can't be saved in our own way," Dickson concluded, but "he shows us just as plainly how we can be saved. Seek him! Go to him in earnest prayer; plead with him for his dear Son's sake; confess your sins; put him in mind of his own promises and calls; ask him to create in you a clean heart and to put a right spirit within you. . . . The Holy Spirit is waiting to be gracious, and the Lord Jesus is longing to save. That's what he died for! Come, all ye weary, heavy-laden, and he will give you rest. Or shall he say to you at last, 'Ye would not come unto me, that you might have life?'"[35]

Another clue to the nature of the sermons addressed to blacks is to be found in a statement of John L. Girardeau, pastor of the Anson Street Colored Church in Charleston. Whites often attended the church and one

34. Jones, *Religious Instruction of the Negroes*, 253, 256–57, 269; *Southern Presbyterian*, July 5, 1856, n.p.; *Southern Christian Advocate*, November 3, 1837, p. 78, April 8, 1842, p. 170.

35. A. F. Dickson, *Plantation Sermons; or Plain and Familiar Discourses for the Instruction of the Unlearned* (Philadelphia, 1856), 89–90, 99–100.

of them, Joseph Mack, pointed out the anomalous character of the sermons Girardeau preached. "The minds of the cultured whites would be strained to keep up with the train of thought, while the negroes seemed to clearly understand and fully appreciate the whole sermon. Hence the remark was frequently made, 'How can those ignorant negroes understand such a sermon?'" When Mack asked Girardeau about this, the pastor replied, "The negroes understand my sermon as clearly but not as fully as you do. I have acquired the power to put *key-words* in my sentences, and to emphasize them both in tone and by manner, and as they are vividly impressed by those words they secure the current of my thought." To illustrate Girardeau's technique, Mack described a sermon which dealt with "the vileness of sin and the certainty of its punishment":

There was the phrase "Holy God" spoken in a tone of deep humility and awe— then "sin hateful," with a look of intense abhorrence—then "God angry" with an expression of heartfelt indignation, and then among other words were "judge," "guilty," "doomed," "death," "depart," "hell," "wailing," "forever," and each word or phrase so emphasized in tone and by gesture as to stamp its meaning upon the mind of the hearer. One could easily see how, through such word painting, the ignorant hearer could readily grasp the main line of truth, and without any weakening of its power by trying also to lay hold upon the subordinate thoughts connected with it. The negro got enough to fill his head and heart, not too much so as to overflow and bring confusion to his mind.[36]

Evangelicals agreed that preaching addressed to the blacks, like that addressed to the whites, should be "full of unction." But since they believed that blacks were by nature more emotional than whites, they cautioned against promoting excitement among them. "They need instruction, not feeling; knowledge, not excitement," declared J. S. Law. Evangelicals also emphasized the necessity of preserving "the strictest order" at religious meetings. This was of course partly to allay any fears or suspicions on the part of whites. It also derived from evangelicals' general concern for decorum. Presbyterians tended to be more strict on this matter than Methodists and Baptists. Charles Colcock Jones, for example, insisted that "no *audible* expressions of feeling in the way of groanings, cries, or noises of any kind, should be allowed." William Capers was inclined to be more permissive, not only because Methodists allowed the emotions more latitude but also because he recognized the cultural differences between blacks and whites. Commenting on the way the blacks expressed "Christian emotion," Capers advised that they "not be held to the edge of a rule which af-

36. Blackburn (ed.), *Life Work of Girardeau*, 71, and see also 390.

ter all may not, as it applies to them, be natural or wise." Why should "the tastes and habits of those in refined and polished life . . . be applied as a law to the plantation negro?" It was not so in other areas. "At a funeral," Capers observed, "Sancho's hideous wailing sounds well enough from Sancho. At a wedding, no one hinders them from being happy in their own way." It followed that "in a class-meeting, a shout that comes with a kindling countenance and flowing tears, will never be offensive to a Methodist missionary."[37]

Besides preaching and catechizing, the evangelist to the Negroes performed other duties: visiting the sick, attending funerals, performing marriage ceremonies, admitting church members, and maintaining discipline. The admission of blacks to church membership was a subject that evoked considerable discussion among evangelicals. Some feared that too many Negroes applied for admission to the church "under the impulse of feeling induced by an *exciting* sermon" or in response to the enthusiasm generated at a camp meeting. This was a problem that was not exclusive to the blacks; ministers made the same complaint with regard to whites. But the "excitable" nature of the Negroes seemed to make them especially prone to act impulsively and "without a proper understanding of the nature and import" of the act of offering themselves for church membership. Baptists, especially, expressed concern that not enough care was being exercised in admitting blacks to membership. They were being baptized and received into the church without having demonstrated that they had "a correct idea of the plan of salvation." Too often their religious "experience" included dreams, visions, and voices, which the white brethren condemned as fanaticism and superstition. The remedy for such problems and deficiencies, most evangelicals agreed, was better instruction in the principles of religion—which suggests why catechetical training was regarded as so important a part of the evangelist's work.[38]

Evangelical thinking about the methods of religious instruction remained fairly constant throughout the antebellum period except on two questions. One had to do with the instruction of plantation slaves. When the Meth-

37. *Southern Christian Advocate*, April 8, 1842, p. 170; *Christian Index*, March 22, 1855, p. 45; Jones, *Religious Instruction of the Negroes*, 262.

38. Jones, *Religious Instruction of the Negroes*, 226; *Southern Christian Advocate*, May 15, 1856, p. 199, July 24, 1840, p. 22; *Christian Index*, August 30, 1849, p. 278; *Religious Herald*, July 7, 1837, p. 105, September 15, 1837, p. 146, July 12, 1855, p. 106, August 9, 1855, p. 121. For an interesting discussion of the differences between the conversion experiences of blacks and whites, see Dickson D. Bruce, Jr., "Religion, Society and Culture in the Old South: A Comparative View," *American Quarterly*, XXVI (October, 1974), 399–416.

odist missions to the slaves were first established, the planters insisted on the use of the "plantation plan" of preaching, whereby the missionary preached at different plantations on successive Sabbaths and devoted weekdays to catechizing the children and visiting the sick and infirm. William Capers and other missionaries acquiesced, but by the late 1830s, they were pointing out serious deficiencies in the plan. It required considerable time and labor on the part of the missionary, who had to preach several times on the Sabbath and do a good deal of traveling from one plantation to another. As an example, Capers cited the missionary John Bunch who "preach[ed] five times, and walk[ed] as many miles on the rice-field banks, for his usual sunday task, winter and summer." The plantation plan also deprived most of the blacks of weekly Sabbath services. Missionaries usually served a number of plantations and were able to offer preaching only about every three or four weeks. Capers, Andrew, and other Methodists involved in the missions to the slaves advocated a different and, in their view, more efficient method of instruction. They proposed that the planters build chapels at central points so that the slaves of several plantations might come together for preaching on the Sabbath. Once they were able to persuade planters that it posed no danger, the new plan was increasingly employed, although the plantation plan continued to be used in a few places.[39]

The other question on which evangelical opinion changed had to do with separate churches for blacks. In the early 1830s, most evangelicals were not in favor of separate churches. Their attitude was partly a legacy of the 1820s, a time of increasing opposition to black churches and black preachers, and partly a response to the Turner insurrection. Leaders of the movement for religious instruction seem to have assumed that most of the Negroes would be incorporated into existing white churches. The slaves on the more remote plantations were an exception; they would have to be served by special missionaries in their own chapels. But many other blacks were within reach of a settled minister or circuit preacher and might attend the church he served. Accordingly, congregations were urged to provide accommodations for them and masters were exhorted to encourage their slaves to attend worship services. Once the evangelization of the Negroes began, the number of black church members grew. Although gratified, ministers were quick to recognize the problems created by the increase. Often the churches did not have sufficient room to accommo-

    39. *Southern Christian Advocate*, September 15, 1843, p. 54, October 13, 1854, p. 75, August 30, 1855, p. 49, June 4, 1857, p. 3; Thomas Leonard Williams, "Methodist Mission to the Slaves," 202–203; *Southern Presbyterian*, November 14, 1857, n.p.

date the blacks along with the white congregation. Also, ministers found that many of the blacks either were not interested in or were unable to profit from the sermons which were addressed to the white members. To solve these and other problems, ministers began holding special services on the Sabbath for the blacks, usually in the afternoon. The entire church was given up to them, except for a few seats occupied by white members who chose to attend. The minister preached a sermon especially to and for the blacks. This was the arrangement used by many churches in the 1830s and early 1840s. The blacks were members of the church along with the whites, were under the care of the same pastor, and were subject to the same discipline. However, special worship services and catechetical instruction were provided them, though they were free to attend the Sabbath service for the white congregation if they desired.[40]

The instituting of separate services and instruction for the blacks was the first step in the direction of separate churches. A look at the Baptist churches of Richmond shows the way the one led to the other. In the mid-1830s the pastors of the First and Second Baptist churches were holding separate Sabbath services for the black congregation. By 1838, however, the arrangement was proving inadequate and Baptist leaders were arguing the necessity of establishing a separate church for the blacks. In an address to the citizens of Richmond, which was published in the *Religious Herald*, they explained why. First, the existing churches could not accommodate the blacks. The committee that authored the address estimated that there were as many as six thousand Negroes in the city "of a suitable age for attending religious worship." Yet the accommodations provided them in all the churches of the city were sufficient for not more than one thousand. The committee noted that "in the Baptist churches, particularly in the First, the space alloted for their use is crowded on every Lord's-day; and many seek admission in vain. Large numbers, bringing from their owners, or employers, certificates of their good morals, and fair character, are now asking membership in our churches, already crowded beyond convenience." The committee added that many blacks spent the Sabbath "strolling through the city, . . . in dram shops, and other places of dissipation." Were there sufficient accommodations in the churches, they too might "be brought under the restraining influence of religious instruction."[41]

The second reason which the committee offered in support of a sepa-

40. Ira Berlin, *Slaves Without Masters: The Free Negro in the Antebellum South* (New York, 1974), 285–86, 289–90; *Watchman of the South*, July 21, 1842, p. 189.
41. *Religious Herald*, February 13, 1835, p. 23, September 7, 1838, p. 143.

rate church for the blacks was that the preaching offered in the existing churches was not as well suited to the circumstances of the blacks as it might be. "Ministers generally adapt their discourses to the taste and wants of the whites, who constitute the larger portion of every congregation," the committee observed. "The colored people have their peculiar prejudices and errors, which need to be corrected by clear and pointed refutation; and their peculiar duties, to which they need to be stimulated by direct appeals."[42]

There were other reasons for establishing a separate church, which the committee did not include in its address. Jeremiah Jeter, pastor of the First Baptist Church, cited the difficulty he encountered, having a large white congregation, of paying very much attention to the blacks. "A pastor who should devote his whole time, or the chief part of it, to their interests seemed to be imperatively demanded." The desires of the blacks themselves also were a factor. On at least two occasions, in 1823 and again in 1834, they had petitioned for the right to build their own church, but without success.[43] By the late 1830s, whites were inclined to look more favorably on such requests.

The establishment of a separate church for blacks in Richmond encountered some opposition from people who appealed to the fears excited by the Southampton insurrection and who charged that any effort in behalf of the blacks favored the designs of the abolitionists. Many of the opponents, according to Jeter, were "irreligious persons—sceptics, gamblers, bar-keepers, and the like," but there were also a good many "pious people" who were distrustful of new measures for the religious instruction of the Negroes. Nevertheless, the First Church finally resolved to build a new house of worship and to allow the black congregation exclusive occupancy of the old church. The First African Church was organized in 1842, with a white man, Robert Ryland, president of Richmond College, as pastor. In accordance with state law, the church held meetings only in the daytime and in the presence of white persons. By 1848 it had 2400 members. Though opposition to the church did not die down completely, it dissipated sufficiently so that a few years later the white members of the Second Baptist Church sponsored a Second African Church. In the late 1840s and 1850s other black Baptist churches were established throughout Virginia, making a total of fourteen by the Civil War.[44]

42. *Ibid.*, September 7, 1838, p. 143.
43. Jeter, *Recollections*, 209; Berlin, *Slaves Without Masters*, 287 and 287n.
44. Jeter, *Recollections*, 209–11; *Religious Herald*, August 17, 1848, p. 131; Berlin, *Slaves Without Masters*, 295.

Baptists were not the only ones who came to favor separate churches. When Jeter began his campaign for the First African Church, he talked with William Plumer, pastor of the First Presbyterian Church, about the advisability of calling a meeting of the clergy of Richmond in order to gain support for the venture. Plumer counseled against such action. "The clergy may decide against your plan, but it is right," he told Jeter. He urged him to "go forward in the work, and if you have trouble I will stand by you." Somewhat later, during a time of intense opposition, Plumer came to Jeter and said, "I wish you to understand that in any difficulties you may have concerning the African church I am to go halves with you."[45]

In the late 1840s Plumer's fellow Presbyterians in Charleston began considering the formation of a separate church for the blacks. The leader in this enterprise was John Bailey Adger. Having returned to the city after spending twelve years as a missionary to the Armenians, he had turned his attention to the religious condition of the blacks. In the Second Presbyterian Church, of which Thomas Smyth was pastor, there were some three hundred blacks. "I often looked at them, as they sat in the gallery, and felt how far preaching to his white congregation went over their heads," Adger wrote. The same situation prevailed in the First Presbyterian Church, where there were some five hundred Negro members. The Methodists and Baptists had a great many more black members than the Presbyterians, and Adger contended that those churches did not have sufficient room to accommodate more than one fourth of them. (One of the Methodist ministers, Whitefoord Smith, disputed Adger's claim and insisted on taking him to measure one of the galleries to convince him of his error, but, Adger wrote, "I think the actual measurement rather convinced him that he was wrong.") Adger estimated that there were at least twelve thousand Negroes in Charleston who were not under the care of any church. Nor was he satisfied with the arrangement in the Methodist and Baptist churches whereby the blacks (numbering almost eight thousand) were divided into classes, which were in turn led by Negroes. "The white pastors could not have much oversight of all these classes, or even of all these class-leaders," Adger declared. Moreover, he was inclined to believe that many of the black leaders were "both incompetent and unfaithful." Adger wrote that "it seemed very clear that the men of my race could not properly discharge their duty to their slaves vicariously. . . . I said to myself, it certainly is time for some white minister to make a beginning of public instruction, specially and separately, for the negroes."[46]

45. Jeter, *Recollections*, 213.
46. Adger, *My Life and Times*, 137–38, 164, 172–73.

In May, 1847, Adger preached a sermon in the Second Presbyterian Church in which he set forth his views on the necessity of a separate church for blacks. Thomas Smyth and many leading members were persuaded to support the enterprise. The Charleston Presbytery gave its approval. However, just as in Richmond, the venture aroused considerable opposition, both within and outside the Presbyterian fold. Some of the critics attempted to play on the fears of a community that had not forgotten the Denmark Vesey plot. Ultimately, however, they were defeated, and in 1850 the Anson Street Church was dedicated, with Adger as its pastor.[47]

It was no ordinary dedication. At the time, Adger explained, "the whole Southern country, placed under the ban of the civilized world, had been stung to madness by unjust reproaches against our 'cruelty and inhumanity' as slaveholders." Adger himself had recently dissolved his connection with the American Board of Commissioners for Foreign Missions rather than become the focus of a controversy over whether that body should permit a slaveholder to be a missionary. Accordingly, he decided that the dedication should serve as a vindication of the South and slavery. "Here was a church built by Christian slaveholders for the religious benefit of the slaves." It seemed only proper that the masters, rather than the slaves, should dedicate the church. The congregation that took part in the dedication was composed exclusively of white people, and James Henley Thornwell preached a sermon that was described as "a powerful vindication of the rights of Southern slave-holders and the duties of Southern christians." Reporting on the ceremony, the editor of the *Southern Presbyterian* described the establishment of the Anson Street Church as a "generous and self-denying" effort, but failed to note the strong element of self-congratulation which marked the dedication.[48] The whole enterprise reflected an ambivalence that, to a greater or lesser degree, characterized much of the movement for the religious instruction of the Negroes.

By the 1850s, most evangelicals seem to have favored separate churches for blacks. Not only Baptists and Presbyterians, but Methodists as well supported the new arrangement. In addition to the arguments that had been advanced in its favor in the 1840s, evangelicals placed increasing em-

47. John Bailey Adger, *The Religious Instruction of the Colored Population. A Sermon, Preached by the Rev. John B. Adger, in the Second Presbyterian Church, Charleston, S.C., May 9th, 1847* (Charleston, 1847). For the response to Adger's sermon, see "Critical Notices," *Southern Presbyterian Review*, I (September, 1847), 137–50; *Watchman and Observer*, June 3, 1847, p. 166; Adger, *My Life and Times*, 55, 165–66.

48. Adger, *My Life and Times*, 178, 136–37, 139–43; James Henley Thornwell, *The Rights and Duties of Masters. A Sermon Preached at the Dedication of a Church Erected in Charleston, S.C., for the Benefit and Instruction of the Colored Population* (Charleston, 1850); *Southern Presbyterian*, June 7, 1850, p. 162.

phasis on what one of them termed the "strong social feeling" of the blacks, that is, their desire to worship in congregations of their own color and to perform some part of the worship by themselves. Evangelicals were no doubt aware of similar separatist feelings on the part of some of the whites, who resented the intrusion of the blacks into their worship services.[49]

A minority of evangelicals opposed separate churches. Charles Colcock Jones, in his two works on the religious instruction of the Negroes, advised against them. Arguing for mixed congregations, he wrote that "this mingling of the two classes in churches creates a greater bond of union between them; and kinder feelings; tends to increase subordination; and promotes in a higher degree the improvement of the Negroes, in piety and morality." Some Presbyterians raised the question of whether the separate church arrangement constituted a form of "class-worship" and fostered "that most pernicious of all errors[,] that there is one religion for masters and another for servants." Bishop James O. Andrew also objected to "the separation of the religious interests of the slaves and their masters as unfortunate to the interests of both." His remarks applied not only to separate churches but to separate services as well. "Whenever it may be done," he wrote, "the master and the slave should worship together, have the same preacher, and [be] under the same pastoral oversight. . . . The intelligence and sobriety of the whites may serve to keep in check the wild excitement to which the negro has a sort of constitutional tendency; and the warmth and unaffected and simple piety of many a pious negro, who can never believe that a hearty amen or a warm old fashioned glory to God is a violation of gospel order, or church decency, might serve, to some extent, to correct the strong tendency to worldly fastidiousness and formality which is the course of many a genteel congregation of Christians in these days of wonderful refinement."[50]

Despite such objections and worries, the trend toward separate churches continued. Rural areas remained suspicious of them, and many churches continued the practice of having separate services and instruction for blacks in the white churches, but in the larger towns black churches were increasingly regarded as a decided improvement on that plan. By 1860, in addition to those already mentioned, there were Negro churches in Savannah, Augusta, Mobile, Natchez, and New Orleans, some with memberships close

49. See, for example, "Duties of Masters," 278–82; *Southern Presbyterian*, April 11, 1857, n.p.; Blackburn (ed.), *Life Work of Girardeau*, 38–51; *Southern Christian Advocate*, September 24, 1857, p. 66; Eighmy, *Churches in Cultural Captivity*, 27; Berlin, *Slaves Without Masters*, 291.

50. Jones, *Religious Instruction of the Negroes*, 274; "Report of a Conference by Presbytery," 2–3; *Southern Presbyterian*, April 26, 1856, n.p.; *Southern Christian Advocate*, April 24, 1856, p. 185.

to or over one thousand, all of them attached to and under the supervision of white churches.[51]

Some of the black Baptist and Methodist churches had black preachers. The two denominations had been employing black preachers and exhorters even before the movement for religious instruction and the practice became more widespread in the 1840s and 1850s. Most of the preachers were free Negroes, but some were slaves. For example, the pastor of the First African Baptist Church in Augusta, Georgia, was a slave. His congregation furnished him with sufficient means to purchase his whole time from his master. Methodists also utilized black preachers in their work among plantation slaves.[52]

The majority of Presbyterians opposed the employment of black preachers. They argued, much as John Holt Rice had in the mid-1820s, that "there is too great a proneness to superstition and extravagance among the most enlightened of them" and that "they would soon degrade piety into fanaticism." Moreover, they noted that the laws of most of the southern states prevented blacks from engaging in the preparation and study necessary to becoming a Presbyterian minister. Charles Colcock Jones took exception to this point of view. "From my own observation," he wrote, "Negro preachers may be employed and confided in, and so regulated as to do their own color great good, and community no harm: nor do I see, if we take the word of God for our guide, how we can consistently exclude an entire people from access to the Gospel ministry, as it may please Almighty God from time to time, as he unquestionably does, to call some of them to it 'as Aaron was.'" As Jones pointed out, the Presbyterian policy of discouraging Negro preachers made the blacks more dependent on white ministers, of whom there was not even a sufficient number to supply the needs of the whites.[53]

While Presbyterians opposed employing blacks as preachers, they, like the Methodists and Baptists, approved the use of blacks in lesser capacities —as members of committees to examine candidates for admission to the

51. Berlin, *Slaves Without Masters,* 296–97; *Religious Herald,* April 19, 1855, p. 58; *Christian Index,* September 6, 1844, n.p., November 18, 1852, p. 185, September 15, 1853, p. 145; *Southern Presbyterian,* June 28, 1856, n.p.; *Southern Christian Advocate,* June 27, 1851, p. 14, February 18, 1858, p. 150, April 15, 1858, p. 182; Sydnor, *Slavery in Mississippi,* 59; Stratton, *Memorial of a Quarter-Century's Pastorate,* 40–41.

52. *Religious Herald,* March 21, 1844, p. 46, April 19, 1855, p. 58; *Christian Index,* November 18, 1852, p. 185, September 15, 1853, p. 145; Purifoy, "Methodist Episcopal Church, South, and Slavery," 147–49; Wightman, *Life of Capers,* 126–28, 138–40; Newman, *History of the Baptist Churches,* 320, 331; Harrison, *Gospel Among the Slaves,* 281, 290.

53. [Thornwell], "Report on Slavery," 394; Jones, *Religious Instruction of the Negroes,* 157–58. Presbyterians had employed a few black preachers prior to 1830. See Thompson, *Presbyterians in the South,* I, 207–208.

church or to maintain discipline, as leaders of prayer meetings and singing, and as catechists. The "coloured helpers," or "watchmen," or class leaders, as they were called, served on plantations as well as in the separate black churches and among the Negro congregations of white churches.[54]

The men involved in the work of religious instruction fall into three categories: ministers whose congregations included blacks, ministers of separate black churches, and the missionaries to the plantation Negroes. The first category included such men as Richard Fuller, Edward Baptist, Basil Manly, Jr., Thomas Smyth, Benjamin Mosby Smith, and William Winans. Like many other ministers of the Old South, they held separate services for their black congregations and organized Sunday schools to provide religious instruction. Some also preached regularly on nearby plantations. All of them regarded the blacks as an important part of their pastoral charge. "They are the poor, the ignorant and, comparatively, the friendless portion of the flock," Winans explained. "It becomes the shepherd, as it did his great superior, to consider these as objects of peculiar sympathy, and of peculiar care." In several cases, the activities of evangelicals in behalf of the Negroes were a carry-over from their student days, when they taught in Sunday schools or Bible classes for Negroes.[55]

Of the ministers of separate black churches, John Bailey Adger, Robert Ryland, and John L. Girardeau were probably the best known. They, like the missionaries to the Negroes, seem to have been more completely dedicated to the cause of religious instruction than the ministers of mixed congregations. Girardeau, for example, believed that he had "a *special* vocation to preach the Gospel of Christ to the coloured people." Even before he became a minister, he felt compelled to preach to the Negroes. As a youth he held religious meetings in the cotton house on his father's plantation. Some years later, while teaching school, he visited plantations on weekday afternoons to catechize and exhort the slaves; and on Sunday,

54. "Report of a Conference by Presbytery," 5–6; *Southern Christian Advocate*, March 5, 1841, p. 150; *Religious Herald*, October 8, 1840, p. 163; *Christian Index*, July 29, 1857, p. 120; Jones, *Suggestions on the Religious Instruction of the Negroes*, 46–50; Harrison, *Gospel Among the Slaves*, 359–60; Clarke, "Thomas Smyth," 179, 187; Blackburn (ed.), *Life Work of Girardeau*, 92–95.
55. Cuthbert, *Life of Fuller*, 82, 104–105; E. G. Baptist, "An Account of the Religious Instruction Granted the Negroes, Prior to the War Between the States, in the Bounds of the Goshen Association" (MS dated March, 1890, in Virginia Baptist Historical Society Collection); Cox, "Life and Work of Basil Manly, Jr.," 73–74; Clarke, "Thomas Smyth." 178–79; Flournoy, *Benjamin Mosby Smith*, 49, 73; William Winans to the Reverend W. Hamilton Watkins, February 6, 1851, in Winans Collection; McIlwaine, *Memories*, 105, 178–79; Hickey, "Benjamin Morgan Palmer," 179, 179n, 181.

after the regular church services were over and the white congregation had dispersed, he stood on the pulpit steps and addressed the Negroes who crowded the church building. Upon being licensed to preach, he rejected an invitation to a large and important church because there were few Negroes connected with it. Instead, he accepted a call to a small church in an area where there was a large population of slaves. He remained there for three years, preaching regularly to the blacks on the plantations, before he succeeded Adger in the Anson Street pastorate in 1853. Reminiscing about his work in Charleston, Girardeau wrote, "I have sometimes thought that I devoted too much time to it. I was absorbed in it." Besides offering three Sabbath services, he held two weeknight prayer meetings, catechized classes, administered discipline, performed marriage ceremonies, visited the sick and dying, and conducted all of the funerals. As a result of his efforts, by 1857 the membership of the church had increased four-fold to nearly two hundred.[56]

William Capers and Charles Colcock Jones were the most famous of the missionaries, but there were hundreds of men, mostly Methodists, who also ministered to the slaves. Most missionaries received between $100 and $200 a year for each plantation they served. Few planters were as generous as the Beaufort man who paid a minister $800 for preaching full time to his Negroes or the Mississippi planter who paid $1,200. Generally, missionaries did not complain about the amount of financial support they received, perhaps because they did not expect munificent salaries, or equally likely, because they were glad of any amount, however small. They did complain about poor preaching and living accommodations. Many of the buildings in which they preached were uncomfortable, even dangerous. A missionary in Georgia was afraid of a fire in the cotton house where he held services. Another in South Carolina reported that he had had to terminate one of his appointments because of "the *decayed and unsafe* condition of the house in which we worshiped." On some plantations the dwellings provided the missionaries were in little better condition.[57]

Securing permission from planters to preach to their slaves was some-

56. John L. Girardeau to Thomas Smyth, June 11, 1858, in Smyth, *Autobiographical Notes*, 197; Blackburn (ed.), *Life Work of Girardeau*, 25–30, 75–78, 32, 37; *Southern Presbyterian*, September 12, 1857, n.p.

57. *Christian Index*, March 28, 1850, p. 50; Dunwody, *Reminiscences and Sermons*, 51; Harrison, *Gospel Among the Slaves*, 296, 268–69; Touchstone, "Planters and Slave Religion," 212; Sydnor, *Slavery in Mississippi*, 59; *Religious Herald*, March 21, 1844, p. 46; Charleston *Observer*, August 31, 1833, p. 137; *Southern Christian Advocate*, May 30, 1851, p. 206, October 20, 1848, p. 79, August 30, 1850, p. 50, August 6, 1857, p. 39.

times difficult. Missionaries complained that some planters were indifferent to religion, while others saw "no reason for any such extra pains-taking for the souls" of the slaves. Other planters supported the work of religious instruction but for what the missionaries considered the wrong reasons. J. Nipper of the Wateree Mission in the South Carolina Conference quoted one of the wealthiest and most influential planters on the mission as saying that "negroes under missionary influence, are worth 25 per cent more than those who are not." In Nipper's view, that was "but the smallest consideration for missionary effort: the moral influence, which it exerts is *not* to be, cannot be, counted by dollars and cents." Alexander McBryde, who served a mission in Marengo County, Alabama, also criticized the motives of the slaveowners in his area. "The preacher is employed to serve the people not that they expect many, if any of them to be converted and saved, but that their own skirts may be cleared," he wrote. He regarded such thinking as contrary to the spirit of the movement for religious instruction. "If the missionary had no higher motives in laboring among the slaves of the South than the acquittal of the master in the day of judgment, methinks he would turn to some other field of labor," McBryde declared. Overseers were more likely than planters to object to the religious instruction of the slaves because they believed that it undermined plantation discipline. Indeed, a few missionaries cited overseers as one of the chief obstacles in the way of carrying the Gospel to the slaves. On the other hand, there were overseers as well as planters who supported the missionary efforts and, not surprisingly, missionaries were full of praise for such men. Because they were convinced that godly men were more likely than the religiously indifferent to favor religious instruction, missionaries often took as much interest in the souls of the planters and overseers as they did in those of the slaves. They noted with pride the fact that services for the blacks were being attended by the whites of the plantation, or that some of the planters had joined the church, or that members of the planter's family were helping to catechize the slaves.[58]

The missionary's relation to the planter was often ambiguous. On the one hand, missionaries expected to be treated with respect. James O. Andrew emphasized that planters should not treat the missionary "as though he were unworthy to be classed with gentlemen, else the overseers, who

---

58. *Southern Christian Advocate*, June 24, 1842, p. 6, September 4, 1840, p. 46, September 15, 1843, p. 54, February 19, 1857, p. 149, April 13, 1838, p. 170, November 1, 1850, p. 86, August 8, 1851, p. 39; Harrison, *Gospel Among the Slaves*, 211, 223, 235, 258; William P. Gready to John McLees, January 13, 1859, in McLees Papers.

are very apt to take their cue from the proprietor, will find many opportunities of thwarting the benevolent efforts of the preacher." At the same time, most missionaries agreed that it was desirable to be on friendly terms with the planters in order to win and maintain their support for religious instruction. Bishop John Early contended that it was "essential for the Missionary to become acquainted with the Planters," and said "that when it is prudent and practical, they should visit them and stay in their houses; as it is proper that any man who exercises so much influence over the slaves . . . should be known by the proprietors." The missionary should be "accessible and independent, as well as grave." Only such a man would be able to perform the public relations work necessary to the success of the missionary enterprise. "It is a great work," Early declared, "and the man who either from a timid disposition, association, or a want of self-respect, avoids the presence or shrinks at the approach of those wealthy and, in many instances, accomplished and benevolent gentlemen who have invited us to take charge of their servants, cannot succeed so as to leaven the whole lump." On the other hand, the very type of man who was impelled to become a missionary to the slaves was likely to feel ill at ease with or even alienated from the planter class. There was a marked difference between most planters and missionaries—in social and economic status, in religiosity, in life style. The planter was, more often than not, a worldling. When he treated the missionary "as a member of the family," as some did, the missionary was apt to react as M. L. Banks did. "The planters lived in princely style," he recalled. "The dishes on their tables were of the best quality and in great variety. I declined nothing but the wines and liquors, and it was a trial to do that. To hold to my temperance principles under a perfect battery of both masculine and feminine hospitality was not the easiest thing in the world to do."[59]

Missionaries willingly accommodated their efforts to the plantation regimen, but occasionally they complained about the restrictions it imposed. Peter Haskew, of the Prairie Creek Mission in Alabama, cited a common difficulty, the fact that all of the planters wished the preaching to be on Sunday, which caused the "Sabbath labours to be very laborious." Missionaries on the sugar plantations criticized the practice of requiring the slaves to work on Sundays at harvest time. John Pipes, an evangelist to the slaves in Louisiana, noted the consequences of suspending religious exercises during the 2½-month period:

59. *Southern Christian Advocate*, May 28, 1857, p. 207, April 24, 1856, p. 186; Harrison, *Gospel Among the Slaves*, 270.

Suppose the Missionary commencing with the year, labours and strives to train the children, harmonize the societies, and instruct the congregation; and suppose that in some measure he feels that he has succeeded. Harvesting commences, and the Missionary leaves, say the first of October, to return in January. When he comes, what is the state of the work? To his regret, the children have forgotten their lessons, the membership have backslidden, and are cold; some of them must be tried and expelled; and the state of things taken altogether is but little better than at the first.

The plantation regimen also interfered with the holding of camp meetings for the Negroes. Some planters were willing to allow their slaves to be away from the fields for several days, but many were not. To deal with this problem, the editor of the *Southern Christian Advocate* advised having the meetings include the Sabbath (rather than starting on Monday and ending before Sunday) so as to make it possible for the slaves to attend. He agreed that masters "ought to feel disposed to give them time to attend upon the extra services which the Church may appoint, even if their attendance should interfere with their secular interests." But, he continued, "as the New Testament contains no specific legislation on this subject . . . the church should accommodate her economy to existing circumstances, and do her best to secure whatever benefit may accrue from her extra services to servants as well as their masters." Apparently, some missionaries did alter the camp meeting schedule so as to permit blacks to attend. Nevertheless, camp and protracted meetings were rare in the lives of the plantation slaves.[60]

The plantation regimen was not the only source of frustration for the missionaries. Often they found the slaves unresponsive or even resistant to their efforts. A writer in the *Southern Christian Advocate* described the difficulties of preaching to the blacks:

The Negro Missionary has to contend with depraved ignorance, blind superstition, and extreme stupidity. . . . [He] finds it extremely difficult to make himself so well understood as to interest his hearers. Under his most earnest endeavors to instruct them, he will frequently perceive, not only that some are not interested, but that others have fallen asleep, and are as insensible as stones. And even in reference to those who appear to be interested, he feels a painful anxiety lest they should misconstrue his words, and adopt error for truth. Or should his preaching have produced apparent effect, he may still be fearful lest it prove no more than sympathy; and his only resource is to commend all into the hands of God, relying on his promise.

60. *Southern Christian Advocate*, July 16, 1847, p. 22, March 7, 1851, p. 158, October 6, 1848, p. 70, May 31, 1850, p. 206, September 8, 1848, p. 54, October 16, 1846, p. 74; Harrison, *Gospel Among the Slaves*, 272; Thomas Leonard Williams, "Methodist Mission to the Slaves," 126.

Part of the problem was that the Negro's mind was not a blank slate. One missionary noted that many of the blacks had "formed religious opinions and notions, every way different from ours," as well as "prejudices . . . against our modes and usages." They would have "to be unlearned, and then correctly taught," and this would require "time and pains." The missionaries learned—and cautioned the planters—not to expect an immediate transformation. "We believe in sudden conversions," one of them observed, "but the old habits and doings of a community, will seldom improve otherwise than gradually." [61]

Many of the missionaries blamed the black preachers for what they regarded as the ignorance and prejudice of the slaves. Indeed, they were dismayed to find that the black preachers continued to exert a considerable influence in spite of the missions. "Let it be known that one of these is to preach on such a day," wrote the missionary to the Ogechee Mission in Georgia, "and there is a rush from Mifflin, Santee, Frog Camp, New Hope, Wild Hors, and High Ground, that they may have the pleasure of hearing one of their own colour." He admitted that this was "natural enough," but he contended that nothing but "mischief" could be expected "from the teachings of an ignorant enthusiast, who knows nothing of God's word, and puts his own delusions to the place of divine truth." No doubt his reaction was partly inspired by jealousy. The slaves assembled reluctantly for his preaching, he reported. "They say whenever they come to hear me, it is from duty. They say among themselves, that they ought to come, because I am employed by their owners." On some of the plantations he served even the children refused to be instructed "because of the example of their parents and the older ones." Other missionaries, however, were equally critical of the older Negroes for instilling "many foolish prejudices" against white religion in the minds of the young ones. [62]

"But after all the difficulties and discouragements," declared a writer in the *Southern Christian Advocate*, "the motives to zeal and diligence in the work are most ample." Missionaries noted the rewards as well as the problems of preaching to the blacks—the improvement in their morals, their interest in and gratitude for religious services. Not all the Negroes resisted their efforts. "To witness the interest often manifest while the word of life is held forth to them, and then the hearty shake of the hand, the 'God bless you my preacher,' when the service is over, is enough to stir the best

61. *Southern Christian Advocate*, September 2, 1837, p. 43, July 28, 1843, p. 26, January 19, 1844, p. 126.
62. *Ibid.*, July 28, 1843, p. 26, May 17, 1844, p. 195.

feelings of [the missionary's] soul," one of them wrote. Missionary work satisfied the religious needs of the missionaries as well as the slaves. What better way to prove one's piety and self-denial than by becoming "a negro preacher"? One evangelist wrote that "in simplifying the gospel to them [the slaves], I have simplified it to myself, so that I have fed on it, as it were, anew." Other missionaries were greatly affected by the intensity of religious feeling in the meetings they conducted for the blacks. Their reports celebrated the "artless" and "unaffected" piety of the Negroes, as exhibited in the love feasts, and the moving character of the singing during worship services. Nor was this reaction peculiar to the missionaries. Joseph Stratton, a Presbyterian minister in Natchez, remarked on the "responsive sensibility" of the Negro congregation to whom he preached. "The services I performed among this people were, in some respects, the most satisfactory of any that belong to my public ministrations," he wrote. "The pulpit, in their presence, has fewer of those temptations to self-seeking which in other cases are liable to disturb the purity and simplicity of the preacher's purpose; and the gospel in their hearing, addressing a class of minds where the affections preponderate over the thoughtful judgment and the sober intelligence, is apt to be listened to with an openness of heart, and a responsive sensibility, which are rare in other assemblies." It would appear that in an era of "wonderful refinement," evangelicals found in the religious feeling of the blacks the simple unadorned piety, the purity of heart that they feared was being lost among whites.[63]

Opposition to the movement for the religious instruction of the Negroes never entirely abated. It was strongest and most concerted in the early and mid-1830s when southerners were particularly agitated about the threat of abolitionism. By the mid-1840s, after evangelicals had demonstrated their support of slavery, it began to gain favor, especially among leading planters and politicians. In South Carolina, for example, it had the backing of some of the wealthiest and most influential men of the state, including Charles Cotesworth Pinckney, Daniel Huger, Joel R. Poinsett, Wade Hampton, Robert Barnwell Rhett and many others. Nevertheless, evangelicals always had to be on guard, lest some statement or incident re-

63. *Ibid.*, September 2, 1837, p. 43, November 23, 1849, p. 98, July 27, 1849, p. 29, March 28, 1851, p. 170, April 24, 1856, p. 185; Cuthbert, *Life of Fuller*, 223; *Christian Index*, July 19, 1849, p. 229; Charleston *Observer*, July 2, 1831, p. 106; Stratton, *Memorial of a Quarter-Century's Pastorate*, 36–37; Blackburn (ed.), *Life Work of Girardeau*, 76–77; William Winans to the Reverend W. Hamilton Watkins, February 6, 1851, in Winans Collection.

vive opposition. In 1838 William Wightman was accused of abolitionism for having delivered an address in the presence of slaves in which he censured slaveholders who treated their slaves cruelly and denounced all who opposed religious instruction of the Negroes. In 1852, when some Negro members of the First Baptist Church in Richmond were charged with murder, the efforts of the Baptists among the blacks came under attack. Robert Ryland, pastor of the First African Church, was singled out for special criticism. Even as late as 1859, John L. Girardeau was denounced in some of the secular papers for his work with a "nigger church." Significantly, none of these men felt secure enough to ignore the attacks. Just as evangelicals had protested their innocence during the abolitionist pamphlet campaign in the mid-1830s, Wightman, the Richmond Baptists, and Girardeau felt impelled to answer the charges levelled against them. Girardeau's "card," originally published in the Charleston *Courier*, was typical. On the one hand he affirmed his belief that the Bible sanctioned slavery and his sympathy with the South against "fanatical encroachments upon its constitutional rights." At the same time he declared, "I hold myself bound to regard the souls of the bond as well as the free, since for them too the Saviour died."[64]

There is a certain irony in the fact that southern critics of the movement for religious instruction attacked it as an emancipating scheme. By contrast, northern abolitionists viewed it in just the opposite light, as an effort which strengthened rather than weakened the bonds of slavery. Historians have generally sustained the abolitionist judgment. Nor is this surprising, in view of the fact that many evangelicals promoted the cause by promising planters that their slaves would be more obedient and by assuring whites in general that it offered a safeguard against slave rebellion. On the other hand, what Kenneth K. Bailey has termed "ameliorative and fraternal tendencies" were as important in motivating evangelicals as considerations of self-interest and social control. Evangelicals sought to provide the Negro with something that they themselves valued greatly. Moreover, they contended for religious instruction on the ground that the Negro was a "fellow being," a member of the human family. They insisted that in the matter of religion "God is no respecter of persons, colors, or condi-

64. Touchstone, "Planters and Slave Religion," 93–94; Harrison, *Gospel Among the Slaves*, 282–87; *Southern Christian Advocate*, September 8, 1843, pp. 50–51, October 5, 1838, pp. 62–63, November 2, 1838, p. 79; Thomas Leonard Williams, "Methodist Mission to the Slaves," 189; *Religious Herald*, November 11, 1852, p. 183, December 9, 1852, p. 198; *Watchman and Observer*, November 11, 1852, pp. 54, 56, December 2, 1852, pp. 65, 66; Smyth, *Autobiographical Notes*, 198–200; *Central Presbyterian*, November 12, 1859, p. 182.

tions." William Winans declared that "among the most deeply pious Christians I have known have been many black people who, ignorant in other matters, degraded in conditions—many of them *slaves*, were children of God by Faith, and heirs of the promise of life eternal through Christ Jesus."[65] It is significant that evangelicals affirmed the humanity of the Negro at a time when theories which denied it (for example, ethnology) were gaining strength. Again, while the attitudes of some evangelicals toward the Negro were tainted with condescension and racism, the attitudes of others revealed genuine compassion.

Evangelicals were not entirely oblivious to the conditions in which the slaves lived and worked. To be sure, they generally refrained from making any adverse comments on the way slaveholders treated their slaves. (William Wightman was a rare exception.) They followed Charles Colcock Jones's "rule of action"—"to have nothing to do with the civil condition of the Negroes, or with their plantation affairs." On the other hand, missionaries frequently cited improvements in the "temporal condition" of the slaves in reporting on the achievement of the missions. They remarked that the slaves who attended their meetings were clean and neatly clad, or they noted improvements in the housing and family life of the slaves. Evangelicals believed that these kinds of improvement were the likely result of the religious instruction of the Negroes. Charles Colcock Jones argued that it was bound to affect "the feelings and conduct" of the master as well as the slaves. The slaves would come to "understand their duties better, and to perform them more perfectly and cheerfully." The master would learn "that his servants are fellow-creatures" and that he must account to God for his treatment of them.

[He] will be led to inquiries of this sort. In what kind of houses do I permit them [the slaves] to live; what clothes do I give them to wear; what food to eat; what privileges to enjoy? In what temper and manner, and in what proportion to their crimes do I allow them to be punished? What care do I take of their family relations? What am I doing for their souls' salvation? In fine, what does God require me to do to, and for them and their children, in view of their happiness here and hereafter? Light will insensibly break into his mind. Conscience will be quickened, and before he is aware perhaps, his servants will be greatly elevated in his regards, and he will feel himself bound and willing to do more and more for them. The

65. Smith, *In His Image*, 46–47, 94–95, 153–54; Eugene D. Genovese, *Roll, Jordan, Roll: The World the Slaves Made* (New York, 1972), 202–209; Kenneth K. Bailey, "Protestantism and Afro-Americans in the Old South: Another Look," *Journal of Southern History*, XLI (November, 1975), 452; Mathews, *Slavery and Methodism*, chap. 3; Mathews, "Charles Colcock Jones," 299–320; Touchstone, "Planters and Slave Religion," 206; *Christian Index*, April 29, 1842, p. 261; Winans Autobiography, 10.

government of his plantation will not be so purely selfish as formerly. His interest will not be the sole object of pursuit, nor offences against that visited with sorer punishment than offences against God himself. He will have an eye to the comfort, the interest of his people, and endeavor to identify their interest with his, and also to make them see and feel it to be so. It will be a delight to him to see them enjoy the blessings of the *providence* and the *grace* of God.

James O. Andrew echoed Jones's argument in observing that as a result of the religious instruction of the Negroes and the increase in their faithfulness and obedience, the master "has learned to regard his servant as a fellowman, susceptible of higher and holier influences than operate on merely animal nature." According to Andrew, "the result is apt to be an improvement in the temporal comfort of the negro, his feelings are more regarded, and his comforts more considered."[66] To the extent that Jones's and Andrew's predictions were fulfilled, the movement for religious instruction aided evangelicals in their efforts to ameliorate the system of slavery.

However, few, if any, evangelicals believed that improvements in the temporal condition of the slaves were the most important result of religious instruction. "The phisical [*sic*] condition of man is of little moment, when compared with his moral," declared J. S. Law. This is why evangelicals were able to comply with the restrictions imposed by the slave system. They believed that the most important thing they could do for the Negroes was "to rescue them from spiritual bondage," to convert them to Christianity. Nor did they blink at the fact that religious instruction strengthened the bonds of slavery. In 1839 the South Carolina Conference observed that the missions to the slaves had "thrown a new element into the moral circulation—planted fresh props beneath the established order of things, and reared up additional securities around the charities of home and household affections."[67] There is no doubt that this was one of the effects of the movement for religious instruction. Indeed, although most evangelicals did not subscribe to the positive good theory of slavery, it gained credence as a result of their efforts on behalf of the slaves. Thus, evangelicals not only strengthened the system of slavery, but to some extent, provided ammunition for the defense of the southern way of life.

66. *Watchman of the South*, July 3, 1845, p. 178; *Southern Christian Advocate*, July 22, 1837, p. 18, September 2, 1837, p. 42, July 28, 1843, p. 26, August 30, 1850, p. 50; Jones, *Religious Instruction of the Negroes*, 207–208; Andrew quoted in Thomas Leonard Williams, "Methodist Mission to the Slaves," 308.
67. *Christian Index*, April 29, 1842, p. 261; Mathews, *Slavery and Methodism*, 83.

CHAPTER NINE

The Sectional Controversy

The times are indeed portentous," James Henley Thornwell wrote in March, 1850, to a friend and former colleague. Congress was debating the compromise measures introduced by Henry Clay, while southerners were preparing to discuss the possibility of secession at the forthcoming Nashville Convention. "The prospect of disunion is one which I cannot contemplate without absolute horror," Thornwell continued. "A peaceful dissolution is utterly impossible. . . . And a war between the States of this confederacy would, in my opinion, be the bloodiest, most ferocious, and cruel, in the annals of history. . . . I have hardly been able to sleep in consequence of my deep conviction with which I am oppressed of the evils that threaten us; and my unceasing prayer is, that God would interfere for our relief. Vain, in this crisis, is the help of man."[1]

Thornwell offered a more elaborate statement of his position during the crisis of 1850 in an article which appeared in the *Southern Presbyterian Review*. He argued that the South demanded nothing but "justice," that "she simply insists that the Federal Government shall not take sides on the question of Slavery. It must not attempt either to repress or spread it." This, he maintained, was the position prescribed by the Constitution, which the North was pledged to obey. Indeed, the Union was "the creature of the Constitution," and the destruction of the one would mean the destruction of the other. Thus, Thornwell was as critical of northern abolitionists and Free-Soilers, who were attempting to "prostitute the power of the general

1. James Henley Thornwell to the Reverend Dr. Hooper, March 8, 1850, in Palmer, *Life and Letters of Thornwell*, 477–78.

government to their own fanatical ends," as of southerners who contended that, given the free states' violations of the Constitution, "there is not only no obligation any longer to adhere to it, but that the danger of further aggressions is so great that it is a duty to withdraw from it." He singled out for special criticism the policy which his own state of South Carolina was following. "Single-handed secession," he wrote, "however it might be justified in a crisis in which the Federal Government had become openly pledged to the extinction of slavery, under the present circumstances of our country is recommended by not a single consideration that we are able to discover, of wisdom, patriotism or honour."[2]

Throughout the 1850s, Thornwell adhered to the position he had taken at the beginning of the decade, despite the fact that, as he wrote to Robert J. Breckinridge, his views were "anything but popular" in the Palmetto State. Then, in 1860, he became an advocate of secession. Twelve days after South Carolina had passed the ordinance of secession he wrote, "I believe that we have done right. I do not see any other course that was left to us. I am heart and hand with the State in her move."[3]

Thornwell's views on the sectional controversy were representative of the majority of southern evangelicals. Although opposed to disunion in the 1850s, they supported secession in 1860–1861.[4] A number of factors brought about the shift of opinion. As citizens and, in most cases, slaveholders, they no doubt acted on many of the same impulses as other southerners. As evangelicals they had other, more specialized reasons for ultimately supporting secession.

In the late 1840s and 1850s, the evangelicals' perception of the abolitionists changed. They no longer viewed them as motivated by religious or moral convictions. They contended that abolitionists had repudiated the church, the Bible, and Christianity, and were motivated by a "political radicalism" which threatened "all the sacred rights and holy institutions of mankind." Thornwell expressed the view of most southern evangelicals

2. [James Henley Thornwell], "Critical Notices," *Southern Presbyterian Review*, IV (January, 1851), 444–45, 448–52.

3. James Henley Thornwell to R. J. Breckinridge, March 28, 1851, and to John Douglas, December 31, 1860, in Palmer, *Life and Letters of Thornwell*, 477, 486.

4. For evangelicals' opposition to disunion in the 1850s see, for example, Peyton Harrison Hoge, *Moses Drury Hoge*, 137–38, Robert Hall Morrison to James Morrison, November 20, 1850, and September 1, 1851, in Morrison Papers, Jeter, *Life of Witt*, 201, Flournoy, *Benjamin Mosby Smith*, 75, George G. Smith, *Life and Letters of Andrew*, 436, McIlwaine, *Memories*, 184, Stratton Diary, March 9, 1850.

when he described the conflict between abolitionists and slaveholders as a conflict between "Atheists, Socialists, Communists, Red Republicans, Jacobins on the one side, and the friends of order and regulated freedom on the other." Evangelicals were particularly alarmed at the abolitionists' entry into the political arena. The question of slavery had "passed from Church to State," the Synod of South Carolina observed in 1851; it was "no longer a debate among Christian ministers and Christian men as to the terms of communion and the rights of particular communities to the Christian name." The synod declared that the efforts of the abolitionists to gain support for their policies in the national government "justified the gloomiest forebodings in relation to the integrity of the union and the stability of our free institutions."[5]

As evangelicals altered their perception of the abolitionists, they also adopted an increasingly derogatory view of northern society in general and of New England in particular. Southern religious journals regularly printed articles picturing the North as a region whose people had little reverence for the authority of the laws and where, as a consequence, vice, crime, and mob rule were rampant. Religion was said to be in a declining state—fanaticism had supplanted true Christianity, revivals were few in number, and church membership was dwindling. The evidences of religious and moral declension were even more evident in New England. There the mighty religious edifice built by "her Edwardses, her Bellamys, her Dwights and her Woods" was but "the memorial of a dead faith." The people had turned away from "the simplicity of the Gospel" and, lacking "fixed principles of belief," were now "willing to take up any nonsense that comes along." New England had become a land of isms. Perfectionism, abolitionism, Fanny Wrightism, and a hundred other species of heresy and humbug all found advocates and supporters there. Nor did southern evangelicals forego the opportunity to make a comparison with the South, which was experiencing powerful revivals of religion. Moreover, noted the editor of the *Southern Christian Advocate*, "our societies enjoy profound tranquillity so far as doctrinal speculations or *pseudo* reform of organic principles of government are concerned. We are not troubled—as they are in New England, with Mormonism, Millerism, Comeoutism, Universalism,

5. "North and South," *Southern Presbyterian Review*, III (January, 1850), 344; Thornwell quoted in Philip Leonard, "The Contributions of Presbyterian Orthodoxy to the Pro-Slavery Argument as Exemplified by the Writings of James Henley Thornwell, 1838–1860" (M.A. thesis, University of Virginia, 1967), 57; Synod of South Carolina quoted in Todd, "Slavery Issue and the Organization of a Southern Baptist Convention," 353.

or with an Americanized edition of German Rationalism. The Southern States are not the soil or [*sic*] which such absurdities flourish."[6]

The editor's sense of the distinctiveness of the southern religious order is significant, for it suggests the extent to which evangelicals had come to think of the churches in their section as having a different ethos from those of the North. The idea had been developing for several decades. As early as the 1820s, southern Presbyterians were arguing that Princeton was not supplying the special needs of "the Southern country" and that a theological seminary should be established south of the Mason and Dixon line. In the late 1830s and early 1840s, during the controversy over slavery within their churches, southern Baptists and Methodists expressed their growing sense of distinctiveness. "The Baptists of the South . . . are now in many important respects a distinct and separate people," declared William T. Brantley in 1837; he added, prophetically, "On some very exciting questions they are becoming every year more and more distant from each other." After the divisions of the mid-1840s, such feelings became even more pronounced among Methodists and Baptists and were reinforced by the work of building and maintaining separate southern denominations. Old School Presbyterians remained united, but in the forties and fifties, southerners expressed mounting resentment that the church was being dominated by the North and that their interests were being neglected. In 1837 and again in 1860, the Synod of South Carolina debated the organization of a separate church. The fact that southern Presbyterians often referred in their writings and sermons to "our Southern Zion," "our Southern Church," and "the Southern Presbyterian Church" also indicates the development of feelings of distinctiveness similar to those of the Baptists and Methodists.[7] What all of this suggests is that ecclesiastical divisions conditioned many evangelicals to think along lines that were compatible with secession, enabling them to see it as confirming a separation that had already taken place, either in fact, as in the case of the Baptists and Methodists, or in feeling, as with the Presbyterians.

Perhaps even more important in leading southern evangelicals ultimately to support secession was their realization that the sectional contro-

6. *Central Presbyterian*, January 26, 1856, p. 14; *Christian Index*, May 16, 1845, n.p.; *Southern Christian Advocate*, August 31, 1849, p. 50.

7. Thompson, *Presbyterians in the South*, I, 276, 284; DesChamps, "Presbyterian Church in the South Atlantic States," 181–83; Smith, *Presbyterian Ministry*, 166; *Southern Watchman and General Intelligencer*, November 24, 1837, p. 187; T. Watson Street, *The Story of Southern Presbyterians* (Richmond, 1961), 54; *Central Presbyterian*, January 5, 1856, p. 2; Lewis G. Vander Velde, *The Presbyterian Churches and the Federal Union, 1861–1869* (Cambridge, 1932), 27.

versy was not simply a political conflict but one involving fundamental moral and religious principles. As long as they perceived it as a political conflict, they took the position that as ministers they should not become involved. Indeed, they sharply criticized clergymen and editors of religious newspapers in the free states who were "presuming to settle the affairs of State." Commenting on northern efforts to secure the defeat of the Nebraska bill, the editor of the *Christian Index* declared, "Let politicians and statesmen discuss questions pertaining to banks, tariffs and territories, but let the religious press, and the ministers of the gospel, go preach the kingdom of God." During the 1850s, however, many southern evangelicals began to feel that the sectional controversy involved more than "banks, tariffs and territories." In an address before the American Colonization Society, Richard Fuller contended that the conflict over slavery was primarily a religious, not a political question, and until the politicians recognized that—and recognized also that "politics is the science of compromises, but religion allows no compromises with evil"—there would be no peace. "There will be a deep and deepening feeling at the North, a consequent resentment at the South, and a growing estrangement between North and South, until something is done to meet the religious convictions connected with slavery," Fuller predicted. Given the southern evangelicals' insistence that the Bible sanctioned slavery, it is not surprising that they more and more tended to view the sectional controversy as a conflict between those who acknowledged the authority of the Bible and those who repudiated it—in other words, between Christians and infidels. Evangelicals also began to worry about the implications of the controversy for "the peace and happiness of the church." Most of them believed that disunion would bring a war that the intense religious feelings on the slavery issue would render particularly ferocious and cruel. They were equally certain that the "age of benevolence" would be the first casualty of the war, Christianity would "sicken and droop," and all the schemes for the conversion of the world would be ruined. Forebodings such as these contributed to the evangelicals' increasing awareness that "the interests of the Saviour's kingdom" were "intimately connected with the permanence and prosperity" of the nation.[8]

Events of the 1850s also sharpened the evangelicals' original animus to-

8. *Southern Christian Advocate*, December 20, 1850, p. 114; *Christian Index*, April 6, 1854, p. 54, October 23, 1856, p. 170; Fuller, *Address*, 8; *Central Presbyterian*, March 29, 1856, p. 50; James Henley Thornwell to the Reverend Dr. Hooper, March 8, 1850, in Palmer, *Life and Letters of Thornwell*, 478.

ward politicians. As sectional tensions increased, evangelicals viewed politicians on both sides as "reckless and . . . desperate" men, demagogues who appealed to the worst passions and prejudices of the people. These "hotspurs" and "faction-mongers" inspired little confidence in their ability to prevent disunion. Indeed, many evangelicals were coming to believe that it was the politicians who were leading the country to disunion against the wishes of the "intelligent, reflecting, sober-minded men of all parties, and in all sections of the country." Thus, Moses Drury Hoge declared in 1856 that the crisis had "been produced by a few, reckless, misguided men— some of them deliberately unprincipled—perhaps more of them honestly fanatical—with exaggerated and monstrously perverted views of the magnitude of some particular evil, to remove which they would imperil everything." Hoge thought that the time had come for "the true men" of both sections of the Union "to speak out in tones that cannot be mistaken."[9]

Hoge did not specifically name clergymen in his call, but the more evangelicals recognized a moral and religious dimension to the sectional controversy and the more they deprecated the part played by the politicians, the more they felt justified in abandoning their position of noninvolvement. A few evangelicals participated in state conventions or meetings called to discuss the crisis. Others prepared articles, editorials, and addresses defending the Union, the Constitution, and the South against northern encroachments.[10] The number of such items increased dramatically in the decade preceding the Civil War.

Perhaps the most significant instance of evangelical involvement in the sectional controversy prior to 1860 occurred in June, 1856, when the clergy of Richmond issued an "Appeal" addressed to their "brethren and fellow citizens." The letter, which was published in the religious and secular newspapers and signed by twenty-three ministers, including Jeremiah Jeter,

9. Robert Hall Morrison to James Morrison, September 1, 1851, in Morrison Papers; Basil Manly, Jr., to his parents, December 12, 1850, in Manly Family Papers; *Central Presbyterian*, March 29, 1856, p. 50, June 21, 1856, p. 89.

10. See, for example, *Southern Christian Advocate*, September 27, 1850, p. 65, *Southern Presbyterian*, September 18, 1851, p. 10, February 23, 1854, p. 74, Griffith, *Life and Times of Landrum*, 160, Stratton Diary, March 9, 1850, Thomas Smyth, "The Sin and the Curse; or, The Union, the True Source of Disunion, and Our Duty in the Present Crisis. A Discourse Preached on the Occasion of the Day of Humiliation and Prayer Appointed by the Governor of South Carolina, on November 21st, 1860, in the Second Presbyterian Church, Charleston, S.C.," in *Complete Works*, VII, 537–61, James Henley Thornwell, "National Sins.—A Fast-Day Sermon, Preached in the Presbyterian Church, Columbia, Wednesday, November 21, 1860," *Southern Presbyterian Review*, XIII (January, 1861), 649–88, and B. M. Palmer, *The South: Her Peril, and Her Duty. A Discourse, Delivered in the First Presbyterian Church, New Orleans, on Thursday, November 29, 1860* (New Orleans, 1860).

Moses Drury Hoge, and W. A. Smith, provides insight into the motives which led evangelicals to intervene, as well as the kind of counsel they offered in the crisis.[11] The clergy began their appeal with the hope that they would not be regarded as transcending their "proper sphere" in offering "a few conservative remarks on the present alarming crisis in our national affairs." They pointed out that, though membership in the clerical profession had restrained them from taking "an active part in political matters," it had not quenched their patriotic ardor. "We love our country—our whole country—our country with all its faults," they declared, adding that they considered it their "solemn duty, as patriots and Christians," to do everything lawful to preserve the country from ruin.

That duty seemed especially pressing in view of the events of the day. The recent Brooks-Sumner incident, the fighting in Kansas, and other equally alarming events demonstrated the extent to which "sectional jealousies and bitterness" had "usurped the place of patriotism and brotherly love." In a thinly veiled criticism of politicians in both sections, the clergy noted that "in various parts of the country, meetings are called, conventions are held, speeches are delivered, resolutions are adopted, and all, or nearly all, are designed to agitate, inflame, excite the worst passions of the human heart, and add fuel to the flames that threatens [*sic*] to consume the noble fabric of our government." The clergymen sought to do exactly the opposite—to allay "the popular excitement" and to awaken "the conservative spirit of the people." Thus, they urged Americans "to cherish a patriotic, candid, kind and forbearing spirit," to "avoid every word and deed, which can tend to increase the public excitement and irritation," to "give no countenance to lawless violence, whether in low or high places," and to "seek, by every practicable method, to strengthen and brighten the bond of fraternal union, which should embrace every citizen of our favored States and Territories."

But the chief remedy which the clergy offered was the familiar evangelical one of penitence and prayer. "We are called individually to self-examination, the confession of our sins, penitence, and a reformation of our lives," they declared. By such means, "far more readily than by fierce discussions, we may avert the dangers which are impending over our beloved land." Concluding the appeal, they invited their fellow citizens to join them on the Sunday preceding the Fourth of July in a day of special

11. *Central Presbyterian*, June 28, 1856, pp. 102–103. Also published in the *Religious Herald*, June 26, 1856, p. 98, *Christian Index*, July 3, 1856, p. 106, Richmond *Whig and Public Advertiser*, June 24, 1856, n.p., and Richmond *Enquirer*, June 24, 1856, n.p.

prayer "to the God of nations, that he would mercifully restrain the angry passions of men, inspire our rulers with a moderate and pacific spirit, disperse the clouds over-hanging our favored republic, [and] restore the harmony which once existed among the States of this Union."

In exhorting Americans to seek divine guidance, the Richmond clergy appealed to a theory of providence which was widely shared by other southern evangelicals and which, perhaps more than anything else, shaped their response to the sectional crisis. According to the theory, the whole of the nation's history revealed "the finger of the Lord." God had kept the American continent "veiled from the view and knowledge of mankind" until it would be settled by "a race ordained and trained by heaven to be worthy of the heritage." He had seen to it that the colonists "were defended in all perils, and prospered in all noble enterprises until they were permitted to lay the broad and deep foundations of our civil and religious institutions." Many crises had occurred since then, but always, when the "country appeared on the very verge of ruin, and the heart of the christian patriot had begun to 'wax faint,'" God had brought deliverance. Even in the 1850s, evangelicals found evidence that "a wise and merciful Providence" continued to watch over the affairs of the country. In 1851, pointing to the defeat of the secessionists in South Carolina, Robert Morrison declared, "He that can survey the State of things in this Land for the last year and not see & admire & adore the wisdom & power & mercy of God must be blind indeed!" Morrison did not doubt that "the Croakers" would "bluster on," but he believed that God had saved the country from "impending danger" by "opening the eyes of the wisest & best men to the folly & madness of self distruction [*sic*]." As each new crisis developed, Morrison and other evangelicals continued to trust in "that good Providence which has kept us under its wing so long." This is why they urged prayer and repentance—as a means of insuring divine guidance. "If ever there was a time which demanded humiliation & earnest prayer to God, that time is *now*," Daniel Witt wrote to Jeremiah Jeter in December, 1860. "It may be the Lord will hear, & avert from us the threatening storm." Witt, like other evangelicals, looked to God rather than to "the mad counsels of corrupt political men." [12] One is reminded of Thornwell's statement ten years earlier: "Vain, in this crisis, is the help of men."

12. James Henley Thornwell to Robert J. Breckinridge, March 28, 1851, in Palmer, *Life and Letters of Thornwell*, 477; *Central Presbyterian*, July 5, 1856, p. 106; *Christian Index*, February 15, 1849, p. 54; Robert Hall Morrison to James Morrison, October 21, 1851, in Morrison Papers; Daniel Witt to Jeremiah Jeter, November 20, 1860, and December 1, 1860, in Virginia Baptist Historical Society Collection.

Given their lack of confidence in the political leadership of the country, evangelicals must have found the theory of providence especially comforting. Once they accepted its primary assumption, that every occurrence was a result of the working of providence, they were able to resign themselves to whatever happened, believing that it was God's will. "The prospects in politics [are] dark. We [are] driftg we know not whither," Basil Manly, Jr., wrote in October, 1860. Yet, he added, "God knows, & God rules: & is all, & that is enough." Their belief in the theory of providence enabled evangelicals to accept secession. When their states withdrew from the Union, most of them accepted the action as part of the providential design. Indeed, the more ardent supporters of secession, such as Benjamin Morgan Palmer, argued that it was the only way the South could carry out its providential task of preserving slavery and defending "the cause of God and religion."[13]

Thus, southern evangelicals relied on God to settle the sectional controversy just as they trusted in him to resolve the slavery question and to bring about the temperance reformation. They were as dubious of human ability in social and political matters as in the matter of salvation. The belief in the sovereignty and omnipotence of God and the dependence of man informed the whole of their thinking, and more than any other single element, contributed to the distinctiveness of southern evangelical thought in the nineteenth century.

13. Basil Manly, Jr., to his parents, October 26, 1860, in Manly Family Papers; Palmer, *The South: Her Peril, and Her Duty*, 6–7, 10–11.

Bibliography

PRIMARY SOURCES

MANUSCRIPTS

Historical Foundation of the Presbyterian and Reformed Churches, Montreat, N.C.
    Francis McFarland Collection
    Henry Ruffner Papers
    Thomas Smyth Papers
    James Henley Thornwell, Sr., Materials
Louisiana State University Archives, Baton Rouge
    John C. Burruss and Family Papers
    Thomas Railey Markham Papers
    Joseph A. Montgomery and Family Papers
    Joseph B. Stratton Papers
    Sereno Taylor Papers
Mississippi Conference Historical Society, Millsaps-Wilson Library, Millsaps College, Jackson
    William Winans Collection
South Caroliniana Library, University of South Carolina, Columbia
    Iveson L. Brookes Papers
    John McLees Papers
    Francis Asbury Mood Papers
    James Henley Thornwell Papers
Southern Historical Collection, University of North Carolina Library, Chapel Hill
    Anderson and Thornwell Family Papers
    Iveson Lewis Brookes Papers
    Bumpas Family Papers
    John Lyle Campbell Papers
    Joseph Benson Cottrell Papers
    John Early Diary

Solomon Hilary Helsabeck Papers
Drury Lacy Papers
William Parsons McCorkle Papers
Mangum Family Papers
Robert Hall Morrison Papers
Abram David Pollock Papers
Thomas Bog Slade Papers
George Gilman Smith Books
Witherspoon and McDowall Family Papers
Special Collections, Furman University Library, Greenville, S.C.
Edmund Botsford Letters
James Clement Furman Papers
Richard Furman Papers
Basil Manly, Jr., Papers
Manly Family Papers
Virginia Baptist Historical Society, University of Richmond, Richmond
Manuscript Collection
Virginia Historical Society, Richmond
Edward Baptist Diary
Hoge Family Papers
Norvell Robertson Autobiography
Union Theological Seminary Library, Richmond, Va.
Moses Drury Hoge Letters
Drury Lacy Record Group
University of Alabama Library, Tuscaloosa
Iveson L. Brookes Collection
William R. Perkins Library, Duke University, Durham, N.C.
Iveson L. Brookes Papers
Eli Washington Caruthers Papers
Peter Doub Journal, in William Clark Doub Papers
Whitefoord Smith Papers

NEWSPAPERS AND PERIODICALS

Nonsectarian
Christian Mirror, 1814
Baptist
Christian Index, 1833–1860
Georgia Analytical Repository, 1802–1803
Religious Herald, 1828–1860
Roanoke *Religious Correspondent, or Monthly Evangelical Visitant*, 1821–1823
Southern Baptist and General Intelligencer, 1835–1836
Southern Watchman and General Intelligencer, 1837–1838
Methodist
Methodist Quarterly Review, 1848–1860
Richmond *Christian Advocate*, 1846–1859
Southern Christian Advocate, 1837–1859

Southern Methodist Pulpit, 1848–1852
Wesleyan Journal, 1825–1827
Presbyterian
    Central Presbyterian, 1856–1860
    Charleston *Observer*, 1827–1828, 1830–1837
    Christian Monitor, 1815–1817
    Presbyterial Critic and Monthly Review, 1855–1856
    Southern Evangelical Intelligencer, 1819–1821
    Southern Intelligencer, 1822–1823
    Southern Presbyterian, 1847–1860
    Southern Presbyterian Review, 1847–1861
    Virginia Evangelical and Literary Magazine, 1818–1828
    Virginia Religious Magazine, 1804–1807
    Watchman and Observer, 1845–1855
    Watchman of the South, 1837–1845
Secular
    Richmond *Enquirer*, June 24, 1856
    Richmond *Whig and Public Advertiser*, June 24, 1856
    Virginia Semi-Weekly Examiner, June 27, 1856

PUBLISHED SOURCES

Abbey, Rev. R. "The Punishment of Death." *Methodist Quarterly Review*, II (July, 1848), 375–433.

——. "A Response to 'J.B.' on Capital Punishment." *Methodist Quarterly Review*, III (January, 1849), 112–20.

Adger, John B., D.D. *My Life and Times, 1810–1899*. Richmond: Presbyterian Committee of Publication, 1899.

——. *The Religious Instruction of the Colored Population. A Sermon, Preached by the Rev. John B. Adger, in the Second Presbyterian Church, Charleston, S.C., May 9th, 1847*. Charleston: T. W. Haynes, 1847.

——. "The Revival of the Slave Trade." *Southern Presbyterian Review*, XI (April, 1858), 100–35.

The American Christian Record: Containing the History, Confession of Faith, and Statistics of Each Religious Denomination in the United States and Europe; A List of All Clergymen With Their Post Office Address, Etc., Etc., Etc. New York: W. R. C. Clark & Meeker, 1860.

Andrew, James Osgood. *Family Government. A Treatise on Conjugal, Parental, and Filial Duties*. Philadelphia: Sorin & Hall, 1846.

Bailey, Rev. Rufus William. *The Family Preacher; or Domestic Duties Illustrated and Enforced in Eight Discourses*. New York: John Taylor, 1837.

Baker, Rev. Daniel. *Revival Sermons. First Series. With an Appendix*. Philadelphia: William S. Martien, 1855.

[Baker, J. S.] *A Calm Appeal to Southern Baptists, in Advocacy of Separation From the North in All the Works of Christian Benevolence. By a Southern Baptist.* [1845?]

Baker, William M. *The Life and Labours of the Rev. Daniel Baker, D.D.* Philadelphia: W. S. & A. Martien, 1859.

"The Baptism of Servants." *Southern Presbyterian Review,* I (June, 1847), 63–102.

Benedict, David. *Fifty Years Among the Baptists.* New York: 1860; rpr., Glen Rose, Tex.: Newman & Collings, 1913.

[Birney, James G.] *The American Churches, The Bulwarks of American Slavery. By an American.* London: Johnston and Barrett, 1840.

Bishop, Isabella Lucy (Bird). *The Aspects of Religion in the United States of America. By the Author of "The Englishwoman in America."* London: Sampson, Low, Son, and Co., 1859; rpr., New York: Arno Press, 1972.

Blackburn, George A., comp. and ed. *The Life Work of John Girardeau, D.D., LL.D.* Columbia: The State Company, 1916.

[Botsford, Edmund.] *Sambo & Toney, A Dialogue in Three Parts.* Georgetown: Printed by Francis M. Baxter, 1808.

[Bowman, John G.] *Address to Legislators on Temperance.* Nashville: Published by E. Stevenson & F. A. Owen, for the M. E. Church, South, 1855.

Boyce, Rev. James P. *Life and Death the Christian's Portion. A Discourse Occasioned by the Funeral Services of the Rev. Basil Manly, D.D. At Greenville, S. C., Dec. 22, 1868.* New York: Sheldon & Co., 1869.

Boyd, William K., ed. "Rev. Brantley York on Early Days in Randolph County and Union Institute." *Historical Papers of the Historical Society of Trinity College,* Series VIII (1908–09), 15–34.

Brisbane, Rev. W. H. *Speech of the Rev. W. H. Brisbane, Lately a Slaveholder in South Carolina: Delivered Before the Female Anti-Slavery Society of Cincinnati, February 12, 1840.* Cincinnati: Samuel A. Alley, 1840.

Broaddus, Andrew. *The Sermons and Other Writings of the Rev. Andrew Broaddus, With a Memoir of His Life, by J. B. Jeter.* New York: Lewis Colby, 1852.

Brookes, Iveson L. *A Defence of the South Against the Reproaches and Incroachments of the North: In Which Slavery Is Shown to be an Institution of God Intended to Form the Basis of the Best Social State and the Only Safeguard to the Permanence of a Republican Government.* Hamburg: Printed at the Republican Office, 1850.

Bryan, Samuel J. *A Plain and Easy Catechism: Designed for the Benefit of Colored Children, With Several Verses and Hymns, With an Appendix: Compiled by a Missionary.* Savannah: n.p., 1833.

Capers, William. *A Catechism for Little Children and for Use on the Missions to the Slaves in South Carolina.* Charleston: J. W. Burges, 1833.

Cartwright, Peter. *Autobiography of Peter Cartwright, The Backwoods Preacher.* Edited by W. P. Strickland. New York: Carlton & Porter, 1856.

Cassels, Rev. Samuel J. "The Relation of Justice to Benevolence in the Conduct of Society." *Southern Presbyterian Review,* VII (July, 1853), 85–103.

Cater, Rev. R. B. *An Address, Delivered Before the Greenville Temperance Society, On the 17th March, 1832.* Greenville: O. H. Wells, 1832.

Chambliss, Alexander Wilds. *The Catechetical Instructor, In Which the Leading Doctrines and Practices of Christianity Are Familiarly Exhibited; Designed for the Use of Families, Sabbath Schools, and Bible Classes: and Especially for the Oral Instruction of the Colored Population.* Montgomery: Bates, Hooper & Co., 1847.

"The Christian Doctrine of Human Rights and Slavery." *Southern Presbyterian Review,* II (March, 1849), 569–87.

Cody, C. C. *Life and Labours of Francis Asbury Mood, D.D.* Chicago: F. H. Revell, 1886.

Coit, Rev. J. C. *A Discourse Upon Governments, Divine and Human, Prepared by Appointment of the Presbytery of Harmony, and Delivered Before that Body During Its Sessions in Indiantown Church, Williamsburg District, S. C., April, 1853.* Columbia: T. F. Greneker, 1853.

"Critical Notice." *Southern Presbyterian Review,* II (March, 1849), 550–62.

"Critical Notices." *Southern Presbyterian Review,* I (September, 1847), 137–50.

"Critical Notices." *Southern Presbyterian Review,* III (October, 1849), 324–25.

"Critical Notices." *Southern Presbyterian Review,* XI (October, 1858), 500–502.

Cuthbert, J. H. *Life of Richard Fuller, D.D.* New York: Sheldon and Company, 1879.

Deems, Charles Force. *Autobiography of Charles Force Deems, D.D., LL. D. Pastor of the Church of the Strangers, New York City and President of the American Institute of Christian Philosophy and Memoir by His Sons Rev. Edward M. Deems, A.M., Ph.D. and Francis M. Deems, M.D., Ph.D.* New York: Fleming H. Revell Company, 1897.

———. *What It Has Done, and What It Must Do. An Address Delivered Before the Grand Division of the Order of the Sons of Temperance of North Carolina, in the Presbyterian Church, Raleigh, On the Evening of the 19th of October, 1847.* Philadelphia: T. K. & P. G. Collins, 1847.

Dickson, A. F. *Plantation Sermons, or Plain and Familiar Discourses for the Instruction of the Unlearned.* Philadelphia: Presbyterian Board of Publication, 1856.

"The Divine Appointment and Obligation of Capital Punishment." *Southern Presbyterian Review,* I (December, 1847), 1–29.

The Doctrines and Discipline of the Methodist Episcopal Church, South. Richmond: Published by John Early, for the Methodist Episcopal Church, South, 1846.

The Doctrines and Discipline of the Methodist Episcopal Church, South. Louisville: Published by John Early, for the Methodist Episcopal Church, South, 1851.

The Doctrines and Discipline of the Methodist Episcopal Church, South. Nashville: E. Stevenson and F. A. Owen, M. E. Church, South, 1855.

Doub, Rev. Peter. *Address delivered before the Grand Division of North Carolina, Sons of Temperance, at the October Session, 1852.* Raleigh: Spirit of the Age Office, 1852.

"Dr. Smith's Philosophy and Practice of Slavery." *Methodist Quarterly Review,* XI (April, 1857), 242–58.

"Duelling." *Southern Presbyterian Review,* X (April, 1857), 126–37.

Dunwody, James. *Reminiscences and Sermons.* Macon: J. W. Burke & Co., 1872.

Dunwody, Samuel. *A Sermon Upon the Subject of Slavery.* Columbia: Printed by S. Weir, State Printer, 1837.

"Duties of Masters." *Southern Presbyterian Review,* VIII (October, 1854), 266–83.

Ely, Ezra Stiles. *The Duty of Christian Freemen to Elect Christian Rulers: A Discourse Delivered on the Fourth of July, 1827, in the Seventh Presbyterian Church, in Philadelphia. With an Appendix, Designed to Vindicate the Liberty of Christians, and of the American Sunday School Union.* Philadelphia: William F. Geddes, 1828.

Emory, Robert. *The Life of the Rev. John Emory, D.D.* New York: George Lane, 1841.

E. M. P. "The Church and Temperance Societies." *Methodist Quarterly Review,* IV (July, 1850), 362–87.

Fair, Robert A. *Our Slaves Should Have the Bible. An Address Delivered Before the Abbe-*

ville Bible Society, at Its Anniversary, July, 1854. Due West, S.C.: Telescope Press, 1854.

Finley, James B. *Autobiography of Rev. James B. Finley; or, Pioneer Life in the West*. Edited by W. P. Strickland. Cincinnati: Methodist Book Concern, 1854.

First Annual Report of the Mississippi State Colonization Society, Auxiliary to the American Colonization Society, for Colonizing the Free People of Colour of the United States. Natchez: Printed at "The Natchez" Office, 1832.

Fitzgerald, O. P. *John B. McFerrin: A Biography*. Nashville: Publishing House of the M. E. Church, South, 1888.

Fuller, Richard. *Address before the American Colonization Society. Delivered at Washington, D. C., January 21, 1851*. Baltimore: Office of the True Union, 1851.

Fuller, Richard, and Francis Wayland. *Domestic Slavery Considered as a Scriptural Institution: in a Correspondence between the Rev. Richard Fuller, of Beaufort, S. C., and the Rev. Francis Wayland, of Providence, R.I.* Rev. ed. New York: Lewis Colby, 1845.

Furman, Richard. *America's Deliverance and Duty. A Sermon. Preached at the Baptist Church, in Charleston, South-Carolina, on the Fourth Day of July, 1802, Before the State Society of the Cincinnati, the American Revolution Society, and the Congregation Which Usually Attends Divine Service in the Said Church*. Charleston: W. P. Young, 1802.

———. *Exposition of the Views of the Baptists, Relative to the Coloured Population in the United States, in a Communication to the Governor of South Carolina*. Charleston: Printed by A. E. Miller, 1833.

[Furman, Wood.] *A Biography of Richard Furman*. Edited and supplemented by Harvey T. Cook. Greenville: Baptist Courier Job Rooms, 1913.

[———,] comp. *A History of the Charleston Baptist Association; With an Appendix Containing the Principal Letters to the Churches*. [Charleston: n.p., 1811.]

A Georgia Pastor. "The Church a Spiritual Power." *Southern Presbyterian Review*, XII (October, 1859), 476–90.

Gillette, W. B. and A. D. *Memoir of Rev. Daniel Holbrook Gillette, of Mobile, Alabama*. Philadelphia: J. B. Lippincott & Co., 1846.

Girardeau, John L. *A Catechism for the Oral Instruction of Coloured Persons Who Are Inquirers Concerning Religion, or Candidates for Admission Into the Church*. Charleston: Evans & Cogswell, 1850.

———. *Conscience and Civil Government. An Oration Delivered Before the Society of Alumni of the College of Charleston, on Commencement Day, March 27th, 1860*. Charleston: Evans & Cogswell, 1860.

Gorrie, Rev. P. Douglass. *The Churches and Sects of the United States: Containing a Brief Account of the Origin, History, Doctrines, Church Government, Mode of Worship, Usages, and Statistics of Each Religious Denomination, So Far As Known*. New York: Lewis Colby, 1850.

Griffith, H. P. *The Life and Times of Rev. John G. Landrum*. Philadelphia: H. B. Garner, 1885.

Grimke, Thomas S. *The Temperance Reformation the Cause of Christian Morals. An Address Delivered Before the Charleston Temperance Society and the Young Men's Temperance Society, of Charleston, On Tuesday Evening, February 25th, 1834, In St. Stephen's Chapel*. Charleston: Observer Office Press, 1834.

Harrison, W. P. *The Gospel Among the Slaves. A Short Account of Missionary Operations Among the African Slaves of the Southern States.* Nashville: Publishing House of the M. E. Church, South, 1893.

Hayward, John. *The Religious Creeds and Statistics of Every Christian Denomination in the United States and British Provinces. With Some Account of the Religious Sentiments of Jews, American Indians, Deists, Mahometans, &c. Alphabetically Arranged.* Boston: John Hayward, 1836.

Hoge, Moses. *Sermons Selected from the Manuscripts of the Late Moses Hoge, D.D.* Richmond: S. Pollard, 1821.

Hoge, Peyton Harrison. *Moses Drury Hoge: Life and Letters.* Richmond: Presbyterian Committee of Publication, 1899.

Holcombe, Henry. *The First Fruits, in a Series of Letters.* Philadelphia: Ann Cochran, 1812.

Humphrey, Edward P., and Thomas H. Cleland. *Memoirs of the Rev. Thomas Cleland, D.D., Compiled From his Private Papers.* Cincinnati: Moore, Wilstach, Keys & Co., 1859.

"The Inefficiency of the Pulpit." *Southern Literary Messenger,* XXIV (February, 1857), 81–112.

Jeter, J. B. *The Life of Rev. Daniel Witt, D.D.* Richmond: J. T. Ellyson, 1875.

————. *A Memoir of Abner W. Clopton, A.M.* Richmond: Yale & Wyatt, 1837.

————. *The Mirror; or, A Delineation of Different Classes of Christians, in a Series of Lectures. With an Introduction, By Rev. A. M. Poindexter.* New York: Sheldon, Lamport & Blakeman, 1855.

————. *The Recollections of a Long Life.* Richmond: The Religious Herald Co., 1891.

Johnson, Thomas Cary. *The Life and Letters of Benjamin Morgan Palmer.* Richmond: Presbyterian Committee of Publication, 1906.

————. *The Life and Letters of Robert Lewis Dabney.* Richmond: The Presbyterian Committee of Publication, 1903.

Jones, Charles C. *A Catechism for Colored Persons.* Charleston: Observer Office Press, 1834.

————. *The Religious Instruction of the Negroes. A Sermon, Delivered before Associations of Planters in Liberty and M'Intosh Counties, Georgia, by the Rev. Charles Colcock Jones, of Savannah.* Princeton: D'Hart & Connolly, 1832.

————. *The Religious Instruction of the Negroes. In the United States.* Savannah: Thomas Purse, 1842; rpr., Freeport, N.Y.: Books for Libraries Press, 1971.

————. *Suggestions on the Religious Instruction of the Negroes in the Southern States: Together With an Appendix Containing Forms of Church Registers, Form of a Constitution, and Plans of Different Denominations of Christians.* Philadelphia: Presbyterian Board of Publication, [1847].

Justice. *The Slavery Question: Comprising the Doctrines of the Bible on the Subject of Slavery.* Spartanburg: Printed at the Spartan Office, 1849.

Kendrick, Rev. J. R. "Address to Christians." In *Course of Lectures on the Claims of Temperance, Delivered Before the Charleston Total Abstinence Society, by Fourteen of Its Members, on Successive Monday Evenings, From the 31st March 1851.* Charleston: George Parks and Co., 1852.

————. *Dueling. A Sermon Preached at the First Baptist Church, Charleston, S.C., on Sunday Morning, August 7, 1853.* Charleston: Printed by A. J. Burke, 1853.

Lee, Leroy M. *The Life and Times of the Rev. Jesse Lee*. Richmond: John Early, 1848.

Leland, A. W. *A Discourse Delivered Before the State Temperance Society of South Carolina, at Its First Anniversary, in the Representatives' Hall, Columbia, Nov. 29, 1838, With an Appendix of the Minutes of the Meeting*. Columbia: I. C. Morgan, 1838.

Leland, John. *The Writings of the Late Elder John Leland, Including Some Events in His Life, Written by Himself, With Additional Sketches, &c. by Miss L. F. Greene, Lanesboro, Mass*. New York: G. W. Wood, 1845.

Lewis, Rev. G. *Impressions of America and the American Churches: From Journal of the Rev. G. Lewis, One of the Deputation of the Free Church of Scotland to the United States*. Edinburgh: W. P. Kennedy, 1848; rpr., New York: Negro University Press, 1968.

Lindsay, J. O. "The Religious Awakening of 1858." *Southern Presbyterian Review*, XI (July, 1858), 246–63.

McIlwaine, Richard. *Memories of Three Score Years and Ten*. New York: Neale Publishing Co., 1908.

McSwain, Rev. W. A. *The Connection Between Temperance and Religion: An Address, Delivered Before Head's Spring Temperance Society, Newberry District, S.C., August 4th, 1855*. Charleston: Walker & Evans, 1856.

McTyeire, H. N., C. F. Sturgis, A. T. Holmes. *Duties of Masters to Servants: Three Premium Essays*. Charleston: Southern Baptist Publication Society, 1851.

Mallard, R. Q. *Montevideo-Maybank: Some Memoirs of a Southern Christian Household in the Olden Time; or, The Family Life of the Rev. Charles Colcock Jones, D.D., of Liberty County, Ga*. Richmond: Presbyterian Committee of Publication, 1898.

Mallory, Charles D. *Memoirs of Elder Edmund Botsford*. Charleston: W. Riley, 1832.

Maxwell, William. *A Memoir of the Rev. John H. Rice, D.D.* Philadelphia: J. Whetham, 1835.

[Mell, Patrick Hues.] *Slavery. A Treatise, Showing That Slavery Is Neither a Moral, Political, nor Social Evil. By a Baptist Minister*. Penfield, Ga.: Benj. Brantley, 1844.

Minutes of the Forty-Eighth Anniversary of the Mississippi Baptist Association, Held With the Sarepta Church, Franklin County, Miss., September 30th, and October 1st and 2d, 1854. Natchez: 1854.

Minutes of the Forty-Ninth Anniversary of the Mississippi Baptist Association, Held With the Ebenezer Church, Amite Co., Miss., October 6th, 7th and 8th, 1855. Natchez: 1855.

Minutes of the Forty-Seventh Anniversary of the Mississippi Baptist Association, Held With the New Providence Church, Amite County, Miss., October 1st, 2nd, and 3rd, 1853. Natchez: 1853.

Moore, John Hammond, ed. "The Abiel Abbot Journals: A Yankee Preacher in Charleston Society, 1818–1827." *South Carolina Historical Magazine*, LXVIII (April, 1967), 51–73, (July, 1967), 115–39, (October, 1967), 232–54.

Moore, Rev. T. V. "God's Method of Saving the World." *Methodist Quarterly Review*, IX (January, 1855), 72–87.

Myers, Robert Manson, ed. *The Children of Pride: A True Story of Georgia and the Civil War*. New Haven: Yale University Press, 1972.

"North and South." *Southern Presbyterian Review*, III (January, 1850), 337–81.

"Objections to the German Transcendental Philosophy." *Southern Presbyterian Review*, IV (January, 1851), 338–41.

The Old Pine Farm: Or, The Southern Side. Comprising Loose Sketches From the Experi-
   ence of a Southern Country Minister, S.C. Nashville: Southwestern Publishing
   House, 1860.
"Our Problem." *Southern Presbyterian Review*, X (October, 1857), 451–63.
[Palmer, Benjamin Morgan.] "Church and State." *Southern Presbyterain Review*, III
   (April, 1850), 604–608.
————. *The Life and Letters of James Henley Thornwell, D.D., LL.D., Ex-President of*
   the South Carolina College, Late Professor of Theology in the Theological Seminary at
   Columbia, South Carolina. Richmond: Whittet & Shepperson, 1875.
[————.] *A Plain and Easy Catechism, Designed Chiefly for the Benefit of Coloured Per-*
   sons. To Which Are Annexed Suitable Prayers and Hymns. Charleston: Observer
   Office Press, 1828.
————. *The South: Her Peril, and Her Duty. A Discourse delivered in the First Presby-*
   terian Church, New Orleans, on Thursday, November 29, 1860. New Orleans: Of-
   fice of the True Witness and Sentinel, 1860.
Pinckney, C. C. *An Address Delivered in Charleston, Before the Agricultural Society of*
   South-Carolina, at Its Anniversary Meeting, on Tuesday, the 18th of August, 1829.
   Charleston: A. E. Miller, 1829.
Plumer, William S. *Thoughts on Religious Education and Early Piety.* New York: John S.
   Taylor, 1836.
————. *Thoughts on the Religious Instruction of the Negroes of This Country.* Savannah:
   Edward J. Purse, Printer, 1848.
"The Power of the Pulpit." *Southern Presbyterian Review*, II (September, 1848),
   207–93.
Preamble and Regulations of the Savannah River Anti-Slave Traffick Association. Adopted
   November, 21st, 1846. N.p.: n.d.
Presbytery of Tombeckbee [Mississippi]. *The Religious Instruction of Our Colored*
   Population. A Pastoral Letter From the Presbytery of Tombeckbee to the Churches and
   People Under Its Care. Columbia: Steam-Power Press of R. W. Gibbes, 1859.
Proceedings of the S. Carolina Anti-Intemperance Society, With an Address to the Public.
   Charleston: W. Riley, [1827?].
[Read, Rev. Clement.] *Reasons for Not Joining the Temperance Society. By a Clergyman.*
   Richmond: T. W. White, [1836].
"Religious Instruction of the Black Population." *Southern Presbyterian Review*, I
   (December, 1847), 89–120.
"Report of a Conference by Presbytery, on the Subject of 'The Organization, In-
   struction and Discipline of the Coloured People.'" *Southern Presbyterian Re-*
   view, VIII (July, 1854), 1–17.
"Report of the Columbia Temperance Society." In S. Henry Dickson, *Address Be-*
   fore the South Carolina Society for the Promotion of Temperance, April 6th, 1830.
   Charleston: Observer Office Press, 1830.
Report of the Committee to Whom Was Referred the Subject of the Religious Instruction of
   the Colored Population, of the Synod of South-Carolina and Georgia, at Its Late Session
   in Columbia, (South-Carolina.) December 5th–9th, 1833. Charleston: Observer
   Office Press, 1834.
Rice, John H. *The Importance of the Gospel Ministry. A Sermon, Preached at the Opening*
   of the Synod of Virginia, on the Sixteenth of October, 1817. Richmond: Printed by

Shepherd and Pollard, 1817.

Riley, B. F. *A History of the Baptists in the Southern States East of the Mississippi*. Philadelphia: American Baptist Publication Society, 1898.

[Ruffner, Henry.] *Address to the People of West Virginia; Shewing That Slavery Is Injurious to the Public Welfare, and That It May Be Gradually Abolished, Without Detriment to the Rights and Interests of Slaveholders. By a Slaveholder of West Virginia*. Lexington: R. C. Noel, 1847; rpr., Bridgewater, Va.: The Green Bookman, 1933.

[Ruffner, William Henry.] *Charity and the Clergy: Being a Review, by a Protestant Clergyman, of the "New Themes" Controversy; Together with Sundry Serious Reflections Upon the Religious Press, Theological Seminaries, Ecclesiastical Ambition, Growth of Moderatism, Prostitution of the Pulpit, and General Decay of Christianity*. Philadelphia: Lippincott, Grambo & Co., 1853.

Ryland, Robert. *The Scripture Catechism for Coloured People*. Richmond: Harrold & Murray, 1848.

Sammet, W. J. "American Society." *Methodist Quarterly Review*, IX (July, 1855), 402–421.

Semple, Robert B. *A History of the Rise and Progress of the Baptists in Virginia*. Richmond: Pitt & Dickinson, 1894.

Smith, Rev. B. M. *Family Religion, or the Domestic Relations Regulated by Christian Principles. A Prize Essay*. Philadelphia: Presbyterian Board of Publication, 1859.

Smith, George G. *The Life and Letters of James Osgood Andrew, Bishop of the Methodist Episcopal Church, South*. Nashville: Southern Methodist Publishing House, 1883.

Smylie, Rev. James. *A Review of a Letter, From the Presbytery of Chillicothe, to the Presbytery of Mississippi, on the Subject of Slavery*. Woodville, Miss.: William A. Norris and Co., 1836.

Smyth, Thomas. *Autobiographical Notes, Letters and Reflections*. Edited by Louisa Cheves Stoney. Charleston: Walker, Evans & Cogswell Co., 1914.

———. "National Righteousness." *Southern Presbyterian Review*, XII (April, 1859), 25–35.

———. *Complete Works of Rev. Thomas Smyth*. Edited by J. William Flinn. 10 vols. Columbia: R. L. Bryan Company, 1908–12.

Stratton, Joseph B. *Memorial of a Quarter-Century's Pastorate. A Sermon Preached on the Sabbaths, Jan. 3d and 17th, 1869, in the Presbyterian Church, Natchez, Miss*. Philadelphia: J. B. Lippincott & Co., 1869.

Stringfellow, Thornton. *A Brief Examination of Scripture Testimony on the Institution of Slavery, in an Essay, First Published in the Religious Herald and Republished by Request: With Remarks on a Review of the Essay*. Richmond: Printed at the Office of the Religious Herald, 1841.

Summers, Rev. Thomas O. "Philosophy of the Temperance Cause." In Rev. James Young, ed., *The Lights of Temperance*. Louisville: Morton & Griswold, 1851.

"The Sunday Question." *Southern Presbyterian Review*, XIII (October, 1860), 629–30.

[Thornwell, James Henley.] "Critical Notices." *Southern Presbyterian Review*, IV (January, 1851), 443–52.

———. *Judgments, A Call to Repentance. A Sermon Preached by Appointment of the Legis-*

lature in the Hall of the House of Representatives, . . . Saturday, Dec. 9, 1854. Columbia: R. W. Gibbes, 1854.

―――. "National Sins.—A Fast-Day Sermon, preached in the Presbyterian Church, Columbia, Wednesday, November 21, 1860." *Southern Presbyterian Review*, XIII (January, 1861), 649–88.

―――. "Report on Slavery." *Southern Presbyterian Review*, V (January, 1852), 380–94.

―――. *The Rights and Duties of Masters. A Sermon Preached at the Dedication of a Church Erected in Charleston, S.C., for the Benefit and Instruction of the Colored Population*. Charleston: Press of Walker & James, 1850.

[―――.] "Slavery and the Religious Instruction of the Coloured Population." *Southern Presbyterian Review*, IV (July, 1850), 105–41.

[―――.] "The State of the Country." *Southern Presbyterian Review*, XIII (January, 1861), 860–89.

Waddel, John N. *Memorials of Academic Life: Being an Historical Sketch of the Waddel Family*. Richmond: Presbyterian Committee of Publication, 1891.

Wigfall, Rev. Arthur. *Sermon upon Duelling. Together with the Constitution of the Grahamville Association, for the suppression of Duelling*. Charleston: A. E. Miller, 1856.

Wightman, W. M., and Whitefoord Smith. *The Discipline of the Methodist E. Church, South, In Regard to Slavery*. Charleston: 1849.

Wightman, William M. *Life of William Capers, D.D., One of the Bishops of the Methodist Episcopal Church, South; Including an Autobiography*. Nashville: Southern Methodist Publishing House, 1858.

[Wilson, J. L.] "The Foreign Slave Trade.—Can It Be Revived Without Violating the Most Sacred Principles of Honor, Humanity and Religion?" *Southern Presbyterian Review*, XII (October, 1859), 491–512.

Wilson, John Lyde. *The Code of Honor; or Rules for the Government of Principals and Seconds in Duelling*. Charleston: James Phynney, 1858.

York, Brantley. *The Autobiography of Brantley York*. Durham: The Seeman Printery, 1910.

SECONDARY SOURCES

BOOKS

Adams, Alice Dana. *The Neglected Period of Anti-Slavery in America, 1808–1831*. Boston: Ginn and Company, 1908.

Ahlstrom, Sydney E. *A Religious History of the American People*. New Haven: Yale University Press, 1972.

Ballagh, James Curtis. *A History of Slavery in Virginia*. Baltimore: The Johns Hopkins Press, 1902.

Barnes, William Wright. *The Southern Baptist Convention, 1845–1953*. Nashville: Broadman Press, 1954.

Bassett, John Spencer. *Slavery in the State of North Carolina*. Baltimore: The Johns Hopkins Press, 1899.

Berlin, Ira. *Slaves Without Masters: The Free Negro in the Antebellum South*. New York: Random House, Inc., 1974.

Blanton, Wyndham B. *The Making of a Downtown Church: The History of the Second*

Presbyterian Church, Richmond, Virginia, 1845–1945. Richmond: John Knox Press, 1945.

Bodo, John R. *The Protestant Clergy and Public Issues, 1812–1848*. Princeton: Princeton University Press, 1954.

Boles, John B. *The Great Revival, 1787–1805: The Origins of the Southern Evangelical Mind*. Lexington: The University Press of Kentucky, 1972.

Bruce, Dickson D., Jr. *And They All Sang Hallelujah: Plain-Folk Camp-Meeting Religion, 1800–1845*. Knoxville: University of Tennessee Press, 1974.

Bucke, Emory Stevens, ed. *The History of American Methodism*. 3 vols. New York: Abingdon Press, 1964.

Butts, R. Freeman, and Lawrence A. Cremin. *A History of Education in American Culture*. New York: Holt, Rinehart, and Winston, 1953.

Calhoun, Daniel H. *Professional Lives in America: Structure and Aspiration, 1750–1850*. Cambridge: Harvard University Press, 1965.

Cameron, Richard M. *Methodism and Society in Historical Perspective*. New York: Abingdon Press, 1961.

Cherrington, Ernest H. *The Evolution of Prohibition in the United States of America*. Westerville, Ohio: The American Issue Press, 1920.

Chiles, Robert E. *Theological Transition in American Methodism: 1790–1935*. Nashville: Abingdon Press, 1965.

Davis, David Brion. *The Problem of Slavery in the Age of Revolution, 1770–1823*. Ithaca: Cornell University Press, 1975.

Eaton, Clement. *Freedom of Thought in the Old South*. Durham: Duke University Press, 1940.

Eighmy, John Lee. *Churches in Cultural Captivity: A History of the Social Attitudes of Southern Baptists*. Knoxville: University of Tennessee Press, 1972.

Faust, Drew Gilpin. *A Sacred Circle: The Dilemma of the Intellectual in the Old South, 1840–1860*. Baltimore: The Johns Hopkins University Press, 1977.

Flanders, Ralph Betts. *Plantation Slavery in Georgia*. Chapel Hill: The University of North Carolina Press, 1933.

Flournoy, Francis R. *Benjamin Mosby Smith, 1811–1893*. Richmond: Richmond Press, Inc., 1947.

Foner, Eric, ed. *Nat Turner*. Englewood Cliffs, N.J.: Prentice-Hall, Inc., 1971.

Foster, Charles I. *An Errand of Mercy: The Evangelical United Front, 1790–1837*. Chapel Hill: University of North Carolina Press, 1954.

Franklin, John Hope. *The Militant South, 1800–1861*. Boston: Beacon Press, 1968.

Freehling, William W. *Prelude to Civil War: The Nullification Controversy in South Carolina, 1816–1836*. New York: Harper and Row, 1965.

Gamble, Thomas. *Savannah Duels and Duellists, 1733–1877*. Savannah: Review Publishing and Printing Company, 1923.

Genovese, Eugene D. *Roll, Jordan, Roll: The World the Slaves Made*. New York: Pantheon Books, 1972.

———. *The World the Slaveholders Made: Two Essays in Interpretation*. New York: Pantheon Books, 1969.

Godbold, Albea. *The Church College of the Old South*. Durham: Duke University Press, 1944.

Gusfield, Joseph R. *Symbolic Crusade: Status Politics and the American Temperance Movement*. Urbana: University of Illinois Press, 1963.

Hartz, Louis. *The Liberal Tradition in America*. New York: Harcourt Brace, 1955.

Hofstadter, Richard. *The Idea of a Party System: The Rise of Legitimate Opposition in the United States, 1780–1840*. Berkeley: University of California Press, 1970.

Hopkins, C. Howard. *History of the Y.M.C.A. in North America*. New York: Association Press, 1951.

Jenkins, William Sumner. *Pro-Slavery Thought in the Old South*. Chapel Hill: The University of North Carolina Press, 1935.

Johnson, Charles A. *The Frontier Camp Meeting: Religion's Harvest Time*. Dallas: Southern Methodist University Press, 1955.

Johnson, Guion Griffis. *Ante-Bellum North Carolina: A Social History*. Chapel Hill: University of North Carolina Press, 1937.

Krout, John Allen. *The Origins of Prohibition*. New York: Russell & Russell, 1925.

LaMotte, Louis C. *Colored Light: The Story of the Influence of Columbia Theological Seminary, 1828–1936*. Richmond: Presbyterian Committee of Publication, 1937.

McLoughlin, William G., Jr. *Modern Revivalism: Charles Grandison Finney to Billy Graham*. New York: The Ronald Press Co., 1959.

Malone, Dumas. *The Public Life of Thomas Cooper, 1783–1839*. Columbia: University of South Carolina Press, 1961.

Mathews, Donald G. *Religion in the Old South*. Chicago: University of Chicago Press, 1977.

———. *Slavery and Methodism: A Chapter in American Morality, 1780–1845*. Princeton: Princeton University Press, 1965.

Mead, Sidney E. *The Lively Experiment: The Shaping of Christianity in America*. New York: Harper and Row, Publishers, 1963.

Miyakawa, T. Scott. *Protestants and Pioneers: Individualism and Conformity on the American Frontier*. Chicago: University of Chicago Press, 1964.

Newman, A. H. *A History of the Baptist Churches in the United States*. New York: Charles Scribner's Sons, 1894.

Owsley, Frank Lawrence. *Plain Folk of the Old South*. Baton Rouge: Louisiana State University Press, 1949.

Peters, John Leland. *Christian Perfection and American Methodism*. New York: Abingdon Press, 1956.

Pfeffer, Leo. *Church, State and Freedom*. Rev. ed. Boston: Beacon Press, 1967.

Posey, Walter Brownlow. *The Baptist Church in the Lower Mississippi Valley, 1776–1845*. Lexington: University of Kentucky Press, 1957.

———. *The Development of Methodism in the Old Southwest, 1783–1824*. Tuscaloosa: Weatherford Printing Co., 1933.

———. *The Presbyterian Church in the Old Southwest, 1778–1838*. Richmond: John Knox Press, 1952.

Putnam, Mary Burnham. *The Baptists and Slavery, 1840–1845*. Ann Arbor: George Wahr, 1913.

Sellers, James Benson. *The Prohibition Movement in Alabama, 1702 to 1943*. Chapel Hill: University of North Carolina Press, 1943.

————. *Slavery in Alabama*. University: University of Alabama Press, 1950.

Smith, Edwin W. *The Life and Times of Daniel Lindley, 1801–80*. London: The Epworth Press, 1949.

Smith, Elwyn Allen. *The Presbyterian Ministry in American Culture: A Study in Changing Concepts, 1700–1900*. Philadelphia: Westminster Press, 1962.

Smith, H. Shelton. *In His Image, But . . . Racism in Southern Religion, 1780–1910*. Durham: Duke University Press, 1972.

Smith, Timothy L. *Revivalism and Social Reform: American Protestantism on the Eve of the Civil War*. New York: Harper and Row, 1957.

Spain, Rufus B. *At Ease in Zion: Social History of Southern Baptists, 1865–1900*. Nashville: Vanderbilt University Press, 1961.

Stanton, William. *The Leopard's Spots: Scientific Attitudes Toward Race in America, 1815–59*. Chicago: University of Chicago Press, 1960.

Stokes, Anson Phelps. *Church and State in the United States*. 3 vols. New York: Harper & Brothers, 1950.

Street, T. Watson. *The Story of Southern Presbyterians*. Richmond: John Knox Press, 1961.

Stroupe, Henry Smith. *The Religious Press in the South Atlantic States, 1802–1865: An Annotated Bibliography with Historical Introduction and Notes*. Durham: Duke University Press, 1956.

Sweet, William Warren. *Methodism in American History*. Rev. ed. New York: Abingdon Press, 1954.

————. *Religion on the American Frontier: The Baptists, 1783–1830, A Collection of Source Material*, New York: Cooper Square Publishers, Inc., 1964.

————. *Religion on the American Frontier, 1783–1840: The Methodists. A Collection of Source Materials*. Chicago: University of Chicago Press, 1946.

Sydnor, Charles S. *The Development of Southern Sectionalism, 1819–1848*. Baton Rouge: Louisiana State University Press, 1948.

————. *Slavery in Mississippi*. New York: D. Appleton-Century Company, 1933.

Taylor, Joe Gray. *Negro Slavery in Louisiana*. Baton Rouge: The Louisiana Historical Association, 1963.

Thompson, Ernest Trice. *Presbyterians in the South*. 3 vols. Richmond: John Knox Press, 1963.

Torbet, Robert G. *A History of the Baptists*. Philadelphia: The Judson Press, 1950.

Townsend, Leah. *South Carolina Baptists, 1670–1805*. Florence, S.C.: Florence Printing Company, 1935.

Vander Velde, Lewis G. *The Presbyterian Churches and the Federal Union, 1861–1869*. Cambridge: Harvard University Press, 1932.

Whitener, Donald Jay. *Prohibition in North Carolina, 1715–1945*. Chapel Hill: University of North Carolina Press, 1945.

Wooster, Ralph A. *The People in Power: Courthouse and Statehouse in the Lower South, 1850–1860*. Knoxville: University of Tennessee Press, 1969.

Wyatt-Brown, Bertram. *Lewis Tappan and the Evangelical War Against Slavery*. Cleveland: The Press of Case Western Reserve University, 1969.

ARTICLES

Bailey, Kenneth K. "Protestantism and Afro-Americans in the Old South: Another Look." *Journal of Southern History*, XLI (November, 1975), 451–72.

Bellot, Leland J. "Evangelicals and the Defense of Slavery in Britain's Old Colonial Empire." *Journal of Southern History*, XXXVII (February, 1971), 19–40.

Bishop, Charles C. "The Pro-Slavery Argument Reconsidered: James Henley Thornwell, Millennial Abolitionist." *South Carolina Historical Magazine*, LXXIII (January, 1972), 18–26.

Blanks, W. D. "Corrective Church Discipline in the Presbyterian Churches of the Nineteenth Century South." *Journal of Presbyterian History*, XLIV (June, 1966), 89–105.

Boles, John B. "Henry Holcombe, A Southern Baptist Reformer in the Age of Jefferson." *Georgia Historical Quarterly*, LIV (Fall, 1970), 381–407.

———. "John Hersey: Dissenting Theologian of Abolitionism, Perfectionism, and Millennialism." *Methodist History*, XIV (July, 1976), 215–34.

Bozeman, Theodore Dwight. "Science, Nature and Society: A New Approach to James Henley Thornwell." *Journal of Presbyterian History*, L (Winter, 1972), 306–25.

Bruce, Dickson D., Jr. "Religion, Society and Culture in the Old South: A Comparative View." *American Quarterly*, XXVI (October, 1974), 399–416.

Carwardine, Richard. "The Second Great Awakening in the Urban Centers: An Examination of Methodism and the 'New Measures'." *Journal of American History*, LIX (September, 1972), 327–40.

Clarke, T. Erskine. "An Experiment in Paternalism: Presbyterians and Slaves in Charleston, South Carolina." *Journal of Presbyterian History*, LIII (Fall, 1975), 223–38.

Daniel, W. Harrison. "Virginia Baptists and the Negro in the Antebellum Era." *Journal of Negro History*, LVI (January, 1971), 1–16.

———. "Virginia Baptists and the Negro in the Early Republic." *Virginia Magazine of History and Biography*, LXXX (January, 1972), 60–69.

DesChamps, Margaret B. "Antislavery Presbyterians in the Carolina Piedmont." *Proceedings of the South Carolina Historical Association* (1954), 6–13.

———. "Union or Division? South Atlantic Presbyterians and Southern Nationalism, 1820–1861." *Journal of Southern History*, XX (November, 1954), 484–98.

Durden, Robert F. "The Establishment of Calvary Protestant Episcopal Church for Negroes in Charleston." *South Carolina Historical Magazine*, LXV (April, 1964), 63–84.

Faust, Drew Gilpin. "Evangelicalism and the Meaning of the Proslavery Argument: The Reverend Thornton Stringfellow of Virginia." *Virginia Magazine of History and Biography*, LXXXV (January, 1977), 3–17.

Garber, Paul Leslie. "A Centennial Appraisal of James Henley Thornwell." In *A Miscellany of American Christianity: Essays in Honor of H. Shelton Smith*. Edited by Stuart C. Henry. Durham: Duke University Press, 1963.

Gohdes, Clarence. "Some Notes on the Unitarian Church in the Ante-Bellum

South: A Contribution to the History of Southern Liberalism." In *American Studies in Honor of William Kenneth Boyd*. Edited by David K. Jackson. Durham: Duke University Press, 1940.

Gravely, William B. "Methodist Preachers, Slavery and Caste: Types of Social Concern in Antebellum America." *Duke Divinity School Review*, XXXIV (Autumn, 1969), 209–29.

Griffin, Clifford S. "Religious Benevolence as Social Control, 1815–1860." *Mississippi Valley Historical Review*, XLIV (December, 1957), 423–44.

Hayden, J. Carleton. "Conversion and Control: Dilemma of Episcopalians in Providing for the Religious Instruction of Slaves, Charleston, South Carolina, 1845–1860." *Historical Magazine of the Protestant Episcopal Church*, XL (June, 1971), 143–71.

Holifield, E. Brooks. "Thomas Smyth: The Social Ideas of a Southern Evangelist." *Journal of Presbyterian History*, LI (Spring, 1973), 24–39.

Jackson, Gordon E. "Archibald Alexander's *Thoughts on Religious Experience*, a Critical Revisiting." *Journal of Presbyterian History*, LI (Summer, 1973), 141–54.

Johnson, Guion Griffis. "The Camp Meeting in Ante-Bellum North Carolina." *North Carolina Historical Review*, X (April, 1933), 95–110.

———. "Revival Movements in Ante-Bellum North Carolina." *North Carolina Historical Review*, X (January, 1933), 21–43.

Loveland, Anne C. "Evangelicalism and 'Immediate Emancipation' in American Antislavery Thought." *Journal of Southern History*, XXXII (May, 1966), 172–188.

———. "Richard Furman's 'Questions on Slavery.'" *Baptist History and Heritage*, X (July, 1975), 177–81.

Maclear, James F. "'The True American Union' of Church and State: The Reconstruction of the Theocratic Tradition." *Church History*, XXVIII (March, 1959), 41–62.

McLoughlin, William G. "Pietism and the American Character." *American Quarterly*, XVII (Summer, 1965), 163–86.

Maddex, Jack P. "From Theocracy to Spirituality: The Southern Presbyterian Reversal on Church and State." *Journal of Presbyterian History*, LIV (Winter, 1976), 438–57.

Mathews, Donald G. "Charles Colcock Jones and the Southern Evangelical Crusade to Form a Biracial Community." *Journal of Southern History*, XLI (August, 1975), 299–320.

———. "Religion in the Old South: Speculation on Methodology." *South Atlantic Quarterly*, LXXIII (Winter, 1974), 34–52.

———. "The Second Great Awakening as an Organizing Process, 1780–1830: An Hypothesis." *American Quarterly*, XXI (Spring, 1969), 23–43.

Mead, Sidney E. "The Rise of the Evangelical Conception of the Ministry in America." In H. Richard Niebuhr and Daniel D. Williams, eds. *The Ministry in Historical Perspectives*. New York: Harper, 1956.

Monroe, Haskell. "Southern Presbyterians and the Secession Crisis." *Civil War History*, VI (December, 1960), 351–60.

Moore, Margaret DesChamps. "Religion in Mississippi in 1860." *Journal of Mississippi History*, XXII (October, 1960), 233–38.

Perkins, Haven P. "Religion for Slaves: Difficulties and Methods." *Church History*, X (September, 1941), 228–45.

Plyler, Rev. M. T. "Peter Doub, Itinerant of Heroic Days." *Historical Papers of Trinity College Historical Society and the North Carolina Conference Historical Society*, Series IX (1912), 33–50.

Pope, Earl A. "The Rise of the New Haven Theology." *Journal of Presbyterian History*, XLIV (March, 1966), 24–44, (June, 1966), 106–21.

Posey, Walter B. "The Baptists and Slavery in the Lower Mississippi Valley." *Journal of Negro History*, XLI (April, 1956), 117–30.

———. "The Early Baptist Church in the Lower Southwest." *Journal of Southern History*, X (May, 1944), 161–73.

———. "Influence of Slavery upon the Methodist Church in the Early South and Southwest." *Mississippi Valley Historical Review*, XVII (1930–31), 530–42.

———. "The Slavery Question in the Presbyterian Church in the Old Southwest." *Journal of Southern History*, XV (August, 1949), 311–24.

Purifoy, Lewis M. "The Southern Methodist Church and the Proslavery Argument." *Journal of Southern History*, XXXII (August, 1966), 325–41.

Schmidt, Frederika Teute, and Barbara Ripel Wilhelm, "Early Proslavery Petitions in Virginia." *William and Mary Quarterly*, XXX (January, 1973), 133–46.

Sernett, Milton C. "Behold the American Cleric: The Protestant Minister as 'Pattern Man,' 1850–1900." *Winterthur Portfolio*, VIII (1973), 1–18.

Smith, Elwyn Allen. "The Role of the South in the Presbyterian Schism of 1837–1838." *Church History*, XXIX (March, 1960), 44–63.

———. "The Voluntary Establishment of Religion." In Elwyn A. Smith, ed. *The Religion of the Republic*. Philadelphia: Fortress Press, 1971.

Smith, H. Shelton. "The Church and the Social Order in the Old South as Interpreted by James Henley Thornwell." *Church History*, VII (June, 1938), 115–24.

Southall, Eugene Portlette. "The Attitude of the Methodist Episcopal Church, South, Toward the Negro From 1844 to 1870." *Journal of Negro History*, XVI (October, 1931), 359–70.

Staiger, C. Bruce. "Abolitionism and the Presbyterian Schism of 1837–1838." *Mississippi Valley Historical Review*, XXXVI (December, 1949), 391–414.

Stewart, James Brewer. "Evangelicalism and the Radical Strain in Southern Antislavery Thought During the 1820s." *Journal of Southern History*, XXXIX (August, 1973), 379–96.

Sweet, William W. "The Churches as Moral Courts of the Frontier." *Church History*, II (March, 1933), 3–21.

Takaki, Ronald. "The Movement to Reopen the African Slave Trade in South Carolina." *South Carolina Historical Magazine*, LXVI (January, 1965), 38–54.

Thomas, John L. "Romantic Reform in America, 1815–1865." *American Quarterly*, XVII (Winter, 1965), 656–81.

Troxler, George. "Eli Caruthers: A Silent Dissenter in the Old South." *Journal of Presbyterian History*, XLVI (June, 1967), 95–111.
Weaver, R. M. "The Older Religiousness in the South." *Sewanee Review*, LI (Spring, 1943), 237–49.
Whatley, George C., III. "The Alabama Presbyterian and His Slave, 1830–1864." *Alabama Review*, XIII (January, 1960), 46–51.
Williams, Jack Kenny. "The Code of Honor in Ante-Bellum South Carolina." *South Carolina Historical Magazine*, LIV (July, 1953), 113–28.
Woodward, C. Vann. Introduction to George Fitzhugh, *Cannibals All! or Slaves Without Masters*. Cambridge: Harvard University Press, 1960.
Wyatt-Brown, Bertram. "Prelude to Abolitionism: Sabbatarian Politics and the Rise of the Second Party System." *Journal of American History*, LVIII (September, 1971), 316–41.

THESES AND DISSERTATIONS

Allen, Carlos Richard, Jr. "The Great Revival in Virginia, 1783–1812." M.A. thesis, University of Virginia, 1948.
Blanks, William Davidson. "Ideal and Practice; A Study of the Conception of the Christian Life Prevailing in the Presbyterian Churches of the South During the Nineteenth Century." Th.D. dissertation, Union Theological Seminary, 1960.
Clarke, Thomas Erskine. "Thomas Smyth: Moderate of the Old South." Th.D. dissertation, Union Theological Seminary, 1970.
Cox, Joseph Powhatan. "A Study of the Life and Work of Basil Manly, Jr." Th.D. dissertation, Southern Baptist Theological Seminary, 1954.
DesChamps, Margaret Burr. "The Presbyterian Church in the South Atlantic States, 1801–1861." Ph.D. dissertation, Emory University, 1952.
Geer, William Monroe. "The Temperance Movement in Georgia in the Middle Period." M.A. thesis, Emory University, 1936.
Grant, Minnie Spencer. "The American Colonization Society in North Carolina." M.A. thesis, Duke University, 1930.
Hickey, Doralyn Joanne. "Benjamin Morgan Palmer: Churchman of the Old South." Ph.D. dissertation, Duke University, 1962.
Hickin, Patricia P. "Antislavery in Virginia, 1831–1861." Ph.D. dissertation, University of Virginia, 1968.
Holmes, Marjorie Moran. "The Life and Diary of the Reverend John Jeremiah Jacob (1757–1839)." M.A. thesis, Duke University, 1941.
Kuykendall, John Wells. "'Southern Enterprize': The Work of National Evangelical Societies in the Antebellum South." Ph.D. dissertation, Princeton University, 1975.
Kyker, Rex Paxton. "William Winans: Minister and Politician of the Old South." Ph.D. dissertation, University of Florida, 1957.
Leonard, Philip. "The Contributions of Presbyterian Orthodoxy to the Pro-Slavery Argument as Exemplified by the Writings of James Henley Thornwell, 1838–1860." M.A. thesis, University of Virginia, 1967.

Mallard, Annie Hughes. "Religious Work of South Carolina Baptists Among the Slaves From 1781 to 1830." M.A. thesis, University of South Carolina, 1946.

Ott, Philip Wesley. "The Mind of Early American Methodism: 1800–1844." Ph.D. dissertation, University of Pennsylvania, 1968.

Purifoy, Lewis McCarroll, Jr. "The Methodist Episcopal Church, South, and Slavery, 1844–1865." Ph.D. dissertation, University of North Carolina, 1965.

Smith, Cortland Victor. "Church Organization as an Agency of Social Control: Church Discipline in North Carolina, 1800–1860." Ph.D. dissertation, University of North Carolina, 1967.

Stroupe, Henry Smith. "The Religious Press in the South Atlantic States, 1802–1865." Ph.D. dissertation, Duke University, 1942.

Thrift, Charles Tinsley, Jr. "The Operations of the American Home Missionary Society in the South, 1826–1861." Ph.D. dissertation, University of Chicago, 1936.

Todd, Willie Grier. "The Slavery Issue and the Organization of a Southern Baptist Convention." Ph.D. dissertation, University of North Carolina, 1964.

Touchstone, Donald Blake. "Planters and Slave Religion in the Deep South." Ph.D. dissertation, Tulane University, 1973.

Towell, Sherman Everett. "The Features of Southern Baptist Thought, 1845–1879." Th.D. dissertation, Southern Baptist Theological Seminary, 1956.

Watkin, Robert N., Jr. "The Forming of the Southern Presbyterian Minister: From Calvin to the American Civil War." Ph.D. dissertation, Vanderbilt University, 1969.

Williams, Thomas Leonard. "The Methodist Mission to the Slaves." Ph.D. dissertation, Yale University, 1943.

Index

Abolitionism: and New School Presbyterians, 86; and southern benevolence, 174; and impulse to Negro religious instruction, 227. *See also* Antislavery

Abolitionists: evangelicals compared with, 120; and "higher law," 153; activities of, 193, 194; southern evangelicals' view of, 193–99, 202, 258–59; and Negro religious instruction, 233, 253, 254

Adger, John Bailey: conversion, 6–7; on the Christian life, 13–14; and Board of Domestic Missions, 230; and black churches, 243–44; as pastor of Anson Street Church, 247; mentioned, 248.

American and Foreign Sabbath Union, 177

American Bible Society, 34

American Board of Commissioners for Foreign Missions, 244

American Colonization Society, 213, 214, 261

American Education Society, 55

American Seamen's Friend Society, 165, 166

American Society for the Promotion of Temperance, 131, 141

American Sunday School Union, 34

American Tract Society, 34

Amusements, 97–101

Andrew, James O.: on Methodists in New Orleans, 49; holds protracted meeting, 77; on bankruptcy, 107; on politics, 123–24, 125, 126; on the poor, 170; and Negro religious instruction, 220, 221, 222, 224, 226, 227, 256; on missions to the slaves, 240; opposed to black churches,

245; on treatment of missionaries to blacks, 249–50

Anglicanism, 32

Anson Street Church, Charleston, 237, 244, 248

Antidueling societies, 183–84, 184n. *See also* Dueling

Antislavery: among southern evangelicals, 186, 189, 192, 212–13, 212n, 215; among Methodists, 190–91; among Baptists, 191; among Presbyterians, 191–92. *See also* Abolitionism

Anxious seat, 82, 82n, 87–88

Arminianism, 70, 71, 162

Bailey, Kenneth K., 254

Bailey, Rufus W., 78

Baker, Daniel: conversion, 2–3, 7–9, 13, 16; parents of, 5; joins church, 13; decision to enter ministry, 17; ministerial education of, 26; establishes Sunday school, 33–34; as evangelist, 48, 66, 67; on recruiting ministers, 54; on revival in Independent Presbyterian Church, 65–66; preaching, 71, 86–87; and anxious seat, 87; and Negro religious instruction, 222

Baker, Jospeh S., 44

Ball, Eli, 130

Banks, M. L., 250

Baptist, Edward: under conviction, 7; youth, 8; conversion, 9, 12; decision to enter ministry, 20; and Negro religious instruction, 247

Baring, Charles, 219